I0331812

Fouzia Farooq Ahmed is Lecturer in the Department of History at Quaid-i-Azam University, Islamabad, where she received her PhD. She has published several articles in peer-reviewed journals on the topic of the Delhi sultanate.

'In this meticulous study, Fouzia Farooq Ahmed analyses the structure and dynamics of Muslim domination in India. Dr Ahmed's survey deftly depicts the obstacles to establishing a stable foundation of authority in a political landscape of kaleidoscopic complexity, comprised of Turkish military slaves, Afghan warlords, Hindu notables, Indo-Muslim powerbrokers, Persianised administrators, and Arabised religious experts. What emerges from her sifting through the chronicles is a story of sultans and warlords pursuing the elusive formula for lasting power and falling short because of the fragility of patrimonial alliances, vast distances between centre and province, and Mongol military pressure from Central Asia.'

David Commins, Professor of History, Dickinson College

MUSLIM RULE IN MEDIEVAL INDIA

Power and Religion in the Delhi Sultanate

FOUZIA FAROOQ AHMED

I.B.TAURIS
LONDON • NEW YORK • OXFORD • NEW DELHI • SYDNEY

I.B. TAURIS
Bloomsbury Publishing Plc
50 Bedford Square, London, WC1B 3DP, UK
1385 Broadway, New York, NY 10018, USA
29 Earlsfort Terrace, Dublin 2, Ireland

BLOOMSBURY, I.B. TAURIS and the I.B. Tauris logo are
trademarks of Bloomsbury Publishing Plc

First published in Great Britain 2016
Paperback edition published 2021

A catalogue record for this book is available from the British Library.

A catalog record for this book is available from the Library of Congress.

ISBN: HB: 978-1-7845-3550-6
PB: 978-0-7556-4293-9
ePDF: 978-1-7867-3082-4
eBook: 978-1-7867-2082-5

Series: Library of Islamic Law 8

Typeset by OKS Prepress Services, Chennai, India

Dedicated to my parents

CONTENTS

List of Illustrations ix
Preface xi
Transliteration Key xiii
Glossary xiv

Introduction 1

1. Traders, Adventurers, Raiders and Settlers: The Arab Experience in India 14
2. Maḥmūd of Ghazna: Plunderer, Strategist or Iconoclast? 30
3. The Master who Conferred his Empire upon his Slaves: Shihāb al-Dīn Ghūrī 41
4. The 'Mystic Prince': Shams al-Dīn Iltutmish 59
5. The Tale of the '40 Slaves': The Post-Iltutmish Interregnum 73
6. Blood and Iron, Poison and Dagger: Balban's Prescription for Successful Rule 98
7. When History Repeated Itself Repeatedly: Wealth, Betrayal and Success under the Khaljīs 113
8. From Megalomania to Chaos: The Tughluqs 150
9. Vacillating between Order and Disorder: Amir Temür, Sayyids and Lodhis 183

Conclusion 188

LIST OF ILLUSTRATIONS

Figures

Figure 1.1 A Theoretical Construction of the Main State Departments in the Delhi Sultanate 25

Figure 7.1 Gold Tanka of Qutb al-Dīn Mubārak Shāh with a Caliphal Claim. Courtesy British Museum, London. 146

Figure 8.1 Image of Sultan's Reception upon his Return to the Capital. Courtesy Walters Museum, Baltimore. 180

Tables

Table 1.1 Summary Investiture, Coinage and Khutba 26

Table 5.1 Summary: Post Shams al-Dīn Iltutmish Interregnum (1236–66) 95

Table 8.1 Salary in the Time of Muḥammad b. Tughluq 166

Table A.1 Rise and Fall of Dynasties: A Summary 199

Table A.2 Issue of Succession 200

Table A.3 Sultans that Reigned more than Six Years 200

Table A.4 Transition of Power between Strategically Placed Minorities 200

Table A.5 Rise and Fall of the Dynasties in the Delhi Sultanate 201

Maps

Map 4.1 Ghurids in India 1192–1206 71

Map 6.1 The Delhi Sultanate under Iltutmish and Balban 111

Map 7.1 Empire of the Khaljis 1290–1320 147

Map 8.1 The Delhi Sultanate from the 1330s to the Early 1400s 181

PREFACE

This book is an outcome of my long-standing fascination with medieval Indian history. The multi-lingual and multi-form historical evidence of this era speaks many voices and adopts multiple tones but extends brilliant insights into the inner mechanisms of power politics. The political history of the early Muslim rule in northern India is a complex account of conquests and subjugations, patrimonial/trust-based relations, ascribed and attained loyalties, unsystematic and non-hierarchal bureaucratic structures and uneven and vacillating domains of political authority. This book aspires to rationalise the oscillation of the state structure from temporary stability to recurring spells of instability. By probing into the cycles of regime formation, regime perpetuation and regime disintegration this work tries to trace continuities and discontinuities in the power dynamics of major northern Indian Muslim states between the eighth and fourteenth centuries.

While writing this book, I have come to admire exceedingly the existing scholarship on the Delhi sultanate as I now fathom the nature of groundwork this subject requires, ranging from ordeals of learning medieval Indian Farsi to locating and procuring rare manuscripts and out-of-print books. I have greatly benefited from such scholarship and have attempted to assay the phenomenon of instability and its impacts on the sultanate power structure.

This work stems from the dissertation that I submitted to the Department of History, Quaid-i-Azam University, Islamabad as a requirement for my PhD degree. The scholarly feedback of my supervisor Dr Syed Wiqar Ali Shah and discussions with Dr Ilhan Niaz helped me understand the subject and its source material better. The evaluations from my PhD thesis reviewers Dr Zareena Salamat, Dr Lawrence Ziring, Dr Roger D. Long and Dr David Commins emboldened me to develop my thesis into a manuscript. I transformed my work into book form after coming to Oxford and in the process the discussions that followed my presentation at the Oxford Centre for Islamic Studies, especially the valuable observations of Dr Farhan Nizami, Dr George Malagaris, his wife Dr Maya Patrovich and Dr Moin Nizami, inspired me to expand certain themes in my work. At 'Dynastic Change and Legitimacy', a conference organised by the Kings and Queens Network and the University of Lisbon (2015), Dr Jeroen Duindam's insightful perspective on comparative medieval history introduced me to some new concepts. Also, I am very grateful to Tomasz Hoskins and Thomas Stottor, editors at I.B.Tauris, for their valuable input.

On the material collection stage, Dr Tanvir Anjum and Dr Khurram Qadir's generosity in lending me books facilitated my otherwise arduous pursuit for source material. Debts of gratitude are due to the rich Hasam ud-Din Rashidi collection, DRSM Library, Quaid-i-Azam University, Islamabad and its extraordinarily forthcoming staff. I am very thankful to Khizr Jawad for his hospitality in Lahore and for helping me access the unique manuscript folios available at Lahore Museum. I am much obliged to Sadia Aziz for her timely input in the development of the bibliography. I was also able to find some very rare books and manuscripts in the Bodleian Library Oxford, Weston Library Oxford and India Office Library London. I acknowledge the Walters Art Museum, Baltimore for providing me with high-resolution manuscripts containing exquisite sultanate miniature paintings, one of which appears in this book. I am also grateful to the trustees of the British Museum for their permission to use the image of the rare Qutb al-Dīn Mubārak Shāh tanka.

At the end, my foremost gratitude is to my family, supportive at each and every phase of the development of this book.

TRANSLITERATION KEY

Vowels

ā	آ
ē	اے
ī	ای
au	او
ū	اؤ
ü	اُو
a	short **a** sound
i	short **i** sound
o	short **o** sound
ay	aybeg
aw	khusraw
ʿ	ع
ʾ	ء
/	i-

Consonants

ch	چ
ḍ	ذ
dh	ض
gh	غ, گھ
jh	جھ
kh	خ
sh	ش
ث	th
ḥ	ح
ṣ	ص
ṭ	ط
ẓ	ظ

GLOSSARY

ahd-i wāsiq	the condition of capitulation
ahl-i ḥarb	fighting men
ahl-i-qalam	those who maintained civilian offices
ahl-i-saif	those who maintained military offices
'ālim	(pl. *'ulāmā'*) religious scholar
amān	grant of protection
amīr	leader/senior state functionary/a noble/a rank in the army
amīr-i ākhūr/ ākhūr beg	intendant of the stables
amīr-i dad	military justiciar
amīr-i hājib	military chamberlain
amīr-i majlis	intendant of the private assembly
amīr-i sadā	commander of a unit of hundred
'ariḍ	muster-master
bāb al-Islām	gateway of Islam
bait	the formal acceptance of the authority of a sultan or leader by the group he claims to lead or govern
bārbeg	see *amīr-i hājib*
barīd	postal officer (sometimes used interchangeably for intelligence officer/spy)
bistagān	salary
chāshnigīr	the superior of the sultan's kitchen

chatr	ceremonial parasol
crōr	ten million
dādbeg	see *amīr-i dād*
dhimmis	non-Muslims living under Muslim rulers
diwān	finance officer
dīwān-i ʿarḍ	see *ʿariḍ*
dūrbāsh	trumpet
fataḥnāmah	victory dispatch
ghāzīs	voluntary troops
ghulām	slave
ḥawālī	territory in the environs
ihsān	munificence
inʿām	reward
iqṭā'	transferable revenue assignment in lieu of salary
jazyā	protection tax levied upon non-Muslims under Muslim rulers
jītal	a coin
kanīz	female slave
kārkhānā	factory, workshop
khālisa	crown lands
khān	an elite rank in the bureaucracy
khānaqāh	Sufi hospice
khuṭba	religious sermon delivered before Friday or Eid prayers
koshak	residential palace
kōtwāl	Castellan
kurtās	Indian style of shirt
lashkarkash	war leader
malik	an elite rank in the bureaucracy
mamlūk	elite military slaves
mans	scale of weight
mawalzādāh	son of a freed slave
muftīs	expounders of the law
muhrdār	keeper of the seal
mulhid/murtid	apostate
muqṭa'	holder of *iqṭā'*
mushrif-i mamālik	accountant general of imperial revenue
mutatāwīʾā	mercenaries

nā'ib	deputy, viceroy
nama nawīs	reporters
namūd-o parwarish	nurturing and cultivation
n'imāh	blessing/endowment
nuqqad	assayers
paīk	infantryman
pilkhānā	elephant-stable
qāḍi	judicial officers
qāḍi al-qazāt	chief justice
qaṣar	residential palace
ṣadr	officer in charge of religious affairs
ṣāhib-i barīd	officer in charge of postal service
saqi-i-khass	royal cup bearer
sar-i-dawatdar	the royal pen holder
sar-i jāndār	commander of the sultan's guards or executioners
sayyids	descendants of the Prophet Muḥammad
sharia	religious law
shuhnā	intendant; governor; (Mongol) resident at the court of a subject ruler
shuhnā-i pīl	intendant of the elephantry
sipah sālār	commander of the army
ṣulh	peace agreement
tawā'if ul mulukiāt	disintegration of a centralised political setup
umarā'	plural of *amīr*; nobility
wakil-i dār	comptroller of the household
walā	a social institution particular to medieval Muslim societies, where the manumitted slaves were accommodated as lesser family members in the households of their former masters
wālī	governor
wazīr	highest ministerial position
wilāyat	provinces

جهان مضـــبوط تيغـــش طول بـــا عرض

هو ا لســـلطان ظل الله فـــى الارض

His blade establishes order across the realm.

The Sultan is the Shadow of God on Earth.

Ḥasan ʻAlā Sijzī, *Kulliyāt-i Ḥasan ʻAlā Sijzī*, ed. Mas'ūd ʻAlī Maḥwi (Hyderabad Deccan, 1933), p. 563.

INTRODUCTION

The Delhi sultanate was established as a corollary of military expeditions by the Ghaznawids (352–582/962–1186) and Ghūrīds (558–602/1163–1206) that extended the eastern Islamic frontiers into Gangetic plains. The successful rulers of both these dynasties carved out principalities in northern India and established garrison towns and colonies, many of which later became the political and military strongholds of their legatees; the Delhi sultans. This work offers insight into regime formation, regime perpetuation and regime disintegration of Muslim states within Indian settings. It also provides additional understanding of the policies of sultans and their ruling class that formed a religious, racial and linguistic minority whose religious and cultural symbols and rituals captured an attempt at moral validation of their power. In the process, this book describes the political dynamics of medieval Muslim states in non-Muslim societies.

The Delhi sultanate is generally perceived as an exceptionally centralised political structure; nevertheless there was a visible asymmetrical distribution of power on the geographical level, making it a segmentary state,[1] comprised of a cluster of military strongholds and taxed agrarian hinterlands. The Delhi sultans ruled territories of northern India from a core region of control in Delhi and its adjacent territories, which gradually expanded – yet the borders of the sultanate fluctuated frequently. Under stronger rulers the sultanate expanded. These annexations, following this expansion policy, occasionally brought some areas of south India under direct control and reduced others to the status of tributaries. The affiliation of the eastern provinces, including Bengal, also hinged upon the strength of the rulers. The weaker rulers were unable to command and control, leaving these territories to either rebellious governors or unruly local elements. The territories of each ruler also witnessed instability owing to various factors, ranging from strategic preferences of the ruler, to monetary problems, bad weather, or the ill health of the monarch that could impede communication. Penetration of state control and administrative structure was also gradual. Within these fluctuating boundaries there were patches of wayward regions where the Delhi sultans could not succeed in marking their presence. Thus, governance in the Delhi sultanate was a nexus of several directly and indirectly administered regions. Due to the multi-layered nature of state control, geographical centralisation was impossible.

The concentration of power in a single hand also seems a legal myth, as the sultans fell from power as often as they rose. There were frequent and abrupt power shifts and dynastic transitions, an outcome of unstable social and political foundations. It is important to understand the extent to which the sultans' administrative policies were considered legitimate by the people, since the ethnic composition of the sultanate ruling elite was predominantly non-Indian and a tiny minority within the total population of India.

The relevance of sultans' religious and cultural symbols and ritualisation to the locals becomes an important question since the sultans and their subjects hailed from different cultures; their languages, scripts, dresses, customs and religions were considerably divergent. Also, the process of assimilation of the rulers was limited. The sultans promoted an urban culture and did not intervene in traditional Indian village society or its caste structure. Instead, they founded new cities and the native Indians who resided there were generally slave captives of war. Under the Ölberli rulers, the natives were not trusted with important administrative responsibilities. This anti-native bias prevailed until the end of the Delhi sultanate; one of the most prominent historians of the Delhi sultanate, Ḍiyā' al-Dīn Baranī, writing in the times of Tughluqs (720–815/1320–1412), criticised the sultans for trusting the natives. The natives, on the other hand, had few ways to relate to their Muslim rulers. Villages customarily acquiesced to sultans' rule, only occasionally conducting substantive resistance through non-payment of taxes. The Delhi sultanate's flimsy social base remained the urban population of

Delhi and other garrisons. In some instances, this social base was involved in political matters of the sultanate.

Owing to its slender social base, the throne was vulnerable to intrigue and rebellion from three directions. Firstly, the ruler required protection from politically apt kinsmen who, in the absence of any definite law of succession, had their own claims to the throne. Secondly, various mutually hostile groups of *umarā'*[2] desired control of the state apparatus. Thirdly, the local political elite could oust ruling groups with their native support. Monarchs often pre-empted their scheming relatives by either putting them to the sword or physically impairing them to an extent that they become ineligible to rule under Islamic law. The local elements were either ignored or neutralised through raids and annihilation. Rulers dealt with the nobility, with caution, as they were not only the power base of the sultans but also the intermediaries between the rulers and the ruled. No governance was possible without them. It is in the context of the Delhi sultanate *umarā'* that analysis of behavioural and relational dimensions of political power yields the most fruit.

The nobility was the most important pillar of the Delhi sultanate power structure. Yet, the struggle between the sultans and their *umarā'* was a zero sum game as the power of one could only grow at the expense of the other. The *umarā'* did not want a very strong sultan who could curtail their liberties and endanger the existence of certain groups within them. The over-empowered *umarā'* were responsible for most of the misadventures of the sultans: these included enthroning puppet rulers, violent dethronements, and executions. Therefore, the sultans often found themselves at the mercy of the ruling elite that they patronised.

The nobility in the Delhi sultanate decided the issues of succession and ignored the will of the deceased sultans. Except Muḥammad b. Tughluq (725–752/1325–1351), no heir apparent was able to ascend to the throne by virtue of his father's will. In the times of comparatively weaker sultans, the core regions of the Delhi sultanate were ruled through a system that resembled an oligarchy rather than a monarchy. The rulers were usually puppets, enthroned and dethroned by the authority of the nobility. The provinces were generally reduced to *tawā'if ul mulukiat*[3].

In modern political systems where legitimacy emanates from public will, decentralisation, by large, leads to power sharing and accountability. However, pre-modern political systems such as the

Delhi sultanate had their own power matrix where the antonym of centralisation was not decentralisation in the modern sense. Under the rule of a weak sultan, fragmentation of the sultanate resulted in *tawā'if ul mulukiat*, a political condition between anarchy and centralisation where several mutually hostile warlords either proclaimed their autonomy or operated as de facto sultans in their own areas under the banner of the sultan. These warlords used power in similar manner to that of any strong sultan of Delhi, and contested other groups for power, adding to the violence and disorder. At such times the Mongol hoards made their way into the core regions of the Delhi sultanate and wreaked economic relapse.

The nobility became strongest in times of power shifts. Under weak sultans, the strongest group among the nobles would replace the former and inaugurate an entirely new dynasty (see Tables A.1 and A.4). This group of nobility usually had either proven its mettle against the Mongols or under the charge of some other military responsibility; for instance, the Afghans were assigned the task of policing Delhi, its forts, and surrounding areas. This culminated in their political and financial dominance vis-à-vis other groups. Individuals without substantial support from the ruling class would seldom succeed. For example, Balban-i Kushlü Khān, Malik Kāfur (715/1316) and Khusraw Khān (720/1320) could not survive as they had insubstantial support among the power base. The *umarā'* were structurally a privileged group, whose control was enacted by the sultan in direct and indirect ways.

Sultanate history was, therefore, an incessant struggle between the sultans and their *umarā'* to prevail. Every sultan adopted both time-tested and novel solutions to minimise the power of nobility. These mechanisms reflect the behavioural and relational dimensions of political power in the Delhi sultanate and can also be construed as defining elements of the political structure of the Delhi sultanate.

For many sultans, killing rivals was an urgent necessity following their enthronement. Every new sultan tried to purge the nobility of the previous sultan in order to suppress any resistance. Unwanted elements were sometimes secretly murdered when there was a risk of adverse reaction from the *umarā'*; for instance, Sultan Ghiyāth al-Dīn Balban (664–685/1266–1287) poisoned his cousin Sher Khān's wine in order to get rid of him. At other times, punishments made an example of the executed; Ghiyāth al-Dīn Balban's punishment of his favourite slave

Toghril, who rebelled in Bengal, offers a prime example. He and his supporters were skinned, stuffed with hay and hanged in the main bazaar of Lakhnawtī. It is important to note that the blood and iron policy was for nobles who did not have loyal sympathisers within the power structure.

In any political setting trust is a precious resource and the Delhi sultanate was no exception. At the start of a new sultan's reign, the power vacuum created by the purging of distrusted groups of nobles was addressed by importing trustworthy individuals into the realm. The absence of an established law of succession left the office of the sultan excessively vulnerable to intrigues and conspiracies. In order to avoid betrayal, the sultans required reliable confidantes as well as civil and military administrators. These imports helped establish a social base for the new ruler.

The sultans centralised power through a strong personal powerbase. This powerbase could only be reliable when it depended on the ruler for its survival. Émigrés and slaves were, from this perspective, the best source of support. The *umarā'* of every sultan consisted of a visible number of personal slaves and émigrés. These groups, divided on ethnic and cultural lines, were mutually hostile. They were generally loyal to the sultan, since they owed their existence and survival to him exclusively. Their lives, deaths, promotions, dismissals, manumissions, marriages and socialisation were subject to the will of the sultan. A strong sultan personalised the state apparatus and centralised power in his hands by encouraging diversity and personalising political relations.

The Delhi sultanate was a safe haven for Mongol-stricken Muslims from Persia, Central Asia and Arabia. The sultans were cognisant of the risk of dissent or revolt embedded in a monolithic nobility. They made sure that not a single ethnic group dominated. Therefore, all the sultans encouraged foreigners and there was a constant inflow of new additions to the ruling elite. Although the sultanate *umarā'* were mostly Muslim, their ethnic and linguistic differences kept them divided. For instance, we know that Iltutmish's nobility was primarily dominated by mutually hostile Turkish *ahl-i-saif* (sward bearers) and Tajiks *ahl-i-qalam* (pen bearers). It was less risky for the sultan to trust foreigners since their social uprootedness and natal alienation rendered them dependent upon the sultan for their existence.

A strong sultan created a delicate balance between various ethnic groups within the power structure. These groups can best be termed as strategically placed minorities as each group was positioned against potential rivalries and alliances. For instance, while one group was entrusted with the responsibility of taking care of the provinces, the other was responsible for the financial affairs and the third was given the responsibility of policing. Nothing was permanent, however. The power structure perennially re-positioned the various ethnic groups and their responsibilities. Arab and Persian sources describe the office of sultan as a pole star, around which the entire system of politics and administration revolved. It was the gravity of the sultan that kept the power structure functioning, since without it the entire system tended to collapse. In the absence of vertical or horizontal hierarchies each group maintained a special direct relationship with the sultan. Feelings of jealousy and otherness worked as fuel for competition. These strategically placed minorities remained vulnerable, divided, distrustful and lacked the will for collective action. Successful sultans harnessed these divisions effectively using one group against the other. Personalised political relations assisted the sultan in balancing competing interests.

While explaining various types of traditional authority, Weber labelled the Delhi sultanate as a patrimonial state,[4] since economic, political and social favours emanated from the ruler to his followers. Like other patrimonial bureaucracies the Delhi sultanate's power structure was also knitted around the personal will of the sultan due to the instability of the bureaucratic system. The relationship between the ruler and his officials was that of dependency which ensured loyalty.

Patrimonial governance was best suited to the Delhi sultanate, in which an agricultural mode of production prevailed and the transactions of resources were generally undertaken on the basis of barter system. In the Delhi sultanate, the officers were paid in kind in the form of a share in the produce of the land, or through fines, tributes or gifts levied on peasant producers. This system had centrifugal tendencies; it was very difficult for the central government to increase the amount of taxes levied on the hinterlands. Thus, the economy largely operated at subsistence level. In this patrimonial form of authority, the sultan's officers, who were delegated governing powers by the ruler, paid the cost of their administration, and possibly that of their military equipment, by generating income from the assigned land. These patrimonial officers used their positions as personal property and their staff as personal staff, becoming patrons themselves.

The autonomy of local powers in the Delhi sultanate varied according to their proximity to the state apparatus. While in the core areas of state, strict checks and balances were possible, tributary kingdoms could be monitored only with difficulty. A continuous scramble for power existed between the centre and the centrifugal local powers. In order to curtail the power of local honoraries, the sultan not only destroyed them but also, in order to eliminate the possibility of their re-growth, replaced them with his own officers through an elaborate *iqṭā'* system (of land tax administration).

Iqṭā' were the transferable land revenue assignments of the *umarā'* of the Delhi sultanate. Continuing the tradition of older Muslim dynasties, this system enabled the sultan to become more powerful by confining the officers to the status of revenue collectors and not owners. The ability of the sultans to transfer the *umarā'* from one *iqṭā'* to another kept the latter from mustering support from the locals or making the region their constituency. An exceptionally good or ignominiously bad performance while administering an *iqṭā'* bore the same result: the transfer of its *muqṭa'*. Every new sultan had to force the existing *muqṭa's* that were appointed by the previous sultan to swear oaths of allegiance. In case the latter declined, the sultan would not hesitate to embark upon an expedition against the rebel. A sultan could undertake several such expeditions at any given time. By stopping land revenue administrators from becoming members of a landed class, sultans prevented them from establishing deep roots in the regions and retained his power. Nevertheless, if a weak sultan could not transfer the nobility from their respective *iqṭā*'s they eventually became a threat. In the times of Fīrūz Shāh (Tughluq) (751–789/1351–1388) when *iqṭā*'s were not transferred, regional powers mushroomed. The relationship between sultans and *muqṭa*'s reveal the sultan's constant effort to keep bureaucratic intermediaries from becoming a permanent landed class.

The sultans also tried to curtail the abilities of the *umarā'* for interest aggregation and interest articulation through control of social relations. There is a significant body of data that indicates that the sultans controlled the social relations of their *umarā'* including marriages and adoptions. For instance, Shihab al-Dīn Ghūrī (569–602/1173–1206) constructed a cumbersome network of matrimonial alliances among his slaves. The fourteenth-century traveller Ibn Battūtah reports a similar practice in the time of Muḥammad b. Tughluq (724–752/1324–1351). Sometimes marriages without the ruler's permission were strictly prohibited, as can be observed from the orders of 'Alā al-Dīn Khaljī (695–715/1296–1316).

It was an open secret among the sultanate officers that they were under strict surveillance and their interactions with one another were constantly monitored. The sultans kept a close watch on drinking parties, where criticism and plots to dethrone the sultan tended to emerge. If parties occurred, proceedings of such gatherings were discreetly conveyed to the sultans. Some sultans, including Ghiyāth al-Dīn Balban (664–685/1266–1287) and 'Alā al-Dīn Khaljī, banned these parties while others kept a careful watch on these social assemblies. The ban by 'Alā al-Dīn Khaljī was very strict and the violators were given excruciating punishments that proved fatal for many. Those who survived often suffered from permanent handicaps.

Sultans effectively controlled areas where his nobles lived, keeping them well within the boundary of his influence. This spatial control also limited the ability of the *umarā'* to operate as an interest group. Every sultan made a new *qasr* or *koshak* (residential palace) and the residential quarters of the new set of *umarā'* were constructed around this new residential complex. New cities adjacent to Delhi like Siri, Kelokherī and in south Dolatābād were outcomes of this attempt to keep the nobility under a tight leash.

It was a common practice of the sultans to keep a record of their *umarā*'s wealth, since affluence led to dissent. Shams al-Dīn Iltutmish (607–633/1210–1236), Ghiyāth al-Dīn Balban, 'Alā al-Dīn Khaljī (695–715/1296–1316) and Muḥammad b. Tughluq (724–752/1324–1351) were meticulous record keepers. Those who concealed their wealth from the sultans were brutally punished. Sultan 'Alā al-Dīn Khaljī due to his expeditions in south had himself become richer than his uncle, the then-reigning Sultan Jalāl al-Dīn Khaljī (689–695/1290–1296). Using this wealth he recruited an army greater than his uncle, the reigning sultan, and after beheading the latter became the sultan. 'Alā al-Dīn Khaljī confiscated all the wealth from *umarā'* after three years in power, during which time he had deployed spies in the markets to ascertain their purchasing power. The sultans were paranoid about any person possessing surplus wealth and perceived them as potential rivals.

'Alā al-Dīn ordained the death penalty by way of torture for alchemists, who were rumoured to be capable of producing gold.

In this atmosphere of distrust, espionage remained a crucial mechanism used by sultans to pre-empt betrayal. In the provinces, the sultans appointed *nāmāh nawīs* (reporters) with every important officer. These reporters wrote directly to the sultan about the day-to-day performance of the nobles' life. If a report failed to communicate any important development, the reporter was punished before the noble was taken to task. Some sultans were rumoured to have supernatural powers, as they could discover the most intimate details of a noble's life. Information remained an important informal source of power.

Unpredictability in the system of reward and punishment contributed to an atmosphere of uncertainty and distrust. Generosity was one of the most celebrated attributes of the sultans often mentioned by historians. When exultant, sultans would bestow incredible largesse upon favoured individuals. In some cases, such generosity resulted in an empty treasury. On the other hand, the threat of punishments such as flaying, trampling by elephant, or immolation, were so extreme that people preferred to die instantly when sentenced by the sultan. This system of reward and punishment was discretionary and often unpredictable; the divided nature of the bureaucratic class kept it from providing an effective counterbalance to sultans' whims.

Thus, interactions between the sultan and the ruling elite fostered instability within the political structure. While the nobility wanted a weak sultan, a strong sultan prevented the collusion of different groups of *umarā'* and kept their integration into the power structure incomplete. This deliberate instability in the bureaucratic class kept *umarā'* vulnerable and dependent on the office of sultan and resulted in *tawā'if ul mulukiat* which instigated violence and concentrated power in a few hands.

Sultans tried to transform power into legitimate authority through the use of religious and cultural symbols. The sultans of Delhi nominally remained under the aegis of Abbasid caliphs, never claiming to be absolute religious authorities. The investiture and robe from the Abbasid caliph was a much-treasured religious symbol. Shams al-Dīn Iltutmish (607–633/1210–1236) was the first Delhi sultan to have received investiture from the Abbasid caliph Abū J'āfar Manṣūr al-Mustanṣir bi-Allah (r. 623–639/1226–1242) in 626/1229. He received a robe of honour, investiture and title of Nāṣir Amīr al-Muminīn (Helper of the Commander of the Faithful). Theoretically, this allegiance made the sultans of Delhi subservient to the authority of the Abbasid caliphs of Baghdad to whom they had to submit an annual tribute. Practically, however, no regular tribute was sent and the caliph could not interfere in the affairs of the Delhi sultanate, which the sultans ruled independently. In order to project the authority of the caliphs over the sultans, the names of the former were read in the Friday *khuṭba* and coins were struck in their names. Quṭb al-Dīn Mubārak Shāh Khaljī (716–720/1316–1320) was the only sultan who claimed to be the caliph himself and discarded the allegiance to the Abbasid caliph. This audaciousness made him unpopular among the populace of Delhi. Muḥammad b. Tughluq (724–752/1324–1351) transferred reference from the Abbasid caliph of Baghdad in the *khuṭba* to another Abbasid caliph, then residing in Egypt, al-Mustakfī bi-Allah, who subsequently sent approval for the formal investiture in 744/1343. It is generally understood that this strategy appeased the Muslim population of the sultanate. Fīrūz Shāh (Tughluq 751–789/1351–1388) also received investiture from Egypt early in his reign. The sultans did not claim to be the legal religious authority in the Delhi sultanate and exerted their will in the religious domain indirectly by patronizing groups of *'ulāmā'* and Sufis. In addition, royal titles, ceremonies, rituals, literary works, architecture and coinage produced under the sultans are replete with carefully constructed statements about the sultan's religious beliefs. In a state where the majority of the subject population was non-Muslim, the use of Muslim religious symbolism to establish legitimacy is intriguing.

While placing people in a power matrix it is important to understand challenges posed by the dearth of sources. Historical data about the Delhi sultanate is unevenly divided into various eras and reflects little upon the lives of ordinary people. For authors, in all historical genres, common people were never object of interest. Their writings are largely accounts of selected groups and selected events; some historical sources are teleological accounts, others were written to appease the patrons.

The patrimonial culture in the Delhi sultanate was not restricted to politics only. It was visible in every kind of social relationship. Even different literary and artistic genre were patron-centric. Political histories focus on the sultan, and Sufi literature focuses on Sufis themselves. Poetry is generally eulogical, focusing on patrons. Though travelogues mention common people in the markets and bazaars, they seldom mention connections between state and society. The data obtained from political and Sufi histories requires scrutiny because the works are primarily patron-oriented. In many cases, the authors of these works misreport, exaggerate and conceal events in order to glorify their patrons. The textual content of inscriptions, epigraphs and coinage reflects the political idioms and philosophies of the sultan, which they used as a justification for their rule. Also, while the weight and metal of the coins tells much about the economic power of the sultan, the same information tells us little about how common people used them.

These historical sources are also unbalanced, since many of the histories overlooked important events and people. Certain groups of people became important for historians during warfare, when they reflected a strong sultan's ability to exercise control over society. In other cases, focusing on other groups confirmed a weak rulers' administrative incompetence. The groups of people that various authors mention in relation to policy in the same period of time diverge. The populations dwelling in the core regions forming the social base of the state were the only visible groups of people in the Delhi sultanate. Information about the lives of the rural population has been lost to history to a great extent, however.

To the extent possible, this book analyses the nature of the relationship between the sultans, their servants and their subjects. It addresses a core set of questions: Could the power exercised by the Delhi sultans be labelled as legitimate authority? Why did some people adhere to the power of the sultans? To what extent did sultans have the power to intervene in the lives of their subjects? Who were the 'people' in the Delhi sultanate and did public opinion have any influence on the policies of the sultans? This work addresses all of these questions by investigating the politics of de facto and de jure rule, issues of succession and ethnicity of ruling elite, political roles of various power groups including *umarā', 'ulāmā'*, civil and military administrators. This book is organised into eight main chapters, and a concluding Chapter 9.

Chapters 1, 2 and 3 discuss authority patterns and legitimacy under the Arabs, Ghaznawids and Ghūrīds. These chapters set the context for a discussion of power relations in the Delhi sultanate and trace the roots of historical experiences of Muslim rule that led to the emergence of the Delhi sultanate. The evidence available also suggests that in the absence of popular support, these states strove for legitimacy through external sources, such as the Umayyad and Abbasid caliphs, and by creating separate social space for themselves to nurture a social base for their rule. This social base was divided on the lines of ethnicity, race and civil status.

Chapters 4, 5 and 6 explain the relationship between the sultans, the ruling elites and their subjects under the Ölberli rule. These chapters cover two dynasties and a period of approximately 80 years. The hallmark of Shams al-Dīn Iltutmish's rule (607–633/1210–1236) was his patronage of a social base that was racially, ethnically and culturally foreign. He promoted exclusive spaces, such as garrison towns and newly founded cities, for the ruling groups and was able to consolidate his rule in north India. He was able to convert his personalised rule into a dynastic order successfully. However, his inexperienced descendants could not survive in power for long and were eventually replaced by Ghiyāth al-Dīn Balban. The *umarā'* in the Delhi sultanate became king makers; thus, the power relations between the ruler and their *umarā'* are discussed at length. Ghiyāth al-Dīn Balban's reign (664–685/1266–1287) and social acceptance of his policies of state control are critically discussed.

Chapter 7 explores the Delhi sultanate under the Khaljīs, covering a period of approximately 30 years. The dynastic transition from Ölberli to Khaljīs was resented by segments of population in the core areas of the sultanate; nevertheless, the military success and effective centralisation of state apparatus through efficient patrimonial staff converted the sultanate into an empire. State penetration into various regions already governed by the sultan became extensive. Owing to conquests and annexations, the borders of the sultanate stretched southwards. The economic policies and efficient policing system under 'Alā al-Dīn Khaljī (695–715/1296–1316) had a positive impact upon the population of the core regions. Due to relative economic prosperity, peace and stability 'Alā al-Dīn Khaljī (695–715/1296–1316) is considered one of the most successful sultans of Delhi and his fall resulted in a chaotic interregnum. Assumption of power by two Indian slaves Malik Kāfur and Khusraw Shāh and their obliteration due to lack of support in the power base is the most noticeable events of the Khaljī era.

Chapter 8 elucidates the Delhi sultanate under the Tughluqs, a period of about 94 years. It was under this dynasty that the borders of the sultanate grew to an unprecedented extent before it started crumbling. Following the examples of their predecessors, the sultans created their own patrimonial staff, attempting to carve a separate space for themselves in the form of royal cities. The Tughluqs ruled for longer than their predecessors and were better able to convert their rule into a dynasty. Nevertheless, the absence of law of succession paved the way for Temür's invasion, which led to the collapse of the existing political system.

Chapter 9 is an epilogue that briefly alludes to the political interregnum between the invasions of Amīr Timür (802/1399) and his great-great-great-grandson Zahīr al-Dīn Bābur (933/1526). Two dynasties, the Sayyids and the Lodhis, rose and fell during this eventful epoch that were discernibly similar to the dynasties discussed in the earlier chapters. Nevertheless, linguistic complexities and the diversely vast source material of this era calls for an altogether new study.

In most of the pre-modern historical discourses behavioural and relational dimensions of power seem more visible than the political structures and institutions. The Delhi sultanate is amongst such political settings where individuals, rather than the power structures or institutions, are emphasised in the primary sources. However, secondary scholarship on the political history of the Delhi sultanate does not reflect this emphasis and has focused on analysis of structures and institutions.

This book augments existing structural and institutional knowledge about the Delhi sultanate with discussion of additional sources on some aspects of the behavioural and relational dimensions of political power and has four broad facets. First, it sheds light on the relations of the powerful and the powerless within the prism of collective historical experience. Second, it explicates informal behavioural patterns such as trust, paranoia, loyalty, betrayal and patrimonialism that crystallise into norms and traditions and become the identity markers of sultanate political structure. Third, it takes into account distributional aspects of power such as centralisation and hierarchy and rationalises the working of the sultanate administrative system. And lastly, it deals with the issues of authority and legitimacy by investigating claims for moral validation of the sultan's power through culture, tradition and religion.

CHAPTER 1

TRADERS, ADVENTURERS, RAIDERS AND SETTLERS: THE ARAB EXPERIENCE IN INDIA

When a seventeen-year-old Umayyad general conquered Sind...

Long before the advent of Islam, India was a major trading partner with the Arab world.[1] Although there are no pre-Islamic historical sources that elaborate the nature of connections between the regions,[2] India features in the historical discourses of Arabs with reference to the epoch of Muslim conquests and expansions into Asia, Africa and Europe.

Muslim political domination in India coincides with the military expeditions under the Rāshidūn and early Umayyad caliphs. This political domination, however, was primarily confined to western India.[3] These areas remained under Muslim control through the governors appointed either by the central caliphate or in the form of regional Muslim dynasties which held sway over particular regions of Sind, Multan, Gujarat and Makran. Many of these dynasties were able to survive until Maḥmūd of Ghazna invaded India. Despite the sparseness of historical records, the sequence of events and political developments provide insight into the Umayyads' policies of expansion and how its influence persisted in succeeding dynasties. The primary recorded accounts of Arabs in India are *Fūtūh ul-Buldān*[4] and *Chachnāmah*, supplemented by accounts of Arab geographers and travellers.[5] For Arab-Muslim historians, geographers and travellers who mentioned South Asia in their writings, the regions of al Hind and Sind were not synonymous.[6] Ruled by autonomous local Rajas, these regions rarely demonstrated administrative uniformity.[7] Very little is known about the nature and dynamics of relationship between the rulers, the ruling elite and the ruled and the extent of regional kingdoms' political sway. The sources do not delve into the difference between the Muslim administration and the Hindu/Buddhist administration, the public reputation of the non-Hindu rulers and the need to legitimise the political authority on the rulers' end. Despite the problem posed by the dearth of sources with reference to the internal workings of these political structures, it is possible to understand these states' cycles of regime formation, regime perpetuation and regime disintegration.

Sind under Umayyad and Abbasid Rule

The Muslim invasions of Sind under Rāshidūn caliphs were mostly reluctant, perfunctory and abortive ventures. Earliest raids on Makran date from the times of Caliph 'Umar in *c.*23/644. The date of the first expedition to India is a matter of dispute, being assigned to either the 15th or 23rd year of Hijrah (636 AD or 644 AD).[8] The ninth-century Persian historian Balāzari claims that this expedition was executed via Bahrain (Oman) towards Daybul and Thānah (present-day Mumbai).[9] The details about the aftermath of this expedition are provided by his contemporary al-Ṭabrī, who reports that this successful expedition was nevertheless unauthorised by the caliph, who had forbidden the armies to penetrate further in India because of the uncertainty of its prospects for future development. At the end of Caliph 'Umar's reign, an expedition dated around 23/644 under al-Muhallab b. abi Ṣufrah reached Bannāh and al-Ahwār (Lahore), towns situated between Multan and Kabul.[10] The caliph Uthmān also prohibited his forces from invading Sind for logistic and strategic reasons.[11]

Umayyad military campaigns towards India were calculated and strategic. It was under the caliphate of Amīr Mu'āwiyāh (40–60/661–680) that Makran was conquered and colonised.[12] The next wave of significant military invasions is reported in the times of Ḥajjāj b. Yusuf (74–95/694–714),[13] an influential administrator under the Umayyad caliphs Abd-al Malik b. Marwān (66–86/685–705) and his son al-Walīd (86–96/705–715). Ḥajjāj as governor of Persia was indirectly responsible for the Umayyad expansion under al-Walīd since he selected generals such as Musā b. Nuṣayr, who consolidated Muslim rule in North Africa; Ṭariq b. Zayād, who conquered Spain; and Qutaybā b. Muslim, who conquered Turkistan.

After two unsuccessful military campaigns in Sind, Ḥajjāj b. Yusuf assigned the task of conquest to his cousin Muḥammad b. Qāsim. This third and final invasion under Muḥammad b. Qāsim won the Umayyads a foothold in India. Historicity of this invasion is debatable, since, some historians take the final invasion as an actual historical event, but sceptics characterise it as a 'historical romance'.[14] Although the invasion might have been a veracious event in history yet its accounts are not based on contemporary records. Whatever we know about this incursion is an outcome of the historical consciousness of Arabs and Sindhi Muslims. Different narratives of the event reflect more accurately the context of the person writing the account, rather than fact. For Arabs this invasion was one of the many expansions of that era.[15] Balazārī devotes few pages to describe this invasion while al-Ṭabrī confines himself to a few lines only. Sources produced in Sind like *Chachnamāh* and *Tārīkh-i-Ma'sumī* provide an elaborate description of the compassionate, military genius Muḥammad b. Qāsim.

The protagonist of the invasion saga Muḥammad b. Qāsim is sketchily depicted in the Arab sources but his rise and fall reveals personality-centric power dynamics under the Umayyads. From these accounts, a story emerges of a youth of tender age[16] who achieved the rank of a general bypassing all recruitment regulations, training requirements and normal paths of promotion. Two positions are available on his consanguinity with Ḥajjāj: one states that he was a cousin while the other suggests that he was a nephew. No matter what the relationship was Muḥammad's rise to power was connected to his propinquity with Ḥajjāj. Similarly there are multiple accounts of his fall from grace, reasons for dismissal from office and circumstances in which he breathed his last. While it cannot be determined whether he died while being transported to the caliph after arrest from Sind or in prison after a predisposed trial under the Umayyad court, one thing is certain: neither his success nor his military talents could ensure his survival in the system once his patrons Caliphs Walīd and Ḥajjāj were gone.

Long-term aims of Muḥammad b. Qāsim's invasion were to secure the trade route between Arabia and Ceylon and to enact the expansion policy of Caliph al-Walīd (86–96/705–715), in whose reign the Umayyad

Empire stretched visibly. The plunder of Arab ships by pirates, Raja Dāhir's refusal to support the Arabs against pirate raids, as well as the need to capture the 'Alāfī rebels of Makran taking refuge in Daybul formed three immediate catalysts for the invasion. This invasion was far more complex than unilateral application of Muslim power over local populations since regional powers worked as allies as well. The Umayyad military contingent comprised of only 6,000 Syrian troops and local groups, including local Jāts and Mīds who fought from the Arab side. Muḥammad b. Qāsim benefited from constant reinforcements, including six catapults and soldiers, from Syria. Ḥajjāj superintended the conquest from Kufā, and received *fatahnamās* (reports of conquests).[17]

Ḥajjāj's initial orders to Muḥammad b. Qāsim were to extend amnesty to all the inhabitants of Sind except those of Daybul, who had been sheltering 'Alāfī rebels.[18] The massacre of the conquered city Daybul continued for three days[19] and included destruction of the Buddhist temple along with its worshipers. Daybul possibly marks the first Muslim settlement in Sind, since it hosted the first Muslim garrison colony comprising 4,000 soldiers and also housed a mosque.[20] Some among the local population also converted to Islam including the chief of the Hindus of Daybul and received the elevated post of supervisor of the revenue officials under the Arab superintendent.[21] The capture of Daybul was followed by the conquest of other towns in the north, including Nirūn and Sadusān. These conquests were not accomplished by military ventures exclusively; victories also occurred in the form of a grant of protection on the condition of capitulation (*sulh*, *ahd-i wāsiq* and *amān*).[22] Mosques cropped up in conquered towns and a steady stream of wealth flowed from Sind to Ḥajjāj and the caliph. Allied towns that had brokered treaties with the invaders gained special privileges, such as patronage and exemption from taxation.[23] It was through the support of Jāts and the Mīds that Muḥammad b. Qāsim succeeded in killing Raja Dāhir in the battle. Muḥammad b. Qāsim remitted the spoils of war, including slaves and *fatahnamās*, to Ḥajjāj, who exhibited these proofs of victory in the congregation mosque and read *fatahnamās* in a sermon delivered in Kūfā.[24]

Within a few years of his governorship of Sind, Muḥammad b. Qāsim consolidated his hold on Brahmanābād, Alōr, Multan, and the areas surrounding them.[25] He even led an expedition to the foothills of Kashmir.[26] Although details about the Umayyads' political domination established under Muḥammad b. Qāsim are unavailable, sources[27] suggest that Muslims did not form an exclusive Arab ruling class in Sind at that time. Power was shared with the native administrative class under indigenous legal and political systems. The Ummayads' exercise of power over conquered towns was fluid and limited to tax collection. The Umayyad conquerors did not treat the vanquished populations as a monolithic group, distinguishing between different groups with varying policies. Only the *ahl-i ḥarb* (the fighting men) could be killed in battle, with the rest of the population becoming enslaved.[28] Instances of coerced conversion were seldom reported in the sources. When the conversions occurred, the converts were not enslaved and were not liable to pay *jazyā* (the protection tax on non-Muslims under Muslim rule).[29] According to *Fūtūh ul-Buldān* and *Chachnāmah*, many non-Muslim population groups were given *amān* (amnesty followed by protection); these included Brahmans, who could enter into the ruling elite and help the Muslim conquerors to administer and exercise authority. Traders, artisans, cultivators, common and poor people were usually allowed to carry on with their trades and occupations.[30]

Around 96/715 Muḥammad b. Qāsim was dismissed and later executed by Ṣāliḥ b. 'Abd al-Raḥmān, the fiscal manager of Iraq, as a result of the internal politics of the Umayyad ruling family. Ṣālih had been appointed by Caliph Sulaymān, the recent ascendant to the Umayyad throne.[31] According to Balāzarī, Muhamad b. Qāsim's demise saddened the locals, who placed an idol of him at al-Kirāj.[32] There is no evidence of this idol in any other historical record or material remains to verify this claim of popularity.

Under Caliph Sulaymān, the Umayyads lost the expansionist drive of their predecessor al-Walīd. Nevertheless, the Umayyads continued to appoint governors in Sind.[33] The overall political dominance of Muslims deteriorated, causing many of the convert rulers and populations to apostatise. The phenomenon of new converts reverting to their old religions may have been a frequent occurrence. Even so, accusations of apostasy were generally levelled against the populations that refused to pay taxes. The new city of al-Manṣūrah which was the seat of Umayyad governors in Sind was developed as a base for occasional expeditions to collect tax or to quell rebellions.[34]

The Muslim rule in Sind became further destabilised in the Abbasid era. As the Abbasids' administrative grip over Sind weakened, governors began to rebel. Consequently, many Abbasid governors were either killed or replaced by the Arab settlers in Sind who then requested the patronage of the caliph.[35] On some occasions, the governorship embraced a dynastic feature. For instance, the caliph confirmed the appointment of ʻImrān b. Mūsā Barmikī who succeeded his father in 221/836.[36]

The invasions of Muḥammad b. Qāsim and Maḥmūd of Ghazna are separated by approximately 375 years. This long interlude witnessed substantial fluctuation in political boundaries and the shift of Muslim rule from the hands of the caliph's governors to Arab settlers and local people.[37] The region of Sind stood on the western border of two successive central Muslim empires – the Umayyad and the Abbasids. The two empires' efforts to gain political control in a post-Muḥammad b. Qāsim era became desultory and ineffective. Nevertheless, the imperial expansion catalysed the emergence of independent Muslim dynasties that ruled in Hind, Sind, Multan and Makran. These localised Arab dynasties owed nominal allegiance to Abbasid and Fatimid caliphs and consequently had Sunni and Shiʻi orientation respectively. Even within the larger kingdoms that are discussed in next section, there were also major land-owners who maintained diplomatic relations with the Abbasid and Fatmid rulers. Four of the most notable of these dynasties – the Mahāniyā Kingdom of Sanjān-Hind, the Hibariyah Kingdom of Manṣūrāh-Sind, the Kingdom of Banū Sam'ā of Multan-Punjab, and the M'adaniyā Kingdom of Tīz-Makran – are discussed below.

Mahāniyā Kingdom of Sanjān-Hind (198–227/813–841)

The dock of Sanjān (located between present-day Mumbai and Maharashtra) came under Muslim suzerainty when a manumitted slave of Banū Sam'ā Faḍal b. Māhān conquered Sanjān in the times of Abbasid caliph al Mamūn (169–197/786–813). This kingdom remained visible in the Abbasid records until the period of Mū'taṣim (277/841). *Khuṭba* was read in the name of three caliphs and these local rulers sent valuable offerings to the Abbasids.[38] While surviving sources reveal little about the inner workings of the political system that this dynasty adopted, the establishment of the congregational mosque and sending elephants as gifts to the caliph demonstrate that the kingdom had strong religious and political inclinations towards the Abbasids.[39]

Faḍal b. Māhān was succeeded by his son Muḥammad, who wanted to establish his writ outside the capital. When he left the capital to fight bandits, his brother Māhān usurped the throne. Māhān was able to secure investiture from Caliph Mū'taṣim by sending curios including *sagwān* (teak wood).This recognition was a stratagem to legitimise his rule with the approval of the central Muslim government. Nevertheless, this justification did not suffice in the case of Māhān, who in the eyes of his brothers remained an illegitimate ruler. Succession fights followed which lead to the area being lost to local Hindus after a quarter century of rule.[40]

The only reference to this empire exists in Arab histories, emphasising the relationship between the kingdom and the central Muslim rule. The unceremonious end of the dynasty indicated a crisis of legitimacy within the royal family, lack of support for the ruler in his bureaucratic class and the dynasty's lack of roots among the natives who must have had scant investment in its continuation.

Hibariyāh Kingdom of Manṣūrāh-Sind (247–416/861–1025)

Manzar b. Zubair Hibari led the Hibariyāh tribe in Sind during the times of Abbasids.[41] His grandson 'Umar b. Azīz b. Manzar Hibari occupied some regions of Sind and established his seat in Manṣūrāh, by defeating and killing the Abbasid governor of Sind Imrān b. Mūsā Barmikī.[42] Although 'Umar managed to become the de facto ruler, he was not able to declare himself the ruler until next 20 years when he received recognition from Abbasids.[43] According to al-Yā'qūbī, after the death of the governor of Sind Hārūn b. Khālid in 854/240, 'Umar b. Azīz Hibari, who was occupying Sind, successfully wrote to the caliph requesting the governorship of Sind.[44] Even before the grant was awarded, the *khuṭba* was read in the name of Abbasid caliph. This indicated only nominal allegiance and 'Umar b. Azīz Hibari had internal and external freedom to rule. The Hibariyāh rulers dealt with the rebellions in Sind and were able to pacify the region.[45] After the death of Caliph al-Mutawakil in 247/861, the weakness in the central Abbasid caliphate became perceptible and 'Umar b. Azīz al-Hibari declared himself the sovereign.[46] No individual references to the successors of 'Umar are available and Arab and Persian sources only mention this dynasty briefly.

According to Ibn Ḥazm, this dynasty continued to exercise power until the time of Maḥmūd of Ghazna. Ibn Ḥūqal mentioned the Hibariyāh king as a king from Quraysh clan and described the population of Sind as Muslim.[47] Similarly, al-Muqaddasī attributed the Hibariyāh allegiance to the Abbasid caliph.[48] This dynasty ended when Maḥmūd of Ghazna raided the temple of Somnāth in 415/1025. This incident is reported by Ibn Athīr.[49] Ibn Khuldūn claimed that Maḥmūd killed the ruler of Sind, after he had become *murtid* (apostate), bringing the area under his suzerainty.[50] The allegations of being apostate may have been a political rhetoric to refer to populations under Muslim rule who stopped paying tribute to the caliph. The portrayal of the non-Muslim character of the population provided a pretext to Maḥmūd for invading India.[51]

Some sources suggest that this dynasty followed Imam Dāūdi Zāhirī (270/883) that propagated a system of beliefs within Islam that has now become obsolete.[52] Nevertheless, according to Yāqūt in *Majmaul-Buldān*, the dominant religious faith of Sind was Hanafite Islam.[53] These people were loyal to Abbasid rule and had cordial relations with the Abbasid *qāḍi-tul qaḍā* Qadi ibn Abi Shwārib's family.[54] The dynasty also had diplomatic ties with the Bawayids.[55]

According to al Masū'di, who exaggerates the extent of settlements, there were 300,000 settlements and villages under the suzerainty of the Hibariyāh ruler.[56] The ruler of Manṣūrāh, Yahyā b. Muḥammad, according to Yāqūt, is said to have occupied all of Sind including the inland area and coast.[57] This kingdom at its peak would have had many tributary states under Hindu rajas. Smaller kings ruled under the suzerainty of the Hibariyāh ruler Māhrūq b. Raīq[58] who controlled the city of Alōr in the region of Sāth.[59] The other contemporary autonomous neighbouring kingdoms included Banū Manbā in Multan, the Mugharids in Qasdār, and the M'ādānites in Makran while the Hībariyāh ruled directly in the central regions of Sind.[60]

According to al-Muqaddasī, the religious orientation of the indigenous Sindhi people was that of idolatry and many of them belonged to Sabian (a variety of ancient Middle Eastern religions based on Gnosticism and Hermeticism) faith.[61]The civil status of Sindhi people was that of *ḍhimmis* (non-Muslims living under Muslim rule who had been granted amnesty in return of either military service or payment of *jizya*).[62] According to the tenth-century Persian geographer Abu

Isḥāq Ibrāhīm b. Muḥammad al-Farisī al-Iṣtakhrī, the population of Sind comprised of Buddhists and Mīd.[63] Most likely, this was the reason why they adopted the appearance of Hindu Rajas, with long tresses and wore loose-fitting garments similar to *kurtās* worn in contemporary South Asia. The people of Manṣūrāh, in contrast, maintained a lifestyle (and dress code) similar to the people of Iraq.[64]

Kingdom of Banū Samā of Multan-Punjab (*c.*280–370/893–980)

The region of Multan came under Muslim suzerainty after its conquest by Muḥammad b. Qāsim. Until 122/739, governors were appointed by or were attached to Damascus. Their political status fluctuated between autonomy and nominal allegiance towards the caliphs until the advent of Banū Samā.[65] Multiple contradicting versions are available about the lineage of Banū Samā, and whether they claimed Quraysh descent.[66] They were largely considered anti-Shi'i due to their leaning towards Rāshidūn Caliph Uthman. In some instances they were reported to have apostatised.[67] The Banū Samā rose in India after the rise of the Māhāniya kingdom, which was founded by Faḍal b. Māhān, a manumitted slave of the Banū Samā, centuries earlier.[68] Despite a term of rule lasting 75 years, records of this dynasty are scarce.

We find three basic threats to this dynasty: the internal Shi'i elements, the Fatimids and the Hindu ruler of Kannauj (the kingdom of Punjab and Kashmir).[69] The ruler of Kannauj eventually was defeated and the kingdom of Multan expanded into that region.[70] A reflection on Abbasid and Fatimid rivalry also became pronounced,[71] and according to Ibn Khuldūn and Ibn Ḥūqal,[72] there were nine Abbasid caliphs in whose name *khuṭba* was read in the kingdom.[73] The ruling elite of the Multan region resided inside the forts that defended the kingdom and had least contact with the locals.[74] According to al-Muqaddasī, the kingdom of Multan was adjacent to the Manṣūrāh and Kannauj regions, Bathinda and Makran.[75] According to al-Iṣtakhrī who provides a graphic picture of the kingdom, the region was fortified and its population was half the size of Manṣūrāh.[76] The majority of the population comprised of Arabs abiding by the Muslim moral codes. Be that as it may, a temple existed in the middle of the city that looked like a fort surrounded by an ivory market along with the houses of worshippers.[77] Adjacent to this temple was the congregational mosque where the rulers, who lived in a village outside Multan, prayed.[78] This region was later lost to the Ismā'līs, whom Maḥmūd of Ghazna defeated and uprooted in turn.[79]

M'adaniyā Kingdom of Tīz-Makran (340–471/951–1078)

This kingdom was in the region of Makran[80] that had been connected with the Muslim empire since the times of Caliph 'Umar, yet it came directly under the control of the Muslims in the time of the Umayyads. Sanān b. Salmā b. Mahbiq Huzailī, a warrior from Banū Huḍayl tribe, was sent by Ziyād Abu Ṣufyān in the reign of Amīr Mu'āwiyāh to these regions.[81]

According to Balāzarī, Sanān first conquered Makran and then consolidated his rule by introducing an administrative set up in the region.[82] Later Ziyād b. Abu Sufyān sent Rāshid b. Amr Jadaidī from the Izd tribe to rule the region who conquered Qayqān (Gāgān, the region of Qalat). While Rāshid executed conquests of new territories, Sanān tended to administration. Seeing his efficiency, Ziyād had awarded the administrative responsibilities to Sanān who took care of the region for two years. During that time Makran remained a peaceful base for the Umayyad administrators.[83]

During Ḥajjāj b. Yūsūf's governorship of Iraq, he sent Saīd b. Aslam b. Zuhrā Kalabī to administer Makran. Two brothers from the Alāfī tribe, M'āwiyah b. Ḥāris 'Alāfī and Muḥammad b. Ḥāris 'Alāfī, killed Saīd with the help of 500 supporters and took over the region.[84] When Ḥajjāj got this news he sent Muja'ā b. Sār Tamīmī to Makran as the *'āmil* (governor). Muja'ā drove the Alāfīs out of Makran and consolidated the Muslim administration, although he died a year later.[85] There is some evidence available which suggests that Ḥajjāj then sent Muḥammad b. Hārūn b. Zara' to the area to conquer these regions and later his progeny ruled the area but even his rule did not last long.[86] The 'Alāfīs took refuge in Alōr in 85/704 which was short-lived since Muḥammad b. Qāsim conquered these regions soon after. The 'Alāfīs then went to Brahmanābād and later asked Muḥammad b. Qāsim for clemency, which was duly granted in pursuance to the orders issued directly from Ḥajjāj.[87]

'Īsā b. M'ādān occupied Makran in *c.* 340/951[88] and took residence in the region of Kīz. Later, his son M'ādān b. 'Īsā transferred the capital to

Tīz.[89] In this kingdom, cultural assimilation with the natives was visible through dressing and nomenclature choices of the rulers. For instance, the locals addressed M'adaniyā rulers as Māhārāj.[90] Strong heterodox influences were also discernible as according to al-Mas'ūdī, Makran was a region largely populated with the people of Khārjite faith.[91] It is possible that the dynasty belonged to the same faith as no evidence is found regarding M'ādān b. 'Īsā's background or allegiance to the Abbasid rulers[92] or the Fatimids in Egypt, demonstrating that it was neither Shi'i nor Sunni.[93] The local population composed of both Hindu natives and Arabs. Traders wore the clothes in Arabian style while some people wore *kurtās* and pierced their ears like natives.[94] Nevertheless, like the Arab rulers of Multan and Manṣūrāh these rulers preferred to live at a distance from the main city and followed the norms of Arab culture in general.[95]

It will be well to record here that the M'adaniyā Kingdom was not the only Muslim power in the region, as several other autonomous Muslim rulers marked their presence in the surrounding areas. For instance, the autonomous ruler of Mushkī (near Makran) Mutāhir b. Rij'ā pledged nominal allegiance to the caliph of Baghdad.[96] The Khārjites also ruled under Muslim suzerainty in the region of Turān (Qasdār). Maḥmūd of Ghazna targeted these regions and later the Khārjites were dethroned from both Makran and Kirmān by Shīhāb al-Dīn Ghūrī.[97]

Hind, Sind, and Regional Muslim Dynasties

During the pre-Ghaznawid times, the Muslim rule in India was confined to the Sind region. According to Arab geographers of the period, to the east the region of Sind faced the Persian Gulf, to the west the desert of Karman and Sajistān, to the north the cities of Hind and to the south the region of Makran, the middle desert of Baluchistan.[98] Al-Muqaddasī divided Sind into five sub-regions and mentioned important cities of Sind[99] which al Iṣtakhrī endorses, implying a consensus of the sources on information.[100]

The sources for this period are not indigenous and are limited to records of military expeditions, relations with the central Muslim Empires and establishment of mosques. The sources make clear that these areas were conquered and re-conquered, indicating the tenuous nature of Muslim rulers' control over the region. This instability and

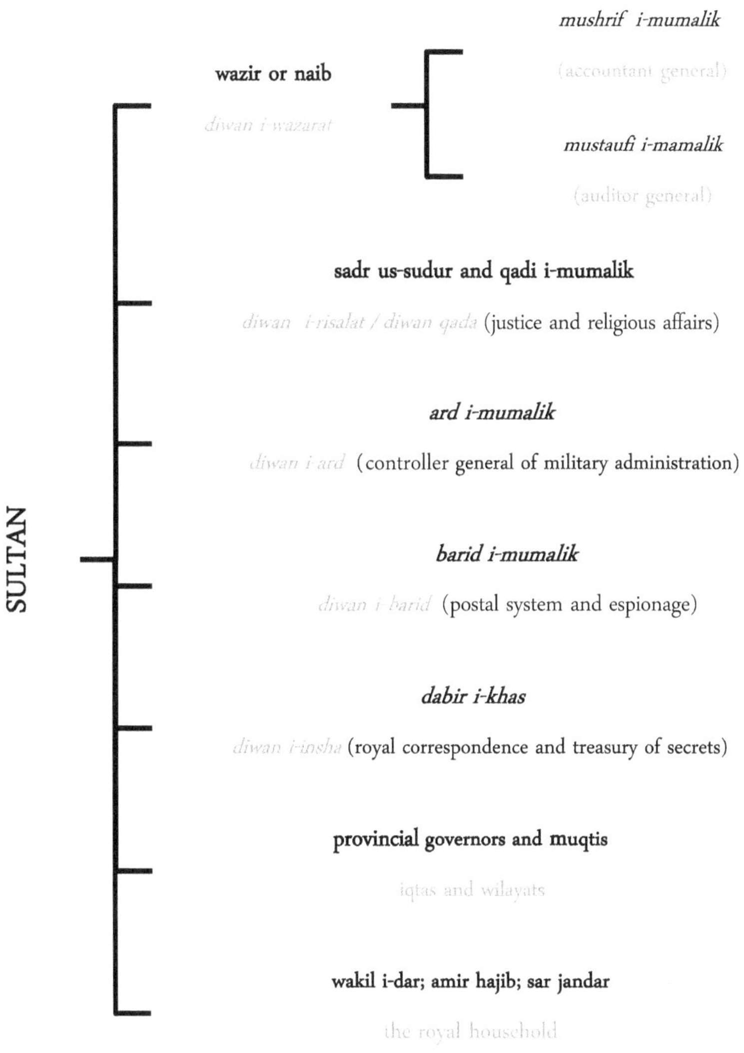

Figure 1.1 A Theoretical Construction of the Main State Departments in the Delhi Sultanate. Based on Qureshi, *Administration of the Delhi Sultanate*. A rough theoretical division of main administrative affairs in the Delhi sultanate helps understand the functions and priorities of the Delhi sultans as administrators. Undoubtedly the sultanate under its spells of better administration was performing most of the functions listed above but neither the departments nor the titles appear consistent during different reigns and in the sources.

Table 1.1 Summary Investiture, Coinage and Khutba

	QUTBI DYNASTY
Title	**Caliphal Reference**
Qutb a l-Din Aybeg (1206–1210)	Insignia granted by Ghiyath al-Din Muhammad (the nephew of Shihab al-Din Ghuri) in 1206.
Aram Shah (1210–1211)	No information.
	SHAMSI DYNASTY
Title	**Caliphal Reference**
Shams al-Din Iltutmish (1211–1236)	1229: Formal award of investiture and *khilat* by Abbasid caliph Abu Jafar Mansur al-Mustansir Billah. Coinage contained caliphs's name since 1225. Title: *Nasir amir al-mumineen*.
Rukn al-Din Firuz (1236) Radiyyah (1236–1240) Muiz al-Din Bahram (1240–1242)	*Khutba* and coinage in the name of Abu Jafar Mansur al-Mustansir Billah Adopted the title: *Nasir amir al-mumineen*.
Ala al-Din Masud (1242–1246)	1243: Abu Jafar Mansur al-Mustansir Billah died and his name was replaced on coinage with the name of his son al-Mustasim Billah.
Nasir al-Din Mahmud (1246–1266)	Al-Mustasim Billah and old coins containing name of Abu Jafar Mansur al-Mustansir Billah. Mustasim was brutally killed by Helegu in 1258 but his name continued to be on coins and was read in *khutba* for the next 40 years.

Ghiyath al-Din Balban (1266–1286) Muiz al-Din Kaiqabad (1286–1290) Shams al-Din Kaykaus (1290)	*Khutba* and coinage in the name of al Mustasim Billah adopted the title: *Nasir amir al-mumineen*

KHALJI DYNASTY

Title	Caliphal Reference
Jalal al-Din Firuz Khalji (1290–1296)	The news of al Mustasim Billah's death had reached the sultanate but Jalal al-Din was reluctant to remove his reference.
Rukn al-Din Ibrahim (1296)	Removed al Mustasim Billah's name from coins but held the title *Nasir amir al-mumineen*.
Ala al-Din Khalji (1296–1316)	Assumed the title *khalifa*. Did not restore al Mustasim Billah's name on coins. At one time held the titles *Nasir amir al-mumineen* and *Yamin al khalifat*.
Qutb al-Din Mubarak Shah (1316–1320)	Assumed the title: *Khalifa al-wathiq billah*.
Khusraw Khan (1320)	Title: *Wali amir al-mumineen*.

TUGHLUQ DYNASTY

Title	Caliphal Reference
Ghiyath al-Din Tughluq (1321–1325)	Restored al Mustasim's reference and the title *Nasir amir al-mumineen*.

Table 1.1 *Continued*

Muhammad b. Tughluq (1325–1351)	1344: Formal award of investiture and *khilat* by al-Mustakhfi bi-Allah (Cairo).
Mahmud b. Muhammad (1351 March)	No information.
Firuz Shah Tughlaq (1351–1388)	Formal award of investiture and *khilat.* Both sons of al-Mustakhfi Billah and al-Mutawakkal Billah were acknowledged as caliphs.
Ghiyath al-Din Tughluq II (1388–9) Abu Bakr Shah (1389–1390) Nasir al-Din Muhammad Shah (1390–1393) Ala al-Din Sikandar Shah I (March–April 1393) Mahmud Nasir al-Din (1393–1394) Nusrat Shah (1394–1399) Nasir al-Din Mahmud Shah (1399–1413)	Not clear if all these rulers were able to mint coins and had *khutbas* read in their names. Nevertheless, both sons of al Mustakhfi Billah and al-Mutawakkal Billah's names appeared whenever coins were minted. Adopted the title: *Naib amir al-mumineen*.
SAIYID DYNASTY	
Title	**Caliphal Reference**
Khizr Khan (1414–1421) Mubarak Shah (1421–1434) Muhammad Shah (1434–1445) Alam Shah (1445–1451)	Adopted the title: *Naib amir al-mumineen*.

absence of large-scale military power might elucidate why Arabs could not expand eastwards to the region of al-Hind. An additional source of difficulty for expansionist rulers was the constant power struggle between orthodox and heterodox religious groups. From the times of the Umayyad dynasty, eastern peripheral regions of the central Muslim empire became the centre of many heterodox Muslim sects, which challenged the orthodox doctrines of the central Muslim state. These sects included Khārjits,[101] Rawāfids,[102] and Ismā'līs (also known as Qaramathians in contemporary texts).[103] Some of the Ismā'līs dynasties maintained regular relations with the Fatimid rulers of Egypt. The interaction of heterodox religious movements and the ensuing political instability might have prevented Muslim rule from expanding into Hind. The prevalence of heterodoxy may also account for the display of symbols of Sunni Islam, claiming Muslim legitimacy in the eyes of the caliphate and even the common people. The policy of adopting Sunni religious symbols continued in the times of Ghaznawids and Ghūrīds. The Delhi sultans also requested the legitimacy conferred by regular acknowledgment from the Abbasid caliphs.

The Arab impact in India was complex, sporadic yet enduring. The available historical sources construct an uneven yet ultimately meaningful picture. The establishment of localised petty Arab kingdoms stands testimony to Muslim political and military domination within Baluchistan, Sind, Multan and Gujarat. The Arab adventurers did settle in the above-mentioned domains, many emerging as hegemon warlords scrambling for power over the native resources. The relationship between the rulers and the ruled was confined to the occasional collection of tribute, indicating the absence of a social base to support these kingdoms. Their connection with the central Arab empires, the Umayyads, Abbasids and Fatimids, remained nominal and symbolic. The warlords used diplomatic relations with the central caliphate as a means to legitimise their power. However, these symbolic relations served as little more than after-the-fact justifications for non-Muslim subjects and the warlord's powerbase alike. As soon as the warlord failed to exercise power effectively, he lost his kingdom as well as political support. While some of these Arab kingdoms lasted only for a few decades, others continued even after the invasions of the legendary Maḥmūd of Ghazna.

CHAPTER 2

MAḤMŪD OF GHAZNA: PLUNDERER, STRATEGIST OR ICONOCLAST?

Somnath: celebrated city of India, situated on the shore of the sea, and washed by its waves. Among the wonders of that place was the temple in which was placed the idol called Somnath. This idol was in the middle of the temple without anything to support it from below, or to suspend it from above. It was held in the highest honour among the Hindus, and whoever beheld it floating in the air was struck with amazement, whether he was a Musulman or an infidel. The Hindus used to go on pilgrimage to it whenever there was an eclipse of the moon, and would then assemble there to the number of more than a hundred thousand ... When the Sultan Yaminu-d Daula Mahmūd Bin Subuktigin went to wage religious war against India, he made great efforts to capture and destroy Somnat, in the hope that the Hindus would then become Muḥammadans. As a result thousands of Hindus were converted to Islam. He arrived there in the middle of Zi-l k'ada, 416 A.H. {December, 1025 A.D.} ... The king looked upon the idol with wonder, and gave orders for the seizing of the spoil, and the appropriation of the treasures.[1]

or

The central object of worship in the temple of Somnath was only the Shiva linga?[2]

Mahmūd of Ghazna's larger than life portrayal as an ideal ruler with extraordinary military and administrative achievements on Indian soil cannot be dismissed as mere magnification by sultanate historians, since his invasions instituted a new epoch of Muslim rule in India. The political control of the Ghaznawids in India was more effective and organised than their Arab predecessors and their successors the Delhi sultans drew enormously from Ghaznawids' military and administrative experience in the regions of the Punjab, Multan, Doab, Gujarat and Makran. The political behaviours of the rulers and the ruled and the patterns of governance under the Delhi sultanate maintain a remarkable resemblance to the Ghaznawids.[3] The Ghaznawid rulers promoted an explicit culture of patrimonial relations. Loyalty from the ruling elite i.e. *umarā', 'ulamā', ghulāms*, émigrés and heterogeneous free stock was achieved through patronisation. This loyalty was not directed towards any institution but was for the patron, who generously rewarded his favoured ones with wealth and privileges. The unsystematic administration was brought to order by the will and strength of the monarch, in the absence of which the system rapidly crumbled. Moreover, the use of religious symbolism was the salient feature of the Ghaznawid rule.

In the latter half of the tenth century, the Ghaznawids led by Abu Manṣūr Sūbūktagin (366–386/977–997) and Raja Jaipāl of the Hindu Shāhī dynasty competed for imperialistic expansion. The core regions of Hindu Shāhī dynasty were the regions of north-western India with its centre in Waihind. Jaipāl was defeated in 375/986–987 and forced to pay tribute to the Ghaznawids. This hegemony was, however, short-lived as Raja Jaipāl refused to pay tribute immediately after he returned to his kingdom. A confederacy of Indian princes led by the Raja made an unsuccessful military attempt to curtail the imperialist designs of the Ghaznawids in 380/991. Consequently, the Ghaznawids demanded heavier tribute and captured additional territory between Lamghān and Peshawar. The military success of Sūbūktagin initiated an era of Ghaznawid expansion and subjugation in the subcontinent.

After the death of Sūbūktagin, his son Maḥmūd (386–420/997–1030)[4] ascended to the throne of Ghazna. Maḥmūd made Lahore the winter capital of his dynasty and established a strong military and administrative base there. Maḥmūd appears to be the first ruler to assume the title of sultan.[5] In Punjab, the dynasty founded by Maḥmūd lasted until the second half of the twelfth century, when Shīhāb al-Dīn Ghūrī ousted its last ruler.

Patrimonial Bureaucratic Staff of the Ghaznawids

Sultan Maḥmūd promoted a patrimonial powerbase to consolidate his rule. He invited notables from foreign lands to his court. These notables comprised émigrés and local slaves, scholars, poets, scientists and artists,[6] who lived on the sultan's wealth. These trusted individuals were appointed on various civil and military positions and reported directly to the sultan.

The sultan was the arbitrator of justice with the extraordinary powers to intervene in judicial decisions. Punishments for political crimes were only his discretion. Nevertheless, like his predecessors, Maḥmūd also patronised a religious class of *'ulāmā'*, who interpreted religious law and performed a legislative function within the state. They were given the designations of *qāḍi*s (judicial officers) and *muftī*s (expounders of the law).[7]

Maḥmūd remained undefeated in his 33-year reign,[8] ensuring the prosperity of his powerbase and preventing any major rebellion in the core regions of his kingdom. His power rested on his ability to provide followers with military appointments and to maintain peace in the realm. The political theory of kingship, extended by Baranī in *Fatāwa-i Jahandāri*,[9] treats Maḥmūd of Ghazna as an ideal ruler, who provided economic relief in the times of drought, war and famine.[10] Although Baranī's statements in his work are largely speculative, it can well be inferred that Maḥmūd's success as a military commander and administrator crystallised his authority among the Muslim elite in India and Afghanistan. His exceptionally long reign, overseeing many successful expeditions, brought a steady stream of wealth from the conquered regions to the core areas of Ghaznawid empire which in turn built his reputation for bringing affluence and stability in the imagination of the Muslims in the Delhi sultanate.

Maḥmūd's success mainly rested on the efficiency of his military machine, since military expeditions provided the main source of the state's income. In keeping with medieval Islamic tradition, Maḥmūd nurtured a patrimonial army comprising his slaves, family members and free men. Maḥmūd capitalised on jealousies that emerged as an outcome of ethnic and religious divisions within his heterogeneous army.[11] With time, this patrimonial army evolved into a more systematic bureaucratic structure and consisted of a large number of regular troops and standing army that were paid in cash instead of kind. There were relatively defined systems of recruitments, standardised salary,[12] and systemisation of duties in the Ghaznawid army.[13] A large number of people in the core regions served in the army and received a salary from the monarch, who in return demanded loyalty.

Maḥmūd's government in the provinces (*wilāyat*) was a military-cum-civil arrangement. The civil and military officers were consciously given distinct yet intersecting realms of responsibilities in order to invite friction. Due to frequent discords, provincial civil and military officers reported directly to the centre and were unable to plot successful rebellions. Abu Bakr Baihaqi's account of Aḥmad-i Yenaltagin reflects upon the tension among the provincial governors.[14]

> After his selection, Aḥmad-i Yenaltagin took the oath of allegiance and signed the articles of agreement that were entrusted to the record keeper. Thereafter, the Khwāja [i.e. Khwājah Aḥmad-i Hasan Maimandi, the *wazīr*] said to him; 'you are a general and must act according to the articles of your agreement. You must not say anything to any person respecting political or revenue matters. But you must perform all the duties of the commander so that the *qāḍi* may not be able to drag you down. His majesty deems it advisable to send with you some of the Dailami Chiefs and some other of whom apprehensions are entertained [. . .] You must take them all and treat them kindly but they must not be allowed to go beyond the river Chenab without the King's order or without your permission. You must be careful not to let them mingle with the garrison of Lahore and not allow them to drink or play at *chōgān* [old version of polo].[15]

The directions given to the *qāḍi* were:

> Your job is management of the finances there and you have nothing to do with the military command or the army. [The new commander in chief] Aḥmad [Yenaltagin] will himself carry out duties required of him, he will exact the stipulated taxation and tribute from the native princes and then go out on plunder raids and bring back large sums of treasury.[16]

These paragraphs denote bureaucratisation and systemisation of governance. It is evident that each officer was to report to the ruler and the absence of hierarchy cultivated spite and distrust among the officers working in various capacities. These divisions among the officers curtailed the possibility of any single element becoming too strong to declare independence. Around 424/1033, Yenaltagin revolted against the centre.[17] Owing to the patrimonial nature of the army, the army of the province did not support him.[18] The sultan then assigned the Hindu general Tilak the task of eliminating the rebel. Tilak was triumphant in this venture and returned victorious to Ghazna in 426/1035, where he was the recipient of largesse and honours.[19] It is difficult to say whether the bureaucratisation of administrative affairs continued under the later Ghaznawids.

Maḥmūd's troops were a combination of *ghāzīs* (professionals) and *mutatāwī'a* (mercenaries). Regular system of recruitment, training and promotion was devised for a standing army that was given standard salaries even when no expeditions were being launched.[20] Maintaining a standing army was an expensive affair, difficult to be sustained solely through booty. Therefore, customary taxation must have been one of the state's paramount objectives. According to Islamic law, part of the spoils of war – including slaves, weapons and other valuables – were divided up amongst the soldiers in addition to their regular pay. Therefore, religious zeal and ambition for gaining enormous amounts of Indian booty encouraged the enrolment in the Ghaznawid army of various groups of professional soldiers or mercenaries from all over the Muslim world. An amount of 50,000 *dinars* from the state treasury was fixed for weapons and equipment of the mercenary troops.[21]

Ghaznawid Rule as Perceived in Subject Indian Regions

For the people of South Asia, the historicity of Maḥmūd and his invasions has long remained a battleground. While people of conflicting perspectives readily accept details given in the sources about the conquests without internal criticism of the historical content, Maḥmūd's intentions and influence inspire debate. Contemporary historical accounts of this episode are confined to Muslim perspective, the hyperbolic claims of which have long created communal tensions among

Hindus and Muslims. Nevertheless, the 'military feats' and 'plundering' of Maḥmūd instil a pride among aspiring '*butshikans*' (iconoclasts) as well as odium among those who contend that the Muslim invaders pushed the prosperous Hindu India centuries backwards into poverty and misery. Due to the absence of contemporary Hindu accounts, we are uncertain if Maḥmūd ushered in an era of ideological destruction in his targeting of temples, or whether he was simply among the many invaders who attacked temples for their copious wealth.

At its greatest extent, the Ghaznawid dynasty spread from the Persian regions of Ray and Isfahan to Hansi in the eastern Punjab.[22] The administrative presence of the Ghaznawid sultanate was distinctly uneven in the subject territories. While some of the areas were directly administered, others were only nominally affiliated. Ghaznawid territories can be classified according to their revenue extraction policy. First, crown lands offered money directly for the expenditure of the sultan. Second, in provinces revenue was extracted through government officials. Third, the tributary states yielded wealth only when the threat of a Ghaznawid attack escalated; and fourth, areas which were adjacent to the Ghaznawid territories but which remained unfeasible to conquer offered the plunder of war.[23]

The methods of revenue extraction from India explain the nature of the state presence in Indian regions and the response of the populations towards the Ghaznawids. Since Ghazna was the seat of governance, the presence of the sultan in the annexed Indian lands was sporadic. The sultan's representatives carried out his will in India. The practice of revenue extraction from India was irregular. Significantly, in the times of early Ghaznawids, there are no references to exclusive *dīwān* or permanent civil administration in northern India. Revenue was extracted occasionally through the medium of military forces. The amount collected had a direct correlation to the scale of threat posed to the subject population. Tribute was generally given either when the Ghaznawid forces reached the gates of the targeted city or the vanquished relinquished their valuables in order to avoid further warfare.[24] In the latter half of his reign, Maḥmūd tried to establish a relatively systematic revenue administration.

The details of Maḥmūd's expeditions in India provide substantial information about his methods of generating tribute. One of Maḥmūd's early expeditions was directed towards the region of Multan, which had experienced Muslim presence since the Arab invasions of Sind in the seventh century. During the course of the tenth century, it fell under Isma'īlī rule. In 395/1005–1006, Maḥmūd conquered Multan. Allegedly, a substantial sum of 20 million *dirhams* was extracted in lieu of tribute and security money, saving the city from devastation.[25] We can infer that regular tribute was extracted from these regions, since the sources do not hint at any further significant violent event for the next three decades. Tribute was paid in the form of cash and kind, including labour, elephants, and indigo. Historical records also mention the seizure of the dyestuff *nīl* (indigo), offered as a curio to the Ghaznawids. While most of the indigo was reserved for the sultans' personal consumption, there are instances when indigo was sent to the caliph and other rulers as presents.[26] Similarly, the Raja of Nārāyanpūr was able to win peace in his expeditions towards Alōr around 399/1009, by offering an annual tribute including 50 elephants and a pledge to provide soldiers for the Ghaznawid army. In an expedition near modern Allahabad around 413/1022–1023, a truce was brokered with the Raja Gandā of Kalinjar who promised an immediate payment of 300 elephants and an annual tribute.[27]

In the latter half of his reign, Maḥmūd attempted to establish systematic bureaucratic control over his territories in India. As mentioned earlier, there were multiple officers appointed to regions of the Punjab. A boundary line between civil and military duties was delineated. While the Turkish *ghulāms* seem to have been responsible for revenue collection and defence, the *qāḍi* was responsible for civil affairs. Yet, it seems that the arrangement was unstable in the long term.[28] It can safely be inferred that the attempt to establish a civil administration in the Punjab with a regular system of taxation was in accordance with the tradition of government in the core areas of the Ghaznawid empire. Nevertheless, later developments in this experiment in separation of state powers are unknown.[29]

Even after taking into account the apparent exaggerations in the Turco-Persian accounts of Maḥmūd's exploits, the spoils of war gathered from India must have been enormous. For instance, in 399/1008–1009, during his raid on a temple in the fort of Nagarkot in the upper Indus valley, Maḥmūd is alleged to have taken 'seventy million *dirhams* in coined money, 70,000 *mans* of gold and silver ingots and rich clothing, a folding house made of silver and a richly decorated throne'.[30] Moreover, the temple of Somnāth gave Maḥmūd 20 million *dinārs* in lieu of plunder and tribute.[31]

During the invasions of Maḥmūd, there was a large-scale transfer of gems, jewels and bullion from the Indian temples to Ghazna.[32] These treasures embellished imperial spaces and served as relics and artefacts. Riches were also converted into exchangeable form by the artisans and assayers (*nuqqad*) at Ghazna and were utilised as circulating currency.[33] Similarly, the wealth became a part of the largesse that the sultan extended towards his patrimonial staff comprising his associates, boon companions, favourites, courtiers, and poets. Since Islam allows for war booty, even the most pious in Ghazna did not hesitate to accept the spoils of war.[34] Keeping in view the enormous amount of wealth extracted from the regions of India, it can be assumed that the flow of wealth from India to Ghazna and its environs must have conferred unprecedented prosperity in the region. As a result, the relationship between the ruler and his subjects in the core regions must have been cordial. Though, the Indian lands of the Ghaznawid sultanate, from which taxes and tribute were demanded regularly, seem to lack the same level of prosperity.

Maḥmūd's achievements in India made him a legend to medieval Muslim historians. His invasions effectively perpetuated Muslim presence within the regions of the Punjab reaching up to the Doab. His military might earned him the reputation of invincibility. He not only eliminated his longstanding rival dynasty, the Hindu Shāhīs of Waihand, around 417/1026, but also undermined the claim of any confederation of Indian princes against his immediate successors. At the time of his attack on Somnath, many of the local rulers deserted their territories, convinced that they could not counter the Ghaznawid invaders.[35] Similarly, Maḥmūd's campaigns against the Qaramathians of Multan weakened their military might until the period of Mas'ūd's son Maūdūd's reign.[36] Although, the momentum of conquest in India was lost after Maḥmūd's death, Mas'ūd was able to keep the regions of Doab and Ganges valley under his control and some new conquests were also made.[37]

India was considered an integral part of the Ghaznawid sultanate. The economic basis of the sultanate of Maḥmūd rested upon his exploits in India. However, in the times of Mas'ūd, India's central status caused uncertainty in strategic aims and policies. A letter that the sister of Maḥmūd Hurra-i Khuttālī wrote to Mas'ūd on Maḥmūd's death reveals that the Ghaznawid family highly valued their possession of Indian lands. In this letter, she describes Ghazna, as the heart (*aṣl*) of the empire with its face towards India; Khorasan was next in importance and the rest were subsidiary.[38] Mas'ūd was killed in his bid to move to India by his *umarā'*, who replaced him with his brother.[39] The decline of the Ghaznawids had started before the death of Mas'ūd. Following his death, the Ghaznawid dynasty could not regain its strength and was consequently expelled from Ghazna by the Shansabanī dynasty of Ghūr. They then fell back on the winter capital of Lahore. The unavailability of historical data about the nature of later Ghaznawid presence in the Punjab blurs any picture of the relationship between the rulers and the ruled. Nevertheless, it can be argued that the majority of the population of Lahore comprised the émigré populations of *ghāzī*s and *'ulāmā'*. Therefore, it is possible that the Ghaznawid sultans of Lahore were in direct connection with the population of Lahore and offered them patronage.[40] The Ghaznawid sultans had cordial relations with the indigenous Indian rulers as well. We see this when the last Ghaznawid ruler Khusraw Shāh made an alliance with the Khokhar tribe in order to fight Shihāb al-Dīn Ghūrī.[41] These alliances proved futile and the Ghaznawid rule in India ended, and with the defeat of Khusraw Shāh the era of Ghūrī supremacy in India began.

Ideological Idioms in the Ghaznawid Empire: Sunni Islam in India

Maḥmūd's cordial attitude towards the Abbasids is one of the most prominent features of his reign. Religion was one of the major sources of legitimacy for the Ghaznawid sultans, both within and outside the sultanate. Maḥmūd sanctified his claims to power with the cachet of Sunni orthodoxy.[42] In the year 389/999, he received the investiture, robe and elevated titles from the caliph.[43] The symbols depicting the sultan's loyalty to the Abbasid caliph were publicised in order to gain legitimacy in the eyes of the locals. This incident had a historical context.

During the tenth century, political Shi'ism was gaining strength in many regions of the Islamic world. While in central Islamic lands the sympathy to Shi'i Islam had increased among the people, it was in this century that the Fatimid caliphate was founded in Egypt. Shi'ism was an expression of Persian national endorsement to the claims of the house of 'Alī. On the other hand, the Ghaznawids, who were ethnically Turk, followed the example of the Samanids in being the orthodox Sunnis, either because the Persians were the flag bearers of Shi'i Islam, or because of the political benefits and security that the association with orthodox Sunni Islam could bring to a nascent sultanate.[44]

Maḥmūd reinstated the name of Caliph al Qāḍīr in the *khuṭba* in Khorasan. He thus received the titles of *wāli-i amīr-ul-mumīnīn* and *yamīn-ud-daulā-wa-amīn-ul-millāh* ('the agent of the leader of the Muslims and right hand of the state' and 'the trustee of the nation on which the responsibility of the group has been bestowed'). These titles symbolised the relationship of cordiality and trust between the caliph and the sultan, and provided Sultan Maḥmūd with religious credibility to undergird his secular military aims. This moral backing not only legitimised the sultan's numerous attacks on non-Muslim populations but also on Muslim rulers of India, who were identified with Ismā'lī[45], Mu'tazilite or Bātinīyah sects[46] or who were declared *murtīd* (apostate) by the standards of Sunni Islam.[47] Although according to 'Utbi, the sultan's motives for attacking Multan were purely religious, yet the sultan also had a strong financial reason. Multan was at that time a rich centre of trade and commercial activity.[48] However, the sultan's hostility against the ruler of Multan was not purely secular in nature, since he had already initiated a purge of Ismā'līs in the Ghaznawid territories, and had promoted the Karamiyyāh sect to persecute Ismā'līs in Khorasan. As a result of his action against the Ismā'līs, who were strong political rivals of the Abbasids, he received the titles of Nizām al-Dīn and Naṣīr al-Haqq from al Qadir.[49] In various contemporary poetical works, Maḥmūd has thus been portrayed as the champion of the Sunni Islam against the Qaramathian '*fitnā*'.[50] The sultan portrayed himself as a religious warrior in his *fatahnamā*s[51] (declarations of victory) and descriptions of a particular battle sent by the ruler to different areas under his rule, to be read in public. These descriptions bolstered the credibility of the ruler among the ruled, who considered victory as a sign that God is on the rulers' side. Maḥmūd' maintained regular connection with the caliph, included the caliph's name on his coinage and sent Baghdad presents from his exploits of wars.[52]

Sultan Maḥmūd's successors continued his successful religious policies,[53] and his son Mas'ūd b. Maḥmūd had a similar orthodox approach. He also vowed to be the champion of Sunni Islam against the

Zinadiqā and Qaramathians. He had cordial relations with the Abbasids. In 421/1030 he received the investiture from the caliph and the illustrious titles Nāṣir Din Allah, Hāfiz 'Ibād Allah, al Muntaqīm min adā Allah and Zāhir Khalifat Allah amīr al Mumīnīn. This was an important development for Mas'ūd who was engaged in a succession struggle with his brother. On receiving the investiture and the titles, the sultan publicised these, in order to gain public support as a legitimate ruler. Three years later, the sultan received another patent investiture from the new Caliph al Qāi'm, who was enthroned in 422/1031 after the death of his father al Qāḍir. The patent was for all of India, Sind, Makran, Qusdār, Walīshtān, Khorasan, Khwārzim, Nīmruz, Zubulīstān, Chaghanīyān, Khuttalān, Qubadhīyān, Tirmidh, Ray, Jībāl, and in Isfahan for the whole of the territory as far as Hulwan, Gurgān and Tabristān.[54] Thus, the Ghaznawids at the time of Mas'ūd claimed authority over entire Hind, Sind, Makran and Qusdār. The last Ghaznawid ruler Khusraw Shāh and the Ghaznawid dynasty were eliminated in the wake of Shihāb al-Dīn Ghūrī's incursions in Punjab. Even then Maḥmūd's ideological idioms as well as his military and administrative practices lived on, as they were adopted by the Ghaznawid's military successors, the Ghūrīds.

CHAPTER 3

THE MASTER WHO CONFERRED HIS EMPIRE UPON HIS SLAVES: SHIHĀB AL-DĪN GHŪRĪ

> *'Let other sultans have one son or two. I have several thousand sons – Turkish slaves – whose inheritance will be my kingdom: after me, they will maintain the khuṭba in {my} name.' And it transpired as that ghāzī monarch pronounced. Since that time, right down until these lines are being written, they have preserved the whole empire of Hindustān and are still preserving it...*[1]
>
> or
>
> *A posthumous concoction to create sultanate history, its heroes and invent continuities?*

The military expeditions of Mu'izz al-Dīn Muḥammad b. Sām[2] famously known as Shihāb al-Dīn Ghūrī in India mark the commencement of an era that can be termed as the formative phase of the Delhi sultanate. The most distinguishing feature of this period was its extensive reliance on patrimonial bureaucratic staff for conquest, annexation and consolidation of rule in the new lands. This patrimonial staff was heterogeneous in its ethnic orientation, comprising Turk, Tajik and Khaljī slaves and free elements. Sultan Shihāb al-Dīn Ghūrī unmethodically appointed these officers as governors of the conquered lands along with the responsibility of civil and military administration. In this age of annexation and consolidation, these patrimonial officers were the sub-sovereigns, who established theoretically quasi-autonomous and practically autonomous political control on their assigned lands. As sub-sovereigns, these officers nurtured their own patrimonial staff through largesse and patronage. In some instances, these patrimonial officers issued investitures for different areas of India and ordained their subordinates' with the right to rule. The religious, racial and cultural differences between the conquered and the vanquished make the nature of political authority and the mediums through which legitimacy was acquired an intriguing subject of investigation.

This chapter explores the patterns of political authority exercised under Shihāb al-Dīn Ghūrī and his patrimonial staff. This era saw contested claims of control along with multiple, indefinite layers of authority in a region marked by a complex system of political control. The selection criteria for particular posts, the training required for service, the system of promotions, trust-based relations and hierarchies among the ruling elite are discussed at length. This chapter also highlights the use of religious, cultural symbols, projection of economic and military success as divine support to the ruler as attempts to establish legitimacy with the common people.

The Persona of Shihāb al-Dīn Ghūrī: A Source of Legitimacy for the Delhi Sultans

Much of what we know about Shihāb al-Dīn Ghūrī is from historical records written posthumously in the sultanate period to magnify his Indian exploits and their aftermath. He is lauded as a warrior of Islam whose patrimonial officers – the Delhi sultans – established Muslim suzerainty over the pagan Indian lands.[3] The Delhi sultans used their connection with Shihāb al-Dīn Ghūrī to legitimise their rule. Measuring this strategy's success is an intriguing issue, since until the end of Ölberli line various rival contenders to the throne drew links to the Ghūrīd line.

The hyperbole in historical accounts can be discerned from their references to Shihāb al-Dīn Ghūrī's ethnicity and religiosity. Multiple versions are available regarding the ethnicity and conversion of the Shansābānī or Ghūrīd tribe to Islam. The sultanate historian Abu Amr Minhāj al-Dīn Juzjāni composed *Tabāqāt-i Nāsiri* six decades[4] after the demise of Shihāb al-Dīn Ghūrī. In order to justify the sultan's right to expand in India and the subsequent rule of his slaves, Juzjāni traced his lineage from Azhd Zahāk, the Persian mythological figure of Firdusī Tūsī's *Shahnamah*,[5] claiming that the Ghūrīds came under the fold of Islam in the times of the Rāshīdūn caliph 'Alī.[6] The modern historians dismiss both of Juzjāni's claims and consider him a man from Tajik stock who had come under the fold of Islam as a result of eleventh-century Muslim invasions of neighbouring areas of Persia and Khorasan.[7]

Like Maḥmūd of Ghazna, the Ghūrīds sought recognition from the Abbasid caliph. Their change of sect was interpreted as opportunism, an attempt to be taken seriously by the central Muslim empire – the Abbasid caliphate. The Ghūrīds had come under the fold of Islam around the eleventh century.[8] As a society recently converted to Islam, they came under the influence of the Kāramiyyah sect.[9] This sect had *madrasah*s (religious education institutions) and *makātib* (schools) in Ghūr. They emphasised asceticism in life, practised austerity and considered Sufism as heretical.[10] Both the Shansabānī princes were initially from the Kāramiyyah sect but later, Sultan Ghiyāth al-Dīn adopted Shāf'ī Islam, and Sultan Shihāb al-Dīn converted to Hanafite Islam.[11] Ghiyāth al-Dīn's conversion was seen with contempt by the *'ulāmā'* of the Kāramiyyah sect. One Imām, Ṣadr al-Dīn 'Alī Hussayn Nīshapurī, who taught in a prestigious *madrasah* of Afshīn in Garjistān composed a satirical poem against the sultan's change in belief. The sultan was displeased but he did not punish the scholar,[12] demonstrating his tolerance towards different sects and religions. He extended lavish patronage to religious scholars and secular scientists, gathering a large number in his court. He sent gifts and stipends to people of piety and learning in cities across Khorasan, Ghazna and India.[13]

The home of the sultans of Shansabānī dynasty was the hilly region of Ghūr in Afghanistan.[14] Maḥmūd of Ghazna invaded this region in 400/1010. The rise of the Shansabānīs of Ghūr, minor warlords under the Ghaznawids, coincided with this episode. The declining power of the Ghaznawids witnessed the rise of the Ghūrīds.[15]

The Ghūrī expansion in other regions followed the tradition of the Ghaznawids, extending towards Central Asia and Persia in the west and India in the east. The Shansabānī sultan, Shihāb al-Dīn Ghūrī, was among those warlords who were carving out principalities outside the Islamic frontiers. Thus in the last decades of the twelfth century, he was able to annex a large portion of north Indian lands into his kingdom. His elder brother Sultan Ghiyāth al-Dīn Muḥammad b. Sām was undoubtedly the most successful ruler of the Shansabānī dynasty. Owing to the efficiency of his arms, he was able to annex a substantial area of Afghanistan and Central Asia, including Herat, Garmsīr, Zamindāwār Gharjistān, Talqān and Jarzvān.[16] After defeating Bahā al-Dīn Toghril, one of the main Seljuk nobles in Herat, he successfully marched on the territories of Qadās, Jalivān, Tīwār, and Saifrud.[17]

Ghiyāth al-Dīn Muḥammad b. Sām's next target was Ghazna. The sultan took a hostile stance against the region. After his victorious return from Sajistān (Sistān), his deputed warriors frequently raided and plundered the region of Ghazna. In 568/1173, following Ghazna's eventual conquest, Shihāb al-Dīn Ghūrī was deployed as the overlord in this region.[18] The new ruler seems to have been successful in ameliorating the conditions of Ghazna since under his rule it caught the attention of traders and merchants, who had moved to other regions during the reign of his predecessor Ghuzz Turks.[19]

Fakhr-i Muddabir, who credited Shihāb al-Dīn Ghūrī for bringing peace and order to the area, also attested to his administrative efficiency. Travellers and caravans were provided with security. Similarly, the Qaramathians, who were reported to have been responsible for pillage and disorder, were strictly curtailed. By securing trade routes towards Ghazna, Shihāb al-Dīn Ghūrī successfully revived commercial activity. Scholars and men of letters gathered in Ghazna were drawn by the sultan's patronage. For the masses the standard of life improved considerably. Under the rule of Shihāb al-Dīn Ghūrī, those who previously could not afford a single menial slave could purchase expensive animals and slaves.[20]

After bringing peace and order to his domain, the sultan started making inroads into Indian lands. Following the example of Maḥmūd, the sultan initiated a series of raids into India. His first prey was the Qaramathian kingdom of Multan and Uchh (upper Sind), which fell in 570–571/1175–1176. After two years, he marched on the region of Gujarat where his forces were routed. He conquered Peshawar with less difficulty in 574–576/1178–1180.[21] His next attempt was towards the fortified city of Lahore in 576–577/1180–1181, where he was defeated. After retreating to his base, he moved towards the region of Sind, to guard against the perceived Qaramathian threat in 578/1182. His raids were successful and he was able to collect a large amount of booty.[22]

The region of Lahore was under the suzerainty of the Ghaznawids at the advent of Shihāb al-Dīn Ghūrī's rule in India. The dynasty had lost the glory it had seen in the time of Maḥmūd of Ghazna. Khusraw Malik, the last Ghaznawid ruler was too weak to be considered a threat but was not an easy target all the same due to his alliances with Hindu kings of Punjab. Shihāb al-Dīn Ghūrī planned to conquer Lahore via stratagem instead of employing a direct attack. This manoeuvre necessitated hitting the enemy while it was defenceless.

In 581/1186, the son of Khusraw Malik, who was kept as hostage in Ghazna to provide an indemnity on behalf of his father, was released. Khusraw Malik perceived the news of release of his son as a gesture of goodwill. Shihāb al-Dīn Ghūrī, on the other hand, reached Lahore before Malik Shāh, the son, by taking a shorter route and caught the Ghaznawids off guard. Khusraw Malik surrendered instantly. He and his son were imprisoned in Gharjistān and subsequently killed in 587/1192 when Khwārazm Shāhī threat to Ghūrīds became grave.[23] Thus the Ghaznawid kingdom of Lahore came under the domination of Shihāb al-Dīn Ghūrī who appointed his officers to rule it. This kingdom had experienced Muslim rule over a span of one and a half centuries and had a significant Muslim population that had migrated to 'little Ghazna' from all over the Muslim world.

Invasions of Rājpūt lands began around 585/1190, when the sultan came into direct contact with Prithvi Rāj (Rai Pathurā of Persian histories) the ruler of Ajmer. The principal victory was at the fort of Tabarhindā (present-day Bathinda in Indian Punjab).[24] Malik Ḍiyā' al-Dīn Tūlakī, who was appointed as guardian of the fort, was the first to confront Prithvi Rāj. Despite the former's courage, control of this region was lost. Sultan Shihāb al-Dīn Ghūrī, in order to regain the control of the fort, came face to face with Prithvi Rāj. In 586/1191, the famous battle of Tarā'īn was fought. The army was routed and the sultan nearly met his end.[25] The sultan, being admirably persistent, was not dispirited by yet another defeat. He returned next year in 587/1192 and was able to defeat Prithvi Rāj on the same plains of Tarā'īn.[26]

Political control within the Ghūrīd sultanate was multi-layered. After his victory in the battle of Tarā'īn, Shihāb al-Dīn Ghūrī sent his brother Ghiyāth al-Dīn at Fīrūzkūh the choicest treasures from booty he had acquired; these included a wheel, a chain, a huge melon with a circumference of five yards and two large drums, all made of gold. Ghiyāth al-Dīn Muḥammad ordered the wheel, the chain and the melons to be hung on the gate of the congregational mosque of Fīrūzkūh to share the spectacle of these victories with the masses.[27]

The Ghūrīds also used their recognition from the caliph to legitimise their rule. The sultan at Fīrūzkūh twice received emissaries and investitures from the caliph of Baghdad.[28] On the other hand, his other Central Asian counterparts (i.e. Sultan Tekish Khwārazm Shāh (596/1200) and the Sultan of Samarqand) did not enjoy the same status since they were the vassals of the Qara-Khitai ruler. The statement of Juzjānī that 'the caliph considered them unworthy Muslims who deserved to be eliminated'[29] testifies that the caliph had chosen the Ghūrīds as his champions and had acknowledged them as the only legitimate political power in the region.

There was no major conflict between Sultan Ghiyāth al-Dīn Muḥammad and Sultan Tekish. Perceiving Tekish's death as an opportunity for expansion, the Ghūrīd brothers decided to go to war against Tekish's son 'Alā al-Dīn Muḥammad Khwārazm Shāh. Subsequently, Khorasan was captured. Nevertheless, after the death of Sultan Ghiyāth al-Dīn Muḥammad, Khwārazm Shāh recaptured the areas that had been lost.[30]

Shihāb al-Dīn Ghūrī became the overlord of the Ghūrī dynasty in 599/1203 after the death of his brother Sultan Ghiyāth al-Dīn Muḥammad. Shihāb al-Dīn Ghūrī emerged as the prime decision maker in his family.[31] He duly divided his brother's territories among his sons under collective sovereignty, a practice dating from the times of 'Alā al-Dīn Jahansūz. While each prince was assigned an area, it was ruled under the name of the Shansabānīs. The notables of Ghūr continued to enjoy the same power as they had previously.[32] Malik Ḍiyā' al-Dīn Muḥammad Alp Ghāzī, the son in law of the deceased sultan, was given the territories of Fīrūzkūh, the seat of Ghūrīd power, along with the regions of Ghūr and the *wilāyat* of Zamindawār. The son of the deceased sultan Prince Muḥammad was given the territories of Faraḥ and Isfizār. Naṣīr al-Dīn, his sister's son, was given the regions of Herat and its adjunct principalities.[33]

This was the time when Sultan Shihāb al-Dīn's patrimonial officers were well established in the Indian territories, ruling quasi-independently. They had been successful in carving out principalities in pagan Indian lands and making inroads into regions that had never experienced Muslim presence. In some regions, this rule had become consolidated to an extent that the Muslim governors were not confined to the fortifications merely. They constructed monuments, patronised various social groups including émigrés, the *'ulāmā'* and intellectuals. At this time, the territories directly under Shihāb al-Dīn's control were significantly less than the empire he ruled through slave officers.[34]

The appointments in the Indian regions included Quṭb al-Dīn Aybeg who was given the region of Delhi. Bahā al-Dīn Toghril was a senior Mu'izzī slave, who had received command of the fortress of Thangīr (Bayana) in 592/1196 and later was given the task of securing the great fortress of Gwalior from Mu'izz al-Dīn in person. He deeply resented his surrender of Gwalior to Aybeg in 596/1200–1201. Similarly, sometime before 600/1204, Nāṣir al-Dīn Aytam held the strategically significant garrisons of Multan and Uchh.[35] After his death the charge of these territories was transferred to Nāṣir al-Dīn Qubacha, a Mu'izzī Turk. Tāj al-Dīn Yildiz, the foster son and the most senior slave of the sultan, who held the *iqṭā'* of Karman (the upper Kurram valley) and controlled the route from Ghazna to India.[36]

After the death of his brother Ghīyath al-Dīn in 599/1203, the sultan's energies were largely absorbed in the developments in Khorasan, where the Khwārazm Shāh sought to recover territories previously lost to the Ghūrīds. He succeeded in 600/1204 at Andkhūd.[37] While victories earned Shihāb al-Dīn Ghūrī followers, failure resulted in desertions and betrayals. In 602/1206, Sultan Shihāb al-Dīn was murdered in Dhamyāk near Jehlum, leaving no male heir. Consequently, a scramble to control his domains ensued among his slaves, relatives and opponent Khwārazm Shāh.[38]

The death of Shihāb al-Dīn proved to be a major disaster for the Ghūrīd dynasty, resulting in secessionist fights among the Ghūrīd princes. The Khwārazm Shāhī dynasty was the major beneficiary of this situation. The Khwārazm Shāh not only re-established his control over the entire Khorasan, but also increased the territory under his suzerainty to encompass the territories of the Ghūrīd dynasty. Within ten years of Ghūrī's death, the entire region of the Ghūrīd Empire up to the Indus River was brought under the suzerainty of the Khwārazm Shāh. Only the region of northern India remained under the slave generals of Shihāb al-Dīn.

The Mu'izzī Patrimonial Officers

The Indian lands under the suzerainty of Shihāb al-Dīn Ghūrī were assigned to different slave and free patrimonial officers known as Mu'izzīs. Although Shihāb al-Dīn Ghūrī oversaw their appointments and transfers, these officers were independent to make crucial administrative decisions. These officers nurtured subordinates, whom they cultivated on patrimonial lines. They acted like sultans of their own regions and were generally free to command and conquer without the knowledge of their master. Four key patrimonial officers took possession of the major portions of Shihāb al-Dīn's empire after his death. Tāj al-Dīn Yildiz took Ghazna. Quṭb al-Dīn Aybeg was enthroned in Lahore, Bahā al-Dīn Toghril took hold of the Bayana region and Nāṣir al-Dīn Qabacha established himself in Sind. All of them acted as the autonomous rulers in their territories.

Tāj al-Dīn Yildiz (602–611/1206–1215)

Tāj al-Dīn Yildiz, purchased by Shihāb al-Dīn as a youth, rose to the office of chief of the Turkish *amīr*s in the contingent of Shihāb al-Dīn.[39] Later, he was granted the *iqṭā'* of Sankurān and Kerman[40] which included, a strategically important area that contained several mountain passes that connected Afghanistan to India, and several populated and fertile regions that yielded high taxes. He was the sub-sovereign of a vast land stretching from the salt range in the north to Gomal Pass in the south and Gardaiz in the west to Indus Basin in the east.[41] On the death of Shihāb al-Dīn, his status rose from malik to sultan. As sultan, Tāj al-Dīn Yildiz claimed regions from Ghazna to northern Punjab as a part of his kingdom.[42] These areas consisted of largely Muslim population with a century of experience with Muslim rule. Yildiz's claims to political legitimacy were manifold. Firstly, he was the most senior among the slaves of Shihāb al-Dīn,[43] who were purchased as children and given special training by the sultan.[44] Second, he was the primus inter pares among Shihāb al-Dīn's officers.[45] Third, Yildiz was awarded a black banner by Shihāb al-Dīn as an indication that he would be the successor.[46] Being the overlord of an important strategic position, he was able to obtain investiture and the royal parasol[47] from Shihāb al-Dīn's nephew.[48] From 602/1206 until 611/1215,[49] the political power in northern Indian regions was contested between Yildiz and Aybeg initially and later between Yildiz and Iltutmish. He was also in constant conflict with Qabacha in Punjab.[50]

In comparison to Aybeg, Yildiz proved to be a stronger monarch, with a more stable political presence and with better support in the Ghazna region. It was due to the threat of encroachment from Yildiz that Aybeg seems to have stayed in Lahore from 602/1206 to 606/1210.[51] It is pertinent to assume that, during the times of Aybeg, the over-lordship of the regions of Koh-i Jūd (salt range) was contested between Aybeg and Yildiz.[52] When Iltutmish rose to power, he inherited the offensive stance of Yildiz from Aybeg. It took Iltutmish almost nine years to eliminate this threat. While Yildiz had obtained the region of Ghazna from the Bamian branch of the Shansabānī dynasty, he regularly conducted raids towards Ghūr, Sajistān and Khorasan and often nominated governors to these areas.[53] Consolidating his stronghold in Sajistān, he went as far as the gates of the city of Sistān but was unable to sustain conquest. Later, he backtracked after concluding a truce with the ruler of Sajistān.[54] Panicked by the presence of Khwārazm Shāh in the region, he fell back to Lahore. His attempt to expand into Delhi was effectually countered by Iltutmish in Tarā'īn. The overpowered Yildiz was imprisoned in Badaun and was subsequently put to death.[55] It is also interesting to note that the coins of Yildiz also bore an image of a horseman and the Hindu God Shiva's bull Nandi. This demonstrates his use of Indian symbols in order to find support for his rule among his Indian subjects.[56]

Naṣīr al-Dīn Qabacha (602–625/1206–1228)

Naṣīr al-Dīn Qabacha was an influential senior Turkish slave of Shihāb al-Dīn Ghūrī who was entrusted with various military and civil administrative capacities during the sultan's life.[57] He ruled Sind for more than two decades and offered asylum and patronage to a large number of Mongol stricken émigré Muslim scholars and notables. Because of this patronage he stands prominent in many historical records, including the *Chachnāmah*,[58] *Tārīkh-i Fakhruddin Mubārik Shāh*,[59] *Lubāb al-Albāb* and *Jawami-'ul Hikayat*.[60]

Qabacha's early career was marked by success and distinction. Qabacha was appointed as governor of Uchh after the battle of Andkhud (599/1203).[61] Later, he was also given the possession of the cities of

Multan, Sindustān (Swistān) and Daybul as far as the coastal region. According to Juzjānī, he subjugated cities, fortresses, and towns of the cities of Sind and assumed two canopies of state.[62] He further annexed eastwards as far as the limits of Tabarhindāh (Bhatinda), Kuhrām and Sursutī.[63]

Qabacha made several efficacious attempts to capture Lahore, yet he was unable to retain the city for a long time. He was at loggerheads with Tāj al-Din Yildiz, who used to invade the Punjab regularly.[64] Qabacha permanently retreated to Sind in 602/1206 when forces of Yildiz defeated him.[65] Since Sind was the gateway to India from the western Islamic lands, during the Mongol invasions, Qabacha received a great number of refugees from Khorasan, Ghūr and Ghazna.[66] The political status of Qabacha's territories after the death of Shihāb al-Dīn Ghūrī had become that of tributary state of the Khwārazm Shāhī dynasty. Unable to resist the Mongol strikes, in 609/1213–1214 the Khwārazm Shāhīs fell upon Ghazna.[67] Dealing with multiple hostile fronts, Tāj al-Dīn Yildiz, as mentioned earlier, was eliminated by Shams al-Dīn Iltutmish around 611/1215. At this point, Qabacha came directly in contact with the Khwarazm Shāhī Prince Jalāl al-Dīn Mingbarnī,[68] who tried to occupy land in the Indus region. As a result, the relationship between Qabacha and Mingbarnī turned hostile.[69] When Genghis Khān raided Afghanistan around 616/1220, Jālāl al-Dīn Mingbarnī fell back to Sind and then proceeded to the regions of Daybul and Makran.[70] Mingbarnī defeated Qabacha who had helped him initially but later opposed him when he could not stand against former's expansionist designs.[71] Later, in a skirmish with Shams al-Dīn Iltutmish, Qabacha accidently drowned in the river.[72]

Despite constant wars and instability in his region, Qabacha is credited with having built schools, colleges and mosques in the Sind that may already have had a predominantly Muslim population. Due to the considerable influx of an émigré population he was able to give the region of Sind a predominantly Muslim character.

Baha al-Dīn Toghril

Bahā al-Dīn Toghril was among the senior slaves of Shihāb al-Dīn Ghūrī. The sultan gave him the fortress of Thangīr in the territory of Bayana, where he administered his authority independent from any other military commander of the sultan.[73] Toghril earned his reputation as an efficient administrator by patronisation of knowledge, art and religion, which encouraged an influx of Muslim émigrés.[74] The prosperity of his region was further symbolised by architectural monuments.[75] Trade and commerce flourished under the aegis of Toghril, as Hindustanī and Khorasanī traders enjoyed special privileges and protection.[76] He also founded the city of Sultānkot. Later, in recognition of his efficiency, the sultan charged him with the duty to take over the fort of Gwalior.[77] Toghril brilliantly weakened the resistance as he built a fortification at the distance of one league from the fort for the cavalry. His military strategy proved to be an utter failure as the enemy surrendered to his arch-rival Aybeg, which was a cause of vexation for Toghril.[78] Later, at the death of Shihāb al-Dīn Ghūrī, Bahā al-Dīn Toghril adopted the title of sultan in the region.[79] Due to limited historical data available about him, there is ambiguity regarding his reign; yet it is certain that he was among notable contenders of power in the post-Shihāb al-Dīn era.[80] The unavailability of any references of Toghril in the accounts of Iltutmish indicates either that he was successfully eliminated at the end of Aybeg's rule or that Iltutmish or some other warlord of the region overthrew him.[81]

Even decades after Toghril's death, his progeny had strong familial claims to Bayana. Sultan Iltutmish developed matrimonial alliances with the family of Toghril, as one of his trusted manumitted slaves Tāj al-Dīn Sanjar Arsalān Khān was married to Toghril's daughter. Ten years after Iltutmish's death, his son Sultan Nāṣir al-Dīn Maḥmūd appointed Tāj al-Dīn Sanjar as the governor of the territories that were earlier ruled by Toghril.[82]

The Khaljī Maliks of Bengal (587–624/1192–1227)

The story of Ikhtiyār al-Dīn Bakhtiyār Khaljī, a freeman of the Gramshīr region, is a classic example of an adventurer endowed with military talents in search of patronage.[83] His fellow Khaljī tribesmen served in the army of Shihāb al-Dīn Ghūrī. Ikhtiyār al-Dīn wanted to test his fortune in Bengal; but, he was unable to impress the *'āriḍ* (muster master) of Shihāb al-Dīn Ghūrī. He then proceeded to Delhi but was unable to gain any substantial military aid from Quṭb al-Dīn Aybeg either.[84] Finally, he managed to gain some help from 'Ali Nagaurī who had recently become the feudatory of Nagaur independent of Malik

Quṭb al-Dīn Aybeg.[85] 'Ali Nagaurī granted the *iqṭā'* of Kashmandī to Ikhtiyār al-Dīn from where he was able to expand further and make incursions in Muner and Bihar.[86] These campaigns won him horses, arms and men that he required for further expeditions. Within a brief period of time he earned a reputation as an able warrior and administrator which attracted the attention of his fellow Khaljī tribesmen, who rallied around him.

His success as a warlord secured him acknowledgment from Quṭb al-Dīn Aybeg who had not assumed the title of sultan yet[87] but was powerful enough to grant him a robe of distinction.[88] Ikhtiyār al-Dīn attacked many fortified cities of Bihar. A seminary in the area was also captured, with the Brahmins annihilated and the books seized. Later Hindus were hired to translate them for the Muslims.[89] Aybeg's superiority over Ikhtiyār al-Dīn is manifested by the latter's sharing of booty with the former and visiting Delhi after this success.[90] As reciprocation, Aybeg again bestowed honour upon him, in the form of an imperial robe that he had received from his own master. This denotes the symmetry of the relationship between Aybeg and Ikhtiyār al-Dīn Bakhtiyār Khaljī.[91] He brought different parts of Bengal under his sway,[92] instituted the reading of *khuṭba* and minted his own coins. Juzjāni does not clarify whether he had issued *khuṭba* and coins in his name or in the name of Shihāb al-Dīn Ghūrī.[93] The fame of his military operations reached the ears of the historian Ibn al-Athīr in Iraq, it also caused a later author to give the Khaljī tribesmen alone the credit for the Muslim conquests in India. Nevertheless, Ikhtiyar's major feat was his acquisition of a considerable tract in the Ganges basin where Shihāb al-Dīn Ghūrī's forces had not penetrated.[94] Some of these regions started acquiring a Muslim character as mosques and colleges were founded in the subjugated areas. However, Ikhtiyār al-Dīn Bakhtiyār's incursions had merely secured the north-western part of Bengal, where Muslim authority now centred on the town of Gaur, renamed Lakhnawtī; eastern Bengal, the region called 'Bang' by the Muslims, remained in the hands of the Senā dynasty.[95]

Ikhtiyār al-Dīn Bakhtiyār Khaljī's career lasted for 12 years[96] before he was murdered by one of his *amīr*s, 'Alī Mardān, in 602/1203. He was killed while he was already breathing his last due to fatal injuries sustained during an unsuccessful military venture eastwards probably in the mountains of Tibet and Turkistan.[97] After the death of Ikhtiyār al-

Dīn Bakhtiyār Khaljī, power was contested between his *umarā'* 'Alī Mardān and Malik 'Izz al-Dīn Muḥammad b. Sherān Khaljī.[98] 'Alī Mardān mustered help from Sultan Quṭb al-Dīn who assigned him the territory of Lakhnawatī.[99] Although it seems evident that the Khaljī rule was a tribal egalitarian system in which the group ruled together, after the death of Quṭb al-Dīn Aybeg, 'Alī Mardān became independent and assumed autonomy. He assumed royal canopy, and established *khuṭba* and issued coins in his name. He tried to build his patrimonial staff by purging the existing nobility of Ikhtiyār al-Dīn's loyalists and later on started granting investitures to his officers for governing different parts of neighbouring regions;[100] he thus posed a threat to the successors of Quṭb al-Dīn Aybeg.

Quṭb al-Dīn Aybeg (587–602/1192–1206)

Quṭb al-Dīn Aybeg distinguished himself from his colleagues with his generosity, material wealth and patronage.[101] Therefore, he was known as Lākh Baksh, giver of hundreds of thousands, a characteristic which made 'the region of Hindustan full of friends and empty of enemies'.[102] Aybeg benevolently patronised émigré scholars as they were needed to staff the administration. Military success also legitimised his position among his subjects.[103]

Quṭb al-Dīn Aybeg had a 14-year career, spanning from 587/1192 to 602/1206, as a commander and governor for Shihāb al-Dīn in various regions of India. He was one of the junior Mu'izzī slaves[104] and is largely credited for the Ghūrīd conquests in the eastern Punjab, Delhi, Ajmer[105] and beyond. Due to his military triumphs, he swiftly ascended in rank and became Shihāb al-Dīn's right-hand man in India briefly after his purchase.[106] He seems to have been constantly backed by his master in his ventures in India.[107]

As one of the representative of Shihāb al-Dīn in India, Aybeg had the authority to appoint his own governors in Indian regions without bringing it to the sultan's attention. The sultan at that time was engaged on multiple military fronts. In 588/1193, a *parwanāh* (letter) of appointment as deputy military commander of Kol that was issued by Aybeg to his slave Malik Ḥassam al-Dīn Ölghbeg extends an interesting insight about the relationship between the Mu'izzī governors and their administrative priorities. The *parwanāh* reads:

> Every effort should be made to render the roads safe and protect the highways and bridges for the convenience of traders who serve as liaison between different countries and come from abroad with the choice products of other countries. The worthy and virtuous people should not be neglected. The travellers and guests should be looked after, no discrimination be made between the rich and the poor in this regard. Money should be saved for charitable purposes, for benevolence serves as a provision for man in the life and hereafter.[108]

This *parwanāh* became the model for drafting the royal *farmāns* in the sultanate era.[109] The content of this *parwanāh* indicates that law and order and economic activity were the primary concern of rulers. The sultan enforced mild taxes on the people for economic reasons and forbade the tax collectors to demand beds and food items from the locals for their personal use. Just as his *parwanāh* was a drafting model, so was the agrarian policy of Aybeg; the basis of similar policies that later sultans formulated.[110]

'Aybeg's attitude towards indigenous belief systems was varied. In many cases, generalised statements in the historical sources tend to mislead the reader. According to Ḥasan Niẓamī, Aybeg was an iconoclast that 'uprooted idolatry and destroyed temples at Kuhrām, Mirath, Banaras (a thousand temples here) and Kalinjar and converted many temples into mosques'.[111] Architectural remains also support the claims made by the historians, since the rubble of Hindu temples was utilised in the construction of mosques in Delhi and for the Arhai Din Ke Jhomprā mosque at Ajmer.[112] However, the claim that Aybeg emancipated the entire region (*diyār*) of Kol from idols and idol worship is hyperbolic.[113] Instead, he obliterated idols in a limited area within the territory. The treatment of the vanquished must have differed according to the circumstances, as occurred during the times of the Arabs in Sind.[114] Stories of Aybeg's attitude toward indigenous religious belief also shed light on the nature of the relationship between the rulers and the ruled, since the Muslim invaders at this stage were seen as *malīcha* (unclean) and hostile usurpers in the accounts of local histories. This account is supported by Sanskrit inscriptions regarding Aybeg.[115]

In 602/1206, after the death of Shihāb al-Dīn, Quṭb al-Dīn Aybeg assumed the title of sultan and advanced from Delhi to Lahore. The people of Lahore including the *qāḍi*s (judges or judicial officers), *imām*s, *saiyid*s, Sufis, officers and military men, traders and merchants extended their *bait* (oath of allegiance) in favour of Aybeg.[116] This ceremonial conduct was as essential a symbol for displaying Aybeg's operational legitimacy as was the reception of *chatar* (parasol) and *dūrbāsh* (trumpet) from the Ghūrīd sultan.[117] The *bait* seems to have been necessary for only the Muslim population here, since none of the non-Muslim classes are mentioned, although they must have comprised a large number in Lahore. The city continued to host heterogeneous religious orientations until the mid-twentieth century.

Although the historical sources of the Delhi sultanate employ deeply religious idioms to describe Aybeg's rule, a close study of the evidence suggests otherwise. For instance, Juzjānī refers to Mu'izz al-Dīn as the holy warrior sultan (*sultan-i ghāzi*), and Muslim historians authorise his forces as the army of Islam. However, we find that Aybeg was busy fighting with his *khwājatāshgān* (slaves of the same masters) and later his inauspicious dealing of the Khwārazm Shāhī Prince Jalāl al-Dīn Mingbarnī testifies that his motives were not exclusively religious. Land, booty and dominance seem to be the secular motives of the Aybeg, for which he also took help from some indigenous non-Muslim groups, many of which served under him in his army.

The career of Quṭb al-Dīn Aybeg as a sultan was brief and precarious. He challenged his father-in-law Yildiz for the domains of Ghazna. After the capture of Ghanza, Quṭb al-Dīn gave himself up to 'wine and debauchery', while Yildiz made a triumphant return.[118] Thus, Aybeg retired to Hindustan without any military encounter, leaving Ghazna to the victor.[119] In India, he had both land and associates, several among them his personal slaves. During the Ghūrīd conquests, Aybeg had appointed several among his personal slaves to important garrisons. Among his most trusted slaves was Iltutmish, who was first appointed to Gwalior and then to Baran and Badaun.[120]

During his reign as a sultan, Quṭb al-Dīn Aybeg took special care to appease the *'ulāmā'* of different religious schools of thought.[121] He did not discontinue their *imlāk* (land grants) and also endowed upon them regular stipends. His generosity and support towards the *'ulāmā'* attracted the scholars living in the neighbouring areas to his domains.[122]

Aybeg's administration was very personalised and spun around the sultan's whims and inclinations; for instance, one émigré scholar was sentenced to imprisonment by a *qāḍi*, on the charges of deceiving a slave merchant. Aybeg, however, intervened with a *farmān* (royal mandate) and settled the issue by paying from the royal treasury to the merchant the price of the slave girl related to the disagreement. The scholar was released, serving in the royal kitchen as a water carrier for a week, after which he was appointed as a *qāḍi*.[123]

Aybeg claimed to have an empire that stretched from 'Peshawar to the shores of the Ocean (Arabian Sea), and in other direction from Siwistān to the borders of the hills of Tibet'.[124] However, his rule was confined practically to a limited area where administrative penetration was partial. He struck coins and had *khuṭba* read in his name. Shortly after, while playing *Chōgān*, 'he fell down from his horse and the raised pommel of the saddle pierced into his ribs'. He died as a result of this unusual accident, and was buried at Lahore in 606/1210.[125]

Aybeg is considered the first sultan of Delhi, despite the fact that he was enthroned in Lahore.[126] There were two simple reasons why Aybeg was not crowned in Delhi. Firstly, Lahore was the Indian capital of the Ghaznawids and Ghūrīds, whereas Delhi was a mere garrison at that time. Only later was it developed by Iltutmish who made it his capital in 606/1210.[127] Secondly, Aybeg had plans for the seizure of Ghazna which could have been materialised only by his staying at Lahore. Nevertheless, Aybeg was not the only sultan of India after Muḥammad Ghūrī's death. As mentioned earlier, there were others who claimed to be the sultan. His brief rule of four years was as rickety as that of the fellow slave grandees Yildiz, Toghril and Qabacha. The reason why Aybeg gets a special treatment in the historical sources is because the next ruler Shams al-Dīn Iltutmish was his emancipated slave who based the legitimacy of his rule on the name of his master. Therefore, most of the primary historical accounts, including *Ṭabaqāt-i Nāṣirī*, which was written under the patronage of the Shamsī slave Balban,[128] connect the Delhi sultanate with Aybeg and consequently Ghūrīds. For this reason, Quṭb al-Dīn Aybeg is considered the first slave sultan of the Delhi sultanate.

The Officers of Ghūrī: An Assessment

In a period of little more than a decade, the Ghūrīd armies in India had made outstanding advances. Muslims by that time held a string of fortresses from which they subjugated more or less the entire north Indo-Gangetic plain and significant lands eastwards towards the region of Bengal. The political authority in the Delhi sultanate was layered. Sultan Ghiyāth al-Dīn Ghūrī paid nominal allegiance to the Abbasid caliph and his younger brother Sultan Shihāb al-Dīn Ghūrī was nominally subservient to Ghiyāth. The military commanders of Shihāb al-Dīn Ghūrī were also independent in exercising their authority in the region and their approaches to military expeditions yet they did not declare absolute autonomy until the death of the sultan Shihāb al-Dīn Ghūrī. It is important to note that victory did not necessitate the displacement of Hindu rulers. For instance, after the death of Prithvirāja, his son briefly ruled Delhi.[129] It appears that the position of Shihāb al-Dīn Ghūrī was of an overlord on whose behalf the military commanders had conquered and colonised certain regions and were collecting tribute from princes, *rai*'s and *rānas*, who according to Ḥasan Niẓāmi approached the court of Aybeg to 'rub the ground'.[130]

Secondly, until the end of the reign of Aybeg, the conquered areas seem to have been divided between various big and small slave and free warlords who were serving as military commanders for Shihāb al-Dīn Ghūrī. There was no administrative uniformity among the Ghūrīd occupations nor was there any administrative uniformity within any individual territorial unit. The prime purpose of the Ghūrīd military commanders seems to have been the protection of territories from each other and the locals. Occupied territories also served as the army base for further military ventures, the aim of which was to expand deeper into the Indian territories.

Thirdly, there was ephemerality in control over conquered lands. Some of the military conquests seemed to be little more than raids to plunder and collect booty. That is why many of the areas that were captured at one point were later lost to the local rulers. For instance, Aybeg's raid on Nahrwālā in 593/1197 did not lead to any territorial gain. The outcomes of his incursions on Malwa in 596/1200 were evenly short-lived.[131] Similarly, in the eastern regions of present-day Uttar Pradesh, the Gahadāvālā kingdom persisted despite raids by Aybeg.[132]

The instances of defeat are not mentioned in the Muslim historical sources but can be inferred from various surviving Sanskrit inscriptions[133] and the folk legends.

Fourthly, the treatment of historical events in the Muslim sources of that era also raises a need for distinguishing eulogy from the pure narration of historical facts; in many cases was the latter not the objective of historians. Historians such as Juzjāni, Fakhr-i Muddabir and Ḥasan Niẓāmi seem concerned to portray Islam's triumph over the non-Muslims. In order to prove their contentions, they either generalise events or make exaggerated claims.[134] For instance, according to Fakhr-i Muddabir:

> Infidel towns have become cities of Islam. In place of images, they worship the most high. Idol temples have become mosques, colleges (*madrassahs*) and hospices (*khānaqahs*). Every year several thousand infidel men and women are being brought to Islam.[135]

Aybeg was followed by Ārām Shāh[136] who was enthroned in Delhi with the support of a faction amongst the Mu'izzī *umarā*.[137] No sooner was he in power than he was replaced by the primus inter pares Shams al-Dīn Iltutmish, a slave/son-in-law, who was mainly supported by his fellow Quṭbī slaves.[138] As a result, the Quṭbī slaves were present amongst the ruling elite in the initial phases of Shams al-Dīn Iltutmish's rule. Jūzjānī stipulates several among them with reference to their roles in power politics. Many Mu'izzī slaves and free nobles were beheaded on the orders of Iltutmish after he ascended the throne[139] and we do not hear of the Mu'izzī *umarā* as a cohesive body henceforward. Nevertheless, two of the strongest Mu'izzī slave 'sultans', Qabacha in Sindh and Yildiz in Ghazna, remained the most daunting challenge for Iltutmish.[140]

CHAPTER 4

THE 'MYSTIC PRINCE': SHAMS AL-DĪN ILTUTMISH[1]

From childhood until his rise to power, his life events follow a pattern similar to the biblical story of the patriarch Joseph ...

The accidental death of Quṭb al-Dīn Aybeg resulted in a leadership crisis in his domains. His immediate successor Ārām Shāh remains an inscrutable character in the accounts of Juzjānī. While at one place he is described as the son of Aybeg, on another occasion reference about his lineage appears mysteriously blur.[2] The historical silence about this figure suggests that his claim to the throne may have been considered stronger than that of Iltutmish.

The death of Aybeg resulted in a leadership crisis in his principalities. With the sultan gone, the delicate balance of power in the ruling elite was disturbed and rival factions tussled for power.[3] Aybeg's successor Ārām Shāh was the candidate of one party of the *umarā'*; others had written letters to Iltutmish in a bid to appoint their own candidate. The status of Iltutmish seems to have been that of primus inter pares. According to Juzjānī, it was *sipāh-salār* (commander of the army) 'Ali-i Isma'īl, who was also the *amīr-i dād* (justicer) of Delhi, in concert with other *amīr*s and high officials of Delhi, who wrote letters to Shams al-Dīn at Badaun inviting him to seize Delhi and assume authority.[4]

Iltutmish's enthronement in 607/1210 commenced an era of consolidation, hence, he can be credited as the founder of the sultanate proper. This ascendance to power was replete with challenges.

Some amongst the Quṭbi and Mu'izzī *amīrs* resisted his rise to power.[5] Following a battle fought near Delhi (*bāgh-i jūd*) Iltutmish was able to put most of the resistance leaders to the sword and pacify the capital.[6] Nonetheless, as mentioned earlier, Iltutmish was not the only ruler of Hindustan. Juzjānī divides Hindustan at the death of Aybeg into four sections. The first section was the territory of Sind governed by Aybeg's son-in-law, Nāṣir al-Dīn Qabacha, who had married Aybeg's two daughters (one after the death of the other). Delhi was under the rule of Shams al-Dīn Iltutmish, and the territory of Lakhnawatī was under the rule of the Khaljī Maliks,[7] where 'Alī Mardān had declared suzerainty.[8] The regions from Ghazna to Punjab were with Tāj al-Dīn Yildiz. Control of the lost Ghaznawid capital Lahore was contested between Qabacha, Yildiz, and Shams al-Dīn Iltutmish[9] since whoever had Lahore would have been considered a successor of Ghaznawid and Ghūrīds. In addition, the Rājpūt chiefs including the chiefs of Jalor and Ranthambor had stopped paying tribute and had declared independence.[10] Aybeg's chief rival, Tāj al-Dīn Yildiz, was the first to recognise Iltutmish through a settlement.[11] This arrangement may have been a result of Qabacha being perceived as more formidable mutual enemy. Yildiz sent a royal canopy and *dūrbāsh* (trumpets) to Iltutmish.[12] The cordiality soon turned sour resulting in the violent end of Yildiz.[13] Iltutmish also had inimical relations with Qabacha regarding the possession of Lahore, Tabarhindāh and Kuhrām. At the very end of his reign Iltutmish was able to kill Qabacha and become the most powerful lord in northern India.[14]

Juzjānī, who wrote almost a decade after the death of Iltutmish,[15] attributes many merits to the sultan. This posthumous aggrandisement of Iltutmish might be a conscious effort to create sultanate history and its heroes. Juzjānī extends a larger than life account of Shams al-Dīn Iltutmish, whose life story resembled that of the Prophet Joseph, from descriptions of his physical beauty to the accounts of his life events.[16] The story of his purchase by Quṭb al-Dīn Aybeg paints him as a youth of a royal descent.[17] The disagreement about his value between Sultan Shihāb al-Dīn Ghūrī and Iltutmish's master, and Iltutmish's later purchase by Aybeg, suggest Iltutmish had invariably been an exceptional slave. An anomaly within this account of purchase contradicts this procurement saga and its implicit meanings. Iltutmish was purchased by Aybeg as a pair with another slave whose name was also Aybeg and later named Ṭamghāj.[18] Raverty correctly notes that

Ṭamghāj was immediately delegated on a better assignment than Iltutmish,[19] as the *amīr* of Tabarhindāh,[20] while Iltutmish initially was maintained as a *sar-i jandār* (royal guard).[21] Iltutmish's rise in ranks was relatively gradual. Aybeg styled Iltutmish as his son and made him *sar-i jandār* shortly before he was promoted to the status of *amīr-i-shikār*.[22] After the conquest of Gwalior by Aybeg, he was made *amīr* of Gwalior. Later, he acquired the *iqṭā'* of Baran and its dependencies as well.[23] Due to his valiance in the battle of Andkhud, Sultan Shihāb al-Dīn ordered his officer Aybeg to manumit Iltutmish.[24]

Many of the secondary researches dismiss Juzjānī's description of Iltutmish's qualities as a ruler as *prolix eulogium*.[25] The selection of words, nonetheless, vividly reflects what was expected from a legitimate ruler. Seven characteristics that are described by Juzjānī in Iltutmish's introductory section are as follows:

> [He was] upright, beneficent, a zealous and steadfast warrior against the infidels, the patroniser of the learned, the dispenser of justice, in pomp like Faridūn, in disposition like Kayquabād, in fame like Kaykaūs, in empire like Sikandar, in majesty like Bahrām, ... [he was] another impetuous 'Alī and in liberality a second Hātim-i Tāi.[26]

These words of appreciation denote his leadership qualities: namely, patronage, military and administrative success and his tendency to represent power through conspicuous wealth. Different historians including Juzjānī, Baranī, Ḥasan Niẓāmī, and Farishtāh admire the sultan for nurturing a patrimonial bureaucratic class that comprised slave and free officers. Juzjānī describes his generosity and remarks that Shams al-Dīn Iltutmish was more generous than Quṭb al-Dīn Aybeg, who was given the title of *lākh bakhsh*.[27] Iltutmish's largesse extended to various groups of *umarā'* including *'ulāmā'*, *sayyid*s, *malik*s, *amīr*s, *ṣadr*s and other notables.[28] It is pertinent to note that initially some *'ulāmā'* questioned his legitimacy as a ruler and demanded evidence for his manumission, since according to Islamic law a slave cannot become a ruler unless manumitted. In his 26-year rule, Iltutmish emerged as a benefactor of the *'ulāmā'*. Their conferral of the title 'mystic prince' on him suggests a long-term geniality.[29] The sultan's patronage and closeness to various Chishti and Suhrawardiā Sufis is evident from political preferences of the Sufis, for instance, the Suhrawardiā Sufi Bahā al-Dīn Ḍhikriyā Multanī wrote letters to Iltutmish opposing the ruler of Multan, Qabacha. Chishti *malfuzat* also mention him as a man possessing extraordinary intelligence and religious devotion who was destined to be a ruler. In Iltutmish's childhood a Sufi 'prophesised' that he would become a ruler. Accustomed to staying awake at night to pray, he appeared posthumously in a mystic's dream and informed him about his own salvation.[30] As a ruler, Iltutmish was able also to create an atmosphere similar to other grand Muslim cities; we find Sufi literature[31] being produced, *manaziras* (religious debates) in progress, and the instances of *'ulāmā'* competing for royal patronage. The Sufis were able to gain popular support through spiritual charisma and reports of other worldly miracles such as *qadam* (commuting supernaturally) mostly through flying, *kashaf* (reading minds) and multiplying food and other basic necessities of life through *barakat* (blessing). These Sufis provided psychological relief to the common people and were their charismatic leaders. The sultan was prudent enough to stay in the good books of the Sufis in order to preserve a positive public image.

The Balancing Act of Maintaining a Powerbase

The most significant move of Iltutmish was to create a personal powerbase through importing slaves and émigrés in the realm. The sultan effectively managed to maintain a delicate balance of power between free and unfree *umarā* as strategically placed minorities.[32] While the control of annexed territories (*iqṭā'*) was maintained through trusted military slaves, most of the important designations of the centre were conferred upon the Ghūrī, Tajik and Persianised *umarā'* of Khwārizm.[33]

Iltutmish was a connoisseur of Turkish slaves. Although Jūzjānī did not explicitly mention the word *'mamlūk'* in his descriptions of Iltutmish's elite military corps, it is plausible that the term 'Turk' might have been an alternative term for *mamlūk*.[34] The sultan's elite slave corps met most of the *mamlūk* characteristics including high quality and 'noble birth'. Iltutmish took special care to purchase highly skilled slaves. To do so he consulted private owners, who had collections of well-bred slaves, as well as professional traders, who dealt in captives of war. Also, the sultan sent his agents to purchase slaves from the slave markets of Baghdad and Egypt.[35] The sultan, according to Baranī, was very conscious about the lineage of his subordinates, and entrusted higher offices to the people of 'noble birth' only.[36] This certainly meant that the Indian *razīls* (meaning people of low lineage) who were enslaved during Iltutmish's military campaigns in India were not included in his elite slave corps.

Jūzjānī's *Tabaqāt-i Nāṣirī*, the key contemporary source of the Delhi sultanate until the reign of Sultan Nāṣir al-Dīn Mahmūd, frequently refers to Shamsī slaves playing important roles in the sultanate's power politics.[37] In *Tabaqāt*, chapter 22 contains 25 biographies of the Shamsī slaves.[38] The author did not specify whether all of these officers held important positions in the times of Iltutmish. Around 14 among these are not known to have held any important offices under the sultan.[39] Jūzjānī noticed them sometime after Iltutmish's death due to the power and influence they held.[40] Many of the slaves who enjoyed greater authority during the times of Iltutmish might have been ignored in this account.[41]

The profiles of military slaves reveal that there was an absence of any formal or standardised training and the slave officials ascended to power in irregular time frames. We find these slaves appointed on important *iqṭā*'s as governors/military commanders at the time of the death of Shams al-Dīn Iltutmish. This indicates Iltutmish's trust in slave elements. This trust was well placed as there is no evidence of any slave rebelling against Iltutmish. The Shamsī slaves either turned rebellious or assumed the role of king makers after their master's death. The slaves who held the most important positions in Iltutmish's era became uncontrollable for his progeny and were eliminated. Important offices were then bestowed upon the junior Shamsī slaves. To identify the Shamsī slaves who held offices during the reign of their master, three clues are helpful: the time of purchase that depicted their status in the hierarchy of the Shamsī corps, their titles and the offices that these slaves held under Iltutmish.

Iltutmish assigned value to his slaves on the basis of intimacy, efficiency and trust.[42] The slaves that were purchased by Iltutmish before his coronation were trusted seniors, who held higher offices than those bought a few years before his death. For instance, Qarāqash Khān, Malik Hindū Khān[43] and Malik Kabīr Khān Ayāz Mu'izzī[44] were among senior slaves who held elevated positions at the time of his death.[45] Junior Shamsī slaves, such as Balban-i Khward (the younger Balban who later became sultan) and his brother Sayf al-Dīn Aybeg, who were purchased only a few years before the sultan's death, were mere royal attendants at the end of Iltutmish's reign. These junior Shamsī slaves only rose to elevated ranks under the rule of the sultan's successors.

According to Habīb, in the early sultanate *khān* was the most exalted title awarded to only the selected few among the *umarā'*. It was an adaptation of the Mongol title 'Khān', since this title was not present among Ghūrīd *umarā'*. It may be inferred, therefore, that the title was an innovation of Iltutmish's times. The rank of *khān* was the highest, allowing the holder of the title to keep nine banners. *Malik* was the second highest rank which conferred entitlement to keep three banners minimum and *amīr* was the third elevated rank.[46] *Sipah sālār* and officer ranks were the fourth and fifth highest ranks.[47] The *muqṭa*s commanded armies as well, though their primary task was to maintain the sultan's writ on a particular *iqṭā'*.[48] Despite the dubiousness of these details of numerical or hierarchal divisions in the army as extended in *Subh ul-Asha* which are not given in any sultanate source, one fact is certainly clear, that there were few Khāns in the service of Iltutmish although the officers numbered in the thousands. At least three or four slaves, mentioned by Jūzjānī, had risen to such stature that Iltutmish endowed them with the title of 'Khān'.[49] Kabīr Khān and Qarāqash Khān were awarded the title of 'Khān' by the sultan around 1228. Since Malik Tāj al-Dīn Sanjar Kezlik Khān died in 1231–1232, Iltutmish must have given him the title of 'Khān'. The fourth Khān was a Turk, Aybeg, who was given the title of Awar Khān, possibly by Iltutmish.[50] However, it is not explicit from the sources that he was a slave.[51] Other slaves, including Nāṣir al-Dīn Aytemür, Sayf al-Dīn Aybeg-i Uchh, Sayf al-Dīn Aybeg Yaghantut and Nūṣrat al-Dīn Tāī'sī, who died in Iltutmish's time or shortly afterwards, were not granted this title.[52] Iltutmish's successors did not seem selective in conferring this title; we come across several 'Khāns' in the later period.[53] Hindū Khān seems an exception, as he was assigned the royal treasury; later he was made *ṭashtdār* (ewer bearer).[54] *Iqṭā'*, important symbols of trust, power and authority, were under the charge of the slave commanders. Seven of these are mentioned by Jūzjānī as holding offices by the time of Iltutmish's death. Bihar was under the command of 'Izz al-Dīn Toghan Khān Toghril.[55] Palwal was administered by Kabīr Khān who was earlier the *muqṭa'* of Multan.[56] Bayana and Gwalior were commanded by Nūṣrat al-Dīn Tāī'sī,

Baran by 'Izz al-Dīn Balban, Kuchat and Nandanā (salt range) by Ikhtiyār al-Dīn Aytagin, Multān by Qarāqash Khān Aytagin and Uchh by Sayf al-Dīn Aybeg-i Uchh.[57] *Iqṭā'* of Lakhnawatī and Bengal were under Awar Khān Aybeg.[58]

It is important to note that 25 slaves mentioned by Jūzjānī were of diverse ethnic and geographic origins, which indicates that Shamsī slaves were not a monolithic ethnic group. The slaves were acquired through diverse means, including purchase, inheritance and war.[59] Among these slaves, the regional identities of only 19 are mentioned.[60] These 'Turkish'[61] slaves were ethnically Indian, Rūmī (presumably referring to Greek or Slavic slaves from Byzantine territory),[62] Khitai or Qara-Khitai (referring to slaves from northern China),[63] Qipchaq (a group of tribes from the steppes north of the Black Sea and Caspian Sea),[64] and Ölberli (the tribe of Iltutmish).[65] Among this group, six were Qipchaq, five were Qara-Khitai, three were Ölberli, two were Rūmīs, one was Georgian and one was Khorasanī.[66] Only Hindū Khān was an Indian slave. He was among the senior slaves, who might have been in charge of the sultan's *mamlūk* department.[67] Some slaves were obtained through purchase and inheritance from other sultans.[68]

Many of Iltutmish's slaves were well established before entering his service as they were neither recently alienated from their homelands nor were socially dead or were malleable youths at the times of their purchase. For instance, Iltutmish purchased two slaves who were a part of trained staff of the sultan Shihāb al-Dīn Ghūrī. The sultan obtained a Mu'izzī slave by an unknown medium, either through purchase or inheritance. These slaves were veterans of service in Afghanistan and northern India. According to the historical records, Hindū Khān was the first indigenous person reported to have been included among the elite slaves of the Delhi sultanate.[69]

The mode and manner of the slave *cursus honorum* is vaguely described by Jūzjānī in his biographies, which is similar to the *mamlūk* style of on job training. The training was purely informal and occurred in multiple stages. Initially, dealers trained elite slaves in marksmanship, religion and social etiquette, augmenting their market value. The rich readily purchased slaves equipped with such skills at higher prices. The most exalted among these made their way to the royal court and began their careers as the personal attendants of the sultan. This phase of progression required investment from both parties. On one hand, the slave had to learn royal etiquette, prove his martial worth, or intellectual ability, show credibility and, above all, demonstrate the capacity to make independent decisions. On the other hand, masters cultivated personal bonds of affection in order to inculcate a sense of loyalty.[70] Many of these slaves were raised as foster sons of the sultans. Those who were able to establish themselves were promoted to the rank of commanders, administrators and *muqṭa*'s. Sunil Kumar describes the slave training system in Shamsī era:

> The slave Malik Taj al-Din Sanjar Kezlik Khān [...] had been bought as a child and was brought up and nourished [*parwarish*] in the royal residence together with the eldest Prince Nāṣir al-Din Maḥmūd. He was then appointed as the superior of the Sultan's kitchen [*chashnigar*], and was promoted thereafter to commander of the horses [*amīr-i-ākhūr*]. In the identical fashion, the slave Malik Izz al-Din Tughan Khān Tughril [. . .] graduated from senior cupbearer [*saqi-yi-khass*], to senior keeper of the royal writing case [*sar-i-dawatdar*], to supervisor of the Sultan's kitchen [*chashnigir*], to commander of the horses [*amīr-i ākhūr*], until he finally received a military and administrative assignment, *iqṭā'*.[71]

The above demonstrates that there was no standard pattern of ranks; while some started as *chāshnīgīr*, others began at the post of *sāqī-i khās*. The period for promotions was not regular either; some officers enjoyed rapid promotions, while others did not. There was no specific age for recruitment, as we can see that the Mu'izzī slaves were obtained when they were already established politically and socially while some of the *mamlūk* such as Yildiz and Kezlik Khān were obtained in their childhood.

The *bandagān-i khās* were the most trusted slaves of the sultan, deployed on important strategic positions and to newly conquered lands.[72] Nevertheless, the junior Shamsī slaves were not ignored either. In many cases, if the senior slaves were made commanders and *muqṭa'*, the juniors were given posts such as *shihna* or superintendent.[73] There were differences in the natures of both positions. The military commanders and *muqṭa'* required freedom of action and power of decision-making. On the other hand, the superintendent worked under the supervision of the sultan. This attitude toward individual slaves was determined by the specific dynamics of each master–slave relationship.[74]

This master–slave relation was a bargain where the sultan demonstrated discretionary benevolence towards his patrimonial staff through *iḥsān* (favours), endowments of *n'imāh* (largesse) and *namūd-o parwarish* (patronage). The bureaucracy was in return expected to reciprocate this generosity with a lifelong commitment to stay loyal only to the sultan. Thus ideally, multiple officers working in a single *iqṭā'* or certain office had to report directly to the sultan. This had been the practice since the times of Maḥmūd of Ghazna and Shihāb al-Dīn Ghūrī and was visible even at the time of Balban. When Iltutmish appointed his eldest son Nāṣir al-Dīn Maḥmūd to the eastern regions of Hindūstān, he was still a minor; a veteran Khorasanī general Bahā al-Dīn Jamī was posted to the same regions for his protection and guidance. This *amīr* suppressed the existing Quṭbī *umarā'* in the region and on account of his services, the sultan awarded him the rank of *malik* along with largesse.[75]

The sultan had consciously appointed free elements in civil offices. For instance, in 629/1231 at the conquest of Gwalior, Malik Ḍiyā' al-Dīn Junaydī was appointed *amīr-i dād*, and probably became responsible for coordinating the division of booty between the centre and the capital as well as coordinating various officers in the region. Juzjānī was appointed as *qāḍi* for dispensation of justice and *sipah sālār* while Rāshid al-Dīn Ali was appointed as *kotwāl*.[76] Thus, a powerful sultan was able to appoint multiple officers in a single region or office to maintain his own control. On the contrary, weak sultans could not make such a move, since various power groups appointed their own patrimonial staff to protect their domains of power.

The Asylum of the Universe: Development of Delhi as Imperial City

Iltutmish also promoted Delhi as royal metropolis and we find the sultan encouraging new settlers from all over the Muslim world to migrate to the new city. Dispensing patronage to and securing loyalty from various groups of Muslim society in Delhi is one of the most prominent features of his rule. Iltutmish patronised various non-military groups, including *qāḍi*s, *imām*s, *muftīs*, *derwaishes*, Sufis, landowners, farmers, traders and travellers from 'great cities'.[77] The sultan was also very particular about high birth and genealogies and extended his full support to Muslim settlers with distinguished family backgrounds. As a result of his encouragement, people from all parts of the Muslim world gathered in the city of Delhi.[78] According to Juzjānī, these people 'had escaped the toils of the calamities sustained by the provinces and cities of 'Ajam; the misfortune caused by the [irruption of the] infidel Mongols, made the capital – the asylum of the universe.'[79] The population of Delhi remained loyal to Iltutmish's name and legacy which symbolised royalty even after his death. The coinage issued by Iltutmish's progeny demonstrates that Iltutmish's name remained a symbol of legitimacy for nearly a century after his death. On the coins of Rukn al-Dīn Fīrūz, Raḍiyyah, Behrām Shāh and 'Alā al-Dīn Mas'ūd, the words used to refer to the current ruler are 'ibn Sultan', 'bint-i Sultan' and the Sultan Mu'izzīm, whereas Iltutmish is referred to as Sultān-i 'Azām (the Grand Sultan).[80] Even matrimonial connection with the women related to the sultan including his daughters and queens provided claims to power. Various slaves who married Iltutmish's daughters were able to claim the throne and Qutlugh Khān, who was the second husband of Iltutmish's wife, was able to instigate a rebellion. Later on, when power shifted from the Olberlis to the Khaljīs, Jalāl al-Dīn Fīrūz Khaljī was unable to enter Delhi for several months. In the revolt of Hājjī Mawlā against 'Alā al-Dīn Khaljī, the plan was to replace the sultan with the maternal grandson of Iltutmish.

The sultan eliminated the undesired *umarā'*,[81] and in order to avoid general resentment this policy was executed covertly. In the account of Saif al-Dīn Aybeg, it is mentioned that he was assigned the task to seize the property of the murdered *umarā'*. Saif al-Dīn abhorred this part of his job.[82] Al-Kasānī, a Transoxanian scholar, who lived in Delhi for six months, noted that the people who revolted against the sultan were removed from the scene and the *rāī*'s of Hindustan had acquiesced.[83] 'Awafī also presents evidence of the same phenomenon by mentioning assassins working for the sultan.[84]

During his 26-year reign, Iltutmish was endlessly busy executing military expeditions, subduing rebels, contesting rivals, and carving out new principalities in the Indian lands. It was only in the last six years that he actually exercised complete power over the regions of Sind and Punjab. Similarly, the regions of Lakhnawatī came under the suzerainty of the sultan in 624/1227. Nevertheless, this control was lost for an interlude and was restored by Iltutmish in 628/1230. The region stayed under the Delhi sultanate for the next 12 years.[85] The expeditions of

Ranthambor, Malwa and Binbān demonstrate that in northern and central India the control was not completely obtained.

In 633/1236, the sultan led an army towards Binbān and it was in this battle that he fell sick and died, having reigned for 26 years.[86] After the death of Iltutmish, rival factions of *umarā'* who were far more powerful than any of the sons and daughters of Iltutmish contested for power. Iltutmish's progeny became titular symbols of legitimacy that the powerful rivalling factions attempted to use.

During his reign Iltutmish's political power gradually came to be accepted as legitimate and thus he was perceived as an authority at least in the core regions. With conquests and annexations in various other parts of north India, he was able to expand the territorial limits of the Delhi sultanate. The extent of state control differed in the empire of Iltutmish and so did his relevance for different groups of subject population. While he was considered legitimate within his social base and among *umarā'*, in the core regions, in the provinces and peripheral regions there were frequent rebellions. At the time of the death of Shams al-Dīn Iltutmish, it is possible to categorise the sultanate into multiple regions according to the penetration of administrative control. The regions of Bihar, Asam, Doab, Hansi, Tabarhindāh, Nagaur, Palwal, Baran and Badaun were among important *iqṭā'* and provinces[87] and the regions of Delhi and its suburbs can be labelled as core regions. The general émigré population of Delhi, the free and unfree bureaucratic class and the royal household were the social base of the Delhi sultanate.

The Delhi sultanate in the time of Iltutmish was a combination of strongholds and wayward regions mentioned as *mawasat* (from the singular *mawas*, shelter and refuge) and *kohpaya* (*koh* = mountain, *paya* = foot, the highlands) in the historical sources. State control was restricted to certain urban centres, important agricultural regions and strategic locations. The state could not extend its writ into *mawasāt* and *kohpaya*, which remained safe havens for rebels.

The regions of Sind, Lahore, Doab, Malwa and Bengal marked the boundaries of the Delhi sultanate. These were the areas that came under the control of Iltutmish very late in his reign and which had earlier been ruled by the strong Mu'izzī warlords such as Yildiz, Qabacha, Baha al-Din Toghril and the Khaljī Maliks who were well established in their areas of domination. There must have been other less significant generals scrambling for new lands that did not find mention in Muslim historical sources. Also, the pattern of capture, loss and recapture of strongholds persisted. At the time of Iltutmish's death, the region of Lakhnawatī or Bengal was held by Awar Khān Aybeg, a Turk who was probably a slave of the sultan.[88] Bengal was sporadically acquired by the sultans throughout the history of the Delhi sultanate, with the population seemingly acquiescent about changes at the centre. There was a reasonable Muslim presence in Lahore, Multan and Uchh. The region of Lahore at the death of Iltutmish was under Malik 'Alā al-Dīn Jānī, a prince of Turkistan and a veteran general who had been assigned important *iqṭā'* of Bihar and then had served in Lakhnawatī.[89] The region of Multan was under Qarāqash Khān Aytagin.[90] In the reign of Behrām Shāh, the population of Lahore was acquiescent towards the governor Qarāqash Khān.[91] According to Juzjānī, the traders of Lahore had acquired letters of protection from Mongols which emboldened them to resist directives of the representative of the Delhi sultan. This apathy of the population of Lahore resulted in its sacking by the Mongols.[92] The salt range regions of Kuchat and Nandanā were under the control of Ikhtiyār al-Dīn Aytigin.[93]

In the provinces and *iqṭā'*, slaves were delegated authority by the sultan to administer and expand. The region of Tabarhindāh was under Malik Tāj al-Dīn-Kazlik Khān Sultānī Shamsī.[94] This region must have come under the suzerainty of the sultan after the fall of Yildiz in 612/1215 and must have been used as a base from which Iltutmish proceeded to attack Qabacha in the year 625/1228. Malik Kābir Khān Ayāz, a senior Shamsī slave, was transferred from Multan to the region of Palwal.[95] The region of Bayana which earlier was the estate of Bahā al-Dīn Toghril was given to Nuṣrāt al-Dīn Tāī'sī,[96] while the region of Baran was in the hands of slave 'Izz al-Dīn Balban-i Kushlü Khān[97] who was also the son in law of the sultan. Kushlü Khān had a substantial patrimonial staff in the region of Sind.[98] The region of Bihar was under the suzerainty of 'Izz al-Dīn Toghān Khān Toghril.[99] Saif al-Dīn Kūchi, a free-born man, held the *iqṭā'* of Hansi and 'Izz al-Dīn Salārī held the *iqṭā'* of Badaun.[100]

Juzjānī's lack of interest in describing the conditions of common people limits our knowledge about the relationship between the rulers and the ruled. We find inscriptions with reference to Muslim rulers as *malecchas* (the filthy), *Turushkas* (Turks) and *Yavanas* (Westerners). Nevertheless, keeping in view the account of later historical records like

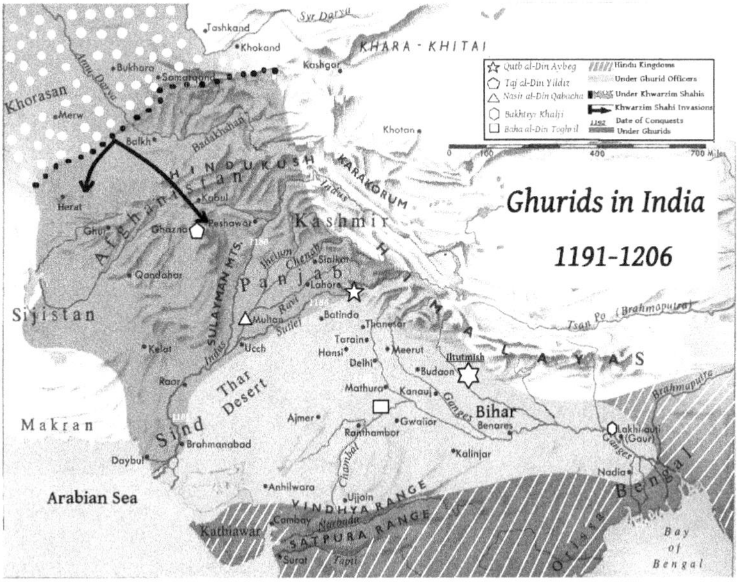

Map 4.1 Ghurids in India 1192–1206

Hammiramahakavya, which was written in the fifteenth century, we can safely assume that Muslims were perceived as outsiders. The *umarā'* appointed in the provinces who were undertaking expeditions had personalised staff among whom they cultivated loyalty by patrimonial relations.

The social base of the Delhi sultanate mainly consisted of the population of Delhi, including the military elite, the émigré population and the menial slaves that were an outcome of the raids of Iltutmish and his predecessor, Quṭb al-Dīn Aybeg. The former's raid in Gujarat in 570/1175, for instance, provided him with 20,000 slaves.[101] These people seem to have been participants in various political happenings in Delhi.

Use of Cultural and Religious Symbols

Prominent cultural symbols of royalty included the regal protocol of *chatar* (royal parasol), *dūrbāsh* (trumpets) and elephants, ostentatious display of artefacts, gems and jewellery in royal processions, regular imperial journeys into various regions of the sultanate, and issuing coinage on which the name of the caliph was inscribed from 626/1229.[102] Emissaries from the caliph's court bearing rich honours reached the capital in 626/1229 and religious symbols were employed with the reading of the caliph's name in the Friday *khuṭba*.[103] These, along with public declaration of the *fatahnāma*s (official written accounts of victory that were read/announced in public) were mechanisms with the help of which the sultan was able to appear legitimate. In addition, relative stability of law and order, revival of trade and communication in the areas where the sultan had strong control, and the presence of *qāḍī*s for dispensation of justice in the core regions, all helped confer legitimacy. Construction works included monuments (mosques, tombs and palaces), roads, inns and water reservoirs.[104] In the case of Iltutmish, we know that he was responsible for transforming the city of Delhi from a mere garrison to one of the most flourishing cities in the Muslim world.

With patrimonialism, elimination of undesirable elements, and effective military and administrative control, Iltutmish seems to have been successful in converting his military power into political authority.[105] Although the sultan continued to confront opposition throughout his reign, there is no evidence of dissent from Iltutmish's social base. Similarly, the regions under the governorship of his slaves stayed connected with the centre even after his death. His dynasty continued to rule for the next 30 years despite the fact that its loss of splendour rendered it vulnerable to the undertakings of the stronger contenders to power. The office of 'sultan' was considered a right of Iltutmish's progeny even during the Khaljī era.

CHAPTER 5

THE TALE OF THE '40 SLAVES': THE POST-ILTUTMISH INTERREGNUM

> *Within ten years of Iltutmish's passing, four of his progeny were enthroned by the nobility. All of them were juvenile and incapable of withstanding the burdens of statesmanship. Most were hedonistic and heedless of the state matters. Therefore during this period the Turkish slaves of Iltutmish, called Chihilgānī, gained power and usurped authority.*[1]

The title Shams (sun) described Iltutmish best, as every political entity in the sultanate orbited around him and was dependent upon him for survival. While delegating offices the sultan maintained a delicate balance between multiple strategically placed minorities and ensured that their hostilities towards one another remained passive but animosity was never forgotten. The passing of Iltutmish disturbed this delicate balance of power and culminated in collisions of mutually hostile factions of nobles. The progeny of Iltutmish were young and inexperienced in comparison with the *umarā'* and proved incapable to manage their office as they neither had patrimonial relations with the existing *umarā'* nor the ability to substitute them. Consequently, within a decade of the death of Iltutmish (d. 634/1236), four of Iltutmish's offspring were enthroned and deposed sequentially. This chapter explains the unsuccessful attempts of the young sultans to control Iltutmish's strategically placed minorities. This chapter also suggests that what Juzjānī perceived as 'incompetence' was essentially the 'inability' to control the veterans.

In their brief reigns, the progeny of Iltutmish were unable to expand or to make a visible presence in the provinces; therefore some provincial governors rose in rebellion and proclaimed autonomy. In centre, the sultans made unsuccessful attempts to eliminate the undesired *umarā'* and to cultivate their own patrimonial staff as was the tradition of their predecessors. Their failure in this bid rattled the targeted *umarā'* that hastily deposed and eliminated the sultans.

The role of the Shamsī nobles became more vital after the Iltutmish's death. Baranī identifies a group of kingmaker Shamsī slaves as *Chihilgānī* (the 40 nobles).[2] The etymology of the term *Chihilgānī*, particularly whether its formation was metaphorical or literal, remains a mystery and a controversy.[3] To date, it is undeniable that the Turkish slaves were among the major power brokers in post-Iltutmish politics. They were among those responsible for the enthronement and dethronement of the sultans in the decade after Iltutmish's death.

Baranī's contention, that a violent power game between a cohesive band of Turkish slaves and free elements resulted in the ultimate destruction of the latter,[4] should not be accepted in a literal sense. Although slaves were striving to retain their positions in power politics, they always had free *umarā'* on their side as well.[5] The nobility did not act as a monolithic group. They acted against each other as well; in fact 'what made the internal crisis in the sultanate so protracted and dangerous was a split among the Shamsīs themselves'.[6] The decade following the death of Iltutmish witnessed greater instability and chaos. The progeny of Iltutmish were unable to centralise power through the office of sultan, which led to amplification in violence and anarchy.

Succession crisis started when Iltutmish's accomplished eldest son and heir-apparent Nāṣir al-Dīn Maḥmūd Shāh was killed in Lakhnawatī on the battleground (*c.* 626/1229).[7] This first instance of a mysteriously accidental death of heir marks the beginning of a sultanate tradition where no heir apparent made it to the throne peacefully. Iltutmish left a will in favour of his daughter Raḍiyyah,[8] who was the eldest born of the sultan. Overlooking this will, Rukn al-Dīn Fīrūz Shāh (633/1236) the eldest surviving son of Iltutmish was enthroned after a bargain of power sharing was struck between his mother Shāh Turkān[9] and provincial nobles.[10] The Turkish queen regent Shāh Turkān was a former *kānīz* (female slave) who was elevated to the position of *malikāh* (chief queen) of the royal *harem*. Juzjānī highlights the ambivalence of her character by appreciating her emphasis on patronage towards *'ulāmā'*, Sayyids, Sufis and recluses[11] on the one hand and mentions her vindictiveness towards other wives of Iltutmish and their children on the other hand.

Among the three characteristics that Juzjānī attributes to Sultan Rukn al-Dīn Fīrūz Shāh are 'beneficence of handsome exterior, gentleness and humanity to perfection, and in bountifulness and liberality, a second Ḥātim'.[12] Yet again, Raverty dismisses this as his hyperbolic verbosity; however, the later evidence testifies that Rukn al-Dīn did squander an extravagant amount of wealth on rewards and gifts for his favoured ones. He used his father's name to buttress his legitimacy, as we can see from the coins that were struck in his name during his brief reign where he mentions his father's name along with his own.[13]

Enthronement of Rukn al-Dīn Fīrūz Shāh (r. 634/1236) and the Rise of Provincial Nobles

Before his ascendancy to the throne, the young sultan had an eight-year administrative career. In 625/1227, Sultan Rukn al-Dīn Fīrūz Shāh obtained the *iqṭā'* of Badaun and a green canopy of state and 'Ain-al Mulk Hussayn-i Asharī who had earlier been the *wazīr* of Nāṣir al-Dīn Qabacha was appointed by Iltutmish as the *wazīr* (guardian) of the young prince.[14] After the death of Iltutmish's heir Nāṣir al-Dīn Maḥmūd Shāh, some groups within nobility expected Rukn al-Dīn, the eldest remaining son, as the next ruler.[15]

There is scholarly consensus that Iltutmish was disappointed by Rukn al-Dīn and had given priority to Raḍiyyah over him, since after Gwalior expedition Raḍiyyah was appointed as *nāi'b-ghaibat* (deputy in absentia) in Delhi and was later announced as his successor. Nonetheless, evidence negates this assumption as after the Gwalior expedition, the territory of Lahore and its environs, which had been 'the seat of government of the Khusraw Malik (the last dynasty of Ghazna)',[16] was conferred upon Rukn al-Dīn. With an ever-increasing Mongol threat, it is unlikely that Iltutmish would have assigned these territories to a son in whose abilities he had little confidence. Similarly, when Sultan Shams al-Dīn returned from his last expedition in 633/1235 from the regions of Sind and Binbān, the sultan brought Rukn al-Dīn along to the capital.[17] This gesture indicated that Iltutmish had some expectations from his eldest surviving son.

Rukn al-Dīn Fīrūz was enthroned with the support of provincial governors who were predominantly slaves.[18] Nevertheless, unable to run state affairs the sultan soon 'gave himself up to pleasure and began to expend in the most profuse fashion the funds of the *bait-ul māl*'.[19] The queen mother Shāh Turkān assumed de facto control over the state.[20] Although the queen and the nobility had each assumed that they could control the other, their mutual inability to dictate the other caused a rift. In order to purge the royal house from potential contenders to the throne, Shāh Turkān killed many ladies of the harem and also one son of Iltutmish known as Quṭb al-Dīn whom Juzjānī called 'a youth of great promise'[21] who might be the grandson of Quṭb al-Dīn Aybeg as the name suggests.

Rukn al-Dīn was too inexperienced to control his father's unruly patrimonial staff and was unable to replace them with his own officers. Various peripheral regions, provinces and *iqṭā'* seceded from the centre. For instance, Malik Saif al-Dīn Aybeg-i Uchh the *muqṭa'* of Uchh declared independence.[22] Another *muqṭa'* Malik Ḥasan Qarlugh established an independent kingdom after capturing Ghazna, Karmān and Binbān[23] and expanded into Uchh by 634/1236 after defeating Saif al-Dīn. Similarly, Malik 'Izz al-Dīn Muḥammad Salārī, who was the *muqṭa'* of Badaun broke out in rebellion. In another direction, Malik 'Izz al-Dīn Kabīr Khān-i Ayāz, the *muqṭa'* of Multan (or Sunam), Malik Saif al-Dīn Kūjī the *muqṭa'* of Hansi, and Malik 'Alā al-Dīn Janī, the *muqṭa'* of Lahore rebelled.[24] Among princes, Malik Ghiyāth al-Dīn Muḥammad Shāh, a younger son of Sultan Shams al-Dīn, declared independence in Awadh. He took possession of the whole treasure of Lakhnawatī that was being conveyed to the capital and wreaked a great financial damage to Rukn al-Dīn.[25]

Seeing the gathering storm, many of the sultan's close associates shifted sides and abandoned him, including his Tajik *wazīr* Niẓām al-Mulk Junaydī, who fled from the imperial town Kelukherī to Kol. He later joined the group of strong rebellious governors located in the west of Delhi, among them were Malik 'Izz al-Dīn Salārī, Malik Janī and Malik Kūjī.[26] The sultan led his army towards Kuhrām[27] to counter the rebels but the situation spun out of control at the centre.

During the absence of the sultan from the centre the hostility between various groups of nobles broke out and took the shape of racial conflict. The tensions aggravated and resulted in a massacre of the Tajiks by Turks.[28] In the meantime bitterness between Shāh Turkān and the eldest daughter of Iltutmish, Raḍiyyah, exploded into an open confrontation. Rukn al-Dīn Fīrūz had to beat a hasty retreat to the capital but it was already too late for him.[29]

In the absence of the sultan, his stepsister Raḍiyyah was able to formulate an alliance with the Turkish *amīr*s, her father's household slaves and groups of people in Delhi, to rebel against the sultan. They attacked the royal palace and seized queen regent Shāh Turkān. When Rukn al-Dīn reached the city he had already lost the battle. Raḍiyyah then dispatched a force consisting of Turkish slaves and *amīr*s to arrest and imprison Rukn al-Dīn. He was subsequently killed in 634/1236 after ruling for six months and 27 days.[30] The brief reign of Rukn al-Dīn was full of turmoil. The *umarā'*, who had become excessively strong, refused to heed a sultan with whom they had no patrimonial relations. The absence of the sultan from the centre resulted in his removal from power, which aggravated the instability rife in the echelons of power. While the relation with Iltutmish did bring Rukn al-Dīn to power, it could not keep him enthroned for more than six months. He was replaced with another contender with the similar claims to the throne.

Implementation of Iltutmish's Will in Favour of Raḍiyyah (633–637/1236–1240) by the 'People' of Delhi

The enthronement of Jalālat al-Raḍiyyah[31] was an outcome of chance and the victory of one faction of *umarā'* over another. Timing also worked in Raḍiyyah's favour since rebellious governors from the western *iqṭā'*s were marching towards Delhi under the leadership of 'Izz al-Dīn Kabīr Khān-i Ayāz, the *muqṭā'* of Multan and a senior Shamsī slave. In order to counter this threat another group of nobles led by influential Shamsī slaves like Malik 'Izz al-Dīn Balban-i Kushlü Khān and Malik Ikhtiyār-al-Dīn Yuzbeg-i-Toghril Khān[32] hastily seized Rukn al-Dīn and set up his sister.[33]

As a sultan, Raḍiyyah was certainly a better choice than her predecessor. K. A. Nizāmi believes that it was Sassanid cultural influence that led to the appointment of the female sultan.[34] Peter Jackson credits it as a Qara-Khitai practice.[35] Sunil Kumar points out that the enthroning of women was a Qara-Khitai practice, but at the time of enthronement of Raḍiyyah, only two or three Qara-Khitai Shamsī *umarā'* were alive.[36] It is possible that the decision maker *umarā'* found it potentially convenient to rule on the behest of a veiled young women since, even in Qara-Khitan, women ruled as a regent to a male heir.[37] However, Juzjānī's statement that if masculinity was not an inviolable norm of a sultan, Raḍiyyah would actually fulfil all the qualities of an efficient ruler, best explains that, as a woman, she was only expected to be a titular ruler.[38]

Raḍiyyah exercised substantial influence even in the times of Shams al-Dīn Iltutmish. Her mother (Turkān Khātūn) was the chief of the royal women of the harem.[39] Raḍiyyah made her mark on the population of Delhi as she served as *nāi'b-ghāi'bat* (deputy of the sultan in his absence) in Delhi while Sultan Iltutmish campaigned in Gwalior.[40] After coming back from the campaign of Gwalior, the sultan ordered Tāj al-Mulk Muḥammad, the secretary who was the Mushrif-i Mumalik to write a decree naming his daughter his heir apparent.[41] On the suggestion of his officers that such a decree could contradict Islam, the sultan replied that Raḍiyyah was more competent than all of his sons.[42] There is some question regarding the credibility of Iltutmish's will in favour of Raḍiyyah, since it might have been forged posthumously with the help of Turkish officers who might have hoped for more extensive de facto powers for themselves, and a more restricted, symbolic role for Raḍiyyah.

Raḍiyyah was able to quell the minor initial rebellions against herself, and appointed and transferred many of the *umarā'*. She effectively commanded the army, and was able to pacify the sultanate as far as the peripheral areas.[43] Immediately after her enthronement Raḍiyyah had to deal with the ongoing rebellion by the governors of the western *iqṭā'*s, involving senior officers such as Malik 'Alā al-Dīn Jānī, Malik Saif al-Dīn Kūjī, Malik 'Izz al-Dīn Kābir Khān-i Ayāz, Malik 'Izz al-Dīn Muḥammad Salārī and *wazīr* Niẓām al-Mulk Junaydī who had put Delhi under siege.[44]

Raḍiyyah was aided by the governors from the eastern borders including Malik Nūṣrat al-Dīn Tāī'sī, the Mu'izzī *muqṭa'* of Awadh, who was appointed by Raḍiyyah after the revolt of her brother Ghiyāth al-Dīn Muḥammad Shāh.[45] Malik 'Izz al-Dīn Toghril-i Toghān Khān on the accession of Raḍiyyah dispatched emissaries to the capital.[46] In order to testify his homage, he continuously sent offerings from

Lakhnawatī. Raḍiyyah conferred a canopy of state, standards and great honour on him.[47]

The siege of Delhi by hostile *malik*s was prolonged for a considerable period. Raḍiyyah came to the field and the rival Turk *amīr*s and the *malik*s had several skirmishes. Eventually the rebellion was quelled. Raḍiyyah was able to break the enemy line, win a temporary alliance with some of the rebels, and eliminate others. The rebellion was repressed only because Malik 'Izz al-Dīn Sālārī and Malik 'Izz al-Dīn Kabīr Khān changed sides in support of Raḍiyyah's camp. Saif al-Dīn Kūjī, Fakhr al-Dīn and Malik 'Alā al-Dīn Jānī were killed. Niẓām al Mulk Junaydī retired to the hills of Sirmūr where he later died. The head of Malik 'Alā al-Dīn Jānī was brought to the capital as a token of victory.[48]

In this reign we see the resurgence of Qaramathians, the conflict between Sunnis and Shiʿas and a general resentment against the *'ulāmā'*. According to the account, during Raḍiyyah's reign Qaramathians became stronger around Delhi, Gujarat, and Sindh and on the banks of river Ganges and Yumna. Nūr Tūrk was the leader of the group and used to preach against the Hanafite and Shafite *'ulāmā'* and had a following in Delhi. His followers attacked the congregation mosque and *madrasah-i mu'izziyah* in Delhi and massacred a large number of *namāzī*s (people offering *namāz*/prayer). This situation was tackled with great difficulty.[49] Nizām al-Dīn Awliyah's Fūā'id ul-Fū'ād provides an alternative picture of Nūr Tūrk as a godly man possessing spiritual charisma who saw the *'ulāmā'* as impure and corrupt. Nonetheless, friction between him and Raḍiyyah is reported even in his account, as Nūr Tūrk refused to accept the gold sent as a present from the ruler.[50] The account of this Sufi is a prime example of varying perspectives held in the multitude of sources. The state account labels him apostate; the Sufi accounts portray him as a pious man. Nonetheless, both the accounts are consistent on his reproachful attitude toward the *'ulāmā'*. Also, it is important to notice that the only form of resistance that people of Delhi formed against the sultans involved rallying around a religious figure that they believed possessed supernatural powers.

Raḍiyyah promoted junior Shamsī patrimonial officers to higher ranks who became king makers in next two decades. Her important decisions regarding appointments and transfers include the promotion of Khwājah Muhazzab (Ghaznavi), who was earlier the deputy of *wazīr* Niẓām al-Mulk Junaydī to the office of *wazīr*. Malik Saif al-Dīn Bihaq (later Qutlugh Khān) was given charge of the army and Malik Kabīr al-Dīn Ayāz was given the *iqṭā'* of Lahore.[51] After some time, Malik Muayyid al-Dīn Hindu Khān was given the *iqṭā'* of Uchh by Raḍiyyah.[52] At the death of Saif al-Dīn Aybeg-i-Bahīq charge of the army was given to Malik Quṭb al-Dīn Hussyn b. Ali Ghūrī.[53] Malik Ikhtiyār al-Dīn Aytegin became the *amīr hājib* and the Abyssinian Malik Jamal al-Dīn Yāqūt, who was the *amīr-i-ākhūr*, acquired favour in attendance of the sultan.[54]

At this point Juzjānī heralds relative peace and the establishment of the writ of state from Punjab until Bengal which did not last long.[55] In 637/1239 'Izz al-Dīn Kabīr the *muqṭa'* of Lahore, with whom Raḍiyyah had earlier won an alliance, rebelled again, surrendering when the sultan led an expedition towards him. The sultan still exercised substantial authority by taking the charge of *iqṭā'* from the rebel, giving the province of Multan (that included region of Lahore) to the charge of Ikhtiyār al-Dīn Qarāqash Khān Aytegin before returning to the capital.[56]

The climate of opinion quickly turned against Raḍiyyah when she started displaying more assertiveness in political matters than was acceptable for her powerbase. Raḍiyyah started to construct a powerbase of her own, by promoting factions other than Turks that were Ghūrīs[57] and Abyssinian[58] thus alienating Turkish *maliks* and *umarā'*, particularly the *amīr-i ḥājib* Ikhtiyār al-Dīn Aytegin.[59] Raḍiyyah's rise to power however became a disappointment for the *umarā'* who had earlier supported her enthronement, since she, contrary to the expectations of the *umarā'*, quitted the veil, assumed a masculine role and commanded the army. It was the promotion of Abyssinian elements as an alternative powerbase in nobility that led to her ultimate downfall. The Turks were well cognisant of the threat of being replaced and tried to counter it; for instance, Malik Yāqūt was killed immediately as Raḍiyyah left the capital to crush the rebellion of Ikhtiyār al-Dīn Altunapa (Altuniya) in Tabarhindāh. Statements in historical sources about her sudden unpopularity are very simple and suggest that within a brief period of three years, Raḍiyyah became unpopular among the urban social base that had supported her rise once she started donning male dress, stopped observing *pardah* and rode elephants in public.[60]

Raḍiyyah's fall bore a remarkable resemblance to that of her predecessor, since it came about as a result of non-cooperation by the *umarā'* at the centre. In 637–8/1239–40, the *amīr* of Tabarhindāh Ikhtiyār al-Dīn Altunapa (Altuniya) rose up in rebellion and Raḍiyyah set out in person to crush the rebel. She, however, was defeated and imprisoned. In the meantime, the Turk *amīrs* at the centre rose up in a rebellion and, as mentioned earlier, killed Malik Yāqūt. They enthroned Raḍiyyah's brother while she was still alive in prison. Raḍiyyah later entered into a matrimonial contract with the rebel Ikhtiyār al-Dīn Altunapa (Altuniya). The rebel, after making an alliance with her, advanced towards Delhi and Malik 'Izz al-Dīn Salārī and Malik Qarāqash the powerful governors of Multan and Uchh joined them.[61] Raḍiyyah and her husband recruited Khokars, Jāts and Rajputs to attack Delhi and reclaim the throne.[62] It can well be suggested that if Raḍiyyah had succeeded in reclaiming the throne, these new elements might have been added to a more racially diverse bureaucracy of the Delhi sultanate.

At the centre, the *umarā'*, who had viewed Raḍiyyah as a lost cause and her brother as the potential protector of their interests, raised Mu'izz al-Dīn Bahrām Shāh to the throne. In 638/1240, Mu'izz al-Dīn Bahrām Shāh came out of Delhi to quash Raḍiyyah's rebellion and claim the throne. Raḍiyyah and Ikhtiyār al-Dīn Altunapa (Altuniya) were routed when they reached Kaithal and were subsequently killed by the locals.[63] Thus, Raḍiyyah's reign ended in 638/1240 after three years and six months.[64] After the fall of Raḍiyyah, none of the progeny of Iltutmish could dominate the *umarā'* and the power struggle between the *umarā'* became more destructive and palpable.

The Turks Finally Take Over: Bahrām Shāh (638–639/1240–1241)

It was during Mu'izz al-Dīn Bahrām Shāh's[65] reign that the *umarā'* were finally able to completely take over the state apparatus. The office of *nāi'b-i Sultanate* had been formally created for Ikhtiyār al-Dīn Aytegin to oversee the governance while the sultan's position was to remain titular.[66] Bahrām Shāh, unlike his sister, was powerless to make appointments and postings.[67] Nonetheless, keeping in view the fate of his predecessors, he remained highly insecure in his office. This insecurity led to a greater amount of hostility towards his *umarā'*, many of whom he tried to eliminate once he became apprehensive about their designs. The sultan's attempt to purge the ruling elite caused his own overthrow. It is in his reign that we find a breakdown of authority in the provinces, *iqṭā'* and core regions. The sultan's preoccupation in the core regions of power resulted in the sack of Lahore by the Mongols.

According to Juzjānī, when Malik Ikhtiyar al-Dīn Aytegin became deputy he took the affairs of the kingdom in his own hands and in concurrence with *wazīr*, Khwājah Muhazzab al-Dīn, Muḥammad 'Iwāz the *mustaufī* (auditor), who assumed the control of the state.[68] After a couple of months, the sultan became highly suspicious of the deputy since Aytegin married one of his sisters who had secured a *khula'* (divorce) from her first husband to marry Aytegin. As a son-in-law of Iltutmish, his qualification as ruler equalled that of Iltutmish, the son-in-law of Aybeg. Aytegin also adopted a protocol specific to royalty, by assuming triple *naubat* and stationing an elephant outside his residence.[69] In his desperate effort to get rid of Ikhtiyar al-Dīn Aytegin and *wazīr* Niẓām al-Mulk Muhazzib, the sultan ordered their assassination; the former died but the latter survived.[70] Nevertheless, Bahrām Shāh's dream of becoming de facto ruler did not materialise and in the new apparatus Badr al-Dīn Sonqur Rūmī, the *amīr ḥājib*, took over the affairs of the state.[71] Soon after the sultan became apprehensive of Badr al-Dīn Sonqur as well. The rivalry between Khwājah Muhazzib and Sonqur caused the former to poison the sultan against the latter.[72] Badr al-Dīn realised that the sultan wanted to replace him.[73] Hastily, he along with the chief nobles including Ṣadr al-Mulk, Sayyid Tāj al-Dīn 'Alī Musawī the *mushrif-i mumālik* (secretary of the kingdom), *qāḍī-i mumalik*, Jālal al-Dīn Kashānī, *qāḍī* Kabīr al-Dīn Sheikh and Sheikh Muḥammad-i Shamī conspired to dethrone the sultan.[74] The *wazīr* who was expected to be a part of the final decision, on the other hand, informed the sultan about the sedition. The sultan immediately reached the venue while the meeting was ongoing. The sultan decided to relocate all the nobles involved in the scheme. Sonqur was transferred to the *iqṭā'* of Badaun and qāḍī Jalāl al-Dīn Kashānī was removed from his position of judge. *Qāḍī* Kābīr al-Dīn and Sheikh Muḥammad-i Shāmi left Delhi in fear of sultan's vindictiveness.[75] Nonetheless, Badr al-Dīn Sonqur returned to Delhi after a period of four months and took up residence in the dwelling of Malik Quṭb al-Din, Hussayn son of 'Alī whose execution is recorded later by Juzjānī.[76]

The sultan soon earned a reputation of being bloodthirsty as he ordered Badr al-Dīn Sonqur's arrest, imprisonment, and execution along with Sayyid Tāj al-Dīn Mūsawī.[77] Also, some nobles started using the credulous sultan for score-settling against one another. For instance, a *derwaish* gained some influence over the sultan and used the royal favour to get his adversary *qāḍi* Shams al-Dīn Mehar thrown under the feet of the elephants and get trampled. This tactless violence alarmed many groups among the masses and sowed further distrust.[78] The *wazīr* Khwājah Muhazzib, who was furtively contemptuous of the sultan, added fuel to fire by creating distrust between the sultan and nobility.[79] The sultan's indiscreet brutality and inability to handle various factions of nobility resulted in his speedy and violent removal from office and public execution.

An Oath at the Mausoleum of Iltutmish and Appointment of 'Alā al-Dīn Mas'ūd Shāh (639–43/1241–6) as Sultan

In the meantime an important slave and son in law[80] of Iltutmish, Balban-i Kushlü Khān, seized the throne and publicly proclaimed himself sultan.[81] Nevertheless, other nobles including Malik Ikhtiyār al-Dīn Aytegin and Malik Tāj al-Dīn Sanjar Qatulaq assembled at the mausoleum of Sultan Iltutmish and denounced his claim.[82] A compromise seems to have been effected between the rival factions of *umarā'* as a result of which Balban-i Kushlü Khān forfeited his claim. In return, he received the *iqṭā'* of Nagaur with the permission to own an elephant, a symbol of either royalty or formidable state power.[83]

The next ruler, 'Alā al-Dīn Mas'ūd Shāh, the son of Rukn al-Dīn Fīrūz Shāh, and thus the grandson of Iltutmish, was brought out from the prison of Qasr-i Sufīd and enthroned by the same *umarā'* who had executed his predecessor.[84] His freedom coincided with the release of his two other potential substitutes, namely Nāṣir al-Dīn and Jalāl al-Dīn.[85] After temporarily silencing dissent among the various groups of *umarā'*, the dominant group facilitated a public pledge of fealty towards the sultan. The offices were divided subsequently. 'Alā al-Dīn Mas'ūd was too powerless to make appointments and subsequently to take decisions. The group of dominant *umarā'* was there to undertake these duties. Malik Quṭb al-Dīn Hussayn son of 'Alī Ghūrī became the deputy of the sultanate, Khwājah Muhazzib was retained as *wazīr* and Malik Ikhtiyār al-Dīn Qarāqash was made *amīr ḥājib* (lord chamberlain).[86] The provinces of Nagaur, Mandōr and Ajmir[87] were given to Balban-i

Kushlü Khān. The territory of Badaun came under the domination of Malik Tāj al-Dīn Sanjar Qatulaq. The office of chief *qāḍi* was given to *qāḍī* 'Imād al-Dīn Muḥammad the Shafurkanī.[88] Malik 'Izz al-Dīn Toghril Toghān Khān, was transferred from Kara[89] to Lakhnawatī. In 641/1243, *qāḍī* Jalāl al-Dīn Kāshānī, as the sultan's envoy, reached Lakhnawatī with a red canopy of state and a robe of honour for Malik Toghril Toghān Khān.[90]

It is at this time that we find the sultan unable to assume any control over the administration and dispensation of state power fell totally in the hands of different segments of *umarā'*. Overt hostility between rival factions of nobility is one of the most salient features of this period of reign. For instance, in the year 641/1243, the conflicts between the forces of Malik Toghril-i Toghān Khān, the governor of Lakhnawtī, and the Rāi' of Jājnagar became obvious. Although the Rāi's forces were initially routed yet the governor requested the centre for help.[91] In the next year, the forces of the rebellious Rāi' of Jājnāgar appeared before the gate of Lakhnawatī. On the commands of the centre, Malik Qamar al-Dīn Qirān-i Temür Khān arrived at Lakhnawatī with troops and *amīrs*,[92] with a secret mission to dethrone the governor.[93] Malik Toghril-i Toghan Khān eventually relinquished Lakhnawatī to Malik Qamar al-Dīn Qirān-i Temür Khān and proceeded to Delhi.[94]

Precariousness in the power equation became more pronounced as each noble tried to assume more power. For instance, Niẓām al-Mulk, Khwājah Muhazzib acquired complete power over the kingdom and appropriated the region of Kol as his own *iqṭā'*. He had already acquired *naubat*, and had stationed an elephant on the gate of his residence, which was definitely a symbol of royalty. He tried to disempower the Turks, who became incensed and killed him near Ḥauz-i Ranī in 640/1242.[95] The de facto command of the sultanate then shifted to the triumphant Turkish *umarā'* and the office of *wazīr* passed to the Ṣadr ul-Mulk Najm al-Dīn, Abu Bakr. Another lasting impact of this era was the rise of Balban who gained power in the centre. He had been promoted to *amīr ḥājīb* from *amīr akhūr*. Balban patronised Juzjānī and gave him the position of *qāḍī* of the region of Gwalior and made him the *khaṭīb* of congregational mosque, he was also granted with a robe of honour and caparisoned horse.[96]

In these four years a number of victories were claimed by nobles on 'Alā al-Dīn Mas'ūd's behalf and wealth poured from vanquished regions into Delhi.[97] These military successes were generally an outcome of the provincial *muqṭa'* operating independently. Raverty correctly observes that these unnamed victories seem to have been minor affairs and did not ensure the longevity of Mas'ūd's reign.

The sons of Iltutmish who had been released earlier during this era also received land revenue assignments. Malik Jalāl al-Dīn was given the province of Kannauj and the 15-year-old Nāṣir al-Dīn was given the preserved city of Bharaij with its dependencies.[98]

During the fourth year of his reign, Mongols under the leadership of Mangutah had advanced towards Uchh. 'Alā al-Dīn Mas'ūd with his troops left the centre to combat the invaders who withdrew and went back to Khorasan.[99] Nonetheless, the sultan's absence from the centre led to intrigues against him and he was subsequently removed. Juzjānī justifies his removal by stating that the sultan came under the influence of 'some worthless people' from the army during the expedition and the sultan made it a 'habit of killing and seizing his maliks'.[100] This expedition must have given the young sultan a chance to interact with groups of *umarā'* other than his Turk patrons – who exercised the de facto powers in state affairs and were too strong for the young sultan to handle. The sultan decided to ally himself with an alternative group of *umarā'* to get rid of his patrons. It is also plausible that the sultan was trying to nurture his own patrimonial staff. Peter Jackson rightly points out that the sultan attempted to cut the Turkish *umarā'* down in size and relied on black African slaves.[101] This might have riled the Turkish nobles who must have become suspicious of his designs. Juzjānī then makes a case for a mysteriously sudden moral decline of the sultan, stating that he became excessively hedonistic with an increasing interest in wine, sensuality and pleasure. The *umarā'* sent letters to Nāṣir al-Dīn Maḥmūd Shāh to this effect and on 644/1246 'Alā al-Dīn Mas'ūd was imprisoned where he died.[102]

A Ruler who Stitched Caps and Calligraphed the Qur'an: Naṣir al-Dīn Maḥmūd (643–664/1246–1266)

In the remarkably long reign of Naṣir al-Dīn Maḥmūd, we find a number of political actors with conflicting interests becoming the de facto regents. Naṣir al-Dīn Maḥmūd ascended to the throne due to the efforts of his mother the Malikā-i Jahān, Jalāl al-dunya o al-Dīn (this title was given to her after her son ascended to the throne).[103] There is no substantial proof that this woman was a concubine of Iltutmish as stated by Elliot and Dowson[104] and she may have been one of the younger wives of Iltutmish. In this era, there were multiple rival factions of *umarā'* and two groups emerged as most prominent, one was led by Bahā al-Dīn Balban (later Sultan Ghiyāth al-Dīn Balban), while Balban-i Kushlü Khān (Balban-i Būzūrg), 'Imād al-Dīn Rayhān and Qutlugh Khān were the ringleaders of the other group.

It is in this period that the region of Lahore was completely lost to Mongols and Nāṣir al-Dīn Maḥmūd's brother Jalāl al-Dīn Mas'ūd Shāh took control of the region as a Mongol satellite. Similarly, the presence of the kingdom of Ḥasan Qurlugh indicates the breakdown of the writ of the state in the north-west. In this era, we find the sultan unable to take decisions of military or civil affairs independent of his patrons. In all instances of promotions and dismissals, we find a number of strong *umarā'* dictating his actions from behind the scenes.

Juzjānī's work was dedicated to Nāṣir al-Dīn Maḥmūd. However, there are some mysterious inconsistencies in it. Firstly, it is an incomplete account of his reign, with the last six years of his reign missing despite the fact that Juzjānī outlived Nāṣir al-Dīn Maḥmūd. Secondly, his account of Nāṣir al-Dīn Maḥmūd somewhat curiously lacks necessary details in some places and includes unnecessary elaborations in others. In the beginning of his account, unlike in his account of the progeny of Iltutmish, Juzjānī provides a list of 18 *umarā'* who most likely were the pillars of the state.[105] According to Raverty, there are some important offices that have not been mentioned in the list, including *qāḍī*s and *malik*s such as Malik Nuṣrat Khān, Badr al-Dīn Sonqar Rumī, Malik Saif al-Dīn Aybeg Shamsī, the chief *dādbeg*, the son of Khislī Khān who was Balban's nephew and many others.[106] Moreover, no list of the sultan's victories is furnished either.

Nāṣir al-Dīn Maḥmūd, possibly one of the youngest surviving sons of Iltutmish, was born in Qasr-i Bāgh in 626/1228, after the death of Nāṣir al-Dīn Maḥmūd Shāh, the eldest son of the sultan. After his father's death, he remained in the royal prison and was released during the reign of his nephew 'Alā al-Dīn Mas'ūd. Bharaij was the first *iqṭā'* that was assigned to him during the reign of his nephew. In this assignment he was accompanied by his mother Malikā-i Jahān, who had made a settlement with the *umarā'* in Delhi, because of which he was replaced with 'Alā al-Dīn Mas'ūd.[107] His entry into Delhi makes an interesting account since he was secretly transported to Delhi in a women's veil.[108] He ascended to the throne at the age of 15.[109] Given that his patrons had a stranglehold in Delhi, 'the *maliks* and *amīrs*, *sadrs*, grandees, *'ulāmā'* and sayyids hastened to present themselves in court to express fealty towards him'.[110] Two days later in the koshak-i Fīrūzī (Fīrūzī Castle) the people made a public pledge of allegiance.[111]

Since the beginning of his reign, the sultan seemed to be dominated by one *amīr* or another. The sultan was credited by Baranī to have copied the Qur'an and to have delegated the affairs of the state to Bahā al-Dīn Balban.[112] These assertions are partially verified by Juzjānī's chronicles. While the historian does not mention the creative talents of the sultan, he does portray a saintly persona of the sultan[113] and Balban as the spirit behind his reign.

After assuming power, the sultan campaigned into the north-western region along with his general Balban. He fought a battle with the Mongols at the river of Sind and Baniān.[114] By this time, the Mongols had played havoc in Lahore, Multan and extorted 30,000 *dirhams*, great amounts of fabric and a hundred captives.[115] By the end of 644/1247, the sultan's forces crossed the river Ravi near Lahore. The expedition near the salt range was led by Balban who successfully raided the regions of north Punjab reaching the banks of the river Sind. The sultan encamped at the bank of river Sudharāh with his followers, heavy materials and elephants, while Balban along with the army ravaged the Koh-i Jūd (salt range) and Jehlum region to subdue Khokars and other rebels.[116]

The following year witnessed a rebellion in Doab region which the royal forces under Balban successfully subdued.[117] In this battle, Balban proved his mettle. On his way back to the capital, the brother of the sultan, Jalāl al-Dīn the *muqṭa'* of Kannauj, presented himself to the sultan and was given additional charge of the territories of Sanbhal and Badaun.[118] Soon after, due to reasons not mentioned by Juzjānī, Jalāl al-Dīn became fearful of his brother and joined the Mongols who later enthroned him in Lahore.[119] In the same year, the royal forces moved again towards Kōh-i Payāh (skirts of the hills of Mewāt) and Ranthambor. The absence of the sultan and his most trusted officers from the centre instigated strife among the *umarā'*. *Qāḍī* Jamāl al-Dīn the Shafurkanī was accused of hatching a conspiracy to dethrone the sultan and was removed from the position of *qāḍī*. He departed towards

Badaun and was later killed due to the endeavours of 'Imād al-Dīn Rayhān, a strong *amīr*.[120]

Balban's influence increased as the sultan married his daughter.[121] From the fifth year of Nāṣir al-Dīn's reign, the Mongol threat in the north-western borders became very formidable. Juzjānī boasts of Ikhtiyār al-Dīn-i Kurez's victory in the vicinity of Multan and extraction of a great number of captives.[122] Raverty, however, finds this statement very doubtful as, according to him, the Mongols were constantly encroaching in the Punjab and were permanently located on the bank of river Bayas.[123] It was the time when, according to Farishtāh, Sher Khān, the cousin of Balban, conducted raids up until Ghazna.[124]

Next year, Malik Saif al-Dīn Hasan Qurlugh, who had founded an independent kingdom in Baniān notwithstanding the Mongol threat, attacked Multan, which was the *iqṭā'* of Malik Balban-i Kushlü Khān. Hasan Qurlugh was killed in a skirmish with Balban-i Kushlü Khān. Nonetheless, his elder son Malik Naṣir al-Dīn Maḥmūd succeeded in seizing Multan. Sometime later Malik Sher Khān was able to recover Multan and install his own patrimonial officer Ikhtiyār al-Dīn-i Kurez there.[125]

Balban's dominance is emphasised in Juzjānī's account of 649/1252, and we find Balban's cousin being placed in charge of the territories of Multan that bordered Balban-i Kushlü Khān's territories of Sind. Both these governors were at loggerheads with each other earlier the same year, Balban-i Kushlü Khān had rebelled in his territory of Nagaur. The imperial army subdued the rebel who presented himself before the royal camp and submitted.[126] The conflict between the centre and Balban-i Kushlü Khān resulted in an encounter between him and Sher Khān. The latter marched from Multan against Uchh and the former pressed on from Nagaur towards Uchh. After the rebel lost, he was detained, forced to relinquish the fort of Uchh to the victor and left for the capital.[127] Balban's brother, Khisli Khān, was put in charge of Nagaur.[128] In 649/1252, Balban-i Kushlü Khān was transferred to the *iqṭā'* of Badaun, which was one of the most important *iqṭā*'s of that time.[129] In the same year, the position of *qāḍī* of the realm and the jurisdiction of the capital was entrusted to Juzjānī.[130] Also, the royal forces marched towards Gwalior, Chanderi, and Narnaul, also reaching Malwa.[131] Balban is reported to have defeated an important local ruler and obtained an enormous amount of booty at the end of this campaign.

In 650/1252, the sultan came under the influence of 'unworthy people' in the same manner that had caused the dethronement and murder of his predecessor. The sultan led an expedition towards Lahore with the intention to march towards Uchh and Multan, where Sher Khān had gathered strength. The sultan was without Balban during the expedition.[132] During this march, the sultan was able to meet the *khāns*, *maliks*, and *amīrs* of the adjacent parts. Qutlugh Khān arrived from the territory of Bayana, and 'Izz al-Dīn Balban-i Kushlü Khān came from Badaun with their respective followings. 'Imād al-Dīn Rayhān also joined the two grand nobles who took the sultan and his companions under their influence and instigated their action against Balban.[133]

Visible changes in the power structure were made to appease the three grand nobles. Within a period of two months Nāṣir al-Dīn issued an order from his encampment of Hisar (siege) against Balban, who was ordered to retire to his *iqṭā'* of Siwālikh and Hansi. Balban's brother was transferred to the far-flung *iqṭā'* of Kara. Then the royal forces returned to the capital where important administrative changes were made. The office of *wazīr* was given to Niẓām ul-Mulk Junaydī and the office of *amīr ḥājib* was given to Malik Saif al-Dīn Aybeg-i Kashlī Khān.[134] 'Imād al-Dīn Rayhān received the office of *wakīl dar*. Soon after, Juzjānī was removed from the position of *qāḍī*. *Qāḍī* Shams al-Dīn Bharaij was brought into office on the recommendation of 'Imād al-Dīn Rayhan, who seems to have been enjoying great power in the current political scenario.[135] In the meantime, the sultan and his new friends raided Hansi to eliminate Balban, who was probably routed and surrendered the region of Hansi and receded to Nagaur. The *iqṭā'* of Hansi and the office of *amīr ḥājib* were entrusted to Prince Rukn al-Dīn Fīrūz Shāh, son of the sultan. Since he must have been very young, some deputy must have been assigned as regent of this child and his offices.[136]

Balban's cousin Sher Khān, who had rebelled in the regions of Sind, withdrew from Sind and was busy raiding Turkistān. The regions of Uchh, Multan and Tabarhindāh were left in the hands of his dependents.[137] The forces at the centre, considering the absence of Sher Khān as an opportunity, marched from Delhi to secure the regions of Uchh and Multan along with the sultan. On arriving at the river of Bayas, a force was dispatched to Tabarhindāh, which was recovered[138] and was assigned to Arsalān Khān, Sanjar-i Chist.[139]

The year 652/1254 witnessed constant rebellions from the rural areas of the core regions. The sultan marched on the hills of *kōh-i pāyāh* to suppress some rebellions.[140] After this, the royal forces turned to suppress a rebellion in Katehar.[141] After this raid, some important changes in the administration took place; the *wazārāt* was conferred on Ṣadar ul-Mulk, Najam al-Dīn Abu Bakar who had served on the same designation some time earlier.[142]

Within a few months, the pro-Balban nobles rallied around Prince Jalāl al-Dīn who had left the Delhi sultanate six year ago in his bid to win the Mongol support to claim the throne.[143] Tabarhindāh was at that time the centre of dissenting *umarā'* that included Malik Tāj al-Dīn Arsalān Khān, Sanjar-i Chist of Tabarhindāh, Malik Saif al-Dīn Bat Khān, Aybeg-i Khitai and Balban.[144] This region was at the western frontiers of the Delhi sultanate that neighboured the Mongols and provided theses nobles a strategic advantage to bargain a potential alliance. The sultan was able to perceive a bigger threat to his throne and decided to reconcile with Balban.

After negotiations with the rebel *umarā'*,[145] who had now overpowered the *umarā'* at the centre, the sultan was forced to dismiss his three friends and their associates. He sent 'Imād al-Dīn Rayhān to Badaun as *muqṭa'* and accommodated the rebels.[146] Lahore was assigned as *iqṭā'* to Prince Jalāl al-Dīn.[147] Soon after[148] the sultan's mother married Qutlugh Khān, who was one of the *amīr*s of his father and was an associate of Balban-i Khuslü Khān and Imad al-Dīn Rayhān. Sultan Nāṣir al-Dīn Maḥmūd sent his mother and Qutlugh Khān to Awadh as *muqṭa'*.[149]

The offices of Balban and his support group were restored subsequently. Juzjānī was restored to the office of *qāḍī* in Delhi.[150] Similarly, the *iqṭā' of* Meerut was assigned to Kishlī Khān.[151] Shortly after the chief adversary of Balban, 'Imād al-Dīn Rayhān, was eliminated.[152] The sultan also ordered the removal of Qutlugh Khān from Awadh to Bharaij. Qutlugh Khān did not comply with this order and thus Malik Baq Temür the Ruknī was directed to expel him. However, the *malik* died before he could perform his job. Then the sultan himself moved towards Awadh and Qutlugh Khān escaped despite the fact that Balban followed him.[153] In the next year, the sultan's forces reached Delhi. Meanwhile, Qutlugh Khān resurged and approached the territories of Kara and Manikpur where he faced the *muqṭa'* Arsalān Khān Sanjar-i Chist. Qutlugh Khān was defeated.[154]

Since it had become difficult for Qutlugh Khān to make further resistance in the territory of Hindustan, he moved northwards towards Lahore and Bayas and then went into the region of Santur, seeking shelter among the independent local tribes. The sultan moved from the capital to quell this rebellion. The locals and a party of the *umarā'* supported Qutlugh Khān. Nevertheless, the royal army won and the enemies were pushed back to the passes of Silmur. The royal army then devastated the Koh-i Silmur and a large number of Hindu rebels were killed.[155]

On the return of the royal forces, Malik 'Izz al-Dīn Balban-i Kushlü Khān, who with the troops of Uchh and Multan, was in the neighbourhood of the bank of River Bayas, advanced still further. Malik Qutlugh Khān and those *amīr*s who were in alliance with him joined Balban-i Kushlü Khān and advanced to the limits of Manṣurpūr and Samanah. When the information reached the capital, Balban left to counter them.[156] After Balban's departure, the centre was an easy target; some of the capital *'ulāmā'* such as Jamāl al-Dīn, Saiyid, Quṭb al-Dīn and *qāḍī* Shams al-Dīn Bharaiji wrote secret letters to the opposing party urging them to come to the capital where everyone would pledge their support. This conspiracy came to the knowledge of Balban, who advised the sultan that the group of 'turban wearers' should be sent away to their *iqṭā'* until the matter was resolved. Thus, the conspiring *'ulāmā'* were removed from the capital.[157]

However, the letters reached Malik Qutlugh Khān and Balban-i Kushlü Khān who arrived at Delhi's gates with their forces within two and a half days. They encamped in the suburbs of Delhi between the bagh-i jud and Kelukherī.[158] The city gates were well guarded by royal authorities[159] giving no opportunity to the rivals to enter the city.

Seeing the strength of the city's defences, Balban-i Kushlü Khān retired and so did the other people along with Malikā-i Jahān and Qutlugh Khān. Juzjānī tells us about the defeated army's response. Firstly, some people at the time of withdrawal took residence in Delhi, some submitted themselves at the royal court and others left with the defeated parties.[160] After the withdrawal of the forces, the royal army under the leadership of Balban (now Ulugh Khān) returned to the court.[161] In this year, certain new appointments were made. Since these appointments are mentioned after Balban's arrival in the capital it can be inferred that just as had happened in the past, Balban directed the same. The designation of *wazīr* was entrusted to Ḍiyā' ul-Mulk Tāj al-Dīn with the title of Niẓām ul-Mulk and the designation of *ashraf-i mamalik* was given to the Ṣadr ul-Mulk. By the end of the year, an army of Mongols from Khorasan reached the territory of Uchh and Multan and Malik 'Izz al-Dīn Balban-i Kushlü Khān entered into a contract with them to join the camp of Sali Noyan, the Mongol.[162] The pact between the Mongols and Balban-i Kushlü Khān marked the end of anti-Balban trio from the Delhi sultanate, after which they disappeared from accounts of the Delhi sultanate.

The last recorded years of the sultan's reign are accounts of Balban's military campaigns, appointments of various provincial officers and the engagement of forces of Delhi with the Mongols.[163] It was during this time that Balban's daughter bore Sultan Nāṣir al-Dīn a second son,[164] who died soon after.[165] It is also worth noticing that the sultan's first son was earlier entrusted with the *iqṭā'* of Hansi.[166]

The rest of the six years' history is missing from the accounts of not only Juzjānī but also from the historians of northern India including Tabaqāt-i Akbarī, Bada'yūnī, Farishtāh and Baranī. It seems safe to infer that Nāṣir al-Dīn fell seriously ill and died. Since no male issue had survived, Balban, who was his father-in-law, ruled instead. The claim by Ibn Battūtah that Nāṣir al-Dīn was poisoned seems to be an outcome of market hearsay. One of the daughters of Nāṣir al-Dīn was married to Balban's son Būghrā Khān, bearing a child (later sultan) Kayqubād.[167]

The history of Iltutmish's successors is generally the story of the rise of the junior Shamsī slaves, including 'Izz al-Dīn Balban (Kushlü Khān), Bahā al-Dīn Balban (the future sultan), his brother Sayf al-Dīn Aybeg (Kishlī Khān) and Tāj al-Dīn Sanjar (Arsalān Khān) and some others. These officers were given rapid promotions to curtail the power of the senior Shamsī slaves like Kabīr Khān and the free elements.[168] These junior slaves, who were appointed at the centre or royal household, seem to be one of the important groups responsible for the dethronement of Rukn al-Dīn and the ascendancy of Raḍiyyah, which explains why Raḍiyyah initially promoted them to higher ranks.[169] The meteoric rise of Iltutmish's junior slaves is a highlight of the post-Iltutmish interregnum and Balban, his brother Kishlī Khān, Tāj al-Dīn Sanjar and Kushlü Khān make apt case studies in this respect.

Bahā al-Dīn Balban-i Khward (the younger)[170] was purchased by Iltutmish and he started his career as a water-bearer.[171] At the death of his master he was a *khāsādār* (falconer). Raḍiyyah designated him as *amīr-i shikār* and Bahrām Shāh promoted him to *amīr-i ākhūr*.[172] He distinguished himself in the siege of Delhi in 640/1242 and received *iqṭā'* of Hansi.[173] In 647/1249, he was designated as *amīr-i ḥājib*.[174] Balban became *nā'ib* or deputy of the state, received the title of Ulugh Khān and Sultan Nāṣir al-Dīn Maḥmūd married his daughter. Successfully concentrating the power in his hands, he became one of the key decision-makers in the Delhi sultanate. After the death of the sultan in 664/1266, he took charge as 'the shadow of God' (the sultan), and remained in power until his death in 685/1287.[175] This information reveals that Balban had established himself within a mere ten years following his recruitment, making his way to important imperial household positions. At no point during his career in the sultanate is there any indication of his extensive military training. However, since he distinguished himself in the siege of Delhi for which he won the *iqṭā'* of Hansi, it may be inferred that he was already well versed in the art of warfare especially in cavalry before his recruitment, as he was given the military offices of *amīr-i shikār* and *amīr-i ākhūr*.

Similarly, 'Izz al-Dīn Balban-i Kushlü Khān (Buzurg the senior),[176] who was one of the chief rivals of Balban-i Khward, was acquired during the siege of Mandhor in 625/1227. By the time of Iltutmish's death in 634/1236, he had become the *muqṭa'* of Baran.[177] His career is that of a powerful *muqṭa'*. He was responsible for enthroning Raḍiyyah and after her fall he proclaimed to be the sultan and adopted the title of Mūghīth al-Dīn; but obviously he failed due to the noncompliance of his colleagues.[178] In 640/1242, he was given the title of Kushlü Khān and an extensive but distant *iqṭā'* of Nagaur and in 644/1246 Multan as well.[179] Later, he acquired the *iqṭā'* of Uchh from Sultan Nāṣir al-Dīn. In approximately 650/1252–3, when Balban-i Khward was demoted from the post of *nā'ib*, Kushlü Khān and his allies controlled the government in the absence of Balban. Kushlü Khān recovered old *iqṭā'* in Sind in the late 630s/1240s.[180] Within the first nine years of his career in the sultanate he obtained an *iqṭā'*, and within ten years he was strong enough to proclaim himself a sultan, later becoming the archrival to the most powerful *nā'ib* Balban-i Khward.[181] Again, we are unable to trace any evidence of military training during his career in the sultanate.

Nevertheless, the fact that he was endowed with an *iqṭā'* or military estate in the sixth year of his career demonstrates that he was already trained in arms before Iltutmish acquired him.

The brother of Balban-i Khward, Sayf al-Dīn Aybeg (Kishlī Khān)[182] was purchased around 629/1231 through a merchant delegation sent to Egypt and Baghdad for procuring military slaves. Until Iltutmish's death, he only served in the sultan's private household. Later, he became *nā'ib-i sar-i jāndār* (commander of the royal guard).[183] Tāj al-Dīn Sonqar (later Arsalān Khān) was purchased around the same date, when he started his career as a *khāsādār* (falconer). Raḍiyyah promoted Sonqar to the post of *chāshnigīr* (senior officer in the royal kitchen) and later he was made *muqṭa'* of Balārām.[184] Thus, we do not observe the patterns of promotions as mentioned by Nizām al-Mulk Tüsi[185] and identified by Bosworth[186] in the *mamlūk* institution of the Delhi sultanate. The slaves mentioned above were undoubtedly men of exceptional characteristics. Still, all of them gained ascendancy in such short time periods that it seems proper to infer that it was primarily the favour of a superior authority that determined the timing of promotions.

The sultan died in 664/1266 in mysterious circumstances. In his account, Ibn Battūtah alleges that Balban murdered Sultan Nāṣir al-Dīn, without explaining the exact circumstances of the sultan's death.[187] The ever-contemptuous Baranī is silent on the issue.[188] With the sultan gone and with the absence of a male heir, the path was clear for Balban; the experienced administrator, successful military commander and astute statesman with matrimonial links to the royal family took over.

In the Delhi sultanate, it seems convenient to assume that the normative notion of a 'legitimate ruler' was different for various social groups. As mentioned earlier, the historical data of the Shamsī dynasty that is largely derived from Juzjānī focused on the relationship between the ruler and his *umarā'*. The references to a Muslim powerbase, however, are very few in number.

In the post-Shamsī interregnum, the absence of any definite law of succession in the Delhi sultanate left multiple contenders to the throne. The problem arose as Iltutmish had tried to convert his personalised rule into a dynastic order, which was unacceptable to his patrimonial bureaucratic staff who wanted to convert the Delhi sultanate into an oligarchy. Iltutmish had developed a delicate balance between various strategically placed minorities which in the absence of a strong sultan

Table 5.1 Summary: Post Shams al-Din Iltutmish Interregnum (1236–66)

Ruler	Reign	Enthroned by	Opponents	Alliances	Nurtured patrimonial staff	Attempted purge	De facto ruler	Outcome of leaving the capital for military campaign
Rukn al-Din Firuz (1236)	6 months	Provincial nobles	Nobles at the centre	No new alliances were formed. The old allies turned enemies	None enjoyed the company of artists and musicians, on whom he showered extraordinary munificence	Yes. The attempted purge of the progeny of Iltutmish had him killed	Shah Turkan	Ousted from throne
Radiyyah (1236–1240)	4 years	Kushlu khan and nobles at centre	Senior Shamsi nobles especially from provinces	Multiple short term alliances were won	Yes. Promoted junior Shamsi nobles, Africans and Ghurids	Yes		Ousted from throne

Muiz al-Din Bahram (1240–1242)	2 years	Mainly by Turkish nobles including Ikhtiyar al-Din Aytagin and Khwajah Muhazzab Ghaznavi	The patrons turned opponents due to his intrigues and tactless hostility	No	No	Yes. The sultan's reputation of killing the umara resulted in his dethronement and murder	Ikhtiyar al-Din Aytagin, Badr al-Din Sonqur and Khwajah Muhazzab Ghaznavi	Ousted from throne. The final agitation against the sultan started when he was on the bank of the river Biyas
Ala al-Din Masud (1242–1246)	4 years	Mainly by Turkish nobles	The patrons turned opponents	Unsuccessful attempt to forge new alliances	Attempted and failed. He was dismissed by the indignant nobles that he tried to replace	No	Turkish nobles	Ousted from throne
Nasir al-Din Mahmud (1246–1266)	20 years	Balban and his support group	Allies continued becoming enemies	Yes	Attempted and failed	No	Balban	Failed conspiracy to oust from throne

regressed to factionalism. The violence between factions determined who was the fittest to influence the reigning sultan. In this era, the political importance of Delhi was augmented due to its population. As soon as any sultan left the centre there were attempts by nobles to oust him or her from power and the city came under siege by the provincial nobles several times. Unlike Shihāb al-Dīn Ghūrī and Aybeg, Iltutmish was able to convert his personal rule into a dynasty by patronising various groups of society and by creating an entirely new space for Muslims by developing the city of Delhi and many other garrisons. This certainly was a reason why Iltutmish's progeny continued to rule the sultanate as de jure rulers despite their inability to coerce power or to cultivate their own patrimonial staff. The bloodline of Iltutmish was a source of legitimacy for the Muslim social base for nearly a century after Iltutmish's death. Nevertheless, Rukn al-Dīn was eliminated as his mother tried to purge the nobility, Raḍiyyah and Behrām Shāh were eliminated due to their attempts to construct an alternative power base and the weak Ala al-Din Mas'ūd died as he riled his patrons. Naṣir al-Dīn was intelligent enough to choose his friends carefully, yet his status as a sultan remained largely titular. The post-Shams al-Din interregnum was a struggle between royal birth and administrative experience. The enthronement of Balban as the successor of Naṣir al-Dīn suggests the triumph of administrative experience over the royal lineage.

CHAPTER 6

BLOOD AND IRON, POISON AND DAGGER: BALBAN'S PRESCRIPTION FOR SUCCESSFUL RULE

Balban claimed to be the descendent of the mythical Turani (Persian/ Turkish) king Afrasiyab. His subjects never saw him laugh or cry ...

Sultan Ghiyāth al-Dīn Balban (d. 684/1286) is known as one of the most successful rulers of the Delhi sultanate. As mentioned in the previous chapter, he was brought to the Delhi sultanate as a slave in early 627/1232–1233.[1] He was among the junior Shamsī slaves, who quickly rose to power after the death of Sultan Shams al-Dīn Iltutmish. Balban became one of the most important officers of the reigning sultan within ten years of his appearance in Delhi and within three decades of his arrival he was the sultan of Delhi.

During the times of Sultan Nāṣir al-Dīn Maḥmūd (d. 664/1266), Balban is alleged by the historian Ḍiyā' al-Dīn Baranī (1285–1357/683–756) to have been the de facto ruler of the Delhi sultanate.[2] According to Baranī's amoral standards of medieval statesmanship, Balban's rule as the sultan was nearly ideal. He efficiently centralised all authority in his hands, successfully eliminated all resistance and 'restored' the prestige of the designation of sultan and sultanate.[3] Interestingly, there are no primary or contemporary accounts of Balban's reign. Baranī documented this period when more than 70 years had elapsed after Balban's death. Baranī authored this work in his late sixties with clear objectives and biases. His statements inspire much of what we read about Balban in the later sultanate, Mughal and secondary literature. By critiquing the available primary sources we discover an alternative perspective on Balban.

Age of Consolidation

Baranī's obsession with normative ideals makes it very difficult to separate his political philosophy and Balban's life. The section on Balban is replete with the ruler's reported[4] monologues addressed to his sons and *umarā'* with the help of which Baranī depicts the mindset of a successful monarch, intending to provide a *naṣhitnāmah* (a mirror of princes) for future monarchs. The incidents relating to the reign of Balban are few, their account is also too general and the statement of events does not follow any specific sequence. These events enable us to understand that the sultan was not able to exercise effective authority throughout his reign which can be divided into four major periods: First, from 664–672/1266–1274 he attempted to re-establish the authority of the Delhi sultanate through military expeditions.[5] He aimed to restore the writ of the state and recapture the tax base that the sultanate had lost due to instability under the descendants of Iltutmish. Second, 673–678/1275–1280 was a period of relative prosperity and stability when Malwa and Gujarat were annexed. The sultan's forces also occasionally countered Mongol raids. Third is the period of 678–681/1280–1283, when rumours of sultan's death resulted in powerful rebellion by Toghril.[6] Fourth is the period of 682–684/1284–1286, when the state authority finally crumbled as a consequence of the failing health of the sultan.[7]

From 664–672/1266–1274, we find the sultan establishing his writ in Delhi, Doab and regions of Hindustan.[8] In the year 664/1266, Tamar Khān, the ruler of Bengal, submitted to him by sending a tribute of 63 elephants.[9] From the beginning of his reign, the sultan was able to cultivate a patrimonial relationship with his *umarā'* by extending largesse. He also reorganised the army along patrimonial lines. In the initial years, the sultan displayed the power of the state through extensive use of cultural and religious symbols. This successfully restored the royal persona in the eyes of the populace of Delhi.

Balban claimed to be the *zil Allah fil arḍ*[10] or 'shadow of god on earth' which was an outcome of the mixture of Sassanid political theory and Muslim political thought.[11] According to Sassanid political theory, the king was god and thus was to be obeyed. This concept was blended into an opinion of Muslim political theory that the ruler derived his authority through divine right. Kingship was considered to be *niyābate khudāwandī* (the deputyship of God); thus the ruler was elevated to the ranks of divinity. Various verses were highlighted to underline this concept: the Qur'anic verse 'obey God, obey the prophet and obey those with authority' and a hadīth that mandated obedience to a ruler 'even if he be black or a slave or mutilated in form'. Another hadīth stated that 'the rebellion against the ruler is sin'.[12] Hence, commentaries were extended by patronised groups among the *'ulāmā'* to help the sultan establish legitimacy through religion. However, such grandiloquent titles were merely post hoc justifications, duly employed by all belligerents to justify their reign and render the masses acquiescent.

The majority of the population of the Delhi sultanate was non-Muslim and their awareness of Muslim religious idioms was sparse. The functionality of religion as a source of legitimacy was limited to Muslims. The extent to which the urban Muslim population, which was the social base, and the ruling elite which was the powerbase of the Delhi sultans adhered to the notions of religiosity are the issues undertaken at length in this chapter.

In the period of the initial three years, the sultan took effective measures to restore law and order in the regions of Delhi and its suburbs by demilitarisation of Mewāties,[13] deforestation of the suburbs of Delhi and fortification of Gopalpur.[14] The sultan repaired and built many forts in the suburbs of Delhi and appointed Afghans as the custodians of these forts.[15] It is from this time that Afghans became visible as a major group policing the suburbs of Delhi.

The raids and deforestation of the region of Doab[16] was a strategic move, since these fertile lands were an important source of agricultural revenue. The sultan successfully eliminated the dissenters and appointed *muqṭa*'s over the regions. In order to make an example the sultan not only eliminated the rebel elements, but also plundered the rebel villages, and enslaved the women and children of the region.[17] In the year 667/1269, the sultan raided Kanpal, Patyāli and Bhojpur; there too he suppressed rebellions, restored the writ of the state and constructed fortifications, the wardenship of which was handed over to Afghans.[18] Similarly, the writ of the state was restored in the regions of Katihar where the opposition was neutralised by arson, plunder and the execution of the male population and deforestation. In addition, control was restored over the areas of Badaun, Amroha, Sanbhal and Gnaur.[19] In 668–669/1270–1271, Baranī reported a successful expedition to Koh-i Jūd (salt range).[20]

The sultan was only able to recapture Lahore after he poisoned and eliminated his cousin Sher Khān in 670/1272.[21] Tamar Khān a veteran Shamsī general was appointed the new governor and, keeping in view the strategic importance of the city, the process of rebuilding of forts started.[22] In 671/1273, the sultan ordered the ousting of the *muqṭa*'s of the Doab appointed during the reign of the Shamsī dynasty but later cancelled his orders on the protest of the nobility.[23] In 672/1274, the sultan appointed Prince Muḥammad the *muqṭa'* of Kol, as governor of Sind and Multan[24] and Prince Būghrā Khān as governor of Sunam and Samana.[25] Thus, through conquest and quelling of rebellions, the sultan was able to pacify the sultanate and appoint his personal staff to key positions.[26]

The period 673–678/1275–1280 is characterised by Balban's successful assertion of power over his realm and expansion into Gujarat and Malwa. In this period, there were regular Mongol raids, which were checked by Prince Muḥammad, Bughrā Khān and Malik Begtars, the favourite slave of Balban.[27]

It seems that Balban's power started waning in the late 670s/early 1280s due to the Mongol raids. The year 679/1281 was marked by the revolt of Balban's slave and governor of Bengal, Toghril Khān. In this year the sultan sent two of his generals to quell these rebellions but they remained unsuccessful.[28] In 680/1282, Balban personally undertook a successful campaign in Bengal with 200,000 men, which resulted in the elimination of Toghril and his associates[29] and the appointment of prince Bughrā Khān in his place.[30] The punishments meted out to the rebels were so dreadful that many who witnessed the spectacle were said to have died from terror.[31] In 681/1283, Balban reached Delhi and ordered the mass execution of rebels of Bengal. Nevertheless, these orders were cancelled at the request of the people of Delhi.[32]

The final breakdown of Balban's power came after the demise of his son, Muḥammad, who died near Lahore in 682/1284 fighting with the Mongols.[33] Thus, Kaykhusraw, the son of the deceased prince, was appointed in his place. Afterwards, the old sultan was unable to control the affairs of state that fell into disarray with his failing health.

Construction of the Ruling Elite

Like his predecessors, Balban's *nobility* was of heterogeneous origins; they included Turks, Indians, Tajiks, Khaljīs and Mongols.[34] The Ghiyāthī notables consisted of a prominent number of slaves and free men with whom Balban had cultivated patrimonial relations. These slaves included 1) Balban's personal slaves, 2) Shamsī slaves and slaves of other *umarā'*, who were patronised and befriended by Balban and 3) Shamsī and Ghiyāthī *mawālzadgān* (sons of the freed slaves).[35] The free *umarā'* were either fresh émigrés[36] who belonged to various racial backgrounds as mentioned earlier or they were descendants of the old notables of Delhi resident in that city from the times of early Muslim settlements.

Balban had a reputation of cultivating patrimonial staff since the times when he had been *muqṭa'*. Before becoming the sultan, Balban had a career exceeding three decades in the royal service. Like other *muqṭa'*s, after taking charge of Hansi in 639/1242, he had started to accumulate his personal force, which included slaves. Before becoming the sultan he already possessed Turkish slaves of his own including Aytagin-i Mū'-i Darāz Amīn Khān,[37] and Sipah Sālār Qarachomaq. Although the tribal origins of these slaves are unknown, they may have been of the sultan's own tribe, the Olberli, as their names suggest that they were Turkish.[38] Balban's favourite slave, according to Baranī, was Ikhtiyār al-Dīn Begtars who was elevated to the office of *amīr-i ḥājib/barbeg*.[39]

Considering Baranī's attestations to Balban's racial prejudice, it can be easily inferred that the Turk freemen and Turkish slaves must have enjoyed eminent positions under the aegis of Balban, and Hindus were not included in the ruling elite.[40] Conversely, Baranī's own account, does not support his avowals. In many instances, Balban does not seem biased towards Hindus. The issue of Balban's hostility towards Kamāl-i Mahyār, a son of the local Hindu slave, for the post of revenue-intendant *(khwājah)* of Amroha[41] is contextualised when we consider that Balban's career was once blighted by a Hindu slave 'Imād al-Dīn Rayhān.[42] Thus, the sultan's antipathy may well have been only for the Indian elite slaves rather than for Hindus particularly.[43] It is also important to note that the sultan did not dismiss Kamāl Mahyār from the nobility, since in the times of his successor Kayqubād he was among the leading *umarā'*.[44] In addition, Balban possessed 1,000 Indian *pā'ik* (foot) slaves in his contingent even before his accession to the throne[45] and he adopted two prisoners of war, sons of a local raja, who later served the sultanate in elevated ranks.[46] Balban's slaves were called the Ghiyāthī slaves due to his royal title Ghiyāth al-Dīn.

Immediately after enthronement, Balban took far-reaching measures to organise the royal army on patrimonial grounds. He put his cavalry and infantry under the guardianship (*supurdagī*) of brave and loyal *amīr*s. He also awarded higher yielding villages as revenue assignments to the best-mounted cavaliers whose loyalty was unquestionable.[47] Balban also patronised people having high lineage, skill and cultivation.

According to Baranī:

> The Sultan Ghiyāth al-Dīn Balban due to his sagacity and experience gave precedence over all other matters to stabilisation and organisation of the army, which is the principal pillar of any government. In the very first year of his reign, he entrusted the cavalry, new and old foot soldiers [*piyādāh*] to the training of experienced *malik*s and prominent *sardār*s that were brave, resourceful and loyal. He promoted a few thousand chosen *sāwār*s whose loyalty was unquestionable, and who had acquired cavalry skills in heritage, to elevated ranks. Instead of salaries [*mawājib*] they were given prosperous villages and lands as *'iqtā*s.[48]

Thus, the sultan cultivated a class of warriors through patronage in order to reorganise the army more efficiently and remunerated them through *iqṭā'* (land revenue military assignments). Although there is no direct mention of military slaves in this passage, it can be inferred that the majority of these elite cavalry troops ('chosen *sāwār*s') must have been the *mamlūk*s or their *mawālzadgān*, for two reasons. Firstly, members of the cavalry must have been foreigners to gain cavalry skills, as in India there was hardly a culture of expert horse riding.[49] Among foreign slaves the Turks were the most prized for their expert riding skills.[50] Secondly, *sāwār*s by Baranī are described as 'high quality'[51] and a 'selected few,'[52] indicating a special status. The number of this group was estimated at a 'few thousand'.[53] We have already seen that the *mamlūk*s were an elite corps consisting of only a few thousand. This evidence supports the argument that many amongst these men must have been *mamlūk*s. In this passage, we are able to record the medium of training and salary in the sultanate also. Some of the elite slaves must have received their training under the guidance of skilled and trusted *malik*s and *sardār*s.

According to the Baranī, Balban aimed to destroy his former colleagues, the Shamsī slaves (*khwājatāshgān*). He stands partially correct here. Balban eliminated all undependable *umarā'* from government with his blood and iron policies[54] and the prime casualties of these policies were the Shamsī slaves. Even his cousin, Sher Khān, the *muqṭa'* of Lahore, Sunam and Deopalpur was poisoned in 668/1269–1270.[55] Nevertheless, some survived by the favour of the sultan: these included Tamar Khān Sonqur-i Ajmī Malik of Kuhrām and *amīr-i dād* Sayf al-Dīn Aybeg Shamsī-i 'Ajmī 'Ādil Khān.[56] Tamar Khān received Sher Khān's *iqṭā'* of Sunam and Samana[57] but had apparently been transferred elsewhere by the time of Toghril's revolt in Bengal.[58] 'Ādil Khān is at one point called Shamsī-i 'Ajmī and hence is doubtless identical to the Aybeg-i Shams-ī 'Ajmī, the *dādbeg* (chief justice) of Nāṣir al-Dīn Mehmūd's reign. His son Muḥammad left an inscription at Farrūkhnagar in Gurgaon dated 674/1276. There are no further references of 'Ādil Khān and Aybeg-i Shamsī in historical annals. The Shamsī slave 'Imād al-Mulk Malik Ḥasām al-Dīn, the *rawāt-i 'āriḍ* (muster master) and maternal grandfather of the poet Amīr Khusraw,[59] seems to have continued in office and died naturally around 671/1273–1274.[60]

One reason that Balban destroyed the Shamsīs could have been to replace them with his own *mamlūk* powerbase and patrimonial staff. His takeover of the sultanate symbolised the end of a dynasty, which had been in power for nearly 60 years. Of the *mamlūk*s of Balban with notable ranks, Baranī only mentions the unfortunate ones, who displeased their master by exceeding their authority or for dereliction of duty, and consequently met fatal ends. Malik Buqubuq[61], the *muqṭa'* of Badaun, was executed for killing a chamberlain,[62] and Ḥaybat Khān *muqṭa'* of Awadh narrowly escaped the same fate for a similar offence by paying a ransom.[63] The most infamous of Balban's *mamlūk*s was certainly Toghril, who usurped control of the isolated province of Lakhnawtī, proclaimed himself Sultan Mūghīhth al-Dīn and compelled the sultan to march against him before he was finally overthrown in 679–680/1281–1282.[64] Earlier, Balban had hanged another of his *mamlūk*s,

Ikhtiyār al-Dīn Aytegin-i mū'-i darāz (the long-haired), for his failure to crush Toghril; he had been a *muqṭa'* of Awadh in the beginning of the reign and had borne the title Amīn Khān.[65]

Nevertheless, Baranī mentions Balban's favourite slave Ikhtiyār al-Dīn Begtars Sultanī, bārbeg (or *amīr-i ḥājib*) around 678/1280s. He seems to have survived longer and was a regular campaigner against the invading Mongols on northern fronts.[66] Balban's *mawālzadgān* included Ikhtiyār al-Dīn Alī b. Aybeg, the *sar-i jāndār*, who at the outset of the reign received the *iqṭā'* of Amroha and was later moved to Awadh. His generosity won him the title of Ḥātim Khān[67] and eulogies from *Amīr* Khusraw.[68] The career of this noble illustrates a distinctive feature of the *mamlūk* institution of the Delhi sultanate that was absent from contemporary *mamlūk* Egypt: in the Delhi sultanate, the son of a slave officer *mawālzadāh* enjoyed political equality and even succeeded to his father's position, whereas in Egypt slave officers had no legitimate share in power politics.

The *mawālzadgān* of the previous sultans in Ghiyāthī nobility included Balban's brother Kishlī Khān's son, 'Alā al-Dīn Muḥammad Chhajjū, who retained the office of *amīr-i ḥājib* which was conferred upon him at the death of his father in 657/1259.[69] Tamar Khān Shamsī's son and Qutlugh Khān Shamsī's son Malik Tāj al-Dīn were sent under the command of Ikhtiyār al-Dīn Aytegin-i mū'-i darāz as *amīr* to subdue the revolt of Toghril.[70] According to Baranī, the sultan purged all threats to his power from the nobility. Those who managed to survive Balban's reign and continued to serve during the reign of his descendants and under the Khaljīs.

Balban did not rely on the slave elements exclusively. Immediate family members[71] as well as Afghan and Mongol émigrés were also important pillars of the Ghiyāthī powerbase. Mongol refugees were heading towards the sultanate for shelter as a civil war broke out in the crumbling Mongol empire.[72] There emerged many matrimonial alliances between the Mongols and slave households by the end of Ghiyāthī era, magnifying the political strength of both the elements.[73] Balban was in his 80s when he died in 685/1287,[74] leaving behind a consolidated and strictly governed sultanate to his young and inexperienced grandsons Kayqubād and Kaykhusraw.[75]

Against Balban's will in favour of Kaykhusraw, the son of his favourite Muḥammad (Khān Shāhīd), the influential Malik al-Umarā'

Fakhr al-Dīn Kōtwāl enthroned Kayqubād, the son of Būghrā Khān.[76] In the reign of Kayqubād the powerful *wazīr* Niẓām al-Dīn, who was the nephew/son-in-law of Fakhr al-Dīn Kōtwāl,[77] and had designs to capture the throne,[78] attempted to curtail all powerful elements through a purge.[79] His first targets were Balban's old slaves and their descendants,[80] including Malik Shāhik Azhdar Khān, the *amīr ḥājib* and *muqṭa'* of Multān, and Malik Turki the *'āriḍ*.[81] Thus, Peter Jackson correctly observes that the *wazīr* of Kayqubād, Niẓām al-Dīn, was more responsible for undermining the power of the Turkish slaves than Balban.[82] Even so, there were nobles who survived Balban's 'overt and covert means of state control', and lived through Nizām al-Dīn's mass liquidation of the notables. Many amongst Balban's officers continued to serve after Sultan Kayqubād had the domineering Niẓām al-Dīn murdered.[83] Early in 688/1290, the incapable sultan fell seriously ill. Despairing of the ailing Kayqubād, Balban's *maliks*, *umarā'* and military commanders replaced the sultan and endeavoured to rule through his infant son, Shams al-Dīn Kayūmarth.[84] A. B. M. Habibullah identifies two of the Turkish slave nobles, Aytemür Kechhan and Aytemür Surkha, who, after Niẓām al-Dīn's downfall attained the key offices of *bārbeg (amīr-i ḥājib)* and *wakīl-i dār* respectively. They were both killed while resisting the Khaljī seizure of power.[85]

Establishing Writ of the State in the Realm

Political domination in Balban's era was complex and uneven. While in the core regions the population had direct contact with the sultan, in the peripheral regions his power was limited. Secondly, Balban ruled through his patrimonial bureaucratic staff, which he used as his personal property. These officers, nurtured with favours and patronage, were dependent upon the sultan for their social survival. The officers of the sultan had personalised their offices and patronised their own staff; thus the state apparatus was distinctly personal in nature. Thirdly, although the implementation of policies was largely a one-sided phenomenon yet a couple of exceptions were also found in Baranī's account. Fourthly, Balban's strategies to obtain legitimacy were only justifications, offered after acquiring power, which could not convert a personalised rule into a dynasty. Fourthly, there are identifiable grey areas in Baranī's own account. In his account, in order to depict a linear state formation, he overlooks the existence of some strong independent states in northern India and other strong political actors, such as Sher Khān, the governor of Lahore, who had been operating independently since the time of Nāṣir al-Dīn. Thus, Balban was not the only political power in northern India. Certain Muslim *muqṭa*'s and Hindu rulers contested his power. Lastly, the growth of Balban's authority was not as linear as Baranī and subsequent primary sources described. The implementation of Balban's authority fluctuated between strength and weakness.

Ghiyāthid rule was perceived differently in different subject regions. These perceptions were dependent upon the functioning of the state apparatus, which also varied according to region. According to functioning of the state, the subject domains can be divided into three broader conceptual categories: core regions, *iqṭā'* and provinces, and peripheral regions. These categories are based on the demographic and territorial administration.

Balban's treatment of his subjects was also not uniform. The ruler defined the nature of his connection with the ruled, using diverse strategies to handle different groups. His treatment of the subjects ranged from pure coercion to use of symbols and patrimonial relations and enslavement. The mass perception of political authority also varied in accordance with an area's proximity or remoteness to the state apparatus. Just as in most medieval states the entire population did not influence decisions of political importance, yet a social base or *khwās-o khalq* (notables and masses) had a political presence.

In this era, the region of Bengal or Lakhnawatī was an important *iqlīm* on the periphery. Due to territorial complexities, it was seldom ruled directly by the Delhi sultans. The control of the sultans was intermittent as the their appointees generally declared autonomy when the centre became weak. According to Baranī, Bengal was *bulghakpūr*, meaning the land of rebels.[86] Due to the Mongol threat, Balban did not expand his territorial domains by conquest and annexation of the Hindu principalities on the borders of the Delhi sultanate. Unlike Ala al-Dīn Khaljī, he raided neither the south nor the central Indian kingdoms and he did not attempt to absorb them into his empire as tributary kingdoms as became the practice of his successors, Khaljīs and Tughluqs.[87]

The perception of the state in the peripheral regions was very different from the centre. According to Baranī, Balban observed that for any newly conquered region on the periphery one of the most trusted governors was needed, with hundreds of bureaucrats and thousands of people as supporting staff. Enormous financial resources were also needed in order to establish the writ of the state and to subdue the conquered natives.[88] For instance, in order to gain control over Bengal, Balban first raided Kanpal, Patyāli and Bhojpur,[89] important routes to Bengal, and restored the writ of the Delhi sultanate. He fortified these regions and set them under command of newly emerging political groups that were mainly Afghans.[90] After taking over Lakhnawatī and Bengal, Balban delegated their governorship to his reliable slave general Toghril Khān. Owing to the distance between Delhi and Lakhnawatī, Balban placed his most trusted men, equipped with able-bodied supporting staff and financial resources, in the region. Soon when Toghril became stable in the *iqlīm* and assumed that Balban was occupied fighting with the Mongols, he heard rumours of the sultan's death and revolted. The supporting staff sent by Balban and the people of the region became Toghril's allies. Later, Baranī described the ghastly suppression of Toghril's revolt.[91] Thus, Balban's handling of Bengal seemed to have been that of a colony, where trusted governors and sub-administrators were appointed and required to extract revenue from this region. Their link with the centre was limited to the payment of regular tribute in the form of cash and kind. The details of the revolt of Toghril suggest that it was not a mass rebellion but the dissent of a governor and his support staff to recognise the over-lordship of the centre. The appalling punishment meted out to the rebel was admonitory and served as a warning to the sultan's own son Būghrā Khān succeeding Toghril in Bengal.[92]

Keeping in view the strategic and administrative requirements of different provinces, diverse administrative policies were adopted. Converting military outposts in north-western India (i.e. Sind and the Punjab), including Multan, Lahore, Sunam, Samana, Deopalpur and Faridkot into strongholds was the highlight of Balban's Mongol policy.

In the fifth and sixth year of his reign, Balban raided these areas to assert his authority over the region. It would be safe to infer that Balban had recaptured these areas in 668/1270, after successfully eliminating his cousin Sher Khān, the governor of this region, who had defeated the Mongols several times and conquered Ghazni in the times of Nāṣir al-Dīn Maḥmūd with the help of a very strong and effective cavalry numbering several thousand. After his death, Balban refortified and reconstructed these areas and appointed both his sons to the north-western military outposts.[93]

Balban's son Muḥammad was the ruler of Sind province,[94] while the *iqṭā'* of Samana belonged to Būghrā Khān,[95] who was later transferred to Lakhnawatī. They sent revenue in the form of cash and kind to their father regularly and were free to have their own patrimonial staff. Muḥammad patronised literary and cultural personalities like amīr Khusraw.[96] Faridkot in Punjab was an important garrison town where significant infrastructural developments were made.[97] The sultan had also appointed other officials such as Tamar Khān Shamsī to safeguard the frontiers.[98] Baranī also mentions that the unruly local tribes that were earlier successfully checked by Sher Khān, including Bhattī, Jāt, Khokhar, Mandahīr and Meneyoan, became a menace after his death.[99] Balban himself raided Koh-i Jūd (salt range) in northern Punjab, subdued resistance and brought back the sons of the defeated Hindu ruler as collateral, where they were raised in the royal house and given important administrative positions.[100]

In the first couple of years, Balban was busy re-conquering some strategically important garrison towns and fertile *iqṭā'* of the Doab region. In the beginning of his reign, one of the most important issues for Balban was to review the taxation patterns of the *iqṭā'* of Doab. His policies targeted two different populations.[101] Firstly, he sought to depoliticise the unruly masses by the use of four methods: to raid the villages of rebels; to eliminate the rebel elements by skinning them alive; to enslave women and children in rebel villages; and by deforesting the entire region. Secondly, the Shamsī patrimonial administrative class was neutralised by depriving them of their administrative responsibilities and thus material resources. However, he could not dismiss the Muslim administrative staff due to the apprehensions of protests or rebellions among the *muqṭa*'s and *jagīrdār*s of Doab.

Baranī refers to the populations of core regions as *khawas-o khalq* (notables and masses). These people were the members of royal household, *umarā'*, *'ulāmā'*, Sufis, other notables, people of Delhi and suburbs. In Balban's era, Baranī describes two major instances when the opinion of the population of Delhi changed the sultan's approach to policy matters. Firstly, when the *iqṭā*'s of Doab were being taken back by the state,[102] and secondly, when the massacre of the rebels of Bengal was ordered (protests by the population of Delhi forced the sultan to change his policy).[103]

The suburbs of Delhi were vulnerable to unruly Mewāties who used to pillage and plunder the environs of Delhi, rendering the trade routes unsafe. The sultan took notice of the dissatisfaction of the people of Delhi and suburban areas, deforesting the Mewāt region.[104] The unruly Mewāties in the suburbs of Delhi were subdued under the command of Balban's Afghan general Fīrūz Khiljī. In order to keep a check over the suburbs, check posts were established and their control was given to the Afghans, who later became powerful enough to replace the Ghāythid dynasty.[105]

A strong ruler centralised power through *umarā'* or nobility, including the civil and military officers, and the *'ulāmā'*. These two groups posed a threat to the rulers too weak to control them. Balban nurtured his own patrimonial staff, divided along lines of ethnicity and interests. Certain new groups were introduced among the *umarā'* to keep them divided and mutually distrustful. He planted his sons, nephew, confidantes and slaves in important positions. He introduced Afghans and Indians groups that did not have visible strength in the reign of Balban's predecessors, into the ruling elite. The sultan eliminated any possible threat to his rule, such as the ever-victorious Sher Khān, whom he eliminated by poison. The *umarā'* were sub-sovereigns in their own domains, personalising their offices and exercising power through their own patrimonial staff. Despite the inculcation of fear and loyalty among his *umarā'*, it can well be assumed that Balban's *umarā'* could not have adhered to their master's will in the absence of his power as demonstrated by their repudiation of his will of succession and later, when his personalised rule failed to convert into a dynasty.

The groups that remained closest to the sultan throughout his reign were: the royal family, members of the household, members of the tribe and *khwājatāshgān* (slaves of the same master). Balban loved his sons and trained them well. Yet as a royal practice, the grandsons of Balban did not live with their fathers but remained with Balban, probably as wards or collateral.[106] While he trained them, he also kept them under strict surveillance. This was an outgrowth of the tradition of keeping the sons of a potential rival in the court as indemnity against rebellion, and to instil loyalty in the young wards.

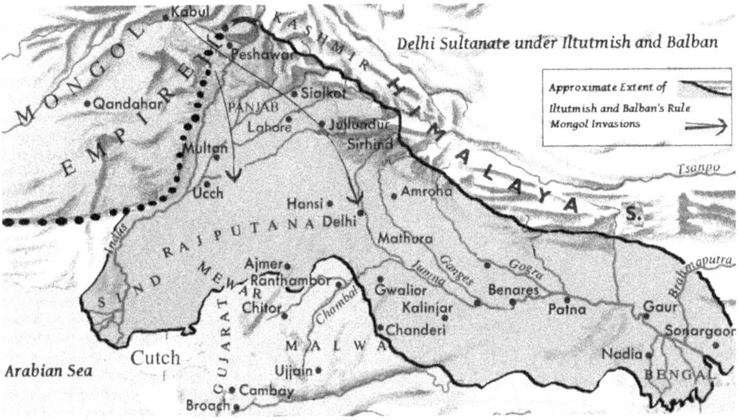

Map 6.1 The Delhi Sultanate under Iltutmish and Balban

Since Balban was highly apprehensive of his *umarā'*, like his predecessors he also appointed multiple officers in a single *iqṭā'*. Each of these officers reported directly to the sultan with no definite spheres of authority visible. The spy system was also one of his means to obtain information about the daily routines of his *umarā'*. Balban, penalised almost any inefficiency or error from the intelligence staff. For instance, the provincial officers Ḥaybat Khān and Malik Buqubuq were punished along with the intelligence officers who did not report their mishandlings.[107]

Balban's distrustfulness of his staff seems justified due to the revolt of Toghril who had been one of the most trusted slaves of the sultan. The geographical distance between Delhi and Lakhnawatī made it impossible for the sultan to obtain adequate reporting from the region, and Toghril rose in rebellion along with the supporting staff that was sent from Delhi to report on him. Thus, the sultan was forced to militarily reclaim the region.

Although Balban was the father-in-law of the deceased sultan and an able military commander, yet these were not the only criteria that could have brought him to power. There were many others who possessed more links to the Shamsī lineage; nevertheless, it was his status of primus inter pares that brought him to power after the death of Iltutmish. The issue of legitimacy becomes more dramatic in the times of Balban as, in addition to coercion, he tried to create an ideological complex by extensive use of various religious, cultural and social symbols in order to sustain his authority. This ideological complex was merely a psychological relief since Balban's success primarily depended upon his ability to coerce, command and conquer. Legitimacy, which converted power into authority, seems to have been missing in Balban's era as his successors could not convert his rule into a dynastic order. The bellicose Khaljīs abruptly replaced his dynasty within four years of his demise.

CHAPTER 7

WHEN HISTORY REPEATED ITSELF REPEATEDLY: WEALTH, BETRAYAL AND SUCCESS UNDER THE KHALJĪS

A Ruler who wanted to be the second Alexander . . . 'Alā al-Dīn Khaljī

The last decade of the thirteenth century witnessed the fall of the Ghiyāthid dynasty and the rise of the Khaljī dynasty. The Khaljī dynasty is credited with extending the Delhi sultanate's reach from north India to the far south and from Bengal to Sind. 'Alā al-Dīn's military and administrative policies initiated a new era in the history of the sultanate leading to the more extensive writ of the state. Many indirectly administered regions were brought under direct control and a uniform fiscal policy, including agrarian and market reforms, was implemented. The state established an efficient intelligence and policing system, and secured the north-western borders from the Mongols.

Despite his administrative success, Balban was unable to convert his personal rule into a dynasty. As happened with his predecessor Iltutmish, his will in favour of Kaykhusraw was not honoured after his death. Weak successors coupled with weak *umarā'* led to the end of the Ghiyāthid dynasty. The Khaljī *coup d'état* was neither supported by the *umarā'*, the social base of the sultanate, nor the masses. In addition, religion and lineage played no part in the rise of the Khaljīs who were able to capture the throne through a display of sheer power. However, Jalāl al-Dīn and

'Alā al-Dīn both fostered their own officers and reached out to people in their own ways.

The Khaljīs[1] were able to replace the Ghiyāthids as a result of ineffective sultans and the inability of the Turkish *umarā'* to counterbalance their growing power. The Ghiyāthid dynasty collapsed due to the violent purge of nobility first by Balban[2] and later by Niẓām al-Dīn the *wakīl-i dar*[3] of Kayquabād who at one point became the de facto ruler. Niẓām al-Dīn first convinced Kayquabād to murder his cousin Kaykhusraw since he was a possible replacement for the existing sultan.[4] According to 'Iṣāmī, Kaykhusraw went to Ghazni in order to solicit Mongol help after a bootless attempt to claim the throne. Later, he returned to Multan, unsuccessful, before he was slayed. There was a massacre of the new Muslim *umarā'* (newly converted *umarā'* of Mongol origin) who were alleged to have conspired against the sultan; their families were banished to distant fortresses.[5] Various Ghiyāthid *umarā'* were eliminated on one pretext or another.[6] Later, Niẓām al-Dīn fell victim to his own intrigue. In his attempt to poison the young sultan, Nizām al-Dīn poisoned himself as he was forced to take the deadly drink he made for the sultan.[7] After the death of Niẓām al-Dīn, owing to his incompetence and failing health Kayquabād was unable to control the government. Kayquabād at this point tried to bail himself out by making some new appointments. He invited Jalāl al-Dīn Khaljī apparently a less ambitious *amīr,* serving as governor of Samana and *sarjandār* of the sultan, to the centre in order to counter the influence of existing groups of *umarā'* in Delhi that were predominantly Turkish.[8]

Jalāl al-Dīn Khaljī, who had proven his mettle against the Mongols, was entrusted with important offices such as the *'ariḍ-i mumālīk*. Furthermore, the two Aytemürs, Malik Aytemür Sūrkhah and Malik Aytemür Kachhan from the Ghiyāthid *umarā'*, were appointed *wakīl-i dar* and *bar bāg*. The declining physical health of the sultan as well as his inability to administer the state, led to a power struggle between the Turks and the Khaljīs. Shortly after, the sultan fell victim to paralysis with little chance of recovery. Without waiting for his death his nobles hastily enthroned a minor son of Kayquabād with the title Shams al-Dīn.[9] In the new order Jalāl al-Dīn Fīrūz Khaljī became the *nā'ib* (deputy) of the sultanate.[10] The misgivings between the Turks and the Khaljīs galvanised. The Turks struck first. After two unsuccessful intrigues to murder Fīrūz Shāh, the chief Turkish noble Aytemür

Kachhan was killed and the Khaljīs took hostage the fledgling sultan Shams al-Dīn Kaykaū's.[11] The Khaljīs abducted Kaykaū's and relatives of malik-ul umarā' Fakhr al-Dīn Kōtwāl and took them to Bahārpur.[12]

The transfer of power from the 'slave' Olberli Turks to the free Khaljīs[13] was not supported by the *umarā'* of the centre and provinces. The notables of Delhi, which included many of the old Turkish households, resented the rise of the Khaljīs.[14] After the abduction of the young sultan, some groups of the people of Delhi became enraged and gathered at Badaun gate. They wanted to march to Bahārpūr and bring the sultan back. The *umarā'* and notables of Delhi resolved to retrieve the hostage sultan and counter the Khaljīs. Nevertheless, the malik-al umarā' Fakhr al-Dīn, in order to save his relatives forbade people from doing so. At this point the deposed Sultan Kayqubād was eliminated on the orders of Khaljīs and was thrown into the river Jamna.[15] Jalāl al-Dīn became the regent of the infant Sultan Kaykaū's and offered Malik Chhajjū, the nephew of Balban on his behalf to come and assume the duties of the regent. Later, an arrangement was made and Malik Chhajjū was given the *iqṭā'* of Kara while the regency and *wizārat* were retained by Jalāl al-Dīn Khaljī.[16] Shortly afterwards, Jalāl al-Dīn Khaljī marched to Kelukherī and took over the throne as sultan. The infant Kaykaū's, who was incarcerated, died shortly after.[17] As sultan, Jalāl al-Dīn did not enter Delhi and instead settled in Kelukherī (the *shehr-i naw*) along with his associates and developed it as the new royal city.[18]

Jalāl al-Dīn's rise to power – it is often labelled as the Khaljī revolution[19] – was not a revolution proper in the sense that the composition of Jalālī nobility was predominantly Ghiyāthid and the change in the power structure was gradual. The Khaljī *coup d'état* was a joint venture of the Khaljī and non-Khaljī elements in the Ghiyāthid *umarā'*. Thus, Jalāl al-Dīn not only extended important offices to his fellow Khaljī tribesmen and male family members but also maintained many of the old nobility. He was unable to foster patrimonial staff or nurture trust-based relations with the existing nobles who tended to plot intrigues and rebel as a result of the sultan's resistance to violent punishments.[20]

The Khaljī kinsmen who were promoted to higher offices were mainly Balban's servicemen. Baranī mentions three sons of Jalāl al-Dīn among the *umarā'*. The eldest son Ikhtiyār al-Dīn, was given the title of *khān-i khānān* and he received the environs of Delhi as his *iqṭā'*. The second son was given the title of Irkalī Khān, and the third son was given the title of Qadar Khān. Malik Khāmush, Jalāl al-Dīn's brother, was given the office of *'āriḍ* and his uncle received the title of *tāj ul-mulk*. We also find references to his four nephews: 'Alā al-Dīn Muḥammad became *amīr-i tuzak* and Mu'izz al-Dīn (Almas Beg) was given the office of *ākhūr beg*. Both of them were the sons of Jalāl al-Dīn's deceased elder brother, Shihāb al-Dīn Mas'ūd. Another nephew of Jalāl al-Dīn, Malik 'Izz al-Dīn became *ākhūrbeg mainā*.[21] Some of the Khaljī tribesmen who earlier had minor offices under various *umarā'* of Balban became eminent. These included Aḥmad-i Chap, who at one time served as chamberlain to Aytemür Sūrkha, was now given the office of *nā'ib barbeg*.[22]

A significant number of the notables and old *umarā'* resented the rise of Khaljīs but with the passage of time they started joining their ranks. The sultan seemed to have been intimidated by them as a majority of the offices were entrusted to the old Ghiyāthid *umarā'*. For instance, Khwājah Khatīr al-Dīn, who was humiliated by Niẓām al-Dīn in Kayqubād's reign, was restored as *wazīr*, and the *kotwāl* Fakhr al-Dīn, was confirmed in his previous office.[23] Ikhtiyār al-Dīn-i Hindū Khān-i Ghiyāthī who was a Ghiyāthid *mawālzadāh*,[24] Malik 'Ayn al-Dīn 'Alī Shāh Kūh i-jūdī and his brother Ikhtiyār al-Dīn Khurām[25] who were the sons of a local raja of the Koh-i Jūd (salt range) also served under Jalāl al-Dīn. As mentioned in the previous chapter, the two princes from Koh-i Jūd were acquired by Balban around 664/1266–1267 as captives of war. It is difficult to determine whether these captives were slaves, since there is no definite indication given in available primary sources.[26] Yet, it is certain that they served Jalāl al-Dīn in his campaign against Malik Chhajjū.[27] The *umarā'* belonging to the time-honoured aristocratic families of Delhi, such as Malik Fakhar al-Dīn Kuchī and his brother Malik Tāj al-Dīn Kuch,ī were given the offices of *dād beg* and *muqṭa'* of Awadh respectively.[28] During the first year of his reign, Jalāl al-Dīn could not enter Delhi. Although later when he shifted to Delhi, he faced many intrigues and insurgencies, in which both the Olberlis and Khaljī elements were involved.

Around 688/1290, Malik Chhajjū, the nephew of Balban,[29] revolted against the new sultan Jalāl al-Dīn Fīrūz Khaljī in Awadh.[30] He received substantial support from the old Turkish *umarā'* of Balban and their households.[31] Nevertheless, some of the Ghiyāthid *umarā'*, including the kōh-judī brothers and Tāj al-Dīn Kuchī, fought under the banner of the Khaljīs. Malik Chhajjū declared independence, assumed the title of Sultan Mūghīs al-Dīn, had the *khuṭba* read in his name, struck coins and advanced with a modest force to capture Delhi.[32] He was defeated by the sultan,[33] who arrested the rebel but displayed leniency.[34] There were no servile measures taken against the rebel slaves and other supporters of Malik Chhajjū either.[35]

This was certainly not the only attempt to remove the old sultan, since in a drinking party Malik Tāj al-Dīn Kuchī and some other Ghiyāthī *umarā'* swore that they would murder Jalāl al-Dīn and that the crown would sit on Malik Tāj al-Dīn Kuchī's head. This information reached the sultan somehow and culprits were apprehended. In spite of this, after the reassurance of Nuṣrat Shāh, an *amīr* who himself had uttered harsh words against Jalāl al-Dīn at the party (he asserted that they could never utter such insolent statements against such a kind and benevolent sultan)[36] the sultan was mollified and the conspirators were exonerated. This forbearing manner of the sultan, according to Baranī, not only emboldened the conspirators but also cultivated resentment among his own folk who became disgruntled with Jalāl al-Dīn's 'unkingly' demeanours.[37] Thus, in the Delhi sultanate's political culture, a mild and trusting sultan was unworthy to rule. The sultan was expected to inflict harsh punishments on people and mistrustfully monitor their day-to-day affairs.

This era also witnessed religious influence being translated into a political power, parallel to that of the sultan. According to Baranī, the *mawālzadgān* of Balban were among those who conspired to assassinate the old sultan and replace him with an enigmatic dervish Sīddī Muwallih.[38] Belonging to the Sufi cult Muwallih,[39] this charismatic dervish[40] was extremely lavish in his spending, though his source of wealth was bafflingly unknown.[41] Furthermore, the dervish had close links with various groups of *umarā'* whom he used to counsel on their official affairs. He was popular with the masses and had a large following. According to Baranī, the aggrieved Turkish population and dissatisfied Khaljī *umarā'* gathered around him. Jalāl al-Dīn Khaljī was more than 70 years old and both of his sons, Khān-i Khānān and Irkalī Khān, expected to claim the throne after their father died. The eldest son of the sultan, Khān-i Khānān was a follower of Sīddī Māwallih. His unexplained absence from the contemporary accounts after the plot described below suggests that he was a part of this conspiracy.

The plan was to assassinate Sultan Jalāl al-Dīn during his weekly attendance in the public procession by one Haytā Pā'ik. Sīdī Māwallih was to be declared as the caliph and subsequently to be married to the daughter of late sultan Nāṣir al-Dīn. The information spilled out through means not specified in the sources, and the intrigue failed. The sultan ordered capital punishment for the chief culprits. In order to make an example, the main offenders were punished publicly in the most vicious manner; for instance, Sīdī Māwallih was trampled under elephant's feet. Conversely, the minor perpetrators were dealt with mildly, as they only had their properties confiscated and were exiled from the capital.[42]

Many politically unwise decisions justified the sultan's unpopularity among his nobility. The sultan was lenient in his treatment to criminals. For instance, when 1,000 thugs were captured the sultan only exiled them from Delhi.[43] Later an abortive expedition to Ranthambor further riled the *umarā'*.[44] It is also evident that his truce with the Mongol raiders worsened the situation.[45] In his bid to include a new ethnic element among the chief nobles, the sultan not only established a matrimonial alliance with the Mongols by marrying the daughter of Alghü[46] but also gave 40,000[47] Mongols quarters in the vicinity of Delhi that probably aroused general dissatisfaction. These Mongols were allowed to make their colonies in Indrapāt, Kelukherī, and Ghiyāthpur, in areas known as Mughalpurā.[48] Later on, these people, known as new Muslims, were massacred due to their image as conspirators against 'Alā al-Dīn.[49]

The economic and social conditions of the common people, in this era, seemed dilapidated; Baranī mentions a number of natural calamities such as famine and drought. Consequently, the prices of food items became exorbitant resulting in mass suicides which were graphically described by Baranī stating that Hindus[50] or peasants,[51] of Sawālik region came to Delhi in sets of 20 and drowned themselves in the river Jumna. The sultan did little to help them, and the heavy rain of the following year thus exacerbated the situation.[52] The food deficiency continued for two years out of his four-year reign. Even so, Baranī admits that common people approved of the sultan's leniency and continued to support him.[53] Nevertheless, adversaries of the sultan relentlessly attempted to dethrone him. The groups, which had earlier supported the rebel Malik Chhajjū,[54] also seem to have participated in a scheme to murder Sultan Jalāl al-Dīn, hatched by his ambitious nephew/son-in-law 'Alā al-Dīn.[55] The intrigue proved to be successful and 'Alā al-Dīn took over his uncle's throne in 695/1296.

Unlike any other ruler of the Delhi sultanate, Jalāl al-Dīn made no deliberate effort to foster a patrimonial staff or to administer on the basis of coercion and thus he became victim of one of the many intrigues against him. It is important here to identify the ambivalence in the portrayal of Jalāl al-Dīn in sultanate sources. The record of Jalāl al-Dīn as a warrior was that of a man of success. Later in the times of the Khaljī seizure of power, he seems to have shown no compassion, the cold-blooded murder of Kayqubād and imprisonment and killing of his infant son being two prime examples. Conversely, in his career as a sultan he seems to have been incapable of making harsh decisions. In addition, the mildness of the sultan was interpreted as unfitness to rule by the *umarā'*, causing general resentment among them. His reign is replete with intrigues and rebellions by the *umarā'*. It seems that the normative portrait of a legitimate ruler among the *umarā'* was that of a person capable of sustaining power through coercion.

Regicide and Showering of Gold: Rise of 'Alā al-Dīn Khaljī

The shift of government from Jalāl al-Dīn Khaljī to his nephew 'Alā al-Dīn was a result of a violent assertion of power. The murder of Jalāl al-Dīn was a result of mutual distrust between the two. After his return from the expedition from Deogīr, 'Alā al-Dīn had gathered an enormous amount of booty and numerous war elephants.[56] This aroused the suspicions of Aḥmad-i Chap who could now see that 'Alā al-Dīn was becoming more powerful than the sultan himself. The *amīr* tried to warn the sultan[57] but the other *umarā'* of the sultan including Malik Fakhr al-Dīn Kuchī, Kamal al-Dīn Abu al-Muali and Nāṣir al-Dīn Khurāmī argued on 'Alā al-Dīn's behalf and convinced the sultan not to initiate any action.[58] 'Alā al-Dīn was apprehensive that since he had become more powerful than the sultan, he would be perceived as a potential threat to the government and if he visited Jalāl al-Dīn he would be eliminated.[59] Thus, he pre-empted and beheaded his uncle publicly.[60]

In Delhi, Malikā-i Jahān the wife of the deceased sultan enthroned her youngest son as Rukn al-Dīn Ibrahīm and became de facto ruler herself. Irkalī Khān, the elder son of Jalāl al-Dīn, was disregarded; then stayed at his *iqṭā'* in Multan and differences formed between him and Malikā-i Jahān.[61] Within five months, 'Alā al-Dīn reached the capital and his display of wealth and power earned him a great following among the *umarā'* and people of Delhi.[62] Using catapults, he literally showered money on people. Important *umarā'* left Delhi and hasted for Baran to join 'Alā al-Dīn and were allegedly rewarded with 20, 30 and even 50 *man (maund)* of gold.[63] After a frail and abortive effort to counter 'Alā al-Dīn the family of Jalāl al-Dīn quietly quitted Delhi and left for Multan.[64]

Successful administration and ability to command and conquer were the means through which 'Alā al-Dīn Khaljī sustained his rule. He was the only distinguished ruler of the Khaljī dynasty, and is credited with transforming the Delhi sultanate into a great empire. He is also among the few Delhi sultans whose policies had a far-reaching impact on the people. The Khaljī armies conquered the south and reached the Deccan peninsula, triumphed over the Mongol hordes in the north-west and effectively secured the allegiance of the generally defiant eastern provinces as well. The sultan gathered nearly 50,000 slaves, most of which were native captives of war, and undertook large-scale construction works to display his wealth and power. The locals were employed in the state machinery and were promoted to the highest civil and military offices. Interestingly, not all of these locals were converts to Islām, as Amīr Khusraw referred to them as 'infidels fighting against infidels'.[65]

'Alā al-Dīn Khaljī's achievements as an administrator and conqueror were due to his success in nurturing trust in an efficient body of patrimonial officers. Baranī identifies three major periods of 'Alā al-Dīn's reign with the composition and character of *umarā'* clearly different from the other periods. In the first era, which was relatively brief, 'Alā al-Dīn rewarded those persons with offices who had been participants in his seizure of power. This group primarily comprised Ghiyāthī and Jalālī *umarā'*. Thus, in the initial years of 'Alā al-Dīn the composition of *umarā'* was more or less the same as it had been in Jalāl al-Dīn Khaljī's era. Gradually, 'Alā al-Dīn was able to get rid of the undesired elements from his *umarā'* and inaugurate an era of empire building. With the help of the remaining *umarā'* 'Alā al-Dīn was not only able to continue his conquests of various Indian regions but was also able to sustain control. The third era, spanning the last three or four years of 'Alā al-Dīn's reign, was dominated by his catamite Malik Nā'ib (Kāfūr).[66]

According to Baranī, the people who sided with 'Alā al-Dīn in his seizure of the throne by plotting the elimination of Jalāl al-Dīn did not last longer than an initial three or four years among the 'Alā'ī *umarā'*. Many from the patrimonial staff of 'Alā al-Dīn from the times of his pre-monarchical career were either eliminated in military ventures or were eliminated as they earned the displeasure of the sultan.[67] Also, there was a purge of Jalālī *umarā'* after 'Alā al-Dīn subdued Jalāl al-Dīn's family in Multan. Once settled in his office, the sultan, who had earlier extended largesse and offices to Jalālī *umarā'* not only deposed them from their offices but also confiscated their properties and killed some of them, blinding and imprisoning others.[68]

Like their predecessors, 'Alā al-Dīn's *umarā'* were diverse and included freemen and slaves. Some of the Ghiyāthī and Jalālī *umarā'* were given important designations, while others were retained at their previous ranks.[69] Although some of the *umarā'* did belong to Khaljī stock there was by no means a monopoly of Khaljī elements. 'Alā al-Dīn's brother Almas Beg, now Ulugh Khān,[70] was given the office of *barbeg* (*amīr-ḥājib*) and the *iqṭā'* of Bayana; later, around 700/1301, he was given the recently reconquered regions of Ranthambor and Jhayin.[71] The sultan's brother in law (wife's brother) Alp Khān Sanjar, about whom 'Iṣāmī states that he was brought up by 'Alā al-Dīn since his childhood, was earlier 'Alā al-Dīn's *amīr-i majlis*. He then received charge of Multan and subsequently accepted governorship of Gujarat in 709/1310 as *iqṭā'*.[72] A maternal nephew of 'Alā al-Dīn, Ḥizabr al-Dīn Yūsūf, was given the title of Zafar Khān and was made *'ariḍ*.[73] 'Alā al-Dīn's nephew Sulaymān Shāh was given the title of Ikhit Khān and was given the office of *wakīl-i dar*. The younger brother of Sulaymān was given the title of Qutlugh Khwājah.[74] Two other maternal nephews, 'Umar and Mangu Khān, were made the *muqṭa'* of Badaun and Awadh respectively.[75] Later, these nephews were killed since they tried to seize the throne.[76]

The second interlude of 'Alā'ī *umarā'* was dominated by the sons of 'Alā al-Dīn: *dabīr* Malik Ḥamīd al-Dīn as *wakīl-i dar*, Malik 'Izz al-Dīn as *dabīr ul mumalīk*, Malik 'Ainu'l Mulk Multanī *dabīr*, Ulugh Khān, Malik Sharaf Qāi' as *nā'ib wazīr* and Khwājah Ḥājjī as *nā'ib 'ariḍ*. Baranī praised these *umarā'* for their efficiency and credited them with taking the empire of 'Alā al-Dīn to its zenith.[77]

The institution of military slavery witnessed some major changes under 'Alā al-Dīn. In the new order, the Turkish slaves seem to have lost their share of power in the government, as compared to the earlier two dynasties.[78] There are hardly any references to newly recruited Turkish slaves in historical accounts. This situation seems to have arisen for two reasons. Firstly, there may have been a revision in the policy of slave recruitment, as the sultan did not want the Turkish slaves to enjoy the monopoly of power that they enjoyed under his predecessors. Secondly, by introducing two new groups into power politics, namely the Afghans and local Indian slaves, the emperor may have precluded the need for the Turkish slave warriors.[79] Peter Jackson puts forward another explanation that the rise in the prices of the Turkish slaves could be the reason for their reduced deployment, an impression taken from Baranī who complains of high prices of foreign slaves. This seems an insufficient explanation, since if rarity and expense did not keep Muḥammad b. Tughluq from purchasing Turkish slaves in an adequate number, then it was improbable that the most resourceful Sultan of Delhi would reduce his purchase of valuable slaves due to financial constraints. Besides, the 'Alā'ī army relied on elephants and foot soldiers instead of mounted archers.[80] This was a more Indian style of warfare that was rapidly replacing the Turco-Afghan military machine of the Olberlis. Therefore, the need for mounted archers might have diminished. Still, there are references to two *muqṭa*'s namely, Ikhtiyār al-Dīn Temür *sultānī* the *muqṭa'* of Chanderi and Erich and Ikhtiyār al-Dīn Tagin the *muqṭa'* of Awadh – who seem to have been Turkish slaves as indicated by their names.[81] Some important Turkish families continued to retain influence, for instance, *mawālzadāh* Malik Qīrān-i 'Alā'ī who was the son of Balban's Turkish slave Ḥaybat Khān held an important office.[82]

There are a reasonable number of references about some prominent 'Alā'ī slaves in the contemporary sources. The first among these relates to a slave of obscure origin[83] named Shāhīn, who 'Isāmī identified as the adopted son and predecessor of Malik Kāfūr. This slave was given command of Chitor on its capture in 702/1303, and was entitled as the Malik Nā'ib. Shortly after, he feared for his life as he suspected that he had displeased the sultan. He fled from Chitor and joined the exiled ruler of Gujarat.[84] Nevertheless, in Khāzā'in al-Fūtūh, Amīr Khusraw reported that, after the conquest of Chitor, the command was given to the crown-prince Khiḍr Khān, thus making no reference to Shāhīn.[85]

Mālik was among those *pā'ik* slaves who saved the life of 'Alā al-Dīn with their shrewdness, while the sultan's nephew Sulaymān Shāh Ikhit

Khān tried to seize the throne around 700/1301.[86] The sultan at this point was on his way to conquer the neighbouring region of Ranthambor. He had reached Tilpat where the royal army camped for a few days. The sultan used to go for hunting or performing drills on daily basis. Once the sultan lost his way and could not return to his abode for the night. On getting an opportunity, his nephew Ikhit Khān with his Mongol new-Muslim associates attempted to assassinate the sultan in a similar fashion to that undertaken by 'Alā al-Dīn himself to kill his uncle Jalāl al-Dīn. According to Baranī, when the new-Muslim converts showered Sultan 'Alā al-Dīn with arrows, Mālik became a human shield for his master. Taking all arrows targeted on the sultan, he saved the sultan from fatal injuries. The other *pā'ik* slaves then covered the sultan with their armour-shields. Ikhit Khān wanted to behead the sultan, and show the head to the people as a substantiation of the sultan's death, but the *pā'ik*s drew their swords. This kept the rebels from coming near the wounded sultan. In the meantime, the *pā'ik*s slaves shrewdly raised an uproar informing the attackers that the sultan had been murdered. Ikhit believed them and dashed back towards the jungle of Tilpat, without the head or any other verification.[87] Then he took over the royal court in Delhi where his authority was accepted. Nevertheless, another 'Alā'ī slave Malik Dīnār,[88] who was the guardian of the *harem* at that time, barred Ikhit Khān from entering the harem, as he did not have the head of the allegedly murdered sultan.

Shortly after, 'Alā al-Dīn made a successful return to the court. The conspirers were given exemplary punishments and the loyalists were rewarded immensely for their services. Mālik seems to have been given a swift series of promotions. By 704/1305, this slave was *akhūr beg* and *muqṭa'* of Samana and Sunam when he defeated the Mongol army.[89] Malik Dinār later served 'Alā al-Dīn as the governor of Badaun, Kol (Aligarh) and Kark (probably Katehar).[90] He was also *shihna-i pīl* (keeper of elephants).[91] He acquired greater ascendancy in the post-'Alā'ī era, when he was given important offices. Malik Nānak was an Indian slave who triumphed over the Mongols.[92] Malik Kāfūr was the most illustrious 'Alā'ī slave commander who was credited with most of the conquests in the south. He was the right-hand man of the sultan in building the empire. The capable slaves were not just the property of the sultans, but many, with elevated skills and celebrated talents, served the *umarā'* and common people.

Baranī[93] and 'Isāmī[94] report a popular revolt in the Delhi led by a slave in the early years of Khaljī era. This event was an outcome of an opportunity that conspiring elements found in the absence of the sultan from the centre. Although, the *umarā'* of Delhi revolted several times even during the post-Shams al-Dīn interregnum but a manumitted slave, revolting in Delhi accompanied by the common people, was something afresh.[95] It exhibits that there was still a faction among the people who considered Olberlis the legitimate heirs to the throne.[96]

Ḥājjī Maulā was a manumitted slave of the Olberli *malik-ul umarā'* and former *kōtwāl* of Delhi, Malik Fakhr al-Dīn[97] who belonged to one of the oldest families of Delhi and had acquired immense influence during post-Balban interregnum. Ḥājjī served in Ritōl (currently a district in Meerut) as *shihna* (police officer). He was also supported by the Olberlis who wanted to regain power.[98] In 700/1301, he was able to muster under his command a reasonable number of soldiers and other groups in Delhi. Meanwhile, the sultan was on a military campaign in Ranthambor. Tirmaḍī, the *kōtwāl* of the old city, was an unpopular man who was notorious for his severity. Ḥājjī Maulā assassinated this man deceitfully, convincing the people of Delhi that it was by the order of the sultan. The people who were already weary of his inequities breathed a sigh of relief.[99] On the battleground, the royal army was reduced to extreme distress due to a prolonged and ineffective siege. The walls of the fort of Ranthambor had proved to be impregnable. Not a single soldier dared to desert, for fear of the sultan's forfeiture on those who would desert the battlefield, amounting to three-year's pay.[100] Conspiring nobility, dissatisfied masses and a decaying army provided a perfect foundation on which the devious Ḥājjī could build an insurrection.

Ḥājjī's next move was to murder 'Alā al-Dīn Ayāz, the *kōtwāl* of the new fort, but the information leaked out, ruining the plot. Nevertheless, the insurgent was able to gain complete control of the city. The royal stables, treasury, and armoury were seized. Those who joined him were promised largesse. All state prisoners were released and this swelled the ranks of the rebels. The number of the prisoners is not mentioned in this account. Baranī later reports that the 'Alā'ī prisoners numbered around 17,000–18,000.[101] Money was distributed among the masses and arms and horses were supplied to the rebels. Most of the force of *kōtwālī* (police), the *lashkar* (soldiery) and the *khalq* (masses) in Delhi rallied around Ḥājjī Maulā. ʻIsāmī called these people *mard-i kam māya* (meaning impecunious fellows) indicating their plebeian background.

Ḥājjī Maulā did not claim the throne himself, as he lacked the royal lineage or military achievements that could have made him acceptable as sultan.[102] Therefore, he enthroned an ʻAlvī (a descendant of ʻAlī, the fourth Rāshīdūn caliph) who was also related to Shams al-Dīn Iltutmish on his maternal side. Allegedly, Ḥājjī Maulā's design was to rule on behalf of the ʻAlvī. Many of the *umarā'* voluntarily and involuntarily submitted themselves to the puppet sultan as a response to the promises and pressure of the Ḥājjī. Nevertheless, an adequate level of fear still prevailed among the masses who knew that if ʻAlā al-Dīn managed to return he would not forgive anyone for this treason.[103]

Briefly afterwards, the ʻAlā'ī stalwarts successfully reinstated the capital. The rebellion was brutally crushed within a week of its initiation.[104] All the money was reimbursed from the people. Those who had aided Ḥājjī's cause were severely dealt with. Ḥājjī himself was killed fighting with Malik Ḥamīd al-Dīn *amir-i koh* and the puppet sultan was beheaded. The entire line of Malik Fakhr al-Dīn, the *sāhib-i walā* (patron of Hājjī) was terminated, despite the possibility that these people might not have been involved in the conspiracy.[105] Hence, the deed of a *mawāli* proved to be calamitous for the entire line of his patron who had died long before.

The third interlude of the ʻAlā'ī era marked the last days of Sultan ʻAlā al-Dīn. The sultan concentrated power in the hands of his trusted ones, the family and the slaves.[106] He dismissed many of the skilled and experienced administrators,[107] probably sensing their secessionist tendencies. The sultan relied upon what Baranī disapproved as 'lazy slaves [*ghūlāmbachāgān*] and imprudent eunuchs'.[108] He prematurely promoted the crown prince Khiḍr Khān[109] and depended on his favourite slave eunuch Kāfūr excessively.[110] As the sultan's health began to decline and his death seemed inevitable, the family and Kāfūr started to contend for succession. At this stage, the sultan seems to have been under the influence of Kāfūr, on whose intimations several officers were dismissed from the court or were killed. The brother of the chief queen Māhrū and the powerful governor of Gujarat, Alp Khān Sanjar, was the major rival of Kāfūr. Alp Khān had managed to retain influence throughout the ʻAlā'ī era. He married two of his daughters to the princes Khiḍr Khān and Shādī Khān. This was a strategic move to secure the succession. Soon, the animosity between Kāfūr and the chief queen's family was out in the open.[111] Kāfūr dealt with all of them, one by one. Alp Khān was murdered in the royal palace;[112] the chief queen was maltreated. Khiḍr Khān was first banished from the palace and later imprisoned in Gwalior.[113] The succession was altered in favour of a five- or six-year-old prince, Shihāb al-Dīn 'Umar[114] whose mother was the daughter of Rāmādīvā, the Yādavā King of Deōgīr.[115] The sultan, allegedly poisoned by Malik Kāfūr,[116] breathed his last in 716/1316, leaving the abounding resources of his empire to his weak successors.

During the Khaljī period, no historical records indicate standardised selection criterion, an organised military training programme for the officials, nor any firm standards for promotion to office. Similarly, the spheres of authority of the officials were not specialised either. Nevertheless, individuals without prior military knowledge could not have been entrusted with higher military responsibilities. Kāfūr's career makes an interesting case study to address some of these issues.

Kāfūr was a slave eunuch[117] captured from his owner in Kanbhayā (Cambay)[118] during the first invasion of Gujarat during 698/1299. Originally a Hindu, he bore the name Mānik. The sultan purchased him for a sum of 1,000 *dinārs* (*dinār* being used figuratively for *tankā*) and, having a special liking for his ambergris-like locks, nicknamed him Kāfūr Hāzār Dinārī.[119] According to the account of K. S. Lal, Kāfūr's master in Cambay obtained him for 1,000 *dinārs*. The slave was snatched from his master during the plunder after the Muslim conquest.[120] Kāfūr soon became 'Alā al-Dīn's catamite and was promoted to the position of a military general. Later, he was given the governorship of different regions of the empire and he also held significant influence on the court. In the last four or five years of 'Alā'ī rule, he became the principal decision maker and created malice in the heart of the sultan against his *umarā'* and family members, alienating the sultan from his associates and making him more dependent upon himself.

Kāfūr's career was an exceptional one. He fought as *bārbeg* against the Mongols around 705/1306–1307. Then he campaigned against the Yamūnā kingdom of Deōgīr. It appears that the title of Malik Nā'ib was conferred upon him when he was placed in command of an army to proceed against Rāi Rām Deō of Deōgīr.[121] Until 708/1309–1310, he held Rāprī as his *iqṭā'*. Thus, within ten years a slave captive of war had become a land revenue administrator. This development signifies growing trust and reliance of the sultanate on the locals. The date of his becoming *nā'ib* (vice regent) is not reported in the historical sources.[122] Nonetheless, this must have occurred after he had consolidated his reputation as a military commander. His position in the sultanate was one of the most powerful. He was a *nā'ib*, a *muqṭa'* and also a fêted military commander, who, on the weakening of his master, took charge of the situation and eliminated all those individuals who could legitimately or illegitimately claim the throne. Kāfūr's rise was resented by a strong group of *umarā'* who removed him from power within a period of 36 days after the death of the sultan.

'Alā al-Dīn's Empire

The expanse of the areas under 'Alā al-Dīn's empire was unprecedented and the administrative efficiency of 'Alā'ī era is unparallelled in the history of the Delhi sultanate. In order to understand the extent of 'Alā al-Dīn Khaljī's authority, it is important to note that he was the first prominent Muslim invader in the Deccan peninsular regions of India.[123] Also, 'Alā al-Dīn was able to reconquer and re-establish the writ of his state over some of these regions that were earlier under the control of the Delhi sultans. Regions of central India and Rajput strongholds that had experienced occasional Muslim campaigns and temporary control had now come under direct control of the sultan. Various *walī*s and *muqṭa*'s were appointed in these regions and regular tax was extracted from these areas.[124]

Baranī gives the names of 11 territorial units and their governors were appointed by 'Alā al-Dīn in the middle of his reign. Gujarat was given to Ulugh Khān. Multan and Swistān were given to Tāj al-Mulk Kāfūrī. Deopalpur and Lahore were given under the command of Ghāzī Malik Tughluq Shāh. Sunam and Samana were given to Malik Ākhur Beg Tatik. Dahar and Ujjain were given to 'Ainu'l Mulk Multani. Jhayin was given to Fakhr-ul Mulk Mirthī. Chitor was given to Malik Abu Muḥammad.[125] Chanderi and Erich were given to Malik Tamar, Badaun. Koehlā and Kirk were given to Malik Dinār shihnā-i pīl, Awadh was given to Malik Tagin and Kara was given to Malik Naṣir al-Dīn Sotaliyā.[126] There was a change in the composition of the crown lands (*khālsā*). Some new regions such as Kol (Aligārh), Baran, Meeruth, Amroha, Afghanpurā, Kabīr and Doab were made a single unit of administration and all the revenue of which was allocated to the royal standing army.[127] The sultans of Delhi were able to assert authority over much of the areas subjugated by ʿAlā al-Dīn until the times of Muḥammad b. Tughluq despite the multiple shifts and changes in the power of the centre. Keeping in view the extent of exercise of authority, the regions of the Delhi sultanate can be divided into core regions, provinces and *iqṭā'* and peripheral regions.

Controlling the Social Base

In the era of ʿAlā al-Dīn, the range of the direct administration significantly increased. It can safely be inferred that the crown lands (i.e. the regions of Doab, Amroha, Afghanpūrā, Kabīr and Dhābī to Badaun) and the north-western regions (i.e. Sunam, Samana, from Pālam to Deopalpur and Lahore, Kara and Kanudī, Kharak, from Bayana to Jhayin,[128] Koehlā and Katihar) fell under the same agricultural revenue policy.[129] Direct and uniform fiscal policy seems to have been implemented in these areas. The residents of Delhi and suburbs were also included in the core areas. The sultan restored law and order in these regions; also, the economic policies were strictly implemented. In order to curb his *umarā'* from instigating intrigues, the sultan curtailed their financial and social capacities to an extent that they were unable to hatch effective conspiracies. Furthermore, the sultan also established an efficient espionage system due to which he was able to maintain his control over *umarā'* and the common people alike.[130] His economic reforms directly connected him to the native rural elite and for the first time we find the historical sources of the Delhi sultanate comprehensively mentioning *muqaddams* and *khōtts* as responsible persons. However, the penetration of authority was not similar in the entire core region; while some areas were strictly administered, others were relatively loosely controlled. Various policies that the sultan implemented in order to establish his writ in the core regions are discussed below.

After the failed rebellions by the sultan's three nephews,[131] during the sultan's expedition of Gujarat four more rebellions occurred, including those of Mongol new Muslims and Hājjī Maulā. The sultan consulted his confidantes and identified some causes: first, the sultan's lack of information about his people; second, the prevalence of drinking parties and social gatherings where intrigues and alliances took root;

third, the cordial personal relations (i.e. matrimonial alliances) binding the *umarā'* together, and which multiplied the number of dissenters; fourth, wealth and affluence among the *umarā'*.[132] Thus, the sultan took four measures to curtail the rebellions.

Firstly, he ordered his officers to extract money from the people on a number of pretexts, to avoid leaving them with excessive wealth. He took back all the villages and properties from the suburbs of Delhi and included them in the crown lands. In addition, he confiscated all the rewards, stipends and grants from everyone except for the *umarā'*, traders and administrators. People became too absorbed in their financial problems to plan a rebellion.[133]

Secondly, the sultan devised an efficient espionage system. The reports of day-to-day affairs of the *umarā'*, bureaucratic staff and notables were regularly transmitted to the sultan. The activities of the *umarā'* each preceding night were reported to the sultan every morning. According to Baranī, the espionage system was so efficient that the *umarā'* were afraid to say anything even in their solitude which might be considered offensive or illicit by the sultan.[134]

Thirdly, the sultan banned all the drinking parties in Delhi and its suburbs. In order to validate the law, he destroyed all the wine reserves of the royal palace and ordered the *umarā'* to mount elephants and go about publicly announcing the new law. He declared the drinking and selling of wine offences punishable by the state. Water wells and prisons were constructed for the violators. The implementation of this law was so strict that many people were killed by imprisonment in the wells; others were rendered incapacitated by their incarceration. Many people started making bootleg wine that they drank at home and sold to friends. Initially with the help of spies, these people were detected and punished but later the government took a more lenient attitude toward such people. Baranī stated that it was impossible for anyone to defy the orders in the range of five kos (1 kos = 1.8 km) and the suburban towns of Ghiyāthpūr, Indrapat and Kelukherī. One had to travel at least a distance of ten kos in order to drink wine safely, demonstrating that in Delhi and its suburbs the orders of the sultan were strictly extended.[135] Though, as the distance grew, the implementation of the law became milder.

Fourthly, the sultan banned unsanctioned socialisation among the elite. The *umarā'* and notables of the city were prohibited from visiting each other and holding large social gatherings as a hedge against espionage and the instigation of rebellion.[136] In addition the sultan instituted strict surveillance over the financial and social behaviour of his *umarā'*. The sultan employed coercion and fear more than he relied on the trust of his patrimonial staff.

A strict system of taxation was considered one of the means of controlling the rebellions of the local elite (*khōtt* and *muqaddim*) and peasants. In order to make the taxation system efficient and promote agriculture, the sultan took the following measures. Firstly, he reserved half of produce for the state. Secondly, he implemented the cattle tax and even a grazing tax. He severely punished any revenue officials found guilty of corruption.[137]

Extensive taxation neutralised the resistance of the local elite and enabled the officers of 'Alā al-Dīn to control *khōtt*, *muqqadim*s and *chohidrī*s. Due to extensive revenue extraction, local elite's alleged financial destitution progressed to the extent that the wives of *khōtt*s and *muqqadim*s had to work in the houses of the Muslims.[138] The taxation system under 'Alā al-Dīn Khaljī was very extensive and special care was taken to monitor the tax officials.[139]

After the defeat of a Mongol army led by Taraghai who had come to Delhi in order to conquer the city in 701/1302,[140] the sultan took special measures to defend the north-western borders.[141] Firstly, he abandoned the idea of personally launching raids and settled in the city of Sīrī after constructing a royal palace.[142] The fort of Delhi was constructed, the old forts in the north-west regions were repaired, and new ones constructed in order to curtail the inward movement of the Mongols. Efficient *kotwāl*s were designated in these forts to store weapons and grains and build lethal weapons such as catapults. Furthermore, they were encouraged to keep skilful staff. 'Alā al-Dīn stationed large armies and efficient officers in the north-western regions. In addition, the sultan established a standing army in the centre numbering 475,000 soldiers.[143] The soldiers were given a fixed salary in cash: 234 per year or 19.5 *tankā* per month. If the soldier had two horses, he was given an additional 6.5 *tankā* per month or 78 *tankā* per year.[144]

In order to support the growing defence and military expenditure, the sultan extended an extensive price control policy.[145] As Moreland writes: 'The essence of this policy was 1) control of supplies, 2) control of transport, with 3) rationing of consumption when necessary, the whole system resting on 4) a highly organised intelligence, and 5) drastic punishment of evasions.'[146] Due to taxation, the purchasing power of the people had become remarkably weak. If anyone was found purchasing expensive luxury items, the spies reported the purchase to the authorities and the purchaser was punished.[147] The price control policy of the sultan had three purposes. First, it ensured the availability of cheap grain for the army and state. The government strictly checked hoarding and inflation by determining grain prices, advising the *muqṭa*'s to monitor hoarding in their local areas. Storage of grain in the royal reservoirs for the public use in the time of need, appointment of an intendant of market, controlling and registration of the trade caravans from the other cities and regions, extraction of taxes in lieu of grain from the regions of Doab were other measures taken in this regard. No one was allowed to privately store the grain, with the efficient espionage system keeping the sultan informed about the working of the market and trade activity. Finally, in a time of drought no one was able to purchase stockpiled grain until it was absolutely necessary.[148]

The price of the food items remained stable for years, despite the occurrence of drought and boomer crops in turn. The sultan kept such a strict check over hoarding so that the need seldom arose to use the royal reservoirs. Similar measures were taken to control the prices of other essentials such as *ghee* (melted butter) and textiles.[149] In addition, the prices of cattle and slaves[150] were strictly monitored. The sultan's price control policy was meant to maintain a large army. The artificially controlled prices and the rationing of food made the food items affordable for a large number of soldiers stationed near the centre even though they received remarkably low salaries.[151] Interestingly, despite the sultan's disinterest in religion and use of religious symbols[152] he was remembered as one of the ablest administrators of the Delhi sultanate. Price controls made living conditions better for the menial classes living in the core regions. Due to the unfailing supply of necessary food items for cheap prices, the poor remembered the 'Alā'ī era as a golden age long after his death.[153] Baranī also expresses his surprise over the fact that the accumulation of talented people all around the Muslim world came about without a deliberate state policy to encourage foreigners which made the city of Delhi as grand as Baghdad and Constantinople. Conversely, it is also true that the sultan, through confiscation of property and increased taxes, financially impaired the *umarā'*, citizens of

Delhi, the Hindu rural elite and any segment of society with the potential to rebel against the sultan.[154]

As mentioned earlier, penetration of authority was not uniform in the core regions either. The regions north-west of the Delhi sultanate, including Multan and Swistān, Sunam and Sumana, Deopalpur and Lahore, were the areas which were directly prone to the Mongol threat. In 696/1297, there was a brief encounter with Mongols and 'Alā'ī forces on the bank of the Indus.[155] After one year a battle between the 'Alā'ī forces and the Mongols who had come to capture Delhi occurred.[156] The sultan, after successfully countering the Mongols, took special care to strengthen the defence of the north-western borders with the construction of forts and checkpoints, appointments of vigilant and competent officers and by advising officials to recruit increasingly efficient staff.[157] In addition, the sultan made an example of Mongols by constructing skull towers of the Mongol soldiers and killing Mongol population that had taken residence in Delhi in the time of his predecessor. The regions of Awadh, Kara and Badaun had more than a century of historical experience of Muslim administration.[158] The Muslim administrators were well established in these regions and the Muslim settlements in these regions were also present. Thus, the extent of core regions was expanded in the reign of 'Alā al-Dīn and an unprecedentedly efficient administration was visible under 'Alā al-Dīn.

Indirectly Administered Regions under 'Alā al-Dīn

The regions of Gujarat, Malwa and Rajhistan were among the indirectly administered regions where the sultan appointed governors and *muqṭa's*. The extent of state control was not as far-reaching as it was in the core regions, since the sultan conquered these regions in the early years of his reign and many of these areas were not present on the map of the Delhi sultanate under the previous dynasty. This was the first extensive conquest of these regions by any Delhi sultan, since the earlier ventures were sporadic or were limited to certain domains. Neither Baranī nor any other historical source mentions the administrative reforms of the sultan as being applied on these *iqṭā'*. The sultan was able to wield power through his appointees. The *muqṭa*'s were allowed to retain their patrimonial staff, nevertheless, the sultan kept a watchful eye over his appointees with the help of the *barīd* system.

'Alā'ī expansion in Gujarat was patchy, while it was partly annexed, most of the regions were still under the local elite. These regions had Muslim presence in the form of Arab traders and occasional invaders even prior to 'Alā al-Dīn. For example, the coastal areas of Gujarat had been within the reach of Muslim invaders since the times of the Umayyads and later in the ninth century, when Maḥmūd of Ghazna raided these regions.[159] The trade links between the Arabs and the Gujarat were even older and more permanent, since over the centuries Arab traders had settled in these regions.[160] In terms of its trade activity and agricultural produce, Gujarat was one of the most profitable regions of India. The coastal city of Kanbhayā (Cambay) in Gujarat is reported to have had Muslim lawyers, scholars and traders long before 698–699/1299–1300 when 'Alā al-Dīn first invaded the region. According to some epitaphs, when 'Alā al-Dīn invaded these regions, some of these areas had localised Muslim communities with their own chief.[161]

In the times of 'Alā al-Dīn, the region of Gujarat was ruled by the Vaghela kingdom, with some localised rulers also present in the region. The expeditions in Gujarat started around 698/1299 when 'Alā al-Dīn sent an expedition under the command of his brother Ulugh Khān and the *wazīr* Nuṣrat Khān. Unable to withstand the Muslim forces the Vaghela King Karnadeva's forces were routed. The king fled south-east to the region of Baglana (in the Nasik region). The rich regions of Somanāth and Nahrwala, the wealth of which was legendary for the Muslims of the Delhi sultanate, were plundered. The coastal regions of Kanbhayā were raided under Nuṣrat Khān, around 698/1299, producing immense booty. The forces of 'Alā al-Dīn had a very strong presence in the region and Jain inscriptions reveal that Satyapura (Sachor) 'was saved by a miracle when the sultan's force overran the Kāthiawad peninsula'.[162] The forces of 'Alā al-Dīn were perceived as pillagers and destroyers within the invaded regions. In the middle of the campaign, some new Muslim Mongol commanders within the army rebelled, thwarting the series of victories.[163]

This conquest however did not uproot the existing dynasty, as Baranī tries to suggest in his account of the campaign. According to his account, the ruler of the Vaghela dynasty Karnadeva was able to secure an immediate asylum in the Dēogīr region, which was under the rule of the Yadava King Ramadeva. A bilingual inscription of 704/1304, indicates King Karnadeva after this debacle continued to rule on

Vadodara (Baroda) in the east of his kingdom;[164] it can well be assumed that the asylum was a later development. There was a second invasion of the region in 710/1310, undertaken by Qirā Beg Aḥmad-i Chhitam in which Sachor was sacked. This is the time when Karnadeva the ruler of Vaghela dynasty took asylum in the Deccan and Tilang. Alp Khān was then appointed as the first Muslim governor of the region and this was certainly one of the later developments of the 'Alā'ī era.[165]

The nature of provincial administration was anything but uniform, systemised or effective. While some areas were directly under the rule of the governor, there were many areas where indigenous dynasties persisted. Similarly, the ruling base of the 'Alā'ī governors was mainly the staff that they nurtured. Many regions were impregnable for the Muslim armies that became asylums for those who did not want to live under the governors.[166] It is also noted by a later source dated in the seventeenth century that 'Alā al-Dīn's conquests were more effective in the regions of eastern Gujarat, ranging from Nahrwala to Bharuch, and the complete penetration of the Muslim rulers was a development under later Muslim kingdoms.[167] As for the Kāthiawad peninsula, it was not within the sultan's domains. There were some areas that paid tribute to the sultan as indicated by the later sources, but, this tributary status was largely temporary.[168] The Vaghela dynasty persisted in Gujarat with its seat of government in Dandahidesa, and with the Delhi sultan as an overlord. This type of governance continued until the time of the independent Gujarat sultans.[169]

The region of Ranthambor had been an objective of many of the campaigns since the Ghūrīd rule and Muslim rule was confined to certain fortifications. From the times of Iltutmish, the historical sources often explain the unruly nature of the region, which was often under rebellions. 'Alā al-Dīn Khaljī's forces made a decisive entry into these regions owing to the Mongol border politics. The Raja of Ranthambor, Hammiradeva was an ally of 'Alā al-Dīn; the relations between the two became hostile, after the former provided asylum to the Mongol *amīr*s who had rebelled during the first Gujarat campaign.[170] After Qutlugh Qocha conducted a major Mongol invasion of the Delhi sultanate borders in 699/1299–1300,[171] the sultan wanted to prevent Ranthambor from entering into an alliance with the Mongols. Therefore, Ulugh Khān, then *muqṭa'* of Bayana and Nuṣrat Khān, *muqṭa'* of Kara, were assigned to take the ruler of Ranthambor to task by attacking his fortress. Jhain was the first region to fall. Later, the Ranthambor expedition came directly under the charge of the sultan when Nuṣrat Khān was mortally wounded.[172] Thus, in 700/1301, after a campaign of four months, Ranthambor fell to 'Alā al-Dīn.[173]

The ruler of Ranthambor, Hammiradeva, was eliminated along with his new Muslim allies. This region, therefore, came under the sultanate's direct control and the sultan duly appointed governors. The first governor of this region was Ulugh Khān, whose rule lasted only a few months owing to his death shortly afterwards.[174] The Muslim rule in these regions was somewhat extensive under the new governor Malik 'Izz al-Dīn Bura Khān who renamed the city of Jhayin as Shāhr-i Naw (New City). This city was brought under the same system for collection of land tax (*kharāj*) as the core regions.[175]

Similarly, the region of Chitor was under the authority of Samarasimha before the status of this region was reduced to a tributary of the Delhi sultanate on the eve of the invasion of Gujarat in 698/1299 by Ulugh Khān and Nuṣrat Khān.[176] However, soon enough the Raja denounced this arrangement, owing to which the sultan himself raided this region around 702/1303. The attack resulted in the surrender of the Raja's forces.[177] The story of the conquest of Chitor is immortalised by the legend of Rānī Padmani. Folklore and later a Muslim author have us believe that it was the beauty of the Rānī that drove the sultan to undertake the precarious and expensive campaigns of Chitor, and the Rānī of course preferred to perish by self-immolation than to be a consort to the sultan. The legendary incident of *jauhar* (self-immolation) of all Chitor women folk led by Rānī Padmani has been eternalised by Muḥammad Jayasi's *Padmavat*,[178] a legendary tale that symbolises resistance and revulsion of fourteenth-century Chitor towards the expansion of the Delhi sultans in Rajputana. The historical value of this tragic love poem is certainly questionable since it was produced in 947/1540, some 237 years after the incident. Some of the hyperbolic imagery that the poem employs demonstrates the poem's tendency to take poetic licence. This poem might be a part of an oral history that was recorded by the poet; its popularity through the ages reflects much about how the sultan of Delhi has been envisaged by the people of Chitor. 'Ala al-Dīn Khaljī has been perceived as a tyrannical and scheming invader of little morality who could conquer a city just to add the womenfolk of that town to his already overflowing haram. The legendary beauty of

Rānī Padmani of Chitor brought 'Alā al-Dīn Khaljī to the gates of Chitor, one of the most impregnable forts of India.

The sultan achieved only a pyrrhic victory after all the Rajput men of Chitor, who took a vow of *saka* (to fight until death), accepted an honourable death by combat. When the forces of sultan entered the city they only found burnt ashes and the bones of the valiant women who had performed the act of *jauhar* (group self-immolation). Although the women of Chitor performed two more *jauhar*s during the times of Mughal Emperors Humayun and Akbar, the story of the *jauhar* of Rānī Padmani achieved legendary status. M. S. Ahluwalia rightly points out there were strategic reasons behind the invasion of Chitor.[179] Nevertheless, this tale reflects the local tone and sentiments that have persisted in the folklores and bard literature for centuries about Muslim rule in general and the rule of 'Alā al-Dīn Khaljī in particular. The extension of the writ of the Delhi sultanate on Chitor was somewhat effective. The city was renamed as Khiḍrabād. Khiḍr, the heir apparent and still a minor, was appointed governor of Khiḍrabād but he was too young to run the affairs of the region independently.[180] As stated by 'Īṣāmī, 'Alā al-Dīn's slave Malik Shāhīn was appointed as the regent of the province.[181] The impression that control of these regions was lost immediately after the death of 'Alā al-Dīn does not seem to be accurate[182] as the same were under the Delhi sultans until the times of the Tughluqs.[183]

Although Baranī makes some indication that the region of Jalōr was under the suzerainty of 'Alā al-Dīn, we learn neither details about the nature of the rule, nor how the rule was attained. From the details of various military expeditions as recorded by Amīr Khusraw it can also be inferred that the Delhi forces had been trying to capture the region of Siwanā for five or six years before victory was achieved.[184] In 708/1308, under an expedition by 'Alā al-Dīn, this fortress was captured and the Raja Satal Deo was eliminated. In this region also, visible administrative changes were undertaken; Siwanā was renamed Khayrabād and Malik Kamāl al-Dīn 'Gurg' was appointed its governor.[185] According to Sirhindī, the same *amīr* was able to kill Raja Kanhar Deo (Kanhadadeva, son and successor of Samanatasimh) and conquer Jalōr.[186] According to inscriptions of 718/1318 and 724/1323, the Delhi sultans were able to hold these regions until the Tughluq era.[187] Similarly, we also find that during the Ranthambor campaigns of 700/1301, the territory (*wilayāt*) of Jhayin as far as the frontier of Dhar was also sacked.[188] But, according to Amīr Khusraw, control over these regions was established after the Chitor campaign.[189]

During the time of 'Alā al-Dīn the region of Malwa was ruled by the Paramara kingdom. This kingdom was internally weak since the *wazīr* was more powerful even than the king himself. The hostility between the two provided an opportunity to the sultan of Delhi to seize the kingdom. Thus, in 705/1305, a campaign was launched under 'Ayn al-Mulk Multanī and within a period of few months the conquest was completed. 'Ayn ul-Mulk, who was already made the governor of Malwa, was rewarded with the further grant of Mandu.[190] We do not find the details of these expeditions in Baranī's account. Nevertheless, he does mention that in 'Alā al-Dīn's reign Mandal-Khur, Dhar, Ujjain, Mandugārh (Mandu), 'Alāī'pur, Chanderi and Erich were all allotted to governors (*wālīs*) and *mūqti*'s.[191] However, none of the sources provide details about when exactly the said places were taken. We also find different cities renamed; for instance Erich is found renamed as Sultānpūr in the historical sources and reference to it is made as being under Muslim control in 709/1309, when the Muslim forces under Malik Kāfūr encamped there for five days en route to Warangal.[192] Similarly, Chanderi held the status of an *iqṭā'* in 711/1312. Even after 'Alā al-Dīn Khaljī's invasions the Paramara dynasty survived in the north-eastern part of the country and an inscription of 709/1310 at Udayapura (in the present-day Vidisha district) testifies this claim. However, the control of these regions was lost in the times of Muḥammad b. Tughluq, as revealed by an inscription of 739/1338 on a mosque.[193]

The peripheral regions of 'Alā'ī Empire consisted of tributary kingdoms of the south. The 'Alā'ī armies occasionally raided these regions and booty was sent to the centre. Extraction of tribute on a temporary basis also defined the relationship between the centre and the tributary kingdoms. In almost all these areas, the local kingdoms were present and found wielding authority every time the Muslim invaders went back to northern India. Nevertheless, the credit for the decisive forward expansion of the Delhi sultanate goes to 'Alā al-Dīn Khaljī. Earlier, his seizure of the throne had been made possible by immense wealth that was plundered through a raid on the distant Yadava kingdom of Deōgīr. Though, the southern campaigns were a later development of the 'Alā'ī rule. In 695/1296, 'Alā al-Dīn Khaljī had raided Deōgīr and Ram Chandara, the vanquished Raja, had promised to send tribute to 'Alā al-Dīn Khaljī annually. Soon after, the arrangement was overlooked and the Raja ceased to pay tribute. Therefore, in 707/1308 an expedition was sent by 'Alā al-Dīn Khaljī to Deōgīr under the command of Malik Kāfūr. Since the military expedition of the south had won him the kingdom earlier, 'Alā al-Dīn Khaljī hoped for more riches from those regions. This led to a series of invasions that continued until the last days of 'Alā al-Dīn Khaljī's rule.

At that time, the southern peninsula was divided into the following four kingdoms: the kingdom of Deccan ruled by Yadavas,[194] the kingdom of Talinganā ruled by Ganapatis dynasty with its capital in Warangal, the kingdom of Dawarsumandara Hoysalas and the kingdom of Pandya or Mabar. These kingdoms were mutually hostile, though wealthy due to their numerous docks, fertile lands, mines and domestic and international trade.

The relationship between these areas and 'Alā al-Dīn was purely indirect. The target regions were simply the raiding grounds for the 'Alā'ī army. 'Alā al-Dīn never visited these regions during his rule and relied upon his generals. According to Baranī, at the first successful invasion of Tilang, 'Alā al-Dīn advised his general, Malik Kāfūr, not to make any effort to take the fortress of Warangal or to overthrow its king if treasure, jewels, elephants and horses were offered, and tribute guaranteed for future years.[195] The people in these regions must have only known about the Muslim rulers from a distance as a large invading army. Local dynasties continued ruling through their own administration systems. The status of Deōgīr region changed by the end of 'Alā al-Dīn Khaljī's reign and a regular governor was appointed to take care of the matters of the state.

The Pandiyas ruled Malabar region at the time of 'Alā al-Dīn's invasions. The people of the Malabar coast had old connections with Arab traders, who had traded and settled in these regions for centuries. Writing in the times of Muḥammad b. Tughluq, Ibn Battūtah mentions the Malabar coast as a region where a Muslim community was well settled, and mosques and hospices were constructed in these regions as well.[196] He recounts Muslim traders, *qāḍī*s and one of the rajas, converted to Islam.[197]

The geographical location of Deōgīr earned it wealth through trade. Yet, it was unlucky to be within ready reach of the sultans of Delhi.

It was in the interest of the ruler of this region to comply with the needs of the Muslim invaders from the north. King Ramadeva's kingdom of Deōgīr was one of the important military bases that provided enormous help to Malik Kāfūr who was to raid in the far south.[198] The 695/1296 invasions of Deōgīr had brought 'Alā al-Dīn immense wealth through tribute, as mentioned earlier. This wealth had won him the sultanate of Delhi. Nevertheless, King Ramadeva's agreement to pay regular tribute was short-lived, instigating a new round of raids. The first campaign was against Deōgīr in 706/1306–1307, when Malik Nā'ib Kāfūr Hazardinari defeated Ramadeva,[199] who was captured and taken to Delhi. From Delhi he was sent back as an appointee of the Delhi sultan. He was given the title of *rāī'-yi rayan* (rāī'of rais) and a *chatr.*[200] We do not find this region rebelling against the Delhi sultan again in his lifetime. This alliance with Ramadeva made the penetration of 'Alā'ī armies into the southern peninsula safer and more convenient. In 710/1310–1311 Kāfūr's attack on Mabar was facilitated by Ramadeva when he delivered supplies for reinforcements and provided a route to Dvarasamudra.[201] Nevertheless, the son of Ramadeva was hostile to the Delhi sultanate, and Deōgīr was annexed and included among one of the provinces by the end of the 'Alā al-Dīn's era. Malik Khān was made governor of these regions and he took care of military and civil affairs. From 714/1314–1315 coins were struck in the name of 'Alā al-Dīn in Deōgīr.[202] Similarly, Quṭb al-Dīn Mubārak Shāh 717/1317 and Khusraw Khān also made a number of raids into these regions.[203]

The regions of Dvarasamudra and Mabar held legendary wealth and treasure.[204] Malik Nā'ib Kāfūr reached this region with the help of Hoysala king, Ballala III of Dvarasamudra, who not only acquiesced in 710/1310–1311 but also guided the armies towards his neighbours. After the campaign, Kāfūr took Ballala III's son Vira Ballala to Delhi where he was awarded a robe (*khi'lat*), *chatr* and treasure and sent back to his kingdom. The Delhi sultanate chronicles do not reflect upon this kingdom further.[205]

When Malik Kāfūr reached the borders of Mabar around 710/1311 it had been going through a war of succession since 709/1309–1310, and princes Sundara Pandya and Vira Pandya after the murder of their king father were at loggerheads with each other.[206] While Kāfūr sided with Vira Pandya, the other brother Sundra Pandya battled with Kāfūr. Still, the most dangerous enemy of all was the monsoon rain, owing to which the army retreated with the least plunder possible under the circumstances.[207] Afterwards, in a battle with his brother, Sundara Pandya's forces were routed. He then joined 'Alā al-Dīn's camp (presumably at Deōgīr), and thus he was restored in the South Arcot district in 713/1314.[208] The second campaign in these regions is recorded in 718/1318 when Quṭb al-Dīn Mubārak Shāh came to Deōgīr to suppress a rebellion. He then dispatched an army under Khusraw towards Mabar, where from a substantial amount of booty was drawn out.[209]

The administrative and military successes of 'Alā al-Dīn Khaljī were short-lived and their benefits perished as soon as the sultan's strength and senses began declining. The very image of Malik Kāfūr in the Muslim historical sources is that of a malevolent and conspiring slave who killed his master and tried to usurp the throne. Baranī accuses him of destroying the empire built by 'Alā al-Dīn Khaljī, reflecting the contemporary mind-set. Kāfūr enthroned a young prince Shihāb al-Dīn,[210] and subsequently married the queen mother to obtain a connection with the Khaljī royal house and thus to have a legitimate claim to the throne. At this point Kāfūr became the de facto ruler. Nevertheless, his support among the *umarā'* was inconsequential.[211] The allegation of poisoning his master must have been a prevalent impression. Kāfūr was assisted by a coterie of nobility with relatively recent appointments. These *umarā'* belonged to different ethnic origins. For instance, one of the prominent associates of Kāfūr was Kamāl al-Dīn 'Gūrg' (wolf), whose family belonged to Kabul.[212]

In the presence of 'Alā al-Dīn's offspring and other wives, the position of Kāfūr was highly insecure, since any of the former could have become a challenge to his authority. Therefore, it was important for Kāfūr to eliminate 'Alā al-Dīn's family. In his bid to wipe out all the possible heirs of the throne, including sons, wives and the slaves of the deceased sultan,[213] Kāfūr imprisoned, blinded and murdered several princes. Many royal women were maltreated. In an attempt to murder the prince Mūbārak Khān (later Sultan Quṭb al-Dīn Mūbārak Shāh), Kāfūr was slayed by four *pā'ik* slaves of 'Alā al-Dīn.[214] Baranī and Ibn Battūtah report the same tradition with a slight variation. According to Ibn Battūtah, the widow of 'Alā al-Dīn sent a message regarding the assassination of Kāfūr to these slaves, who already had similar designs.[215] Whereas, according to Baranī, when these four slaves reached the dungeon to assassinate prince Mūbārak Khān, the prince beseeched loyalty in them for their old master. Consequently, the slaves changed their mind and went to Kāfūr and killed him instead. The four slaves took Mūbārak Khān out of the prison and placed him on the throne.[216] Thus, the first rule of an Indian slave was concluded within 35 days of its inception.[217] Kāfūr's career lasted a total of 26 years. His appointments, as a war leader and *muqṭa'* and later as the deputy of the sultanate were due to his competence that won him proximity to the sultan.[218]

Quṭb al-Dīn Mubārak Shāh

The next ruler, Mubārak Khān, started his regal career by becoming the co-sultan of his stepbrother Shihāb al-Dīn 'Umar. Soon after, he took over completely, with the title of Quṭb al-Dīn Mubārak Shāh, discarding the sultan in the process.[219] Kāfūr's example did not eliminate the influence of the Indian slave elements from the court, as the new sultan bestowed many key designations and important *iqṭā*'s upon his slaves. In addition, many of the *iqṭā*'s remained under the administration of 'Alā al-Dīn's slaves[220] who must have been appointed during the last phase of 'Alā'ī rule.

In the first year of his enthronement, the sultan executed the four *pā'ik* slaves who had rescued and later enthroned him. This was because the slaves publicly boasted about their role as kingmakers and often demanded greater rewards, status and wealth. The attitude of these slaves became intolerable for the young sultan. Consequently, they were taken to the suburbs and beheaded.[221]

In the same year, before the sultan left for an expedition to Deōgīr to suppress a revolt, he handed over his capital and royal treasury to an 'Alā'ī slave Shāhīn, who was given the title Malik Wāfā (= reliable)[222] and endorsed to the rank of *nā'ib* (deputy) sultan.[223] The sultan's calculations about trust immediately proved wrong as Malik Wāfā had the coins struck using the title of Shams al-Dīn Maḥmūd Shāh and claimed the throne. Finding little support in the capital, the conspiracy failed. Along with many other conspirers, Malik Wāfā was executed when the sultan returned to Delhi.[224]

In this era, efficient administrative control over the core regions, which was the hallmark of 'Alā al-Dīn's reign, seem to have been lost as well. The sultan did not continue with the price control system that was introduced by his father, weakening the system of checks and balances on the market.[225]

Under Mubārak Shāh, Malik Dinār, an 'Alā'ī slave, was conferred the title of Zafar Khān and made governor of Gujarat. From Gujarat, he gathered enormous revenues and sent them to the capital. The sultan married the daughter of Malik Dinār, thus developing matrimonial links with the slave elements. This amicable relationship did not last long as shortly after the sultan in his bid to eliminate all possible threats to the rule executed Dinār in 717/1318.[226]

The four years and four-month[227] reign of this 17/18-year-old[228] sultan witnessed the rise of a Barvārī[229] slave of 'Alā al-Dīn Khaljī. This slave was captured in the Malwa campaign around 704/1305. He was converted and named Hasan.[230] He was raised by Malik Shādī the *nā'ib-i khās*[231] of 'Alā al-Dīn but later was obtained by Mubārak Shāh. In a short period he rose to the position of *wazīr* with the title Khusraw Khān.[232] This exceedingly treasured eunuch and catamite[233] was also given the military contingent and *iqṭā*'s of Malik Kāfūr.[234]

Soon after, Mubārak Shāh handed over one of the wealthiest province of Gujarat to Hasām al-Dīn who was the brother of Khuraw Khān. Hasām in return, accumulated support from his Barvārī kinsmen, converted back to Hinduism and rebelled. The rebellion was ineffective and he was arrested by the *umarā'* of Gujarat who sent him back to the sultan. The sultan, blinded in his adoration of Khusraw Khān, treated him mildly and made him a confidante, which made the *umarā'* feel even more disgruntled.[235]

Many Hindus and rebel associates of Malik Kāfūr, whom he used to consult regarding the instigation of a rebellion against the sultan, befriended Khusraw Khān.[236] Initially, Khusraw Khān tried to revolt during a campaign in the south in which he wanted to rule autonomously, but he failed when his fellow officers refused to cooperate. The officers handed Khusraw Khān over to the sultan with reports of treason. The sultan, who would not hear any word against his favourite slave, in return punished these officers.[237] The resentment against the sultan was mounting amongst the *umarā'*, many of whom had been mistreated on the orders of Khusraw Khān.[238] However, the *umarā'* were probably not as strong a group as they had been in the time of Iltutmish. Due to the blind trust and favour of the sultan, Khusraw was able to accumulate his own support group consisting of 40,000 Barvārī warriors.[239] This was a crucial development in the plan to murder the sultan and seize the sultanate.

The intrigue to assassinate the sultan was well known among some of the *umarā'*, but none dared to warn the irascible sultan about it. Qāḍī al-Dīn, the one-time teacher and the bearer of the door-keys of the royal palace, revealed the plot to the sultan. The unfortunate man was badly insulted by the sultan,[240] and later killed by the rebels.[241]

In 719/1320, Khusraw was able to murder Sultan Mubārak Shāh in cold blood at the Hazār Sūtūn Palace.[242] After the murder of the sultan, Khusraw took all important officials of the state into his custody and successfully pressured them to extend public allegiance,[243] and thus was enthroned as Nāṣir al-Dīn Khusraw Shāh. The associates of the new sultan plundered the royal harem and slayed all possible heirs to the throne. The sultan took the chief wife of Quṭb al-Dīn[244] and married his brother to 'Alā al-Dīn's daughter.[245] Trusted individuals were appointed to important posts.[246] Randhol, the uncle of the new sultan, was given the title of Ra'i Rayhān with the house and property of Qāḍī Khān, whose family had absconded after his murder in the royal palace the subsequent night.[247]

Khusraw Khān and Ghāzī Malik

The new sultan tried to appease all those who had opposed him or had accepted him unwillingly. 'Ayn al-Mulk Multanī and Malik Fakhr al-Dīn Juna were given important positions.[248] The idea of a convert ascending to the throne with a Hindu power base was appalling to the Muslims. According to Baranī, the rise of Khusraw was the rise of Hindu values, damaging to the Muslim cause. Copies of the Qur'an were used as chairs and idol worship had begun in the palace.[249]

Baranī describes the entire scene as the rise of Hindu influence. A detached analysis of the situation will attest that it was not the rise of Hindus, but individual motives that underlined the entire conspiracy. Khusraw Khān's words or actions do not match the historian's account for a number of reasons. Firstly, on his expedition to the south, Khusraw Khān was as pitiless to the Hindu kings of Deccan as any other Muslim general.[250] Secondly, he also desecrated Hindu temples during his military expeditions.[251] Thirdly, his actions seem to have been influenced by the example of Malik Kāfūr. He was driven by the desire for political domination, since many of his associates were the friends of Malik Kāfūr. Although the support group of Khusraw Khān consisted of Hindu Barvārīs imported from Gujarat, this was only because he could not win unreserved support by the existing *umarā'*. These Hindus seem to have performed religious rituals that created the impression among Muslims of the rise of Hindu influence. Conversely, it is important to note that, in his brief reign,[252] Khusraw Khān neither formally reverted to Hinduism nor did anything seriously against Muslim values. He did not disturb the Muslim population in the capital nor the governors of the provinces. Instead, he had *khuṭba* read in the caliph's name and many officers of the previous ruler continued to serve under the new ruler. Soon enough, many of the Barvārīs who had supported Khusraw Khān in a coup receded to the background.[253]

Like his predecessors, Khusraw did not have noticeable support among the nobility. Just as had happened in the times of earlier sultans, dissatisfied elements waited for an opportunity to oust him. Religion, a possible slogan for his opponents, had limited practical effectiveness. Malik Fakhr al-Dīn Jūna (the future Sultan Muḥammad b. Tughluq), an *amīr* stationed at Delhi, took advantage of the situation and fled to join his father Ghāzī Malik (the future Sultan Ghiyāth al-Dīn Tughluq) warden of the marches at Deopalpur.[254] Ghāzī Malik decided to overthrow Khusraw Khān using the idiom of religion. He sent letters to the governors of various provinces requesting them to join him against Khusraw, the alleged infidel who killed his patron.[255] Ghāzī Malik asked his *dabīr* (secretary) to draft letters, intended for the six governors and *muqṭa'* of the northern provinces and *iqṭā'* including Amir Mughlatī the (*mīr*) governor of Multan, Muḥammad Shāh the governor of Swistān, Behrām Aybā the governor of Uchh, Yaklakhī the governor of Samana, Hoshang the *muqṭa'* of Jalōr and 'Ayn al-Mulk Multanī.[256] When 'Ayn al-Mulk Multanī received the letter he was already in the centre and Khusraw Khān had already appointed him the *wazīr*. Although he received this letter, the response from him was not encouraging. Few governors responded positively, most reacting with disbelief. Thus, according to *Tārīkh-i Mubārak Shāhī* and *Tughluq Namāh*, Ghiyāth al-Dīn was enraged by the replies that he received to his letters.[257] 'Alī al-Kā'ūs, the *amīr* of Deopalpur and Bahrām Aybā, governor of Uchh, joined him readily. Two Khōkhar chiefs, Gūl Chandār and Sahaj Rāi, also joined the banner of Ghāzī Malik. Malik Mughlatī, the governor of Multan, refused to support him.[258] Malik Yakhlakhī, who wrote letters to Khusraw and expressed confidence in him, also refused.[259] Ghāzī instigated subjects against their governor and had him killed by his own men. Similarly, Muḥammad Shāh, the *amīr* of Swistān who had been imprisoned by his *umarā'* on the enthronement of Khusraw, was released by the letter of Ghāzī Malik. Subsequently, the *amīr* worked for his saviour.[260]

Consequently, Ghāzī Malik was able to gather adequate support to oust Khusraw Khān.[261] His first encounter was with the sultan's brother Khān-i Khānān who had an army numbering 40,000. After a brief skirmish, the royal forces were utterly routed and their inexperienced commander fled from the battlefield, leaving behind elephants, horses and treasures to be seized by the victors. Many of the vanquished soldiers were taken as prisoners. Ghāzī Malik's financial resources swelled after this triumph, equipping him for the final battle for the throne.

Like 'Alā al-Dīn, Khusraw Khān had killed his master and thus decided to use measures similar to those used by 'Alā al-Dīn to gain public espousal. In order to win public support and the confidence of his soldiers he spent lavishly without leaving much in the imperial treasury. He also burnt the state records.[262] Yet so overwhelming was Ghāzī Malik's victory that the soldiers abandoned the idea of fighting for Khusraw Khān. Having no other respectable way open to him, Khusraw Khān decided to fight to the end. In the beginning of the battle, 'Ayn al-Mulk Multanī deserted the sultan,[263] who lost the battle and absconded to Tilpat.[264]

The following night, Khusraw Khān successfully concealed himself in a garden of Malik Shādī, his patron of yore.[265] In the morning, he asked for food from the gardener and offered him a ring that was probably the royal seal.[266] The ring when reached to the market revealed its owner, who was consequently captured. Ghāzī Malik first treated him kindly but later executed him in 719/1320 at the same spot where Mubārak Shāh was murdered. Khusraw Khān's corpse was displayed in the same way as he had displayed the body of his master.[267] The rule of Khusraw lasted for four months and four days.[268] Although there are no special references to his military training in the records, Khusraw's Barvārīs kinsmen were prized for their military skills. Furthermore, he had once served as *'alā'ī pāsbān* (watch guard) and he was given the command of the expeditions in the south. Thus, he must have been familiar with the art of warfare even before his capture.

While examining the accounts about both the powerful slaves Malik Kāfūr and Khusraw Khān, it is interesting to identify a number of similarities between their careers: their capture in the war, conversion from the Hindu religion, nature of their relationship with the sultans, immense political influence, swift promotions, usurpation of throne, marriage with the chief wives of the late sultans to gain legitimacy, brief reigns, inability to win adequate support among the powerful Muslim elite, and a grisly end. The activities of these slaves proved to be a deathblow to the strength of the dynasty already weakened by the slaughter of Mubārak Shāh.

Power was the only rule of domination in the Delhi sultanate; it was only power that could legitimise rule. For instance, in the case of dynastic transition from Ghiyāthids to Khaljīs, the accession of ʻAlā al-Dīn, and in the rise and fall of Malik Kāfūr and Khusraw Khān, the ability to coerce seems to have been the most important determinant of who came to power. In the absence of any definite law of succession, only the most aggressive and pugnacious among the *umarā'* was able to assert power whether as de facto or de jure rulers. Despite mass resentment against Jalāl al-Dīn and later ʻAlā al-Dīn, both were able to retain control due to the effective exercise of power. Malik Kāfūr sought dominance on the basis of his sheer ability to manipulate and Khusraw Khān was deposed not due to the resentment of the people but due to the successful campaign of Ghāzī Malik who had already made his mark as an efficient administrator since the times of ʻAlā al-Dīn.

Figure 7.1 Gold Tanka of Qutb al-Dīn Mubārak Shāh with a Caliphal Claim. Courtesy British Museum.

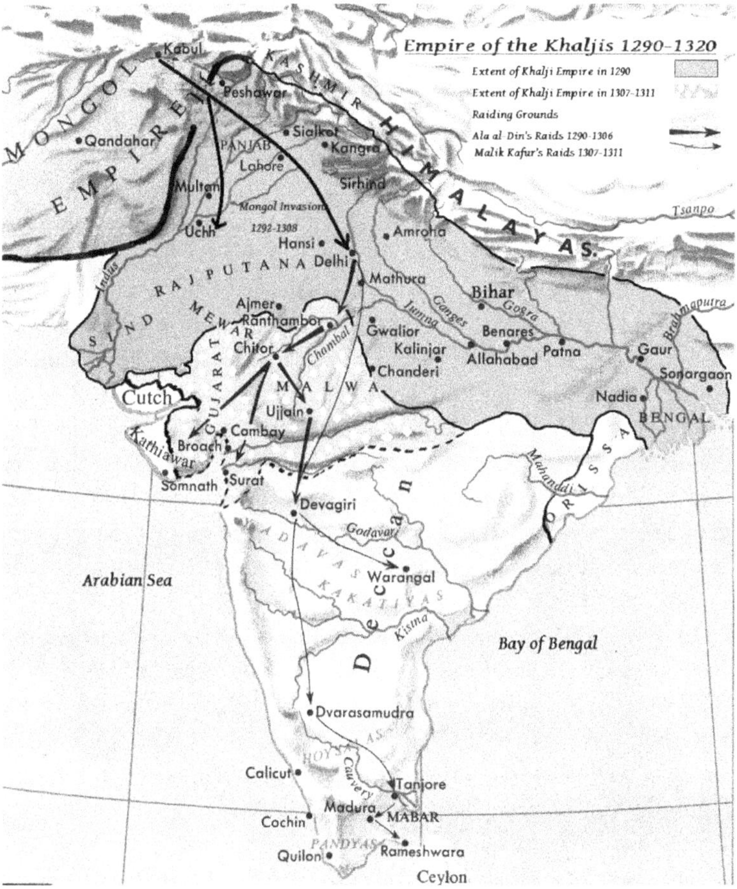

Map 7.1 Empire of the Khaljis 1290–1320

Dissent against power seems to have been a trend among the nobility that was not monolithic in its composition. Conspiracies were a matter of chance as evident in the earlier Delhi sultanate. It was neither the mildness of Jalāl al-Dīn nor the administrative success of 'Alā al-Dīn that prevented the nobility from hatching conspiracies. The nobility considered Jalāl al-Dīn, who was neither suspicious about the plans of his nobility nor willing to punish the offenders, an aberration. Historians of the sultanate also consider Jalāl al-Dīn an anomaly in the universe of the sultanate. 'Alā al-Dīn's strict surveillance of his nobility kept them from conspiring effectively and not his military or administrative success. Thus, in most cases intrigue was a matter of opportunity rather than inspired by a real reason.

Wealth and its efficient use seem to have played an important role in winning the throne. The rift between 'Alā al-Dīn and Jalāl al-Dīn that led to the murder of the latter emerged because 'Alā al-Dīn had become financially stronger than the sultan. Learning from the experience of his own life, 'Alā al-Dīn, after becoming sultan, did not let anyone become stronger than himself in terms of finance and military strength. 'Alā al-Dīn Khaljī, though having the reputation of a murderer, was accepted by the people and *umarā'* alike, since he showered wealth on people with catapults. The same policy seems to have been adopted by Khusraw Khān, who had murdered his patron Quṭb al-Dīn Mubārak Shāh in the same way as 'Alā al-Dīn. He also showered money on his subjects until the treasury was drained. From the hagiographical sources, we find that even the eminent Sufi saints such as Nizām al-Dīn Awliya had accepted grants sent by Khusraw Khān. It was only the fear of the powerful army of Ghāzī Malik, which was marching towards Delhi that forced the supporters of Khusraw Khān to abandon him.

In the Delhi sultanate, it seems that powerful political actors considered it their right to seize the throne. The fittest had the right to rule. Once this ability or fitness diminished, they were eliminated violently. For instance, during the reign of Jalāl al-Dīn, 'Alā al-Dīn emerged as *primus inter pares* and seized the throne after regicide; Malik Kāfūr, Khusraw Khān and later Ghāzī Malik seized power on the same logic.

The response to Khaljī rule was mixed in different regions. While the people of Delhi resented the rise of the Khaljīs and considered it illegitimate, they were unable to dethrone Jalāl al-Dīn Khaljī, despite their intention to raid Bihārpūr and rescue the infant son of Kayquabād. Similarly, the murderers 'Alā al-Dīn and the Hindu Khusraw Khān were accepted due to their military power and wealth. Sultan 'Alā al-Dīn was able to find the only solution which could keep people from rebelling and conspiring: he made them financially weak and dependent on the state. On the other hand, the ultimate feat of Khaljīs was to save the Delhi sultanate from Mongols. Rationing of food and a regular supply of grains earned him praise from the lower ranks in the core regions. Nevertheless, this praise could not convert his personal reign into a dynastic order.

Like its forerunners, the 26-year history of the Khaljī dynasty is full of betrayals, intrigues, conspiracies, revolts and rebellions. However, one can identify some unique phenomena characterising political authority and legitimacy under the Khaljīs. Significantly, the religious and cultural symbols employed by Iltutmish or Balban seem to have been missing in the times of 'Alā al-Dīn. Similarly, the socio-religious influence of Sidi Mawillah was materialised in his bid to attain political authority. Thus, we can see political power not only as the product of military might but also as something supported by religious influence.

CHAPTER 8

FROM MEGALOMANIA TO CHAOS: THE TUGHLUQS

The king's compassion, generosity and hospitality were unmatched and extraordinary, as I have reported earlier. However, the king was overtly brutal as well. It was a rare day when no one was killed at the doorway of his castle. The corpses of the slain remained putrefying at the entrance. Once I was going inside the castle and my horse took a fright after seeing something hoary. I enquired what it was, and my companion replied that it was a human torso that had been busted into three pieces. This king used to punish indiscriminately and extensively major and minor crimes; he made no exceptions for scholars, nobles or the pious. Every day several hundred of men were brought in chains into the dīwan khāna (hall of audience); some were slaughtered, some were tortured and others were beaten up.[1]

or

Superfluity of Historical Evidence and the Making of a Zālim (cruel) *Sultan, Muḥammad b. Tughluq*[2]

By the first quarter of the fourteenth century, the Delhi sultanate had become an empire the political frontiers of which stretched from Mabar in the south to Sirhind in the north and from Swistān in the west to Satgaon (Saptagram) in the east. 'Alā al-Dīn's empire survived the interregnum of Quṭb al-Dīn Mubārak Shāh and Khusraw Khān and was able to endure as a political entity until the rise of the Tughluq[3] dynasty which succeeded the Khaljīs.

The founder of the dynasty, Ghāzī Malik, entitled Ghīyāth al-Dīn, is speculated to have been the descendant of a Balbanid slave, whose name was also 'Tughluq'. His wife, the mother of Ghīyāth al-Dīn Tughluq, was a woman of the Jāt tribe. This view is supported by Farishtāh who investigated the issue in the last decades of the sixteenth century under the patronage of Ibrāhīm 'Ādil Shāh of Bijāpūr.[4] Fifteenth-century Egyptian sources also testify that Ghīyāth al-Dīn had been a military slave.[5] Nevertheless, contemporary observers, including Amīr Khusraw,[6] Ibn Battūtah,[7] 'Afīf[8] and Baranī, contradict this claim.[9] In Baranī's account, Ghīyāth al-Dīn Tughluq expressed emotional attachment to Jalāl al-Dīn Khaljī at the time of the former's coronation.[10] He dealt with the Khaljī *umarā'* with kindness and tolerance, as if they were his colleagues. In *Tārīkh-i Fīrūz Shāhī*, the Khaljī nobles and the sultan were referred to as *khwājatāshgān* meaning 'fellow slaves of the same master'. If Ghīyāth al-Dīn Tughluq had been a slave of Balban, he would have mentioned him instead of Jalāl al-Dīn Khaljī at his coronation. In the Tughluq era, there was a renewed dependence on Turkish *mamlūk*.[11] Thus, it can be inferred that although Ghīyāth al-Dīn Tughluq belonged to the nobility yet his family was newly emergent and not an old Delhi sultanate household.

Max Weber uses the example of Muḥammad b. Tughluq's reign to demonstrate the ideal type of patrimonial authority and sultanism in his work *Society and Economy*.[12] Many contemporary research works also describe the nature of authority under the Delhi sultanate as patrimonial authority, particularly keeping in view Muḥammad b. Tughluq. The present chapter approaches the question of authority versus power and evaluates the advantages and disadvantages of a patrimonial system.

Dynastic Change: Power versus Religion

As mentioned in the previous chapter, the dynastic change from the Khaljīs to the Tughluqs occurred as a result of explicit power play in which religion played only a nugatory role. While Ghāzī Malik received inappreciable help from the *umarā'* of the north-western provinces to whom he wrote letters,[13] the population of Delhi had been placated by the new Sultan Khusraw. The grandees were given important designations and many of the *umarā'* and notables including Niẓām al-Dīn Awliyā'[14] accepted royal grants.

It was a display of sheer power that brought Ghīyāth al-Dīn success. During his career as an 'Alā'ī *amīr*, Ghīyāth al-Dīn Tughluq made his reputation as a capable administrator and as a general fighting against the Mongols in Deopalpur. Despite the fact that Deopalpur was not a major city like Multan,[15] Ghīyāth al-Dīn Tughluq's administrative efficiency was well known beyond that immediate locality.[16] It is interesting to note that three founders of dynasties – Balban, Jalāl al-Dīn Khaljī and Ghīyāth al-Dīn Tughluq – were celebrated generals who had fought against the Mongols. Their success against the Mongols established their reputations as veteran military generals who earned the most important designations and strategic positions. Keeping in view 'Alā al-Dīn Khaljī's defence policy, it can be inferred that as the governor of Deopalpur Ghīyāth al-Dīn Tughluq must have been supplied with ample funds, arms and ammunitions by the centre in order to strengthen the north-western borders. The very survival of the Delhi sultanate depended on the successful defence of those borders.[17]

As the centre grew weak, a replacement would have emerged either from the centre, as was the case in the times of the progeny of Iltutmish, or from the nearest provinces where efficient military means existed. The Khaljī dynasty ended when their replacement in the capital the Baravarī clan of Gujarat took over. The nobility in the capital had lost will and cohesion in the wake of two successive purges by 'Alā al-Dīn and later Mubārak Shāh's advisor Niẓām al-Dīn to counter Khusraw Khān and dissent was only latent. Malik Fakhr al-Dīn Juna Khān (the future Sultan Muḥammad) was able to foster this dissent to his own ends. Moreover for northern governors, military efficiency, financial resources and a weak centre helped to catalyse this dynastic change.

Although Ghiyāth al-Dīn's rule was supported by the people from the north-west,[18] yet 'Alā al-Dīn Khaljī's *umarā'* who outlived the purges prevailed in the new set up,[19] as neither Mubārak Shāh nor Khusraw Shāh had significantly altered the administrative machinery.[20] During his last days, 'Alā al-Dīn chiefly relied upon his patrimonial staff and family. Since, his family had been eliminated, the patrimonial staff continued to serve even in this era.[21] Baranī's statement that the sultan took special care of the fellow 'Alā'ī *umarā'* and generally overlooked trivial faults strengthens this view.[22] The unprecedented persistence might have given unparallelled power to the nobility for interest aggregation and interest articulation.

The *Umarā'* of Ghiyāth al-Dīn Tughluq

Like his predecessors, on his accession to the throne Ghiyāth al-Dīn Tughluq ensured that his *umarā'* hailed from heterogeneous ethnic backgrounds and various interest groups. The Ghiyāthī nobility was predominantly composed of the sultan's family members and kinsmen, his patrimonial staff from his prior postings as an *amīr*, and the *umarā'* of 'Alā al-Dīn Khaljī and Quṭb al-Dīn Mubārak Shāh. Nonetheless, unlike Iltutmish, Balban and 'Alā al-Dīn Khaljī, the sultan was not able to nurture a nobility comprised of only his own patrimonial bureaucratic staff, a tactic crucial to establish effective, centralised rule.

The most important group of the sultan's *umarā'* were his kinsmen. None of the sultan's *umarā'* except his sons seems to have been elevated to the ranks of Khān; though, the relatives of the sultan were given important offices at the centre along with the charge of some territories in the provinces. Tughluq's son Malik Juna Khān [23] (the future Sultan Muḥammad) was designated as heir apparent and was bestowed with the title of Ulugh Khān. Baranī also mentions five other sons with the titles of Bahrām Khān, Mubarāk Khān, Nuṣrat Khān, Mas'ūd Khān and Maḥumad Khān although none of these sons appeared on the list of Muḥammad b. Tughluq's *umarā'*. The sultan's nephew, Ṣadr al-Dīn Arsalān, was raised to the rank of *nā'ib barbeg*. Another nephew, Bahā al-Dīn (his sister's son), was given the title of Garshāsp along with the rank of 'malik'. He was given the office of *diwān-i ariḍ-i mumālīk*. One of the sultan's sons-in-law Shādi Dāwar was also given the rank of 'malik' along with the office of *nā'ib -i diwān-i wizarāt*. The sultan's Mongol foster son was given the title of Tatar Khān and the governorship of Zafarabād.[24] From 'Afīf's account one can infer that the sultan's brother Rajab must have been given an important office as well. A slave of the sultan, Shihāb al-Dīn, was also given the titles of *malik* and Tāj-ul Mulk.[25]

Since Ghiyāth al-Dīn ascended the throne with the help of the elements from the north-west, it can be observed that he promoted officers from those parts.[26] The sultan greatly trusted his staff from Deopalpur and the people of the north-west. Yusuf, the sultan's *nā'ib* during his governorship at Deopalpur, was inducted in the central administration. Similarly, Burhān al-Dīn, a scholar cum civil officer, was appointed as the *kotwāl* of Delhi and given the title of 'Ālam Malik.[27]

Qwām al-Dīn, the son of 'Ālam Malik who had tutored Muḥammad b. Tughluq in calligraphy, was appointed as *wazīr* of Deogīr and held high positions even in Muḥammad b. Tughluq's reign.[28] Another son of 'Ālam Malik Niẓām al-Dīn, was conferred with the title of 'malik' and was a prominent noble. Malik 'Ali-yi Ḥaydar, an old companion of the sultan, was entrusted with the office of *wakīl-i dar*.[29] The Ghiyāthī army was mainly from the upper country (*iqlīm-i bālā*) and comprised warriors of different ethnicities including the Khokhars and Mongols.[30]

When Ghiyāth al-Dīn declared war over Khusraw, he enjoyed thin support from the 'Alā'ī and Quṭbī *umarā'*, although the sultanate-era historians portrayed the victory of Ghīyāth al-Dīn as a popular uprising in which the *umarā'* and the people supported him. Baranī, 'Isāmī and Amir Khusraw depicted the success of Ghīyāth al-Dīn against Khusraw as a triumph of Islam against idolatry.[31]'Isāmī maintains that Ghīyāth al-Dīn was supported by many 'Alā'ī and Quṭbī maliks;[32] however, we are unable to find details. *Tughluq Nāmā* and *Tārīkh-i Mubārak Shāhī* suggest that few of the provincial governors supported Ghiyāth al-Dīn.[33] The only *amīr* who supported him was Bahrām-i Aybā, *muqta'* of Uchh, whose father may have been one of Sultan 'Alā al-Dīn's boon companions (*nadīmān*).[34] He was given the title of Kushlü Khān and the governorship of the regions of Multan, Uchh and Sind (Swistān).[35] The *umarā'* obstructive to Tughluq were: Yaklakhī the governor of Samana who was ethnically an Indian; Malik Mughaltaī, the *amīr* of Multan; Muḥammad Shāh Lur at Swistān; and Malik Hushang at Jalōr. The governor of Multan and Samanā were eliminated by popular revolts and [36] none of these nobles were present in Ghīyāth al-Dīn's nobility. Although 'Ayn-al Mulk Multānī fought against Ghīyāth al-Dīn, he deserted Khusraw on the eve of the battle and retreated towards his *iqṭā'* of Dhar and Ujjain in Malwa.[37]

So well-grounded were the 'Alā'ī nobility in the provinces that the approximately four-year interregnum of the Quṭbī and Khusrawī era did not seriously damage the 'Alā'ī empire. The *umarā'* (with some exceptions) seem to have been faithful to the centre despite the uncertainty engendered by power struggles. The old Quṭbī and 'Alā'ī *umarā'* supported Khusraw. The *muqta'* of Chanderi supported the centre, and Khusraw sent Qutlugh the *amīr-i shikār* and Tulabugha Bughdā to counter the rebels in Sarsatī.[38] In the second round of the battle, when Khusraw came out of Delhi to counter Tughluq, he was accompanied by members of the old Quṭbī and 'Alā'ī nobility including Tulabugha Bughda, Tulabugha Nagwrī, Tegin, the *muqṭa'* of Awadh, Ikhtiyār al-Dīn Sunbul the *amīr hajib*, Kāfūrmuhrdār (the keeper of the seal), and Qabūlshihna-yi mandā (the supervisor of the market).[39] Thus, once Ghīyāth al-Dīn Tughluq had seized the throne by force, he took special care to appease the *umarā'* by maintaining them in their offices and offering rewards in the form of *iqṭā'*.[40] For example, Khwājah Hajjī was retained as *'āriḍ*,[41] and his brother Malik Ali was also retained in the nobility. 'Ayn al-Mulk Multanī remained governor of Malwa, though he does not seem to have endured the Tughluq era (this 'Ayn al-Mulk is to be distinguished from Ibn Mahrū),[42] who later bore the same title.

Ghīyāth al-Dīn was able to get rid of some of the 'Alā'ī notables including Temür, Tagīn and Kāfūr by sending them to a campaign in Warangal in 721/1321–1322 where many were killed on the battlefield. One Ubayd-i Hakīm was also mentioned as one of the boon companions of 'Alā al-Dīn, therefore it is difficult to dismiss the possibility that the Ubayd who allegedly started the revolt in Warangal was an 'Alā'ī *amīr*.[43] Nothing emerges in the sources to elucidate the sultan's motivation for this purge but it is impossible to dismiss the idea that these senior 'Alā'ī officers fell victim to a plot by the sultan.[44] It seems that the expeditions to Warangal and Talangana served two broader purposes: first, as Baranī states, after the death of 'Alā al-Dīn, military expeditions were necessary to deal with governors of distant provinces who had declared independence. Secondly, these expeditions displayed the power of the sultan in far-flung regions.[45] These expeditions were a customary practice for every sultan after his ascension to the throne.

During his four-year reign, the sultan is admired by Baranī for his efficient tax administration, reorganisation of army, fortifications, construction works and agrarian reforms. When the sultan ascended the throne he found the royal treasury empty and state records burnt by his predecessor; nevertheless, much of the wealth was recovered but it severed his relations with many notables including Niẓām al-Dīn Awaliyāh. Within a brief period, the sultan was able to annex Bengal and claim victories in Bihar. The sultan's armies defeated the Mongols who raided Delhi while he was away at Warangal.[46] According to Ibn Battūtah, during his campaign he grew weary of his heir Muḥammad and probably wanted to replace him with another son. Nevertheless, before he could reach the capital Muḥammad had him killed by constructing a fragile timber palace for his reception that crumbled when the elephants paraded outside.[47] The allegations of patricide are only unique to Ibn Battūtah and 'Isāmī's[48] account and despite the sultanate historian's portrayal of Muḥammad as a callous sultan, none of the other source charges him with murder.

Genius or Lunatic: Muḥammad b. Tughluq (725–52/1325–1351)

Muḥammad b. Tughluq's accession to power is unique in the history of the Delhi sultanate, as honouring of the will of a sultan in favour of his heir apparent was an unprecedented incident. Unlike with other sultans of Delhi there was no hostile event associated with his rise to power. He was enthroned in Tughluqabad and on the 40th day of his accession to the throne, he entered Delhi. The celebrations recorded by Baranī,[49] 'Iṣāmī[50] and Ibn Battūtah indicate enthronement as an event of unmatched munificence in which wealth was showered upon the population of Delhi in the form of gold and silver *tanka*s. The population of Delhi actively participated in the revelry as the sultan took his oath sitting on an elephant. Ibn Battūtah, who arrived in Delhi approximately eight years (733/1333) after this occurrence, reported that the extraordinary illumination of fireworks on this event blinded the queen mother.[51] It is interesting to note that after the rise of 'Alā al-Dīn Khaljī, we find every sultan lavishing large amounts of money at the time of their accession to the throne.

Muḥammad b. Tughluq's *Umarā'*

When he ascended the throne, Muḥammad b. Tughluq's position was far more secure vis-à-vis his nobility as compared to his father's position.[52] The links of Muḥammad b. Tughluq to the existing *umarā'* were probably well established since the reign of his father. He was an established military general who had served as an *amīr-i ākhūr* of the previous dynasty; he had served in 'Alā al-Dīn's campaign in Warangal.[53] The existing nobility had acknowledged him as the heir apparent and must have been inclined towards him because of his military prowess. Ghiyāth al-Dīn Tughluq's support base from Deopalpur and the regions of the north continued to support the new sultan.

Thus, nobles of Muḥammad b. Tughluq, like those of his father, consisted of his kinsmen, the grandees of the previous regime and his patrimonial staff.

Baranī provides a list of the nobles in the beginning of the narrative of Muḥammad, in which the brothers of the sultan, Maḥmūd Khān, Mubārak Khān and Nuṣrat Khān, are mentioned.[54] Before the end of Muḥammad's reign all of them disappeared furtively from the records.[55] While the brothers were not given such importance in this reign, the adopted sons of Ghiyāth al-Dīn enjoyed relatively higher positions. According to Ibn Battūtah, while the foster brother of the sultan, Prince Mubārak Khān, served as a judicial officer in this era,[56] the step-brother of the sultan, Prince Mas'ūd Khān, whose mother was a daughter of 'Alā al-Dīn Khaljī, was eliminated as he allegedly intrigued against the sultan.[57] Two years earlier his mother was stoned to death on charges of adultery.[58] This ignominious death must have neutralised Prince Mas'ūd Khān's claim to the throne, which was formidable due to his being descended from both Ghiyāth al-Dīn and 'Alā al-Dīn Khaljī. Although Prince Maḥmūd Khān is mentioned in the list of *umarā'* given in the beginning of the reign of Muḥammad b. Tughluq,[59] he was with Sultan Ghīyāth al-Dīn when the palace roof fell. When the rubble was removed, the sultan was found leaning over his favourite son, as if he had tried to save him from the calamity that lead to their deaths.[60] The foster sons of Tughluq held important positions under Muḥammad because they could not claim the throne for themselves. Bahrām Khān was given the region of Sonargaon. Similarly, although evicted from the administration due to a misunderstanding with the sultan, Tatar Malik was among the prominent *umarā'* of this reign.[61] According to Ibn Battūtah, Fīrūz (b. Rajab/ Tughluq) the cousin of the sultan was given the office of *barbeg*.[62]

On his enthronement, Muḥammad b. Tughluq promoted the *umarā'* of the previous regime, who had helped him to ascend the throne. Many of them belonged to the north-west.[63] Although, initially Muḥammad did not displace the grandees that had served under his father, with the passage of time he was able to replace many with his own patrimonial staff. Other notables including Bahā al-Dīn Garshāsp,[64] Kishlī Khān,[65] and Behrām-i Aybā[66] revolted against him and were immediately removed. There were some replacements among the ministerial posts; Malik Shādī Dawar, the brother-in-law of the sultan, was replaced with

Aḥmad b. Ayāz who acquired the *wazārāt* entitled Khwājah Jahānin in 732/1331–1332.[67]

The sultan took special care to introduce among his *umarā'* new elements who were dependent upon the sultan for their survival in the power structure. This new staff belonged to various ethnic groups that had no prior links to the echelons of power. These included émigrés,[68] Afghans, Mongols[69] and slaves. Although these groups had been part of the nobility under earlier sultans, under Muḥammad b. Tughluq 'base-born' native Indians were also given important positions among the *umarā'* for the first time.[70]

The political structure of the Delhi sultanate due to its pro-émigré character had been a haven for immigrants who came from deposed royal families, fortune hunters and mercenaries. These immigrants included Arabs, Central Asians, Afghans and Europeans. The sultan generously provided them with fiscal and financial support, encouraging an influx of immigrants from the western borders. One of the first things that Ibn Battūtah noticed in the Delhi sultanate was the sultan's regard for foreigners. Foreigners were addressed as *azīz*[71] instead of *gharīb*,[72] and many of the sultan's officers, including judges and administrators, were foreigners.[73] Ibn Battūtah mentions *amīr*s from Khorasan among Muḥammad's important officers.[74] The sultan also had matrimonial links with these foreigners and many of his sons-in-law were foreigners.[75] The historical accounts of this era suggest that the sultan's army comprised Turks, Afghans, Khorasanis, Persians and people from Khitān. Ibn Battūtah himself is an example of such fortune hunters who were incorporated in the royal administrative staff and given the lucrative position of *qāḍī* of Delhi despite his inability to understand Persian. The fiscal favours bestowed by the sultan were most extraordinary.[76] The émigrés from west and north-west India were promoted and through them the sultan stayed informed about the neighbouring courts. The Mongols[77] that came to the court of the sultan included the *qāḍī* of Temürid ethnic stock, Khudāwandzādah Qiwām al-Dīn; his cousin Ghiyāth al-Dīn; Qabtagha and Aḥmad-i Iqbāl; Bahrām, *malik* of Ghazna; and two grandees from Transoxania.[78] Similarly, around 733/1332–1333, Niẓām al-Dīn, a member of the former ruling dynasty of Qays in the Persian Gulf, arrived at Muḥammad's court, where he struggled two years in vain to secure the sultan's help.[79] A few years later, Ibn Battūtah observed that and Ilkhānid Prince Hājjī Keun, the brother of the Ilkhān Mūsā, was the sultan's guest; the prince returned to south-west Persia in 743/1342 and was killed while endeavouring to occupy Shabankarā.[80] According to Ibn Battūtah, the sultan sent his agents into the Persian Gulf in order to recruit Arabs, who were given extreme respect in the Delhi sultanate, demonstrated by their common title 'sayyids'.[81]

Baranī disapproved of Muḥammad b. Tughluq's support for native Indians, holding that base-born people were untrustworthy.[82] Nevertheless, these people were given high positions, governorships and ministerial ranks on an unprecedented scale. Ibn Battūtah mentions Ratan, an accomplished person in regard to calculation and writing, who was given the charge of fiscal administration of Sind.[83] Dhārā was designated as *nā'ib wazīr* to Dōlatabād (earlier mentioned as Deogīr) around 745/1344–1245; however, he was unable to maintain power resulting in the rise of the Bahmāinī dynasty. According to Baranī, Najīb, a musician of obscure origin, was given the charge of Multan, Gujarat and Badaun, while another, Pirā Mālī (the gardener), was entrusted with the charge of *diwān-i wizārāt* and was raised above the *malik*s, *wālī*s, *muqṭa*'s and senior grandees. Azīz Khummār (the vintner) was endowed with the governorship of Malwa.[84] Samara Singh was appointed as the ruler of Tilang by the sultan.[85] Maqbul, the slave of Aḥmad Ayāz, was given the office of assistant governor of Gujarat in which capacity he looked after regional matters in the absence of his master.[86] There are other native Hindus mentioned in Baranī's account as lowly persons, along with their professions: Fīrūz the barber, Nanak the weaver, Ladhā the gardener, Mankā the cook, Mas 'ūd Kumhār the liquor brewer and Azīz the potter.[87] While many of them were converted Muslims, it was to Baranī's horror that some were non-Muslims as well – such as Bhirān, auditor (*mutasarrif*) at Gulbaragā.[88]

Muḥammad b. Tughluq encouraged the institution of slavery. The sultan had *mamlūk*s numbering in the thousands. According to Ibn Battūtah, 4,000 slaves were stationed in Amroha alone.[89] Al-'Umrī reported that the sultan's slaves numbered 20,000.[90] His personal collection of slaves was multi-ethnic, comprising elements of Indian, African and Turkish origins. When he was the crown prince, his father Ghiyāth al-Dīn disapproved of his practice of amassing Turkish slaves.[91] Muḥammad b. Tughluq employed slaves in the court for the purposes of security and pageantry.[92] During his reign, many amongst the slaves rose to high positions. These slaves had been both purchased and captives of war, with many said to be *mamlūks*[93] employed in military services. However, there is no evidence indicating extensive military training.[94]

The sultan had matrimonial links with some slaves as well. Ibn Battūtah mentions a Turk slave commander Imād ul-Mulk Sirtīz who was stationed in Swistān (Sind). Sirtīz received the traveller on his arrival at the Delhi sultanate's borders in Sind. This slave was the son-in-law of the sultan, *amīr* of Sind and Bakshī in the army. He was a strict administrator mentioned in the traveller's account as suppressing an insurgency in Swistān.[95] Around 748/1348, Sirtīz died while subduing the insurrection of Hasan Kankoī Bahmanī in the Deccan.[96]

Many among the most respected *umarā'* of Sultan Muḥammad were originally slaves. Malik Qabūl, a royal slave and confidante, was probably Indian.[97] Qiwām al-Mulk Maqbūl (later Khān Jahān), the governor of Multan and Tilang, was a slave as well.[98] He had been a Brahman (by the name Kannū) taken as a prisoner of war during the conquest of Tilang in 721/1322.[99] He entered the service of the sultan and converted to Islam. He was named Maqbūl and subsequently given the title of Qiwām al-Mulk. Although he did not know official Persian, his administrative genius[100] attracted the approval of Muḥammad, who appointed him the governor of Multan on the suppression of Kushlü Khān's rising in 727/1327–1328.[101] He also governed Tilang until its revolt in 736/1336. Maqbūl played an important role in the next reign.[102] Badr al-Habashī the governor at 'Alāpūr was a black slave. Other slaves who were probably Turks included: Imād al-Mulk Sirtīz, the *'āriḍ* and governor of Multan; Malik Qiran Safdar Malik Sultānī; and Taghai who later revolted in Gujarat at the end of Muḥammad's reign.[103]

The sultan is reported to have received an emissary from the Chinese Emperor Sūntī, better known as Tōgān Temür. The purpose of this emissary was to obtain permission of the sultan to build a temple in Qarachil mountains near Sambhal, a popular location for pilgrimage among the Chinese. The Emperor Sūntī sent the sultan lavish gifts including 100 slaves of both sexes. Sultan Muḥammad accepted the request, with an imposition of *jazyā* (poll tax). In response to the emissary, the sultan sent a delegation of his own, accompanied by gifts that included 100 male slaves, 100 female slaves, and

15 eunuchs,[104] thus becoming the only Delhi sultan to have diplomatic relations with the far east.

The surveillance and espionage system of the sultan was one of the most notable features of his rule. He increased the centralisation of his rule by keeping the patrimonial staff under strict surveillance through espionage and brutally punished those whom he suspected of having plotted conspiracies. The sultan employed royal slaves in the households of the *umarā'* tasked with reporting to the authority domestic and political activities.[105] In several instances these espionage networks assisted the sultan in uncovering powerful conspiracies aimed to oust him. According to Ibn Battūtah, during a drought in Delhi, 'Aynul-Mulk, the governor of Awadh, Zafarābād and Lucknow decided to overthrow the sultan. He had an ample store of provisions that he was supplying to the sultan. His clandestine plan was almost underway when a slave woman reported the plot to royal spies. The conspiracy having been disclosed, the sultan overcame the rebels after a brief skirmish.[106] In another case, Sayyid Ibrāhīm, the keeper of royal pen and stationary and governor of Hansi and Sarsā, rebelled when it was rumoured that the sultan had died while returning to Dolatābād from an expedition. When accounts of the sultan's death proved to be false, he aborted his plan to revolt. After two and a half years, one of his slaves revealed Ibrāhīm's rebellious intentions to the sultan; he was subsequently tortured to death.[107] Ibn Battūtah described the efficient *barīd* system (postal system and domestic intelligence service) under the sultan scrupulously that was the primary constituent of espionage system.[108]

Baranī refers to *diwān-i sīyāsat* where persons alleged to have conspired against the state were interrogated, tortured to confess, and subsequently punished.[109] When Ibn Battūtah entered Multan he found an efficient spy system in the regions of Sind. On his arrival to the bank of the river Sind, his presence was reported to Quṭb ul-Mulk, the ruler of Multan.[110] Similarly, the traveller mentions that, in the absence of the sultan from Delhi, the activities were kept under strict surveillance. When the sultan came back from his campaigns he heard reports of the activities of the *umarā'* and dismissed those involved in questionable activities; Ibn Battūtah was one of those stripped of his position after the sultan's return.[111] Masālik al-Absār mentions that spies were called *munhin*.[112] The sultan used to dismiss, punish and kill provincial governors if he became apprehensive of their designs. Ibn Battūtah writes regarding spy networks:

> it is the tradition of the sultans of Hindustan that, in the household of every important or less important *amīr*, slaves of the sultan are appointed, who update the sultan about the *amīr*. The female slaves report to the sweepers, who inform to the investigation officers.[113]

Muḥammad b. Tughluq killed an *amīr* when a chambermaid reported the preceding night's squabble between an *amīr* and his wife.[114] Similarly, a slave of an *amīr* named 'Ayn al-Mulk reported his treason to the sultan.[115] The espionage system of the sultan was efficient in the centre, its suburbs and other important cities. Provincial governors, their staff and important persons in the distant areas were also kept under surveillance.

Recruitments, Promotions and Dismissals

Muḥammad b. Tughluq's reign spans nearly 25 years. In this era, many appointments and dismissals took place. The sultan preferred an ethnically and religiously diverse powerbase, among which he nurtured trust-based loyalties. In order to understand training, promotion patterns and the multiple spheres of responsibilities of the sultan's servants, the case of Aḥmad b. Ayāz is enlightening. According to a hagiographic source, the architect Aḥmad b. Ayāz was the disciple of Niẓām al-Dīn Awliya'.[116] Ibn Battūtah blames Aḥmad b. Ayāz for the death of the sultan Ghiyāth al-Dīn, asserting that he built the roof with technical flaws that led to the collapse of the building.[117] 'Iṣāmī's content suggests a similar theory.[118] Aḥmad b. Ayāz stood among the confidantes of the sultan before the time of his enthronement.[119] While the sultan did not appoint Aḥmad on *wāzārāt* immediately after his ascension to the throne, he appointed Aḥmad *wazīr* in 732/1331–1332 with the title of Khwājah Jahān.[120] He can be identified on a number of occasions leading military forces against rebels.[121] Khwājah Jahān seems to have been among the *umarā'* who survived Muḥammad b. Tughluq's reign. When Muḥammad b. Tughluq left Delhi, he entrusted authority over the capital to Khwājah Jahān, his cousin Fīrūz and Malik

Qabul Khilāfatī (also known as Malik Kabīr).[122] His role as a kingmaker during the transfer of power marked his end, since he opposed Fīrūz Shāh's accession.

The cases of Ibn Battūtah and Baranī shed light on the nature of promotions and dismissals from the government. Regarding Baranī, we know that he was among the boon companions of the sultan, who served him for seven or eight years before he fell from favour and was dismissed. Until the time of Fīrūz Shāh, this man remained in a state of destitution.[123] Similarly, we know that Ibn Battūtah entered Delhi around 733/1333. Due to the sultan's privileged treatment of foreigners, Muslims in general and Arabs in particular, he was able to obtain the office of *qāḍī* of Delhi. On the suspicion of interacting with one Sufi Sheikh Shihāb al-Dīn Jām, who had already fallen from sultan's favour, he was dismissed and feared for his life.[124] Later the sultan offered to restore him. Although he begged to be excused from the offer, the sultan gave him the responsibility to convey a message to the Chinese emperor.[125] The very incident conveys the instability of the system. The system was such that it gave advantage to anyone, be it the sultan or a strong faction of *umarā'*, who possessed the power to appoint and dismiss without any professional and cogent reasons. Ibn Battūtah discussed the cases of many who rose in and fell from the sultan's favour. While the sultan favoured his *umarā'* with largesse in the form of one-time gifts of cash, kind and *iqtā*'s, he also sponsored their day-to-day expenditures and paid off their debts. He oversaw matrimonial decisions[126] and kept a close eye on their social activities.[127] The sultan considered it his right to kill and penalise those who offended him.[128] There was general resentment and aversion against the sultan's viciousness but none of the several rebellions[129] was powerful enough to remove the sultan from office.

Patronage of heterogeneous groups of *umarā'* has been a time-tested advice found in multiple mirrors to princes that were written before the foundation of the Delhi sultanate was laid. Niẓām-al Mulk Tusī (485/1092) recommends this in *Sīyāsatnāmah* as an efficient means to keep *umarā'* mutually distrustful, thus curtailing their ability to socialise, build alliances and plot conspiracies.[130] A weak, divided and mutually hostile nobility helped the sultan centralise his power. Furthermore, a patrimonial bureaucratic structure enabled the sultan to make unilateral decisions about fiscal policy, recruitment and dismissals.

Baranī's statements may allude to the enmity between the immigrants and the native born (known as *razīls*) in the power structure. Similarly, Ibn Battūtah asserts that Muḥammad's preferential treatment of foreigners, and specifically of Khorasanīs, generated contempt among the existing nobility as well.[131] The sultan not only had lifted the two-century ban on Shī'is from Iraq and Arab lands entering the Delhi sultanate but also occasionally treated these foreigners with favour. They were mainly posted in Deccan but many of them settled down in Delhi.[132] Despite this mutual distrust there was an ever-increasing presence of the native Hindus in the power structure; for instance, Kannū Brahman, who was enslaved during the conquest of Tilang in 721/1322.[133] He was named Maqbūl after his conversion to Islam when he entered the royal service.[134] Although he was not literate, his discipline and strictness in collecting revenue from the *umarā'* entitled him to the highest ranks of the Delhi sultanate. He was later given the title of Qiwām al-Mulk.[135] In 728/1327–1328, when the sultan suppressed the rebellions of Kushlü Khān, he was assigned the regions of Multan.[136] Later he was transferred to Tilang until its revolt in 736/1336[137] and soon afterward he was appointed as deputy to the *wazīr* Khwājah Jahān Ahmed b. Ayāz.[138] Maqbul rose to a position of eminence under the next sultan and was made the *wazīr* of the empire, a designation he kept until the end of his life.[139] Later, his son, titled as Khwājah Jahān, was responsible for vicious fighting among the progeny and slaves of Fīrūz Shāh.[140] However, despite the obvious mutual resentment social interaction among the classes was not as restricted as it may have first appeared. For example, Ibn Battūtah befriended *muhrdār*, Abū Muslim, one of the many sons of the Rāi' of Kampila whom Muḥammad had maintained at his court after the conquest of that territory.

No records of the specific criteria for appointment to Muḥammad's administration are available. However, the appointments of Ibn Battūtah, Ratan and Kannū Brahman indicate that the sultan was ready to employable-minded people from any group of society. Ratan was an expert in mathematics and writing,[141] and Kannū Brahman was an able tax collector.[142] Although Ibn Battūtah was not familiar with Persian and could only communicate in Arabic, he was appointed as a judge and assisted the sultan with translations.[143]

Although officers rose quickly, their fall could be equally precipitous. Baranī, 'Iṣāmī and Ibn Battūtah mention the sultan's violent tendencies.[144] All three of the authors agreed that although the sultan initially had been humane in his treatment of his *umarā'*, when his projects started failing, he became excessively paranoid and hostile. Any hint of conspiracy or a disagreement led to capital punishment administered in a gruesome manner. Ibn Battūtah mentions his own anxiety, manifest in endless prayers and fasting, to avoid the wrath of the sultan, who suspected he had met with Sheikh Shihāb al-Dīn Jām in his absence.[145] According to Ibn Battūtah, it was a rare day that murdered criminals were not showcased on the castle gates; hundreds of men in shackles were brought forward every day.[146] Some were killed and others were tortured. On Friday, the living prisoners were allowed to take rest and bathe. Dead bodies were laid on the gates until the officers appointed could dispose of them.[147] Therefore, many among the relatives of the dead bribed the officers in order to take the corpses. The killings of Sheikh Shihāb, his brother Mas'ūd Khān and stepmother, who was a daughter of 'Alā al-Dīn,[148] Afif al-Dīn Kashānī, the two Maulvīs of Sind, Sheikh Hūd, and Ḥaider Qalandārī were a few examples of his brutal murders, animated by suspicion.[149]

Other instances showed that even a noble's fall from grace was not necessarily permanent. In one example, the sultan had married his sister to an Arab named Saif al-Dīn Ghada b. Hatba b. Mahna who received both respect and office. After sometime, he was deposed on the pretext of unstable behaviour. Four years later, he was restored to office and once again came into favour.[150] Above all, the sultan's whims ruled the lives and deaths of his servants.

Hierarchy

Despite the different levels of the officers and variance in their pay as mentioned by al-'Umarī, we are unable to find any regular hierarchy among them. Table 8.1 shows some examples of recorded salaries assigned to given ranks.

Similarly, unlike 'Alā al-Dīn Khaljī who had subsidised necessities of life for his army through his price control policy but had paid in cash, Muḥammad b. Tughluq nurtured a sense of patrimony in his army by paying his soldiers in both cash and kind. The army officers were assigned *iqṭā'* in lieu of a cash salary. However, the soldiers and Turkish slaves were paid a salary by the royal exchequer. Every slave of the sultan

Table 8.1 Salary in the Time of Muḥammad b. Tughluq[151]

Rank	Salary in *Tankās*
Khān	200,000
Malik	50,000 to 60,000
Amīr	30,000 to 40,000
Isfahla	20,000
Soldier	1,000 to 10,000
Turkish slaves	1,000 to 5,000

received one *maund* of wheat and rice, along with his monthly salary. Aside from this, he received three *seers* of meat with other necessary cooking essentials daily. He was also paid ten silver *tankās* every month and received four suits of clothes every year.[152]

Despite being profligate, the sultan was extraordinarily mistrusting and hostile as well. Owing to his surveillance and his harsh punishments administered to dissenters the sultan earned a reputation of being extremely callous. He seems to have considered such treatment necessary to rule.[153] It is undeniable that he had been exceedingly generous; this was one reason his treasury had bled dry, forcing him to devise a token currency.[154] In his interview with Baranī, his view seems to be that of a ruler for whom coercion was the only means to power.[155] The capriciousness of the sultan made insecurity in terms of personal safety and livelihood the norm for the people of his era. While many among the common people, who had little to lose except their lives, must have fled;[156] others might have resorted to prayers and reclusiveness as Ibn Battūtah did.[157] Still others, among them the strong *amīrs*, rebelled as the last option.[158] After coming back to Delhi after the unsuccessful experience of Dolatābād (earlier Deōgīr), the sultan made an additional effort to rehabilitate the villages of Doab, the population of which had decreased due to his harsh taxation policies and undue strictness.[159] The uprising of 'Ayn al-Mulk b. Mahrū in Awadh may be taken as a case study of the *umarā'* rebellions under Muḥammad. The *amīr* had ruled this principality with great efficiency and faithfulness to the centre. Owing to his good administration, Ibn Mahrū had an ample supply of edibles in his region. In times of famine in some of the regions of north India, he supplied goods and food from Awadh to Sargadwarī and Delhi.

The reduced amount of monetary output of Deccan province, in those days, led the sultan to suspect that his tutor and governor Qutlugh Khān's officials were misappropriating money. The sultan, keeping in view the administrative efficiency of Ibn Mahrū, decided to appoint him to Deccan as governor, a far wealthier province than Awadh where he could extract more revenue through the *amīr*.[160] The sultan was also disquieted by the fact that the residents of Delhi were migrating towards Awadh, demanding their return. Ibn Mahrū understood this as a manoeuvre of the sultan to deprive him of his powerbase. Keeping in view the sultan's capriciousness, and the nature of punishments he could inflict over his *umarā'*, Ibn Mahrū and his brothers rebelled. The forces of the rebels were no match for those of the sultan, and were therefore pulverised. Ibn Mahrū's brothers were killed in the fight or disappeared. Ibn Mahrū was taken as prisoner, but since he was too valuable to be executed he was soon restored to favour.[161] We find him appointed as governor of Multan at the time of Muḥammad's final campaign against the rebel Taghai and his Sumra allies in Sind;[162] Ibn Mahrū then again rose in rebellion and was killed.[163]

The Empire of Muḥammad b. Tughluq

During the times of Muḥammad b. Tughluq, the sultanate's territorial expansion reached its zenith. The sultanate stretched from the regions of Dāvār Samundrā and Mabar in the south to Multan and Lahore in the north. *Masālikal-Abṣār* provides a list of the 23 provinces.[164]

Al-'Umarī claims to have obtained the list from an administrator from Malwa,[165] Although Baranī's list is generic, there is a consensus amongst the authors. Ibn Battūtah's travels inform us that the sultan of Delhi was feared even in the islands of the Maldives.[166] Despite the detailed account of his reign in multiple historical sources, few details are available about patchy fiscal administration or rebellions.

Much that we know about the nature of fiscal administration in the Delhi sultanate comes from Baranī. However, the details that Baranī provides are few. He mentions that Muḥammad b. Tughluq tried to bring those areas under a unitary system of administration. The sultan had assigned trusted servants the duty to collect taxes of some regions.[167] He had the ability to appoint, transfer and kill the officers who disappointed him.[168] Except for the offices of *wazīr* and *nā'ib wazīr* and some other offices, no information about the regions is available. Baranī concentrates on his six policies, two among which (expeditions to Iraq, Khorasan and Qarachil, and maintaining a large-scale army) were related to territorial expansion.[169]

At the beginning of Muḥammad's reign, the territorial boundaries of the Khaljī and Tughluq empire were nearly similar but the sultan was able to add new regions to his empire.[170] Nevertheless, the sultan's expansionist plans and policies financially devastated the core regions of the khalisā (crown land) and areas at the north-western borders.[171] The Doab region was destroyed due to over-taxation;[172] the region of Delhi was deserted; and the *umarā'* of Swistān region rebelled.[173] The peripheral regions of the sultanate started throwing off the shackles of the centre and the regions such as Bengal, Warangal and Deccan were lost forever.[174] The geographical extent of the sultanate was too great for a single monarch to rule. While the transfer of the capital might have retained central control, the sultan's lack of trust in his *umarā'* prevented his effective delegation of that authority.[175] The absence of any stable horizontal and vertical hierarchy in the times of Muḥammad b. Tughluq rendered his centralisation of power unsustainable.

The Social Base of the Sultan: Drought, Displacement of Populations and a Currency Fiasco

Bad administration in the core regions led to a drought, which must have fostered resentment against the sultan among the cultivators and the residents of the core regions. Around 732/1332, three harsh revenue demands led to a widespread revolt in the Doab region. People burned their harvests, drove off their livestock and fled to the forest areas.[176] Initially the sultan ordered his *shiqqdarān* (revenue officers) and *fawjdarān* (military commanders) to pillage the refractory principalities; later the sultan personally attacked the regions of Baran and Kol.[177] He also embarked upon expeditions to the regions of Kannauj and Dalmaw in 734/1334.[178] The heavy taxation thus led to a population decrease in the Doab region and a drought ensued that lasted for seven years.[179]

The drought affected the regions from Doab to eastern Punjab and from Delhi to the boundaries of Awadh.[180] After returning from his campaigns the sultan attempted to provide relief through supplying grain and encouraging cultivators; however his efforts did not bear fruit.[181] The sultan also plundered the region of Katihar in order to obtain grain but the supplies provided little help.[182] He then allowed the residents of Delhi to migrate to the region of Awadh in order to find food. The sultan himself stayed in an area of Saragadwarī on the bank of Ganges for two years instead of Delhi.[183] He also extended generous monetary grants to the cultivators and the landlords for restoring agriculture.[184]

Although Muḥammad b. Tughluq was said to be 'the prince of the moneyers', his project of token currency benefited forgers more than it did the government. The failed project led to a depletion of currency and resulted in a substantial surge in inflation. According to Peter Jackson, token currency produced a nearly fivefold rise in prices.[185] The token currency was disaster-prone, requiring reimbursement of actual currency, which led to greater resentment in the core regions.

The Empire Crumbles

Bengal

According to Masālik al-Abṣār, the empire of Sultan Muḥammad b. Tughluq was so vast that it required three years to cover it by an ordinary journey.[186] During the initial years the sultan received regular revenue from the provinces and *iqṭā'*. From 734/1334 onwards administrative blunders of the sultan spurred a wave of revolts in more distant provinces, notably those in Mabar, Bengal and Tilang.[187] The revolt of Sayyid Jalāl al-Dīn Hussayn, the *kotwāl* of Madura, who assumed the title of Sultan Jalāl al-Dīn Ahsān Shāh, was probably the first and occurred in *c.*734/1333–1334. Muḥammad's representatives were killed, and the troops supposedly garrisoning the province did nothing.[188] This crisis was closely followed by the loss of Bengal. Fakhr al-Dīn (also known as Fakhra) was the former *silahdār* (armour-bearer) of the sultan's adopted brother Bahrām Khān, and had already made an unsuccessful bid to seize power at Sonargaun after his master's death. Qadr Khān, Muḥammad's representative at Lakhnawatī checked the uprising but not long afterwards a prolonged struggle broke out for control of the province. First Qadr Khān's troops mutinied, slew their leader and transferred their loyalty to the rebel Fakhr al-Dīn, who established his residence at Sonargaun. Then Qadr Khān's former *'āriḍ*, 'Alī Mubārak, at the head of loyalist troops, killed Fakhr al-Dīn's lieutenant at Lakhnawatī. When the sultan proved unable to comply with his request, a new governor was dispatched from Delhi, and 'Alī Mubārak found himself obliged to assume the royal title himself as Sultan 'Alā al-Dīn 'Alī Shāh in order to rally support against the hostile activities of Fakhr al-Dīn. In the early 1340s, Ilyas Hajji, a third candidate for sovereignty, overthrew 'Alī Shāh and in the 1350s overthrew Fakhr al-Dīn's son and successor, Ikhtiyar al-Dīn Ghāzī Shāh. He was a former *chākir* (retainer) of 'Alī Mubārak, and ruled as Sultan Shams al-Dīn.[189] Like 'Alī Shāh, Ilyas seems to have recognised the authority of Delhi, since a *farmān* of Muḥammad's successor Fīrūz Shāh would later claim that he had remained submissive until after Muḥammad's death.[190]

It may have been the presence of actively loyal troops in Bengal that induced Muḥammad to give priority to the suppression of Aḥsan Shāh in Mabar. With a sizeable army, he moved towards the south in 735/1334–1335 and passed through the Deccan. Nevertheless, on its arrival in Tilang, the army was struck by some kind of *wabā* (epidemic), and the sultan was obliged to retreat. He fell gravely ill when he reached Dolatābād, recovering only after his return to Delhi. That the campaign had been a major disaster was apparent to Ibn Battūtah, who dates the falling-away of outlying provinces after this incident.[191] The failure to recover Mabar gave the signal to the other potential dissidents, and rumours of Muḥammad's death started circulating widely. Already, as the sultan marched southwards, one of his officers, Tāj al-Dīn Hoshang (the son of Kamāl al-Dīn Gurg) *muqṭa'* of Hansi, fled to the Vindhyas and thence into the Konkan region; Qutlugh Khān, Muḥammad's old tutor and governor of the Deccan, rebelled but was eventually pardoned and restored.[192]

Sahu's Rebellion in Punjab

While the sultan was busy in the south, the north-western region rose in rebellion. Around the same time a Mongol commander named Hulechu occupied Lahore in alliance with the Khokhar chief Gūl Chand, the one-time ally of Muḥammad's father; the rebels were defeated and the city retaken by the *wazīr* Khwājah Jahān.[193] The seizure of Multan by the rebel Afghan chief Shāhu, was a formidable challenge that awaited the sultan in the western Punjab. Muḥammad, who had now returned to Delhi, viewed this revolt as sufficiently threatening to warrant dealing with it directly; but Shāhū fled upon his approach and sent a message of submission.[194]

South is Lost

More serious were the loss of Kampila (present northern Karnataka), which now became the nucleus of the kingdom of Vijayanagara, and an uprising in Tilang where the governor, Malik Maqbūl, was expelled by Nayak and fled to Delhi.[195] The loss of Tilang, the province the conquest of which during the previous reign had been Muḥammad's personal achievement, dealt an especially severe blow to him. He is said to have wanted to launch an expedition to recover it, but was prevented from doing so because of the famine.[196] At this stage Muḥammad's military strength had depleted noticeably. If 'Iṣāmī is to be trusted, half the army commanders and a third of the troops perished in the *wabā* (epidemic)[197] and the Qarachil (Kumaon hills) campaign had gravely weakened the army of the Delhi sultanate.[198] Both these quagmires – a heavy reduction in the number of troops and a considerable loss of revenue owing to a decline in cultivation – bedevilled Muḥammad's government for several years to come and he was unable to rebuild the army.

The above-mentioned revolts reflect opportunistic responses to a prolonged crisis, whether on the part of disaffected *amīr*s or by Hindu elements on the periphery of the Delhi sultanate. However, the ineffectiveness of these rebellions indicates evolution in the sultanate power dynamics as now there was a direct link between the imperial treasury and the ordinary trooper. The *amīr*s had lost the capacity to bind troops to their own interests with *iqṭā'* grants from their assignments, which were intended exclusively for their personal maintenance.[199] In addition, Ibn Battūtah reveals that the military command had become completely separate from the fiscal administration of the *iqṭā*'s, so that within the territory of Amroha, for instance, a *wālī al-kharāj*, responsible directly to the sultan, was found alongside the *amīr*.[200] These assaults on the position of provincial commanders were one factor underlying the revolts in Gujarat and the Deccan that plagued the sultan's last years.[201]

The loss of revenue accompanying the secession of a number of major provinces also had an insidious effect of increasing pressure on Muḥammad to demand larger sums from the regions that remained loyal. Officers who had entered into contracts for the farming of revenue transmitted unrealistically high sums to the sultan. Ibn Battūtah was told of a Hindu who contracted to farm the revenues of the entire Deccan province for 17 *crores* (170,000,000 *tankā*s), but was unable to meet his obligations and was flayed alive on Muḥammad's orders.[202] Incidents such as these must have instilled a fear of failing to meet financial commitments to the sultan. The impossibility of supplying the government's needs in this fashion engendered rebellion by hitherto loyal servitors. Two uprisings, which occurred during Muḥammad's stay at Sargadwarī, fell into this category. Niẓām Mian, who farmed the revenues of Kara, and Shihāb Sultānī, styled Nuṣrat Khān, who had undertaken to extract one *crores* (10,000,000 *tankā*s) from Bidar and its *iqṭā'* over three years, were both pushed to rebel by their failure to raise the sums promised. Nuṣrat Khān is said to have been unable to recover even a third or a quarter of the amount of his promised revenue. The governor of Awadh, 'Ayn al-Mulk B. Mahrū, and his brothers, snuffed out Niẓām Mian's feeble bid for independence. He then rose in rebellion with the troops from Dolatābād but was eventually persuaded by Qutlugh Khān to surrender under a guarantee of safe conduit.[203]

At the death of Muḥammad b. Tughluq in 751/1351, his *wazīr* Khwājah Jahān Aḥmad b. Ayāz enthroned a son of the late sultan in Delhi. At this time the late sultan's cousin, Fīrūz Shāh, was attempting to capture the capital. The balance of power shifted in favour of Fīrūz Shāh when the slave *nā'ib wazīr* Qwām al-Mulk Maqbūl Khān Jāhān switched sides and joined him. Fīrūz consequently took over the capital and Khān Jāhān was rewarded by an appointment to *wazīr* in the new administration.[204]

Fīrūz Shāh (751–789/1351–1388) and his Patrimonial Staff

Free Elements

Like his predecessors, the *umarā'* of Fīrūz Shāh were ethnically heterogeneous and belonged to multiple social groups ranging from *'ulāmā'* to slaves, and had old and new elements. During the transition, the revolt of Aḥmad b. Ayāz resulted in a conflict that divided the *umarā'* into two groups.[205] Aḥmad b. Ayāz lost after his supporters deserted him. Baranī states that unlike in previous reigns, in this era bloodshed was avoided and only a few among the protagonists of this revolt, including Aḥmad Ayāz, Nathu Sudhal, Ḥasan, Ḥasām Adhung and two slaves of Aḥmad Ayāz's son, were executed, while their families were spared.[206] Ahmed Ayāz's son Husayn later served the sultan and married his daughter.[207] The old noble families were retained on their previous honour.[208] Nevertheless, the nobility of Fīrūz Shāh had fewer officers of

Sultan Muḥammad. A comparison of the list of *umarā'*, provided in the beginning of the reigns of Muḥammad and Fīrūz Shāh, reveals that except for Tatar Khān none of the chief *amīrs* of the previous sultan is included on the list of the new sultan.[209] This discontinuity was primarily due to two causes. Firstly, many of the *umarā'* had failed to outlive the 25-year reign of Muḥammad. Secondly, the punishments of Muḥammad and the risks of warfare must have become a mechanism of attrition for the unwanted elements of the old *umarā'*. Thus by the end of the reign of Muḥammad the composition of the ruling class had changed drastically. Fīrūz Shāh, who himself had worked under Ghiyāth al-Dīn and Muḥammad as an important *amīr*, must have nurtured his trusted staff over a period of thirty years. These *umarā'* became an important part of Fīrūz Shāhī ruling elite.

The free *umarā'* of Fīrūz Shāh included: Malikzādah Fīrūz, the son of Tāj al-Dīn Turk, who had served Ghiyāth al-Dīn Tughluq. This *amīr* held the new *shiqq* of Fīrūzpūr.[210] According to a seventeenth-century historian of Gujarat, Sadharan (renamed as Wajih al-Mulk), the ancestor of the independent sultans of Gujarat was the brother of one of Fīrūz Shāh's wives; he had accompanied the sultan to Delhi and adopted Islam.[211] By this time, leading figures among the local princes enjoyed a place at court. After his campaign against Damrila, the sultan took its princes, Jām and his brother Banbhina, back to Delhi.[212] By his death Uddharan, brother of the Tomara Rāi' of Gwalior, and Sumer, the Chawhān Rāi' of Etawa, were both in attendance.[213] Zafar Khān (II), the *muqṭa'* of Gujarat,[214] was the son and successor of Zafar Khān (I), whose full name, Tāj al-Dīn Muḥammad Lur Farsi, indicated that his family probably came from south-west Persia.[215] The free *maliks* also comprised a group of Afghan *amīrs*: Malik Bayyu, *muqṭa'* of Bihar; Malik Khaṭṭāb, appointed to the *shiqq* of Sambhal in 782/1380; and Malik Muḥammad Shāh, *muqṭa'* of Tughluqpūr in Etawa.[216] Indian converts related to the sultan by marriage also found a place in the ranks of the elite.

It is also believed that the *'ulāmā'* played an important role in the enthronement of Fīrūz Shāh.[217] Therefore, the sultan took special care to include the *'ulāmā'* among his *umarā'*. The first person mentioned in the list of *umarā'* as given by Baranī is Ṣadr us-Ṣudur Saiyid Jalāl al-Dīn Karamānī;[218] several other *'ulamā'*, including Sheikh Farīd al-Dīn, Sheikh Baha al-Dīn, Sheikh Niẓam al-Dīn, Sheik Rukn al-Dīn and Sheik Jamal al-Dīn Uchhī, were given land, villages and gardens as grants.[219]

Fīrūz Shāh's sons and other kinsmen also seem to have been the prime beneficiaries of the new government.[220] An associate of Aḥmad b. Ayāz, Ā'ẓam Malik Shaykhzadah Bistāmī, had been banished from Fīrūz Shāh's territory initially but he was later forgiven when he reappeared with a caliphate robe. This *amīr* was given the title of Ā'ẓam Khān.[221] We also see the second generation of many of the Muḥammad b. Tughluq's *umarā'* serving under Fīrūz Shāh. Malik Mubārak, the son of Muḥammad's leading *amīr* Malik Qabūl Khalifati, served as *Silahdār-i Khaṣ* and later *wakīl-i dar*, surviving Fīrūz Shāh himself.[222] Husam al-Dīn, son of Malik Nuwa, became *nā'ib* of Awadh and received the title of Husām al-Malik.[223]

Despite Baranī's statement that Fīrūz dismissed the fortune hunter émigrés from Herat, Sistān, Aden and Qusdār,[224] some of Fīrūz Shāh's *umarā'* were foreigners who were given important designations. The Mongol *amīr*s Qabtagha and Aḥmad-i Iqbāl[225] were given offices, similarly Khudawandzādah Qiwām al-Dīn Tirmiḍi, Muḥammad's *nā'ib -i wakīl-i dar*, became Khudāwand Khān and *wakīl-i dar*, while his nephew was entitled as Sayf al-Mulk and made *amīr-i shikār-i maymanā*.[226]

Slaves

Fīrūz Shāh's patrimonial staff largely consisted of his slaves. He extensively reformed and systematised the institution of slavery. His efforts to acquire slaves appear to have been more emphatic than those of his predecessors. The *muqṭa'* were instructed to send the finest slaves to the centre as annual presents to the sultan. Fīrūz Shāh's personal slaves, as reported by 'Afīf, amounted to one *lac* 80,000. These slaves were employed in every department of the government.[227] The sultan used them as his alternative powerbase, or as a self-created fifth column for personal security and power.[228]

A large number of the slaves were included in the administration of the centre and the provinces. In the centre, 40,000 slaves were appointed as the royal attendants of the sultan. These slaves were trained archers, swordsmen, horsemen and cow riders, which the sultan used to exhibit in royal processions as a symbol of his strength.[229] Slaves operated even the royal household department. They held posts that gave them the responsibility for key aspects of royal household management; the *ābdār* was in charge of water, *jāmādār*, clothing, *chitrdār*, the royal canopy, *pārdahdār*, curtains, *shārābdār*, drinks, *shamādār*, light, *'itrdār*, perfumery[230] and *pīl bān* was keeper of the elephants. Moreover, slaves were appointed in the libraries and communication department and as *gharyāl kāhanā* (timekeepers). In the provinces, slaves were employed as *muqṭa'*, *jagirdār*, *paragnā dār* and *shihnagān* (officer in charge).[231] Others were given to provincial governors and senior nobles for education and training. The slaves were raised by the *umarā'* as they would bring up their own children. Accomplished slaves were presented to the sultan who used to reward the *umarā'* for their good training of the slaves.[232]

The *umarā'* of Fīrūz Shāh also nurtured personal patrimonial staff members. Many of theses *umarā'* had their personal slaves numbering in thousands. In addition, it seems that the practice, reported in the eras of 'Alā al-Dīn Khaljī and Muḥammad b. Tughluq, of employing royal slaves in the households of the *umarā'* to monitor their activities, continued. Since Fīrūz Shāh gave the slaves to his *umarā'* and *mumlūk* for training, these men must have been used as tools for espionage. 'Afīf reports an incident when two slaves reported to the sultan about disorders in the royal mint and the sultan ordered inquiries.[233] Slaves were employed in various vocations according to their capacities. Artisans and skilled workers were employed in *kārkhānā*s.[234] Some slaves were stationed permanently in Ḥijjāz to perform religious rituals for the prosperity of the empire.

So great was the number of slaves under Fīrūz Shāh that *diwān-i bandāgān* (the slave department), separate from the *diwān-i wazārāt*, was introduced to administer the affairs of the slaves.[235] These royal slaves were given salaries from the royal treasury.[236] Some of the slaves were employed in the army and were also made *muqṭa'*. Those living in cities were given allowances of 100, 50, 30, 25 or 10 *tankā*s at intervals of six, four or three months.[237] Those living on *iqṭā'* were paid through their revenue assignments.[238] By the end of Fīrūz Shāh's reign, his slaves had become an important part of the nobility and army. They played an important role in the wars of succession during the life of Fīrūz Shāh and after his death. In the post-Fīrūz Shāhi era, slaves became the principal kingmakers and continued to play this role even after the invasion of Temür in 800/1398–1399. Their capricious political attitude seriously damaged the stability of the sultanate.

Many of the slaves were given major offices and *iqṭā'*. Muḥammad b. Tughluq's slave *nā'ibwazīr* Khwājah Jahān became *wazīr* and served the sultan under the same designation his entire life. A purchased slave, Malik Dilan 'Imād al-Mulk Malik Bashīr the *amīr-i shikār*, was a confidante of the sultan even before the sultan's accession to the throne.[239] Other notable slaves during this era included: Malik Qabūl Torāband, the *amīr* of Badaun; Malik Qabūl Quran Khwān, the *amīr-i majlis* and *muqṭa'* of Samana; and Farhat al-Mulk, Malik Ikhtiyār al-Dīn Mūfarrij Sultānī, the *dawadār*, later *nā'ib* of the *iqṭā'* of Gujarat.[240]

Power and Wealth of the Patrimonial Staff of Fīrūz

'Afīf mentions the power and wealth of three powerful slave *umarā'*, 'Imād al-Dīn Shabīr *'āriḍ-i mumālīk*,[241] Malik Dilān *amīr shikār*[242] and Qawām al-Mulk Maqbūl Khwājah Jahān, the *wāzīr*.[243] Brief biographical sketches of the three will facilitate understanding of the extent of privilege enjoyed by the elite slaves and the fact that they themselves maintained patrimonial relations. 'Imād al-Mulk was among the confidants of the sultan, holding the title *'āriḍ-i mumālīk*. 'Imād al-Mulk was one of the most capable and dependable slaves of the sultan.[244] Due to his competence, he held immense influence over the sultan and was able to install or depose any *amīr* he desired.[245] Therefore, he promoted his patrimonial staff through favours. A reasonable number of *parganāh* and *jāgir*s were under the command of his staff.[246] He had enormous wealth amounting to 13 *crore tankā*s and other valuables,[247] which outweighed the riches of any other Khān and Malik. The slave 'Imād al-Mulk Shabīr personally owned families of 4,000 slaves that he manumitted in his last days.[248] At his death, the sultan seized 12 *crore tankā*s (one *crore* had already been taken by the sultan during his life).[249] From the recovered amount, three *crore* were given to family and slaves. His son Malik Isḥāq inherited his title and designation.[250] Nevertheless, the treasure of 'Imād al-Mulk fostered anarchy and civil war in the realm after the death of Fīrūz Shāh.[251]

The *wazīr* Khān Jāhān, as mentioned earlier, was a slave of Muḥammad b. Tughluq.[252] He was also the keeper of the royal treasury, which he administered efficiently.[253] In the first seven years of his reign, the sultan stayed in the capital for only 13 days.[254] In the absence of the sultan he was the designated *nā'ib*.[255] The sultan used to visit the capital after two or three years and within a few days depart after giving the trusted *wazīr* orders about administration.[256] The *wazīr* administered the city efficiently and kept the masses subdued through pomp and show.[257] Khān Jāhān is said to have had 2,000 concubines, imported from all over the world including China and Rome. He had numerous sons, sons-in-law and slaves along with wealth, which included horses and elephants.[258] He was trusted and respected by the sultan throughout his life.[259] He died during the lifetime of Fīrūz Shāh and his son, with the title of Khān Jāhān (II), succeeded him to the post of *wazīr*. Khān JāhānII served the sultan for six years. The sultan was extremely fond of him and respected his opinion on matters of state.[260]

Penetration of State Control under Fīrūz

The crumbling of the empire, which had started during the reign of Muḥammad b. Tughluq, continued during the reign of his cousin Fīrūz who neither was a war leader of the calibre of Ghiyāth al-Dīn Tughluq nor did he have the aptitude to quell rebellions like his cousin Muḥammad possessed. In the peripheral regions, the state power had started disintegrating during the time of Muḥammad after the establishment of the kingdom of Deogīr. Fīrūz was unable to recapture the lost territories. At the times of Fīrūz's accession to the throne, many of the provinces and *iqṭā*'s had become independent and had ceased to pay taxes. Even so, Fīrūz raided Bengal twice and was able to establish Bengal as a tributary through negotiations. He also raided Sind and was able to assert the writ of the state there.

Construction of a Social Base

There is little evidence available to help demarcate the limits of core areas in the Delhi sultanate under Fīrūz. Nevertheless, it can safely be inferred that the following were included in the core areas: Delhi, its suburban cities, Doaband the provinces of the west and north-west, including Multan, Deopalpur, Samana, Sirhind, Lahore, Mahoba including the districts of the Kara and Dalamau, Badaun and Kannauj. In the core regions of sultanate, the slaves and free officers comprised a sizeable proportion of the population. These slaves were also present in large number with the provincial *umarā'* in order to receive proper training. In addition, the slaves were recruited from the provinces on a large scale and thus, a good number of people from different provinces were brought under the employment of the central administration. Although several officers were appointed by the sultan to directly report to him, *nā'ib wazīr*s were also appointed in these regions as sub-sovereigns.

Some part of core regions broke away as well. For instance, parts of Sindh had become autonomous under Sammas, with Fīrūz's two expeditions to recover it ending in failure. The rise of Samma rulers reflected the entrenched establishment of local Muslim rule. On the other hand in the letters of 'Aynul-Mulk, we find a reference to the appointment of Khān-i Ā'ẓam Khān to the governorship of Sind. It therefore can be assumed that the region of Sind was a favourite of Fīrūz. Probably the regions of Multan, Bhakkar and Swistān were part of his empire.[261] The north-western regions of Lahore, Sanam and Deopalpur were also under the suzerainty of the sultan. These regions had witnessed the Muslim and Mongol invasions and the influx of the populations from Transoxania, Persia and Afghanistan. The centuries-long[262] historical experience of Muslim rule and mass migration of the Muslims into the region had transformed these areas into Muslim majority regions. In the Doab region, we find a severe rebellion that kept the sultan busy. Fīrūz Shāh's defence policy was similar to that of his predecessors, although the Mongol invasions had lost their impetus during his reign.

The Provinces and *Iqṭā'*

Important indirectly administered *iqṭā'* under Fīrūz Shāh included Gujarat, Malwa, Khandesh and Awadh. The region of Gujarat was prominent in the sultanate sources dating to the reign of Fīrūz Shāh. We find noticeable changes in the administration of the province in this period. In order to avoid rebellion the old governors were dismissed and the new ones were appointed very frequently. Probably due to trade and commercial activities, this province was one of the richest provinces of South Asia. The sultan first appointed Amīr Ḥussayn and later he was dismissed. Zafar Khān succeeded him and later Darya Khān was given the office. He was succeeded by Shams al-Dīn Damaghanī and, when he was killed, the sultan appointed his slave Malik Mufarrih Sultanī to govern this region.

The region of Awadh was large, including the areas of Sandilah, Gorakhpur and Karosah. It was constantly under attack by the ruler of Bengal, motivating some of the people of Awadh to ask the sultan for support. The sultan raided Bengal and restored his authority over the region. At one time Malik Niẓām al-Dīn Nau was the governor in those areas. The chiefs of Gorakhpur and Kharosh paid tribute to him. In the region between Delhi and Awadh the sultan founded many cities including Fīrūzabad and Jaunpur.[263] The city of Jaunpur became the centre of learning and Islamic culture. After the raid of Temür, the sultanate of Jaunpur was among the successor states that contested the hereditary state of the sultanate.

The Final Breakdown of the Peripheral Regions

Most of the peripheral regions broke away in the times of Fīrūz Shāh who avoided invading the regions of Mabar and Dolatābād. The foundation of the Bahamanī sultanate blocked the way of the sultanate to the southern peninsula. There were no expeditions undertaken in these regions and their control was lost forever. In 742/1341 the region of Bengal became independent under Fakhr al-Dīn, an *amīr* of Muḥammad who ruled from Sonargaon and 'Alī Mubārak who ruled from Lakhnawatī. There was a constant struggle for power between the two. The reign of 'Alī Mubārak ended in 746/1345 with his murder at the hands of his brother Shams al-Dīn (later Hajjī Ilyas Shams al-Dīn Bhangarah) who became the ruler of Bengal. Under Hajjī Ilyas, the kingdom of Bengal began to extend its boundaries by encroaching into the Delhi sultanate. His raids on Tirhut, Bharaich to Banaras and also in the regions of Jajnagar, which was a tributary region of the Delhi sultanate, became frequent. In order to curtail the power of Hajjī Ilyas, Fīrūz Shāh twice attacked these regions but instead of wiping out the enemy he was satisfied with a peace settlement and there were exchanges of gifts between the rulers of two territories. There is no indication that tribute was paid by the ruler of Bengal. Nevertheless, some local rulers of Bengal occasionally accepted the over-lordship of the sultan. In 756/1356 after the second expedition of Bengal, the sultanate armies lost their way and reached Jajnagar. The ruler of Jajnagar, Rāi' Virabhanudeva III of the Eastern Gangā dynasty, accepted the suzerainty of the sultan and paid tribute. He claimed that he and his father had both been servants of the court of Delhi.[264]

Figure 8.1 Image of Sultan's Reception upon his Return to the Capital. Courtesy Walters Museum.

In the last days of Fīrūz Shāh, the rivalry between the all-powerful *wazīr*[265] Khān Jāhān II and the only surviving son of Fīrūz Shāh, Prince Muḥammad, took the shape of an armed conflict.[266] This dispute marked the beginning of a politically volatile era in which Fīrūz Shāhī slaves were the key players. These slaves initially had control over the royal elephant stables and were the dominant group in the royal army. This resourcefulness enabled them to pressurise the sultan to act

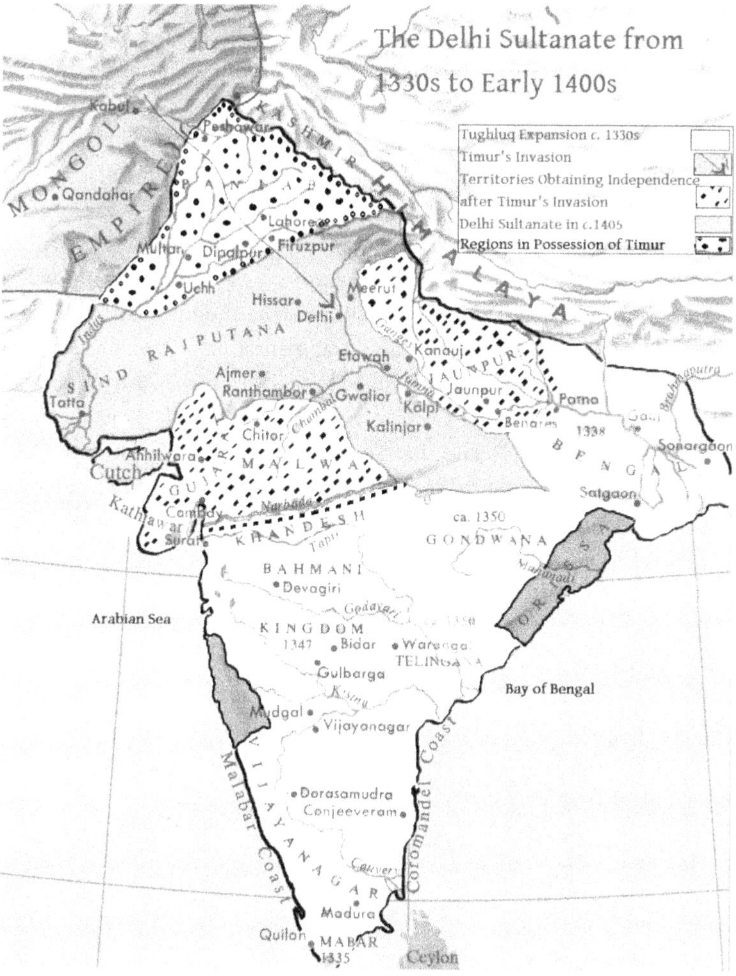

Map 8.1 The Delhi Sultanate from the 1330s to the Early 1400s.

according to their preferences. However, they were not a cohesive group, as inter-slave rivalries existed. They lacked permanent loyalty towards a particular sultan, and shifted sides according to how their interests evolved. Thus, they had the authority to enthrone or dethrone the sultans. Consequently, during the last decade of the Tughluqs, six new rulers acceded to the throne and fell. Several times, two sultans claimed to be rulers of Delhi simultaneously, with slaves playing a major role in their political movements. There were two state-ordered massacres of slaves in the sultanate. Nevertheless, slaves remained in power even after the fall of Delhi to Temür in 801/1399.

The eventful fourteenth century witnessed the height of territorial expansion and the downfall of the Delhi sultanate. Since the historical material of this era is greater than any other sultanate period it facilitates understanding the behavioural and relational dimensions of power in this era. All three monarchs of the Tughluq dynasty were veteran nobles at the time of their enthronement and enjoyed support among the ruling elite as well. Nevertheless the over-ambitiousness of Muḥammad in terms of unnatural expansion and centralisation and his inability to trust and delegate power resulted in rapid fragmentation of the empire. Fīrūz Shāh tried not to repeat Muḥammad's mistakes but in turn made his own; his grand project of slave recruitment stabilised his government but resulted in a civil war that marked the end of the greater Delhi sultanate. Thus the slaves that were architects of the Delhi sultanate became responsible for its ultimate downfall.

CHAPTER 9

VACILLATING BETWEEN ORDER AND DISORDER: AMIR TEMÜR, SAYYIDS AND LODHIS

It is difficult to sum up the eventful post-Fīrūz Shāh period of the Delhi sultanate, which lasted until the first battle of Pānipat in 932/1526, in a few pages and it requires an altogether new research. This era can explain best the case of *tawā'if ul-mulūkīat* or political fragmentation characterised by the absence of strong sultans who could maintain a relative peace within the Delhi sultanate. This phenomenon resulted in a greater amount of chaos and arbitrariness among the power echelons as different warlords scrambled for power.

By the end of the fourteenth century, the political power of the Delhi sultanate was in steady decline. Muḥammad b. Tughluq's ambitious projects drained the treasury and provinces had broken away. Muḥammad's successor Fīrūz Shāh did not make any serious move to re-conquer the lost territories. Furthermore, his policy of making the *iqṭā'* heritable for the landed elite made the *iqṭā'* strongholds of the *umarā'* who held them. As a result, provinces had split into independent states. Some of these independent states aspired to capture Delhi since it could have provided them the ability to claim the successorship of the deceased empire of Delhi. The tributary states had already assumed their independent status during Muḥammad b. Tughluq's time that Fīrūz Shāh had been unable to retrieve. The civil war in the last days of Fīrūz Shāh left the sultanate defenceless and prone to external invaders. This was the time when Amir Temür was gaining ground in Central Asia. Seeing the sultanate's north-western borders unguarded and sensing a power vacuum, he advanced to conquer Delhi. However, like Maḥmūd of Ghazna, it was not his aim to settle there. Temür left no notable generals in the region to administer his conquered territories like Shihāb al-Dīn Ghūrī; no new administrative institutions were established in the sultanate. In brief, the Temürid invasion proved to be a deathblow to the political authority of the Delhi sultanate. For three years after Temür's invasion, the sultanate remained sans sultan. Death, plague and pestilence were the legacy of the Temürid onslaught for the people of the Delhi sultanate who were left unattended in the absence of any state authority. Some who were able to avoid death and disease took the road towards Kabul,[1] while others took shelter in neighbouring villages and towns.[2]

In the post-Temürid sultanates, while multiple contenders to the throne contested for power and privilege, the inherent instability of the system did not give them a chance to reach out to the people through economic or social reforms. The next notable power to rise in Delhi was the Sayyid dynasty (817–855/1414–1451). Its founder Khiḍr Khān (817–824/1414–1421) was one of the warlords competing for power during the post-Temürid invasion. He rose to prominence as a deputy of Temür in the Punjab, yet he became the overlord only when he was able to curb the powers of other warlords such as Mallū Iqbāl Khān, Nāṣir al-Dīn Nuṣrat, Sultan Nāṣir al-Dīn Maḥmūd, Dawlat Khānand and the Sharqi sultan.

Since the primary and contemporary historical records are scarce, the picture of historical events during Sayyid dynasty becomes more sketchy and enigmatic. Not much can be said about the lineage of Khiḍr Khān. Although Khiḍr Khān claimed descent from the Prophet Muḥammad, these claims were unauthentic.[3] In addition, during the reign of Muḥammad b. Tughluq, the Arabs were called Sayyids and it is plausible that he might have been an individual of Arab descent.[4] Khiḍr Khān did not claim sovereign status for himself. His title was never that of a sultan but that of R'ayat-i Ā'alā (exalted standard)[5] – one of the officers appointed by Temür.[6] At the time of Khiḍr Khān, the status of the Delhi sultanate was reduced to that of a tributary of Temür's empire. Khiḍr Khān sent tribute to Temür's youngest son Shāh Rukh and received a *khil'at* (robe) and banner in return.[7] Shāh Rukh at that time ruled the eastern Islamic world from his capital at

Herat. It seems that Khiḍr Khān's son and successor Mubārak Shāh (824–837/1421–1434) had claimed the title of sultan.[8] Nonetheless, he also had links with Herat where he received a *khil'at* (robe) and *chatr* (royal parasol).[9]

Being a tributary to the Temürids did not secure the sultanate borders from Mongol raids.[10] Sheikh 'Alī, who was Shāh Rukh's son's appointed governor of Kabul, took advantage of the weak administration of the Sayyids and at one point occupied Lahore in 836/1432–1433.[11]

The further weakening of the Sayyid dynasty led to the rise of the Lodhis as the most prominent strategically placed minority. Khiḍr Khān utilised Lodhi warriors to counter rivals in several instances. Lodhis were trusted as the newest ethnic element in the sultanate ruling elite. During the times of Islam Shāh the Lodhis were placed in Sirhind. They were later granted Lahore and Deopalpur. So overwhelming was their power that after assisting the Sayyids in countering the forces of Malwa they actually made two attempts to conquer Delhi. The internal strife among the *umarā'* of Delhi, who had become exceedingly powerful in the absence of any strong sultan at the centre, also worked in the Lodhis' favour. The last sultan of the Sayyid dynasty, Alam Shāh, was unable to exercise authority either within or outside Delhi. The rival states of Jaunpur, Malwa and Gujarat were expanding, and he had neither the will nor the ability to withstand these threats and pressures. Thus, he left Delhi to his conspiring nobles and shifted to Badaun in 852/1448. A three-year interregnum followed, in which the tussle of power led to one group of *umarā'* inviting Bahlul to Delhi, where he was enthroned as sultan.

The political situation under the Lodhis was certainly better than that under the Sayyids. The Lodhis were militarily stronger and were well guarded against their enemies both inside and outside. The political system as devised by Bahlul Lodhi was not a monarchy or despotism but that of an oligarchy or confederacy based on tribal egalitarian norms.[12] With the passage of time, he was able to win support of his fellow Afghans. He parcelled out lands to Afghans and advised those Afghans from trans-Roh regions to join him. The territorial extent of the Delhi sultanate was reinforced when the Lodhis finally defeated the sultanate of Jaunpur and annexed it to Delhi in 884/1479. The last Sharqi ruler then resigned to Bihar.

The Afghans in India had maintained a distinct culture. Their power dynamics, social and economic institutions, socialisation and manner of living had distinct tribal traditions. Ibn Khuldūn's theory of dynastic cycle and *asabiyah* applies well to the Afghan settlers in India. Due to their tough mountainous training, they were able to dominate militarily on the relatively civilised northern Indian environment. However, until the Tuqhluq era their settlements were developed individually; therefore, their impact over the sultanate polity was not as strong as it became in the post-Tughluq era when their settlements in India fell along tribal lines. They rose as the Lodhi sultans due to their tribal *asabiyah*. Regardless of their rural, tribal roots, the urbanisation of the Lodhi sultans was rapid. In the first generation, Bahlul Lodhi restricted his governance to the model of tribal egalitarianism, aware of the fact that his strength laid in tribal *asabiyah*. In the second generation, Sikandar tried to adopt the traditional decorum of the sultan's office and curtailed the power of his nobility. In the third generation, Ibrahim Lodhi tried to discard the tradition of tribal egalitarianism and centralise all the authority in his hands. As a result, he was overthrown. The strength of his nobility, who considered themselves the legitimate co-sharers to the throne, caused his fall. Therefore, it can be said that the proliferation of tribal *asabiyah,* which caused the rise of Afghans to power, also caused the fall of the Lodhis and their consequent replacement with the Mughals.

Hence, the Delhi sultanate under the Sayyid (817–855/1414–1451) and Lodhi (855–932/1451–1526) dynasties was reduced to one of the multiple successor states contending to gain the region of Delhi. They strove to seize control of Delhi, since control of Delhi implied a more serious claim to the successorship of Iltutmish, Balban, 'Alā al-Dīn Khaljī and Muḥammad b. Tughluq's Delhi sultanate. The states of Jaunpur, Gujarat, Malwa, Bengal, and Hindu principalities in Mewar, Alor and the Doab had challenged the authority of the Delhi sultanate under the Sayyids several times. Delhi itself was invaded by rival Muslim kingdoms a couple of times. For instance, the sultan of Malwa invaded Delhi in 844/1440 and the sultan of Jaunpur attacked the region four times; first in 810/1407, secondly in 856/1452, thirdly in 870/1466 and finally in 883/1479. Although, Lodhis were able to improve upon the models of political authority established by the Delhi sultanate, even they could not annihilate all rival states. Similarly, although since the times of the Tughluqs, the caliphal investitures in India had been a privilege of the sultan of Delhi, in this period these investitures were now obtained by other rival states.[13] Finally in 932/1526 Babur, a descendent of Amir Temür and Genghis Khān, undertook the final 'Mongol' invasion of Delhi and marked the decisive end of the Delhi sultanate.

CONCLUSION

The political legitimacy of a regime is intrinsically conditional upon the voluntary acceptance of its subjects. Thus, power becomes legitimised only when it is accepted in a society without the use of coercion. In the power dynamics of the Delhi sultanate, the issue of legitimate political authority seems irrelevant, since neither the rise nor fall from power was conditional upon these considerations.

The concept of legitimacy relates to the relationship between the sultan, the ruling elite and the subjects. Due to inadequate historical data about the common people in the historical sources, it is difficult to investigate the relationship between the sultans and their subjects. In the historical records of the Delhi sultanate, socio-political interest groups are seldom mentioned and accounts of their response to the government's policies scanty. Nevertheless, from available evidence it can be deduced that the population of the Delhi sultanate was multiracial and had diverse religious orientations. In addition, it consisted of many social, political and economic interest groups that demonstrated complex and varying interactions with the state. Thus, the sultanate's subjects cannot be treated as a monolithic entity.

The available information suggests that coercion was the major reason that various population groups in the Delhi sultanate obeyed the sultans' power. Justifications were extended by rulers in the form of political philosophies, religious/cultural symbols such as *manshūr*, *khil'at* and honorific titles from the caliph. The issuance of coinage and reading of the caliph's name in *khuṭba*, use of different cultural symbols such as Arabic royal titles, Persianisation of state apparatus, and construction of monuments, seem to have done little to make the sultan appear legitimate in the eyes of different population groups. To begin with, it is difficult to accept that Muslim religious symbols could deem the power of a sultan legitimate in the eyes of the majority non-Muslim population of the Delhi sultanate. In light of Baranī's philosophy, it can well be argued here that the sultan of Delhi was the sultan of Muslims only, referring to the social base of the Delhi sultanate, which is assumed to have comprised Muslims residing in the urban centres.

The idea that the sultans were conscious of their public face and formulated their religious and economic policies in the light of public response is not demonstrable through the empirical evidence. The sultans' actions indicate their awareness regarding their susceptibility vis-à-vis various ruling groups, including *'ulāmā'* and *umarā*. For example, Sultan Shams al-Dīn Iltutmish was asked by the *'ulāmā'* to produce his letter of manumission since, according to Islamic law, a slave, unless manumitted, cannot become a ruler. Sultana Raḍiyyah was brought to the throne with the help of the people of Delhi. Sultan Balban was twice convinced to change his decisions by influential groups: on one occasion, his decision concerned the old officers of Iltutmish in Doab region and, on another occasion, the sultan pardoned the rebels of Bengal who had sided with Toghril. The population of Delhi resented the rise of the Khaljīs. Jalāl al-Dīn could not enter the city of Delhi immediately after enthronement and 'Alā al-Dīn Khaljī aborted the plan of founding a new religion due to public resentment.

Conversely, substantial data is available to indicate that even the social base of the sultan seldom responded to the state's policies as a monolithic entity. Generally, their acceptance of a particular regime was directly related to the display of power, wealth and largesse. Iltutmish had come to power with the help of a dominant group in Quṭbī *umarā'*, nonetheless, his eligibility to rule was questioned by other rival groups also present in the power structure. The sultan gradually eliminated all those who were a challenge to his power. Although various social groups in Delhi seem to have contributed to the rise of Sultana Raḍiyyah, however, this support was absolutely ineffective at preventing her brother Sultan Mu'izz al-Dīn Behrām Shāh being placed on throne while she was alive. Sultana Raḍiyyah was raised to the throne by the *umarā'* of Iltutmish because her predecessor had fallen from favour. Sultana Raḍiyyah as a female was expected to be a de jure ruler while the *umarā'* hoped to exercise the de facto power. Her attempt to create a personalised powerbase riled the *umarā'* and she was replaced.

Sultan Balban seems to have cowed the population of the Delhi sultanate with his overt and covert means of state control. Except for the two examples mentioned above, there is no empirical evidence that suggests the reciprocity of his policies. As mentioned earlier, various social groups in Delhi resented the rise of the Khaljīs; this resentment could not prevent the Khaljīs from assuming power. Although Sultan Jalāl al-Dīn Fīrūz Khaljī was lenient, this leniency generated contempt. Various conspiracies by nobles and an intrigue leading to a popular rebellion that was plotted against him in the hospice of Sidi Muwallah suggests that forbearance was a trait which was not cherished in the Delhi sultanate. In the beginning of 'Alā al-Dīn's reign there were rebellions in Delhi. Various members of the royal household and *umarā'* attempted to replace the sultan. Nevertheless, in his later reign there are no rebellions since the sultan exhausted his social base's ability for interest aggregation and interest articulation. Thus, in the absence of coercion or ineffective assertion of power the social acceptance of the sultan ended.

The power of the sultan was not considered legitimised either in the eyes of people nor in the ruling group including his own family members. The absence of any law of succession was a cause of incessant intrigues within the royal household. Anyone and everyone within the power structure was a potential enemy of the sultan. Potential enemies ranged from multiple political groups within *umarā'*, including the officers at the centre and provincial governors to the religious groups, which included *'ulāmā'* and Sufis. The sultan was able to continue ruling until he had the ability to exercise power upon his *umarā'* and suppressed the rebellions and conspiracies that frequently surfaced in one region of the sultanate or another. From the empirical data available in the historical sources, it is evident that only six sultans out of 27 were able to rule for a period of more than seven years while the rest of the rulers became either victims of court intrigues or rebellions. Only six of the sultans – Iltutmish, Balban, Muḥammad b. Tughluq, Fīrūz Shāh and Nāṣir al-Dīn Muḥammad Shāh I and II (minor Tughluq sultans) – died natural deaths. Some of the historians suggest that the deaths of Nāṣir al-Dīn Maḥmūd b. Iltutmish, 'Alā al-Dīn Khaljī and Ghiyāth al-Dīn Tughluq were the results of conspiracy.

The vulnerability of the office of the sultan made its possessor excessively mistrustful of the people who surrounded him and the subject population. Sultans consolidated their rule by centralising power through nurturing a patrimonial bureaucratic staff and through surveillance of various groups of society through policing and espionage networks. The sultans attempted to knit the fabric of the state around their own selves. Due to the absence of a stable vertical and horizontal hierarchy that is required to govern a vast territory, lack of systemisation in the patterns of recruitment, appointments, transfers and dismissals, and indeterminate areas of operation in offices, the system of governance of the Delhi sultanate was highly unstable, arbitrary and prone to disorder. The strong sultans were able to centralise power. In the absence of a strong sultan at the centre, the sultanate became a portrait of *tawā'if ul-mulūkīat* (group rule) and disintegrated into various power groups in the centre and in the provinces contending for power.

The mode of centralisation in the Delhi sultanate was dissimilar to the mode of centralisation in modern times. The borders of the Delhi sultanate fluctuated frequently and the state's penetration in all the regions was uneven. Governance in the Delhi sultanate was multi-layered. While, the designates of the Delhi sultans operated in the provinces, the local administrative elite including *khōtt*s, *muqqidim*s and *chohadries* were also meaningful sources of authority. Due to uneven state presence in the areas within the Delhi sultanate, the regions can be classified into directly administered areas, indirectly administered areas and tributary kingdoms.

In the directly administered areas, the population was connected to the centre. In the indirectly administered areas, the sultan appointed his governors and the population living there had relatively little contact with the sultan. In the absence of modern means of mobility and communication, the provincial governors were generally free in their conduct and choice of patrimonial bureaucratic staff. The *iqlīm* of Bengal and the tributary kingdoms were temporarily annexed to the sultanate. These outer regions of the sultanate were primarily the semi-autonomous tributary kingdoms; control of these regions depended upon the sultan's ability to annex and conquer. Once control in the centre was lax, the tributary kingdoms ceased to pay tribute and control was lost until the next successful expedition by the sultan of Delhi.

Political control evolved with the growing penetration of the sultan into the areas of the Delhi sultanate. With the passage of time, areas under direct control increased and a greater proportion of the population became directly affected by sultans' policies. In the times of 'Alā al-Dīn, the Doab areas were included in the *khalisā* lands. The middle zone of authority extended to regions of the south and the outer zones of authority extended further south. 'Alā al-Dīn Khaljī was able to appoint bureaucrats that provided stable rule in the provinces. Even the interregnum of Quṭb al-Dīn Mubārak Khaljī and Khusraw Khān did not distort the state structure in the provinces and Ghiyāth al-Dīn Tughluq and Muḥammad b. Tughluq inherited the empire of 'Alā al-Dīn Khaljī without major territorial losses. Thus, the deeper penetration of stable governance consolidated power in the sultanate.

The question emerges: how can a system so loosely knit be labelled as centralised? In a period of two centuries, the sultanate saw 27 rulers, with only six sultans reigning for more than a decade and with the reign of the rest of the sultans not lasting more than six years. The notion that the sultanate was a centralised empire rests on the enormous time span (amounting to 150 years) of these six rulers: Iltutmish ruled for 25 years; his son Nāṣir al-Dīn Maḥmūd and slave Balban ruled for a period of 20 years each; 'Alā al-Dīn Khaljī's reign consisted of two decades; Muḥammad b. Tughluq ruled for a period of 27 years; and Fīrūz Shāh ruled for a period of 37 years. During this period of one and a half centuries, with the exception of Nāṣir al-Dīn Maḥmūd, the sultans nurtured patrimonial staff and centralised the state apparatus. No specific rules and regular patterns regarding the appointment, transfers and dismissals of the bureaucracy can be identified in the sources. In the times of Iltutmish, explicit multi-layered governance patterns are visible; the provinces of the sultanate were divided among the Turkish slaves of Iltutmish, while the freemen, generally Tajik émigrés, served him in the centre. There was bifurcation of duties among various mutually hostile ethnic groups (for instance, Tajiks were *ahl-i qalam* and Turks were *ahl-i saif*). The sultan befriended various religious groups of *'ulāmā'* and Sufis as well. Iltutmish personalised power and the state structure so extensively around himself that in his absence it crumbled immediately. The patrimonial staff of Iltutmish had little regard for the progeny of their deceased master. Iltutmish's descendants became the victims of their inexperience and four of them were overthrown in their bid to remove the untrustworthy *umarā'* and replace them with their own loyalists. The *umarā'* continued to replace the progeny of Iltutmish with one another until the line of Iltutmish was extinguished. From the data available regarding the governance in the provinces, it can well be generalised that a similar pattern of governance was replicated in the provinces where the *muqṭa*'s had their own patrimonial staff, military contingents and workforce employed for policing and espionage. The historian Juzjānī, who sheds light on 14 years of Naṣīr al-Dīn Maḥmūd's rule, explicitly denotes the weaknesses of Nāṣir al-Dīn as a sultan and the rivalries between the factions among the *umarā'*. In this context, eventually Balban assumed greater power and was able to dominate. In mysterious circumstances, Balban assumed power and asserted his will over his *khwājatāshgān* (colleagues) and patrimonial officers through overt and covert means of coercion. Balban's use of religious and cultural symbols seems to have done little to legitimise his rule in the eyes of his patrimonial staff, since he could neither prevent rebellions from occurring nor could he convert his personal rule into a dynastic one. Toghril, one of the sultan's slaves, suspecting the sultan to have grown weak, revolted in Bengal and the population of the region and the staff of Toghril sided with the rebel. The sultan was only able to quell the rebellion with coercion. He publicised the excruciating punishments inflicted upon the rebels in the major centres of sultanate in order to prevent a recurrence of rebellion.

The *umarā'* did not honour Balban's will in favour of his grandson Kaykhusraw and instead enthroned Kayquabād. One camp of *umarā'* controlled the young sultan while others waited, resentful, for any opportunity to alter the power equation. The Khaljī *coup d'état* brought forth Jālal al-Dīn Khaljī, whose clemency and gullibility could neither win him the support and sympathy of the ruling elite nor the lasting loyalty of the population of Delhi. Despite the cold-blooded murder of his uncle Jalāl al-Dīn, 'Alā al-Dīn Khaljī was accepted by the population in the Delhi sultanate due to the strength of his arms and money. 'Alā al-Dīn purged the dissenting elements from *umarā'* and cultivated his patrimonial bureaucratic staff, which comprised his family members, slaves, and patronised émigrés. Social control over them was achieved through surveillance, an espionage system and strict enforcement of the laws limiting interaction among the *umarā'*. The sultan was able to make his mark upon the masses, not through religious or cultural symbols, but through the efficiency of his administration, sound economic policies, enforcement of law and order and efficient communication and transportation. There is ample historical data suggesting that the reign of Alā al-Dīn was viewed as ideal in terms of the economic conditions of the state and society. However, this economic prosperity could not convert the sultan's reign into a dynastic order. As soon as the sultan's strength started to wane, his Indian slave, Malik Kāfūr, assumed power. At the death of the sultan, Kāfūr seized the throne yet due to the presence of other strong contending powers his violent rule could not survive more than 36 days. Quṭbal-Dīn Mubārak Shāh attempted to cultivate patrimonial staff and grew excessively capricious. His Gujarati (Baravarī) slave Khusraw treacherously killed him. He was able to assume power with the help of his tribesmen; however, the Baravarī tribe was routed and later eliminated by Ghazī Malik, the *primus inter pares* among the ruling elite. Ghazī Malik died in a curious accident, for which Ibn Battūtah accused his son Muḥammad b. Tughluq.

Like his deceased father, the new sultan cultivated his patrimonial staff during his career as an *amīr.* In the times of Muḥammad b. Tughluq the empire reached its zenith. Nevertheless, such a large state required both a systematic administration and hierarchy. Although Muḥammad b. Tughluq tried to centralise the state and push through reforms, it was unnatural and thus the rebellions sprang up on an unprecedented scale. The sultan became exceedingly belligerent and commanded the army to quell the rebellions in order to keep his grip on the state. He tried to socially dislocate the population of Delhi including notables and other ruling group by shifting the location of the capital. He also kept the notable people and population of Delhi under strict surveillance via espionage. The mass killings had evoked hatred from various groups of society, including religious groups. However, despite all the distrust of the people, economic fiascos and bad agricultural policies, he was able to sustain his rule as no other person was strong enough to replace him.

In the times of Fīrūz Shāh, the recruitment of unusually large number of royal slaves acquired through equally unusual means, was one of the major reasons that his government prevailed for more than three decades. Even so, in his last days, civil war broke out at the instigation of patrimonial staff and the progeny of the old sultan who could not wait until the confirmation of the rumour of his death. The haphazard enthronement and dethronement of several progeny of Fīrūz Shāh by his slaves and other patrimonial staff led to a greater amount of chaos. The provinces broke away from the centre and assumed autonomy, while the unguarded north-western border and centre resulted in the sack of Delhi by Temür. After Temür's invasion, the majority of the population of Delhi was enslaved and taken to Central Asia. The political system that had emerged and endured by force ultimately collapsed by force.

In the Delhi sultanate, lack of acceptance and trust between rulers, the ruling elite and the subjects led to enormous instability. The political behaviour of the people of the Delhi sultanate can be explained with the help of regularly identifiable cycles of regime formation, regime perpetuation and regime disintegration.

The very basis of regime formation was the ability of a ruler or a ruling group to grasp power. In the event of dynastic change, it was the *primus inter pares* among the *umarā'* who was able to capture the throne; succession within a dynasty primarily depended upon the will of the dominant group among the nobility. Except for Muḥammad b. Tughluq, we do not find any other example where the will of the deceased sultan pertaining to succession was honoured. Factions strove to enthrone their own candidates in the absence of a strong sultan, while a strong sultan tried to curtail the powers of the opposing *umarā'* himself.

Regime perpetuation was primarily dependent upon the sultan's ability to nurture a hetero-racial patrimonial bureaucratic staff. The *umarā'* of any sultan, at the time of his accession to the throne comprised of mutually hostile interest groups. While some of the *umarā'* were the acquiescent members of the previous sultan's powerbase, others had been part of the previous regime and supported the new sultan. In the case of dynastic transition, the founder of the dynasty who himself was a strong noble of the previous regime had his own patrimonial bureaucratic staff which he promoted during his career as *amīr*. Few among the sultans were able to cultivate such personalised support, while the rest either did not get a chance to adopt such political strategies or were eliminated in their bid to replace the existing *umarā'* with their own loyalists. This patrimonial bureaucratic staff was dependent upon the sultan's will in many ways. These people were recruited, appointed, promoted, dismissed and eliminated at the often-unpredictable will of the sultan and no regular patterns of any of the above-mentioned phenomena are available in the historical data. The process of overt and covert liquidation of those whom the sultan suspected of dissent was a frequent occurrence as well. While the weak sultans were eliminated either because they did not get an opportunity to construct their own powerbase or were killed in their attempt to construct their own powerbase, the strong sultans not only nurtured their own patrimonial staff but also controlled their social interaction through surveillance and espionage. The construction of new cities, the transfer of nobles into new cities, the banning of social gatherings and the sultan's control over the marriages of the elite indicate this effective social control.

The use of cultural and religious symbols and ritualisation were the post hoc privilege that a sultan used once he had acquired power to justify his rule and to convert his personal rule into a dynasty. Nonetheless, a ruler was able to maintain power only while he was strong. Once his weakness became evident, intrigues and rebellions started and the sultan only continued ruling as long as he was able to suppress his opponents. The will of a strong ruler regarding succession was never honoured unless the heir was as strong as Muḥammad b. Tughluq. The use of religious and cultural symbols, including the construction of monuments and cities, use of *khi'lat*, *manshūr*, issuance of coinage and reading of *khuṭba* in the caliph's name, and the use of Persian etiquette and protocols in the court were not enough to convert a personal rule into a dynastic order.

A regime disintegrated whenever a sultan was unable to control the state apparatus. The centralised power of the office of sultan was then converted into *tawā'if ul-mulūkīat.* In the times of a weak sultan, various interest groups within the *umarā'* endeavoured to gain influence over the sultan and assume power. While one group was able to dominate, the other group would either use the other members of the royal family as their candidates for the office of sultan or write letters to other strong contenders – usually a powerful general who had made his mark against the Mongols – to assume power at the centre. In the provinces, the governors appointed by the sultan would rebel whenever they found the power at the centre weakening or when they grew apprehensive of having fallen from the favour of a strong sultan.

The Delhi sultanate's instability explains its inability to become a legitimate authority. A stable political system is essential for political authority and legitimacy to prevail in a regime. This stability stems from an enduring historical experience of regime perpetuation and power sharing. Both of these characteristics were rare in the political landscape of the Delhi sultanate. The political system in the Delhi sultanate was highly volatile and unstable. It oscillated back and forth into chaos; it remained either one step away from disaster or in a state of perpetual chaos.

The Delhi sultanate was a conquest state where neither social settings nor the political institutions allowed stability. The subject population of the Delhi sultanate largely comprised native non-Muslims who had come under the rule of the Delhi sultans because of their inability to compete with its military power. These populations were prone to rebel in the absence of power and were at best apathetic to the fate of the sultanate.

Similarly, the ruling group lacked moral relations and was unstable in the absence of any established law of succession. The nobility and the sultan grew stronger only at the cost of each other. Since strong nobility could have the influence to limit the powers of a sultan, the sultan preferred to destroy the old nobility and replace it with his own patrimonial staff. The nobility, being apprehensive of the sultan, would try to intrigue against the sultan. The sultans made a habit of imprisoning, blinding and eliminating all the members of the previous royal family or even those in their own family who were potential claimants to the throne. *Umarā'* at the time of the breakdown of power became autonomous in their regions, cultivating patrimonial staff and ruling in a similar pattern to that of the sultan of Delhi.

In the Delhi sultanate, the state was highly unstable and prone to intrigue. Nevertheless, it was still stronger than a society in which different rival social groups either acquiesced to or supported the sultan for their material vested interests. Power seems to have been the most rational and most prevalent rule in order to gain political and military domination. There was resentment of rulers who could not punish dissenters and criminals and of those rulers who failed to organise military expeditions frequently.

Ruling groups are the core instruments of governance and the state is unstable if the ruling elite are violently precarious. The absence of any cohesive support for the sultan led to a greater amount of chaos. Nevertheless, it was the sultan's preference to avoid the formation of cohesive nobility as a well-grounded nobility could limit his power. Thus, the sultan preferred a nobility that was divided along ethnic, racial and religious lines. Since the instability within the ruling group favoured the sultan, every strong sultan preferred divided nobility. The nobility grew in strength when the sultan grew weak; at the same time, the opposite of centralisation in the Delhi sultanate was not an equal distribution of power. The decline in the sultan's centralising ability led to a greater number of mutually contending nobles, who centralised power in their own domains along a similar pattern adopted by the sultan. Multiple centralising forces led to violence and mayhem, while the centralisation of a single ruler ensured only relative stability and order.

APPENDIX

Table A.1 Rise and Fall of Dynasties: A Summary

1206–1399	27 or 30 as three additional people claimed to be sultans
Total Number of Years = 194	21 = 6 years or less 6 = over a decade
Causes of Death	
Natural	6
Accidents/unknown circumstances/ suspected murders	8
Explicit murders by nobility	13
Stayed alive after being deposed from the office of the sultan	None (in post-Timurid invasion, Shah Alam of Sayyid Dynasty is one example)

Table A.2 Issue of Succession

Instance where the will of a sultan was honoured	Once
Attempt for dynastic continuity	No dynasty could survive more than three decades after its founder's demise.
Succession pattern	1. Son 2. Daughter 3. Former slave and son-in-law 4. Father-in-law 5. Cousin 6. Grandson 7. Nephew

Table A.3 Sultans that Reigned more than Six Years

1210–1236	Shams al-Dīn Iltutmish	26
1246–1266	Nāṣir al-Dīn Mahmūd Shāh	20
1266–1286	Ghiyāth al-Dīn Balaban	20
1296–1316	'Alā al-Dīn Khaljī	20
1325–1351	Muḥammad b. Tughluq	27
1351–1387	Fīruz Shāh (Tughluq)	37

Table A.4 Transition of Power between Strategically Placed Minorities

Dynastic Transition	**Ethnicity**
Qutbīs to Shamsīs (607/1210)	Olberlī Turks
Shamsīs to Ghiyāthids (664/1266)	Olberlī Turks
Ghiyāthids to Khaljīs (689/1290)	Afghans/Afghanised Turks
Khaljīs to Barado Tribe (720/1320)	Gujratīs
Khaljīs to Tughluqs (720/1320)	Qurana Turks
Tughluqs to Sayeds (817/1414)	Arabs
Sayeds to Lodhīs (855/1451)	Afghans

Table A.5 Rise and Fall of the Dynasties in the Delhi Sultanate

Ruler	Reign	Years in Power	Succession Pattern	Death Circumstances	Salient Features of the Reign
Qutbī Dynasty					
Qutb al-Dīn Aybeg, appointed deputy by Shihāb al-Dīn Ghgīrī	588–602/1192–1206	14 years			Territorial expansion
Qutb al-Dīn Aybeg, as Sulten of Delhī	602–606/1206–1210	4 years	Ghulām of Shīhāb al-Dīn Ghgīrī	Freak accident	At loggerheads with other duties of Shīhāb al-Dīn Ghgīrī
Aram Shāh	607–608/1210–1211	Few months	Son of Aybeg/Ambiguous	Killed by *umará*	tawā'iful mulukiat
Shamsī Dynasty					
Shams al-Dīn Iltutmish	607–633/1211–1236	25 years	Ghulām/son-in-law/amīr of Aybeg	Natural	Territorial expansion and consolidation
Rukn al-Dīn Fīrūz Shāh	633–1236	6 months	Son of Iltutmish	Killed by umara´	tawā'iful mulukiat
Jalāl at-Radiyyah	633–637/1236–1240	4 years	Daughter of Iltutmish	Killed in her bid to take the throne back	tawā'iful mulukiat
Mu'izz al-Dīn Bahram Shāh	637–639/1240–1242	2 years	Son of Iltutmish	Killed	tawā'iful mulukiat
Ala al-Dīn Masūd Shāh	639–643/1242–1246	4 years	Son of Rukn al-Dīn Fīrūz Shāh	Killed	tawā'iful mulukiat
Nāsir al-Dīn Mahmūd Shāh	643–664/1246–1266	20 years	Son of Iltutmish	Killed/Ambiguous	Exceptionally long reign but no salient administrative reforms are mentioned
Ghiyāthid Dynasty					
Ghiyāth al-Dīn Balban	664–685/1266–1286	20 years	Warrior, father-in-law of Nāsir al-Dīn Mahmūd Shāh	Natural	Relative stability and administrations reforms
Mu'izz al-Dīn Kayquabād	685–689/1286–1290	4 years	Grandeen of Balban	Killed	tawā'iful mulukiat
Shams al-Dīn Kaykaī's	689–1290	Few months	Son of Mu'izz al-Dīn Kayquabād	Killed	tawā'iful mulukiat
Khaljī Dynasty					
Jalāl al-Dīn Khaljī	689–695/1290–1296	6 years	Amir of Balban	Killed	Instability
'Alā al-Dīn Khaljī	695–716/1296–1316	20 years	Nephew/son-in-law of Jalāl al-Dīn Khaljī	Killed/Ambiguous	Expansion and relative stability

Shihāb al-Dīn Umar	716/1316	35 days	Son of ʻAlā al-Dīn Khaljī	Killed	tawā'iful mulukiat
Qutb al-Dīn Mubārak Shāh	716–720/1216–1320	4 years	Son of ʻAlā al-Dīn Khaljī	Killed	tawā'iful mulukiat
Khusraw Shāh	720/1320	Few months	Ghulām of Qutb al-Dīn Mubārak Shāh	Killed	tawā'iful mulukiat
Tughlaq Dynasty					
Ghiyāth al-Dīn Tughluq I	721–725/1321–1325	4 years	Amir of ʻAlā al-Dīn Khalji	Freak accident/ Ambiguous	Attempt to recapture the territories of east, agricultural developments
Muḥammad b. Tughluq	725–752/1325–1351	26 yesars	Son of Ghiyāth al-Dīn Tughluq I	Died in a battlefield/ sickness	tawā'iful mulukiat
Mahmūd b. Muḥammad	725/March 1351	Few days	Son of Muḥammad b. Tughluq	No further reference	tawā'iful mulukiat
Firūz Shāh (Tughluq)	725–790/1351–1388	37 years	Cousin of Muḥammad b. Tughluq	Natural	Agricultural developments
Ghiyāth al-Dīn Tughluq II	790–791/1388–1389	Few months	Grandson of Firūz Shāh	Killed	tawā'iful mulukiat
Abu Bakr Shāh	791–792/1389–1390	Few months	Grandson of Firūz Shāh	Killed	tawā'iful mulukiat
Nāṣir al-Dīn Muḥammad Shāh	792–795/1390–1393	3 years	Son of Firūz Shāh	Natural	tawā'iful mulukiat
Sikander Shāh I	795/March–April 1393	Few months	Son of Nāṣir al-Dīn Muḥammad Shāh	Ambiguous	tawā'iful mulukiat
Mahmūd Nāṣir al-Dīn (Sultan Mahmūd II)	795–???/1393–???	????	Son of Nāṣir al-Dīn Muḥammad Shāh	No further reference	tawā'iful mulukiat
Nāṣrat Shāh, controlled the west from Firūzābād	796–???/1394–???	????	Grandson of Firūz Shāh	No further reference	tawā'iful mulukiat
Nāṣir al-Dīn Mahmūd Shāh, controlled the east from Delhi	802–815/1400–1412 or 1414	12 years	Son of Mahmūd Nāṣir al-Dīn	Natural	tawā'iful mulukiat
Sayyid Dynasty					
Khiḍr Khān	817–824/1414–1421	7 years	Warlord appointed by Temur	Natural	tawā'iful mulukiat
Mubārak Shāh	824–837/1421–1434	13 years	Son of Khiḍr Khān	Killed	tawā'iful mulukiat
Muḥammad Shāh	837–849/1434–1445	11 years	Nephew and adopted son of Mubārak Shāh	Natural	tawā'iful mulukiat
ʻĀlam Shāh	849–855/1445–1451	6 years	Son of Muḥammad Shāh	Natural	tawā'iful mulukiat
Lodhi Dynasty					
Bahlul Lodhī	855–894/1451–1489	38 years	Amīr of ʻĀlam Shāh and overlord of the Punjab	Natural	tawā'iful mulukiat
Sikandar Lodhī	894–923/1489–1517	28 years	Son of Bahlul Lodhī	Natural	Relative Stability
Ibrahīm Lodhī	923–932/1517–1526	9 years	Son of Sikandar Lodhī	Killed	tawā'iful mulukiat

NOTES

Introduction

1. According to this model, the state had three distinct levels or zones of administration: the central, the intermediate and the peripheral. While in the central regions there was actual political control, in the other regions it was temporary and nominal. Local territories did not constitute administrative regions of the government and local functionaries were not bureaucrats of the center. See: Burton Stein, 'The segmentary state in South Indian history', in *Realm and Region in Traditional India*, ed. R. J. Fox (Durham: Duke University Press, 1977), p. 16; Herman Kulke, ed., *The State in India (1000–1700)* (Delhi: Oxford University Press, 1995), p. 23. For more on this concept see Burton Stein, 'State Formation and Economy Reconsidered: Part One', *Modern Asian Studies*, Vol. 19 (3, Special Issue: Papers Presented at the Conference on Indian Economic and Social History, Cambridge University, April 1984): pp. 387–413; idem, *Vijayanagara (The New Cambridge History of India)* (Cambridge and New York: Cambridge University Press, 1987); idem, 'Notes on "Peasant Insurgency" in Colonial Mysore: Event and Process', *South Asia Research*, Vol. 5 (1985): pp. 11–27. For an elaborate insight into the concept of segmentary state, see: Aidan W. Southall, 'The segmentary state: From the imaginary to the material means of production', in *Early State Economics*, ed. H. J. M. Claessen and P. van de Velde (New Brunswick: Transaction Publishers, 1991).
2. *umarā' (singular = amīr)* refers to the sultanate ruling elite or patrimonial bureaucracy. The nearest English translation is 'nobility' which invokes the hereditary, land-based ruling elite of medieval Europe with a largely feudal character. Since the sultanate ruling elite was neither hereditary nor land based, and the mode of production was agrarian but not feudal, the term *umarā'* is preferable in this context. From this reference onwards the terms

umarā' (singular = amīr) and nobility (singular = noble) are used interchangeably.

3. *tawā'if plural tāifa = group, mulukiat = rule* or 'rule of petty kings'. This term appears frequently in Persian and Urdu literature produced in South Asia however; a similar term was used for eleventh-century Andalusia which developed after the fall of Umayyad caliph in the region. The era of the *mūlūk ul tawā'if* (which is also translated by Arab historians as 'Party Kings'), to means the multitude of mutually hostile successor kingdoms of the Umayyad caliphate. Jamil M. Abun-Nasr, *A History of the Maghrib in the Islamic Period* (Cambridge: Cambridge University Press, 1987), p. 72.
4. The Middle English word patrimonial is derived from the Latin word *pater*, which means 'father'. Patrimonialism generally denotes a patron–client relationship. Weber further situates patrimonialism in two contexts: in historical experience of traditions and in personal rulership. Personal rulership is based upon a culture of patronage through material incentives and does not involve any belief in the ruler and leader's personal qualifications. See: Max Weber, *Economy and Society: An Outline of Interpretative Sociology*, ed. Guenther Roth and Claus Wittich (Berkeley: University of California Press, 1978), pp. 1094–9; Vatro Murvar, 'Some Reflections Weber's Typology of Herrschaft', *The Sociological Quarterly*, Vol. 5, No. 4 (Autumn, 1964): pp. 374–84; Andrew Eisenberg, 'Weberian Patrimonialism and Imperial Chinese History', *Theory and Society*, Vol. 27, No. 1 (1998): pp, 83–102; Rangalal Sen, 'Patrimonialism and Urban Development: A Reflection of Max Weber's Theory of the City', *Bangladesh e- Journal of Sociology*, Vol. 1, No. 1 (2004): pp. 1–13; Gray G. Hamilton, 'Patriarchy, Patrimonialism and Filial Piety: A Comparison of China and Western Europe', *The British Journal of Sociology*, Vol. 41, No. 1 (1990): pp. 77–104. An earlier work that applied the Weberian concept of patrimonialism to the Delhi sultanate was: Stephen Conermann, *Die Beschreibung Indians in der 'Rihla' des Ibn Battuta: Aspekte einer herrschaftssoziologi. Einordunung des Delhi-sultanatesunter Muhammad ibn Tughluq ... Untersuchungen)* (German Edition) (K. Schwarz, 1993). Conermann explains that while the Delhi sultanate rule of Muḥammad b. Tughluq was that of a patrimonial state nevertheless, the prevalence of the *iqṭā'* system makes it resemble prebendalism.

Chapter 1 Traders, Adventurers, Raiders and Settlers: The Arab Experience in India

1. Sayyid Suleyman Nadwi, *Arab Hind kayTa'lluqat* (Allahabad, 1930), pp. 250–300.
2. The later historical sources mention that trade links between Arabia and India existed long before the advent of Islam in India. The medieval Indian historian Ibu al-Qāsim Farishtah mentions that Hindu merchants and pilgrims used to

visit the holy shrine of K'abā in Mecca even before the advent of Muḥammad b. Qāsim. Mohammad Qasim Hindu Shah Astarabadi Farishtah, *Tārīkh-i-Farishtah*, Vol. 2 (Karachi: Sindh University Library, n.d), p. 310. As cited in Mumtaz Hussain Pathan, *Arab Kingdom of Al-Mansurah in Sind* (Karachi: University of Sind, Institute of Sindhology, 1974), p. 34.

3. This includes the regions of present-day Baluchistan, Sind, Indian Gujarat and some regions of Punjab.
4. Al Balazari, *Futuh al-Buldan* (Cairo: n.p., 1967).
5. U. M. Daudpota, ed., *Chachnama* (Hyderabad: Deccan, 1939); P. Hardy, 'Is the ChachNama intelligible to the historian as Political theory?', in H. Khuhro (ed.), *Sind through the Centuries* (Karachi, 1981), pp. 113–15. For selected extracts of the historical sources referring to Sind see: H. M. Elliot, *The History of Sind (being Vol. 1 of Elliot's History of India) as Told by its Own Historians: The Mohammadan Period*, ed. John Dowson (Karachi: Karimsons, 1976). Elliot and Dowson's work cannot be accepted without its internal criticism. For a critique on Elliot and Dowson's history see: K. A. Nizami, *Supplement to Elliot and Dowson's History of India*, Vol. 2 (Delhi: Idārāh-i-Adbiyāt-i-Delhi, 1981), pp. 1–11.
6. Al Hind was a political term used for the regions under the sway of Hindu and Buddhist rulers. In Wink, *Al Hind: The Making of the Indo Islamic World*, Vol. 1 (Brill: 2002), p. 192. Sind on the other hand was used as a geographical term for the land of the river Sindh.
7. Qāḍi Athar Mubarikpurī, *Hindustān main Arabon kī Hukūmatain* (Karachi: Education Press, 1967), p. 23. See also: Yohanan Friedmann, 'A Contribution to the Early History of Islam in India', in M. Rosen-Aylon, ed., *Studies in Memory of Gaston Wiet* (Jerusalem, 1977), pp. 309–33.
8. H. M. Ishaq, 'A peep into the first Arab Expeditions to India under the companions of the prophet', *Islamic Culture*, Vol. 19 (1945): pp. 109–14; B. M. B. K. As-Sindi, 'The probable date of the first Arab expeditions to India', *Islamic Culture*, Vol. 20 (1946): pp. 250–66. Probably, these expeditions were to discourage the Indian rajas from helping the Persians against the Muslims. Qāḍi Athr Mubarikpurī, *Khilafat-i-Rashidah aur Hindustan* (Delhi: Nadwat al-Musannifīn, 1972), p. 103.
9. Al-Balazari, *Futuh al-Buldan*, p 240. According to Balāzari, Caliph 'Umar appointed 'Uthmān b. 'Aṣi from Banu Saqif to Bahrain in 15/636. In the same year, Uthmān sent his brother Ḥākim to Bahrain and he himself went to Omān and dispatched an army to Thānah. When the army returned he wrote to Caliph 'Umar to inform him of it. The caliph replied that 'O brother of Saqif, thou has placed the worm in the wood but I swear by God if our men had been killed I would have taken (slain) an equal number from your tribe.' He also sent a force to Broach and to the bay of Daybul under the command of his brother Mughīrah, who met and defeated the enemy.
10. Al-Balazari, *Futuh al-Buldan*, p. 421. The Muslim governors reached as far as Kashmir and Malwa as a result of occasional skirmishes with their Hindu

neighbours. For details see: J. F. Richards, 'The Islamic Frontier in the East: Expansion into South Asia', *South Asia*, Vol. 4 (1974): pp. 94–8. See also Saiyyid Abu Zafar Nadvi, *Tarikh-i-Sind* (A'zamgarh: Ma'arif Press, 1947), pp. 33–8; M. H. Zotenberg, *al-Tabari*, Translation, Vol. 3 (Paris: Maisonneuve, 1958), p. 519.

11. Zikriyah Qazvini, *Athar al-Bilad wa Akbar al Ibad* (Ustenfield: n.p., 1848/50), pp. 62–3.
12. M. H. Zotenberg, *al-Tabari*, Translation, Vol. 3 (Paris, 1958), p. 519.
13. Wink, *Al Hind*, Vol. 1, p. 202. For a general account on the Umayyads in India see: Qāḍi Athar Mubarikpurī, *Khilafat-i-Umwia aur Hindustan* (Delhi, 1975). Muḥammad b. Qāsim's expedition was the third expedition sent in the reign of Al-Walīd. The two early expeditions under Nabhan and Budayl were defeated by Rājā Dahir. See: Zafar Nadvi, *Tarikh-i-Sindh*, pp. 42–3. For an alternative account of the Arab invasions, suggesting their insignificance, see: A. L. Srivastava, *The Sultanate of Delhi (Including the Arab Invasions of Sindh), A.D. 711–1526* (Agra: Shiva Lal Agra wala & Co., 1950), p. 39.
14. On the evidence of Muḥammad b. Qāsim's invasions of Sind see: F. Gabrieli, 'Muḥammad ibn Qasim al-Thaqafi and the Arab Conquest of Sind', *East and West*, Vol. 15 (1964–5): pp. 281, 289. Muḥammad b. Qāsim has become increasingly relevant in the context of debates concerning Muslim nationalism and the two-nation theory. In the Pakistani imagination Muḥammad b. Qāsim symbolises victory; as a youth he confirmed his military superiority over several veteran military generals of Sind. In some works of fiction he is a symbol to shame Pakistani youth into devoting their lives to proselytisation and jihad. Furthermore, his invasion has been used to assert Sind's historical importance; Pakistani curriculum dubs Sind *Bābul-Islām* (the door for Islam), despite the fact that the region formed one of two routes for the invasion. While Muḥammad came via Baluchistan, his reinforcements and logistics were transported via sea route of Sind.
15. While one popular verse in the account of Balazarī suggests that he was a youth of 17, a less important source suggests that he was in his thirties.
16. ibid., p. 203.
17. Daudpota (ed.), *Chachnama*, p. 105.
18. Al-Balazari, *Futuh al-Buldan*, p. 424. This fact is also reported in the *Chachnāmah*. See: Daudpota, ed., *Chachnama*, p. 100.
19. Wink, *Al Hind*, Vol. 1, p. 203.
20. Daudpota, *Chachnama*, pp. 109–10.
21. ibid., pp. 115–20, 123–4, 132; Al-Balazari, *Futuh al-Buldan*, p. 425.
22. Daudpota, *Chachnama*, pp. 115–20, 123–4, 132; Al-Balazari, *Futuh al Buldan*, pp. 426–7.
23. Wink, *Al Hind*, Vol. 1, p. 205.
24. Daudpota, *Chachnama*, pp. 195–8, 204–7, 237–8; Al-Balazari, *Futuh al-Buldan*, p. 425. According to Yā'qubi, Muḥmmad b. Qāsim also founded a

city by the name of Manṣūrah. Ya'qubi, *Tarikh-i Yaqubi* (Beirut, 1375 AH), pp. 50, 55, 177.

25. Daudpota, *Chachnama*, p. 241.
26. See *Chachnāmah*, *Fūtūh ul-Buldān* and the various *Kūfic* inscriptions found in Sind.
27. Al-Balazari, *Futuh al-Buldan*, p. 426–7; Daudpota, *Chachnama*, pp. 195–8, 204–7, 237–8.
28. Daudpota, *Chachnama*, pp. 200, 204, 208.
29. Al-Balazari, *Futuh al-Buldan*, pp. 426–7; Daudpota, *Chachnama*, pp. 202, 207–10, 214, 216–18, 220–1, 225–6, 237–8.
30. Al-Balazari, *Futuh al-Buldan*, pp. 427–8. The relationship between Ḥajjāj and Sulaymān was antagonistic, since Ḥajjāj died before Sulaymān rose to power. His favoured ones, including Muḥammad b. Qāsim, were brutally eliminated when Sulaymān ascended the throne. For details see: Zakariyau I. Oseni, 'A Study of the Relationship between al-Ḥajjaj ibn Yusuf al-Thaqafi and the Marwanid Royal Family in the Ummayed Era', *Hamdard Islamicus Karachi*, Vol. 10, No. 3 (1987): pp. 20–4.
31. Al-Balazari, *Futuh al-Buldan*, p. 428.
32. Andre Wink, *Al-Hind*, pp. 206–8.
33. Al-Balazari, *Futuh al-Buldan*, p. 431. See also: Ibn al-Athir, *Kamil fi al-Tarīkh*, Vol. 4 (Cairo, 1801), p. 283.
34. For details see: Wink, *Al Hind*, Vol. 1, pp. 209–12.
35. Al-Balazari, *Futuh al-Buldan*, p. 432.
36. M. Aslam, *Mujāhid-i-Kabīr Muḥammad ibn Qāsim aur us kay Janashīn* (Lahore: Riaz Brothers, 1996).
37. Throughout Islamic history *khuṭba* has remained a symbol of royal authority. It is one of the means through which Muslim rulers communicated their ideas with their subjects. *Khuṭba* was more important before the advent of modern means of communication as it informed people about many things concerning their ruler and his ideas. Mubarikpurī, *Hindustān main Arabon kī Hukūmatain*, p. 48.
38. Mubarikpurī, *Hindustān main Arabon kī Hukūmatain*, p. 41. The major references to this dynasty are found in Balāzarī's *Fūtūh ul-Buldān*.
39. ibid., pp. 44–7.
40. ibid., p. 77. Abu Zayd Sirafī, *Silsilat al-Tawarīkh* (Paris, 1811), p. 77; Ibn-Khaldun, *Kitab al-Ibar*, Vol. 2 (Cairo: n.p., 1284), p. 327.
41. M. A. Ghafur, 'Fourteen Kufic Inscriptions of Banbhore, the site of Debal', *Pakistan Archaeology*, Vol. 3 (1966): pp. 81–3.
42. Mubarikpurī, *Hindustān main Arabon kī Hukūmatain*, pp. 84–5.
43. Y'aqubi, *Tārīkh-i-Y'aqubī*, pp. 50, 55, 177.
44. Mubarikpurī, *Hindustān main Arabon kī Hukūmatain*, p. 77.
45. Ibn-i Hazam, *Jamrat ul Ansāb al-Arab*, p. 118 in ibid., p. 86.
46. Ibn-i Hazam, *Jumratul al-Ansāb*, pp. 109–10 in ibid.
47. Al Muqaddasī, *Ahsan al-Taqasīm*, p. 485 in ibid.

48. Ibn al-Athīr, *Kamil fi al-Tārīkh*, Vol. 9, p. 143.
49. Ibn-Khaldun, *Kitab al-Ibar*, Vol. 2, p. 327.
50. *Marūjaz Zahab*, Vol. 1, p. 168. Quoted in: Mubarikpurī, *Hindustān main Arabon kī Hukūmatain*, p. 112.'
51. In the fourth century AH the Dāūdi Zāhirī *maslak* (religious beliefs) became popular in the eastern zones of Muslim Empire, replacing the Hanbali *maslak*. Therefore, al Muqaddasi describes the four *maslaks* of that time as Hanafite, Malikite, Shaf'īte, and Dāūdi. He does not mention Hanbali beliefs. The Dāūdi Zāhirī *maslik* was not only popular in Sind and Manṣūrah but also in Persia. In the times of Bawayids, the followers of this *maslak* were unimportant civil and military administrative positions. See: ibid., p. 120; Al Muqaddasī, *Ahsan al-Taqasīm*, p. 30.
52. Yaqut al-Hamavi, *Mujama al-Buldan*, Vol. 9 (Cairo, 1324 AH), pp. 151–2.
53. *Marūjaz Zahab*, Vol. 1, p. 168. As quoted in: Mubarikpurī, *Hindustān main Arabon kī Hukūmatain*, p. 110.
54. *Zeel Tajarat ul Umam*, pp. 264–5 in ibid., p. 115. In 385/995 Samsām ud-Daulah Dalmi ordered the assassination of the Turks residing in Persia and when some of the Turks fugitives reached Sind they were eliminated by the Hībariyāh ruler of Sind.
55. Al-Muquddasī, *Ahsan al-Taqasīm*, pp. 476–7 in ibid., p. 124.
56. Yaqūt, *Majm'a al-Buldan*, Vol. 5, p. 419 in ibid.
57. Buzurg Ibn Shahriyar, *Aja'ib al-Hind* (Cairo: n.p., 1336 AH), pp. 3–4.
58. ibid.
59. Yaqūt, *Majm'a al-Buldan*, Vol. 5, p. 419. in Mubarikpurī, *Hindustān main Arabon kī Hukūmatain*, p. 124.
60. This could have been one of his cultural misunderstandings; he may have labelled Zoroastrianism as the Sabi religion. For details on Sabian see: Judah Benzion Segal, *The Sabian Mysteries: The planet cult of ancient Harran, Vanished Civilisations*, ed. E. Bacon (London: Thames and Hudson, 1963).
61. The Buddhist population of Sind was probably also considered to be that of idol worshipers. Al Muquddasī, *Ahsan al Taqasīm*, p. 474 in ibid., p. 147.
62. Istakhrī, *Al Masalik al-Mumalik*, p. 176 in ibid.
63. Istakhrī, *Al Masalik al-Mumalik*, p. 172 in ibid., p. 122.
64. Mubarikpurī, *Hindustān main Arabon kī Hukūmatain*, pp. 240–1.
65. Al-Mas'ūdī, *Muruj al-Ḍhahab wa Ma'adin al-Jawahir* (Baghdad, 1283 AH), p. 82.
66. Mubarikpurī, *Hindustān main Arabon kī Hukūmatain*, p. 169.
67. ibid., 205.
68. ibid., p. 231.
69. ibid., p. 236.
70. Mubarikpurī, *Hindustān main Arabon kī Hukūmatain*, p. 232. See also, Muḥammad Aslam, *Mohammad bin Qasim aur us kay Jansaheen* (Lahore: n.p., 1996), p. 69.
71. Ibn-Huqal, *Kitab Surat al-Ard*, p. 319.

72. Mubarikpurī, *Hindustān main Arabon kī Hukūmatain*, pp. 233–4.
73. Al Masūdī mentions the strategy of one Musa ibn Haroon who lived in a fort near Multan. *Maroojaz Zahab*, Vol. 2, pp. 9–11 in ibid., pp. 236–7.
74. *Ahsan al Taqsīm*, p. 478 in ibid., p. 239.
75. *Ahsan al Taqsīm*, pp. 480–1 in ibid., pp. 241–2.
76. *Ahsan al Taqsīm*, pp. 480–1 in ibid., pp. 241–2; Al Muqaddasī, *Masalik al Mumalik*, p. 173. On the temple in Multan see: Ibn al Wardi, *Kharidat al Ajaib* (Cairo: n.p., n.d.), p. 62.
77. Al-Muqaddasī, *Masalik al-Mumalik*, p. 173.
78. Sayyid Muḥammad Masum Bakkarī, *Tarikh-i Masumī* (Bombay: n.p., 1938), p. 32.
79. Its major cities were Kīz, Tīz, Qanzbūr, Beh, and Bind. Al-Iṣtakhrī, *Al-Masalk wa 'l-Mumalik*, p. 178; Al-Maqdisi, *Ahsan al-Taqasim*, p. 477. The three regions that al-Iṣtakhrī describes are Kharūj, Jadrān and Mushki.
80. Mubarikpurī, *Hindustān main Arabon kī Hukūmatain*, p. 255.
81. ibid.
82. ibid., p. 256.
83. ibid., p. 257; Aslam, *Muḥammad ibn Qāsim aur us kay Janashīn*, p. 27.
84. Mubarikpurī, *Hindustān main Arabon kī Hukūmatain*, pp. 257–8.
85. ibid., pp. 258–9.
86. Mubarikpurī, *Hindustān main Arabon kī Hukūmatain*, p. 257.
87. ibid., pp. 257–8. In Yaqūt Hamavī, *Majmaul-Buldan*, Vol. 8, p. 132. The date is mentioned.
88. Mubarikpurī, *Hindustān main Arabon kī Hukūmatain*, pp. 266–7.
89. Al-Iṣtakhrī, *Masalik al-Mamalik*, pp. 176–8.
90. *Marūjaz Zahab*, Vol. 1, p. 110 in ibid., p. 267.
91. ibid., p. 259.
92. ibid., p. 267.
93. ibid., p. 275.
94. ibid., p. 267.
95. ibid., p. 269.
96. ibid., pp. 279–81.
97. Ibn-Huqal, *Kitāb Surat al-Ard* (Leyden: n.p., 1938), p. 317. For an account on geography of Sind and Hind, see also: Al-Idrisi, *Nuzhat al-Mushtaq fi Ikhtiraq al-Afaq* (Aligarh: n.p., 1954), pp. 26–30.
98. Including Manṣūrāh (the capital), Daybul, Zandrīj, Kidār, Mayāl, Tanbalī, Nirūn, Kalarī, Innarī, Ballarī, Maswāhī, Bhēraj, Baniā, Manjabirī, Sadosān, Alar (Alor Sind) Soparā (Mumbai) Kinās, Chīmūr (Mumbai). Bashshari al-Maqdisi, *Ahsan al-Taqasim fi Ma'rifat-al-Aqalim* (Leiden: n.p., 1906), pp. 476–7, 489. Despite Muslim settlements in other cities, the city of Daybul remained the focus of attention for Muslim geographers. Al Sayuti and Ibn al-Athir mention an earthquake in Daybul that destroyed a large number of the population. Al-Sayuti, *Tarikh al-Khulfa* (Lahore: n.p., 1892), p. 254; Ibn al-Athir, *Kamil fi al-Tarikh*, Vol. 7, p. 185.

99. Excluding Soparā and Chīmūr from the aforementioned names. Al-Iṣtakhrī, *Al-Masalkwa 'l-Mumalik* (Leyden: n.p., 1927), p. 173.
100. Khārijites (or *Khāriji*, plural *Khawārij*, literally meaning 'those who went out'), historically known as the *Shurah* (literally: the buyers or 'those who have traded the mortal life – *al-Dunya* – for the other life – the after-life or *al-Aakhirah*) form a Muslim heterodox sect distinct from Shi'a and Sunni Islam on the grounds of the extreme doctrine of *Takfīr* (from *kafir*) and other radical political views. The Khārijites emerged as a distinct group during the times of the final Rāshidūn caliph Ali ibn Abi Talib. They initially supported the caliph but later rejected his leadership on the grounds that any Muslim could be a leader of the Muslim community and had the right to revolt against any ruler who deviated from their interpretation of Islam. Due to their radical religious doctrines, they were viewed as a threat for the central Muslim empire at Damascus and later Baghdad. The Khārijites therefore, had larger concentrations in the peripheral regions of the central Muslim empire. Jeffrey T. Kenney, *Muslim Rebels: Kharijites and the Politics of Extremism in Egypt* (New York: Oxford University Press, 2006); Hussam S. Timani, *Modern Intellectual Readings of the Kharijites*, American University Studies, Series 7: Theology and Religion (New York: Peter Lang Publishing Inc., 2008); John Walker Lindh, Omar Bakri Muḥammad, Mullah Krekar, *Islamists by Sect: Kharijite Islamists, Shi'a Islamists, Sunni Islamists* (Books LLC, 2010).
101. The followers of the fourth Rāshidūn caliph Ali were mentioned as '*Rawāfids*'. See: U. N. Day, *Some Aspects of Medieval Indian History* (Delhi: D. K. Fine Arts Press, 1990), p. 21.
102. Ismā'īlism is the second largest sect of Shi'ism, after *Athna Ashari*. For a detailed account of Ismā'īlism see: Farhad Daftary, *The Ismailis: Their History and Doctrines* (Cambridge: Cambridge University Press, 1990); Bernard Lewis, *The Assassins: A Radical Sect in Islam* (Great Britain: Weidenfeld and Nicolson, 1967). S. M. Stern, 'Ismaili Propaganda and Fatmid Rule in Sind', *Islamic Culture*, Vol. 23 (1949), pp. 298–307; 'Abbas al-Hamdani, *The Beginning of the Ismaili da'wa in Northern India* (Cairo, 1956).

Chapter 2 Maḥmūd of Ghazna: Plunderer, Strategist or Iconoclast?

1. This is one of the most popular accounts supporting the image of Maḥmūd as a brutal plunderer bent on proselytisation. Extracts from 'Wonders of Things Created, and Marvels of Things Existing', in Zakariya al-Qazwini, *The History of India, As Told By Its Own Historian*, transl. into English by Henry Miers Elliot(London: Eli born Classic Series, 1952), pp. 97–9.
2. A comparative analysis of the Turko-Persian and Sanskrit sources suggests that many of these accounts of Somnath temple are historical fantasies. see: Romila

Thapar, *Somanatha: The Many Voices of a History* (New York: Penguin Books, 2005).

3. For the causes of Maḥmūd's invasions in India see Jagadish Narayan Sarkar, *The Art of War in Medieval India* (Delhi: Munshiram Manoharlal, 1984), pp. 36–7.
4. C. E. Bosworth, 'The Imperial Policy of the Early Ghaznavids', *Islamic Studies: Journal of the Central Institute of Islamic Research*, Karachi, Vol. 1, No. 3 (1962), p. 45. See also: M. H. Syed, *History of Delhi Sultanate* (New Delhi: Mehra Offset Press, 2004), p. 7.
5. For debate about the etymology of the word sultan, and its usages, see: C. E. Bosworth, 'The Titulature of the Early Ghaznavids', *Oriens*, Vol. 15 (1962); Mohammad Habib, *Sultan Mahmud of Ghaznin: A Study* (Lahore: Universal Books, 1978), pp. 20–1.
6. Iqtadar Hussain Siddiqui, *Authority and Kingship under the Sultans of Delhi (Thirteenth–Fourteenth Centuries)* (New Delhi: Manohar Publishers, 2006), p. 8.
7. For details see: Muḥammad Nazim, *The Life and Times of Sultan Mahmud of Ghazna* (New Delhi: 1971), pp. 147–9.
8. For an alternative account of Maḥmūd's invasions where he is stated to have been a mixture of success and failure see George Malagaris, *Mahmud of Ghazna* (forthcoming).
9. See: Zia ud-Din Baranī, *Fatawa Jahandarī*, compiled by Riaz Ahmad and trans. by Atiqur Rehman (National Institute of Historical and Cultural Research, 2004). Diya al-Dīn Baranī extends what is considered to be the political theory of the Delhi sultanate. Ḍiya al-Dīn Baranī in his book takes the example of Maḥmūd of Ghazna as an ideal ruler whose conduct should be followed by the sultans of Delhi.
10. ibid., pp. 147–65.
11. See: C. E. Bosworth, *The Ghaznavids: Their Empire in Afghanistan and Eastern Iran 994–1040* (New Delhi: Munshiram Manoharlal Press, 1992). Chapter II discusses the patrimonial bureaucratic staff in the administrative structure and chapter III elaborates on the patrimonial bureaucratic staff in the army.
12. Nizam, *The Life and Times of Sultan Mahmud of Ghazna*, pp. 141–2.
13. Al Maari, *Risalat ul Ghufran*, p. 153 as cited in Nizam, *The Life and Times of Sultan Mahmud of Ghazna*, p. 140, fn. 7.
14. Siddiqui, *Authority and Kingship*, p. 9.
15. AbulFazal Muḥammad al Baihaqi, *Tārīkh-i Mas'ūdī* (Tehran, 1324 AH), pp. 266–7.
16. As quoted in Bosworth, *Ghaznavids*, p. 76.
17. Abul Fazl al Baihaki, *Tarikhus-Subuktigin*, translated and edited by H. M. Elliot and John Dowson (Lahore: Sang-e-Meel Publications, 2006), p. 86.
18. Siddiqui, *Authority and Kingship*, p. 10.
19. Zainal Akhbar Gardezi, p. 497. Cited in Siddiqui, *Authority and Kingship*, p. 10.

20. Bosworth, *The Ghaznavids*, pp. 109–10; Habib, *Sultan Mahmud of Ghazni*, p. 77.
21. Bosworth, *The Ghaznavids*, p. 114; Nazim, *Sultan Mahmud*, p. 133, fn. 4.
22. Bosworth, 'The Imperial Policy of the Early Ghaznavids', *Islamic Studies*, Vol. 1 (1962), part 3, pp. 49–82.
23. Bosworth, *The Ghaznavids*, pp. 67–79. For the causes of Maḥmūd's invasions in India also see: Sarkar, *The Art of War*, pp. 36–7.
24. For a detailed note on the dynamics of revenue extraction please see: ibid., pp. 75–6.
25. Ibn al-Athir, *al-Kamil fit-tarikh*, ed. C. J. Tornberg (Leiden, 1889), p. 132. For Mahmūd's campaigns of Multan, see also: Ashiq Muḥammad Khan Durrani, 'Sultan Mahmud and Multan', *Journal of the Pakistan Historical Society*, Vol. 50, No. 4 (2002): pp. 19–26.
26. Aufi, *Jawami al Hikayat*, in Elliot and Dawson, *History of India*, Vol. 2, p. 189; S. H. Hodivala, *Studies in Indo Muslim History* (Bombay, 1939), p. 176.
27. Utbi and Gardizi as quoted by Nazim, *Sultan Mahmud*, pp. 102, 114.
28. Bosworth, *The Ghaznavids*, pp. 76–7.
29. ibid.
30. ibid., p. 78.
31. ibid; B. K. Thapar, 'The Temple at Somanatha: History by Excavations', in K. M. Munshi, *Somnath: The Shrine Eternal*, Bombay (1951), pp. 105–33; M. A. Dhaky and H. P. Sastri, *The Riddle of the Temple at Somanatha* (Varanasi: 1974).
32. Romila Thapar is of the opinion that the attacks on temples had no communal motives whatsoever and were executed purely for imperialistic and economic reasons. Thapar, *Somnath*. See also: Aziz Ahmad, 'Epic and Counter Epic in Medieval India', *Journal of the American Oriental Studies*, No. 83 (1963): pp. 470–6. For an alternative account from Hindu communal perspective see: Richard M. Eaton, 'Temple Desecration and Indo-Muslim States', in Richard M. Eaton, *Essays on Islam and Indian History* (New Delhi: Oxford University Press, 2000); J. L. Mehta, *Advanced Study in the History of Medieval India (1000–1526)*, Vol. 2 (New Delhi: Sterling Publisher Pvt Ltd, 2007), pp. 58–60.
33. Edward C. Sachau, *Alberuni's India: An Account of the Religion, Philosophy, Literature, Geography, Chronology, Customs, Laws and Astrology of India About AD 1030*, Vol. 1 (Lahore: Ferozesons, 1962), p. vii; See also: Ansar Zahid Khan, 'Mahmud and Al-Biruni: A Reappraisal', *Journal of the Pakistan Historical Society*, Vol. 54, No. (2006): pp. 21–54.
34. Bosworth, *The Ghaznavids*, pp. 75–7.
35. ibid., p. 235.
36. ibid.
37. Baihaqi, *Tārīkh-i Mas'ūdī*, pp. 533–4.
38. ibid., pp, 13, 282–4, 530–1.
39. Bosworth, *The Ghaznavids*, ch. VIII. The relations between Mas'ūd and his *umarā'* were strained. The sultan tried to kill all those *umarā'* (nobility) that he found difficult to handle.

40. Bosworth, *Later Ghaznavids*, p. 64; idem, *Ghaznavids*, pp. 76–8.
41. Jackson, *The Delhi Sultanate*, p. 21.
42. For a general discussion of the sultan's relations with the caliph see: Bosworth, 'The Imperial Policy of the Early Ghaznavids', pp. 49–82.
43. Amir Hasan Siddiqi, *Caliphate and Sultanate in Medieval Persia* (Karachi: Amiyat-ul Falah Publication, 1969), p. 132.
44. In the Samanid and Qarakhānid dynasties the Sunni orthodox *'ulāmā'* were able to execute Aḥmad b. Khiḍr Khān in 488/1095 and Amir b. Nasar b. Aḥmad, who was forced to abdicate the throne in 331/942, because of their adherence to 'extremist' Shi'a ideas. Bosworth, *Ghaznavids*, pp. 51–3.
45. The expedition against the ruler of Multan, Abul Fath Dāūd b. Nasr in 396/1005–6.
46. ibid., p. 53.
47. Abdullah Saeed and Hassan Saeed, *Freedom of Religion, Apostasy and Islam* (Burlington: Ashgate, 2004).
48. Al-Utbi, *at Tarikh al-Yamini*, with commentary by Shaikh Manini, *al-Fath al-Wahbi* (Cairo: 1286/1869), Vol. 2, pp. 72–6; Jurb adhqani, *Tarjuma-yi Tarikh-i Yamini*, ed. Ali Qawim (Tehran, 1334/1955), pp. 180–1.
49. Bosworth, *The Ghaznavids*, pp. 52–3.
50. A *marthiya* (genera in Muslim poetry expressing lament) by Fakhari denotes: 'O woe and misery! The Qarmatiyan must be rejoicing, for they are safe now from stoning and the gallows!', ibid.
51. ibid., p. 53.
52. ibid.
53. For a detailed account see: C. E. Bosworth, *The Later Ghaznavids, Splendour and Decay: The Dynasty in Afghanistan and Northern India, 1040–1186* (New York: Columbia University Press, 1977).
54. ibid., p. 54.

Chapter 3 The Master who Conferred his Empire upon his Slaves: Shihāb al-Dīn Ghūrī

1. Persian extract from *Ṭabaqāt-i Nāṣirī* translated by Peter Jackson, *The Delhi Sultanate: A Political and Military History* (Cambridge: Cambridge University Press, 1999), p. 31.
2. From here onwards Shihāb al-Dīn Ghūrī's officers are mentioned as Mu'izzī.
3. Minhāj al-Dīn Abu 'Umar Usman Jūzjanī, *Ṭabaqāt-i Nāṣirī*, Persian (Lahore: n.p., 1952), p. 46. For a debate on history of the Delhi sultanate, image and reality see Blain H. Auer, *Symbols of Authority in Medieval Islam: History, Religion, and Muslim Legitimacy in the Delhi Sultanate* (New York: I.B.Tauris, 2012), p. 160.
4. Shihāb al-Dīn Ghūrī died in 1206, while Juzjāni wrote his book around 1260 in the reign of Nāṣir al-Dīn Mahmūd. Nāṣir al-Dīn's reign ends in

1266 and it is known that Juzjāni could not cover the last six years of Nāsir al-Dīn's reign. Thus *Tabāqāt-i Nāsiri* was compiled around 1260. For details on Juzjāni see: Mumtaz Moin, 'Qadi Minhaj al-Din Siraj al-Juzjani,' *Journal of the Pakistan Historical Society Karachi*, Vol. 15, No. 3 (July 1967): pp. 163–74.

5. Abu Amr Minhāj al-Dīn 'Uthmān Juzjānī, *Ṭabaqāt-i Nāsrī*, translated from Persian to Urdu by Ghulām Rasul Mahar (Lahore: Urdu Science Board, 1975), pp. 580–3.
6. ibid., p. 581.
7. For details see: K. A. Nizami, *Some Aspects of Religion and Politics in India during the Thirteenth Century* (New Delhi: [publisher], 1961), p. 31; Mohammad Habib, 'Shihab Uddin of Ghur', in *The Collected Works of Professor Mohammad Habib*, ed. K. A. Nizami, Vol. 2 (New Delhi: [publisher], 1981), p. 140; C. E. Bosworth, 'The Early Islamic History of Ghur', *Central Asiatic Journal*, Vol. 6 (1961: Wiesbaden), p. 118.
8. Iqtadar Hussain Siddiqui, *Authority and Kingship under the Sultans of Delhi (Thirteenth–Fourteenth Centuries)* (New Delhi: Manohar Publishers, 2006), p. 36.
9. C. E. Bosworth, 'The Rise of the Karamiyyah in Khorasan', *Muslim World*, Vol. 1 (Jan 1960): pp. 5–14. The Kāramiyya sect was founded by 'Alī Abdullah Muḥammad b. Karam al Sijzī Nishapurī (who was born in Sīstān, lived in Nīshapur and died in 225/869). The sect was popular in Khorasan, Gharjistān and Ghūr. Its doctrine denounced Sunnis and Shi 'i alike. This sect was accused by its rivals of having an anthropomorphic conception of God. However, they denied these charges. They interpreted Qur'an literally, but were sympathetic towards the Hanafite sect because of the pious life style of Imām abū Hanifah. Khorasan was the nucleus of this sect.
10. Iqtadar Hussain Siddiqui, 'Abu Addullah Muḥammad b. Kirām Aur Unki Ta'līmat', *Tahqīqāt-i Islām*, Aligarh, Oct.–Dec. 1991, pp. 226–36. As quoted in Siddiqui, *Authority and Kingship*, p. 36.
11. Juzjani, *Ṭabaqāt-i Nasrī*. As quoted in Siddiqui, *Authority and Kingship*, p. 36.
12. ibid.
13. Juzjani, *Tabaqat-i Nasri I* (English), p. 251.
14. This was near the headwaters of Farah Rūd and Marghab, located in the east and south-east of Herat, south of Gharjistān and Juzjān.
15. Ghiyāth al-Dīn captured Ghazna the capital of Ghaznavids. Later Shihāb al-Dīn captured the second capital of the dynasty, which was Lahore. Juzjani, *Tabaqat-i Nasri I* (English), p. 31.
16. Siddiqui, *Authority and Kingship*, p. 29.
17. Juzjani, *Tabaqat-i Nasri I* (English), p. 448. It was the largest city in the Garmsīr district.
18. Hardy, P. 'Dihlī sultanate,' *Encyclopaedia of Islam, Second Edition*. Brill Online, 1 February 2013, http://referenceworks.brillonline.com/entries/encyclopaedia-of-islam-2/dihli-sultanate-SIM_1848.

19. Siddiqui, *Authority and Kingship*, p. 30.
20. Fakhr-i Mudabbir, *Tarikh-i Fakhr al-Din Mubarak Shah*, ed. E. D. Ross (London: Royal Asiatic Society, 1927), 19–20. See also: M. S. Khan, 'A Study of Fakhr-i Mudabbir's Thoughts on Avoidance of Warfare', *Quarterly Journal of Pakistan Historical Society*, vol. 43, No. 4 (1995): pp. 293–9; idem, 'A Thirteenth Century Persian Source For the Art of Warfare in Early Medieval India', *Quarterly Journal of Pakistan Historical Society*, Vol. 38, No. 4 (1990): pp. 293–307. For a commentary on the religious beliefs of the Ghūrīds see: Anthony Welch, H. Keshani and A. Bain, 'Epigraphs, Scripture, and Architecture', *Muqarnas, an Annual on the Visual Culture of the Islamic World*, Vol. 19 (Leiden: E.J. Brill, 2002): 12–15.
21. A. B. M. Habibullah, *The Foundation of the Muslim Rule in India: A History of the Establishment and Progress of the Turkish Sultanates of Delhi (1206–1290)* (Allahabad: Central Book Depot, 1961), pp. 60–1.
22. Juzjānī, *Tabāqāt-i Nāṣirī* (Persian), p. 31.
23. Sadid ud-din Muḥammad Awfi, *Jawami'ul Hikayat*, Vol. 1, Part 2, ed. Muḥammad Nizam uddin Ahmad (Hyderabad: A.P, 1965–6), pp. 409–10.
24. *The Prithviraja Raso* of Chand Bardai and anonymous and incomplete *Prithviraja-Vijaya-Kavya* are two regional sources that provide details of this issue however, the authenticity of these contents is debated among the historians. Habibullah, *The Foundation of the Muslim Rule*, p. 19. For the account of Prithvi Raj Chauhan, see ibid., pp. 35, 39, 40, 42. See also Jayanaka Kasmiri, *History of Culture of Indian People*, ed. R.C. Majumdar and Pusalkar, Vol. 5: *The Struggle for Empire* (Bombay, 1957), p. 384, note 20. For the historical construction of Prithvi Raj and its impacts on current day Indo-Pak relations see John McLoad and Kanwar P. Bhatnagar, 'The Deaths of Prithvi Raj', *South Asia, The Journal of South Asian Studies*, Vol. 26, No. 2 (2001): pp. 91–205.
25. Juzjani, *Tabaqat-i Nasri I* (English), pp. 458–60.
26. ibid., p. 468; Siddiqui, *Authority and Kingship*, p. 32.
27. Later when the mosque was damaged by flood water, the gold drums, the melon, the wheel and the chain were sent to Herat with instructions that they should be melted and the money from their sale should be spent on the construction of a new congregational mosque. Finbarr B. Flood, *Objects of Translation: Material Culture and Medieval Hindu–Muslim Encounter* (Delhi: Permanent Black, 2009), pp. 126–8.
28. Ata Malik Juvaini, *Tarikh-i-Jahan Qusha*, ed. Mirza Muḥammad Qazwini, Part 2 (Leiden: n.p. 1916), p. 86.
29. Juzjani, *Tabaqat-i Nasri I* (English), pp. 401–2.
30. Siddiqui, *Authority and Kingship*, pp. 33–4.
31. ibid., p. 34.
32. In Juzjānī, *Tabāqāt-i Nāṣirī*, all three dynasties (i.e. the Ghiyāthī dynasty, the dynasty of Bamian and the Mu'izzīs) are included as offshoots of the Shansabānī dynasty.

33. Siddiqui, *Authority and Kingship*, p. 33.
34. ibid., p. 39.
35. Aitam or Aytamar appears to be a Turkish name and there was a later namesake of his who was a slave of Bahā al-Dīn Toghril. See also: Khurram Qadir, 'Implications of the Distinctive Features of the Ghūri Chain of Command', *Journal of History and Culture*, Vol. 22 (January–June 2001): p. 5.
36. Irfan Habib, 'Formation of the Sultanate Ruling Class', *Medieval India 1: Researches in History of India (1200–1750)*, ed. Irfan Habib (1992): p. 6.
37. Jackson, *The Delhi Sultanate*, p. 11.
38. ibid., p. 27.
39. Juzjānī, *Tabāqāt-i Nāṣirī* (Persian), p. 46.
40. ibid.
41. Juzjani, *Tabaqat-i Nasri I* (English), pp. 498–9, fn. 7.
42. Juzjānī, *Tabāqāt-i Nāṣirī* (Persian), pp. 45–9.
43. ibid., p. 46.
44. Sunil Kumar, *Emergence of the Delhi Sultanate* (New Delhi: Permanent Black, 2007), p. 80.
45. Juzjānī, *Tabāqāt-i Nāṣirī* (Persian), pp. 46–7.
46. ibid., p. 47.
47. The royal parasol, like the investiture, royal banner, seal (emblem) and robe, was part of the sultan's regalia. Though identifying a systematic colour code for parasols that indicates royal hierarchy is now impossible, colour-specific mentions within sources indicate that such a colour-coding of royal parasols did exist.
48. ibid., pp. 47–8.
49. He reigned for nine years.
50. For details see: Hasan Nizami, *Taj al-M'athir*, Vol. 2, pp. 239, 241–2. See also: Mumtaz Ali Khan, *Some Important Persian Prose Writing of the Thirteenth Century A.D. in India* (Aligarh: Department of History, Aligarh Muslim University, 1970), pp. 70–86; Habibullah, *The Foundations of the Muslim Rule*, p. 77; Ahmad, *Political Institutions*, p. 165; Jackson, 'Mongols in India', p. 69.
51. Juzjānī, *Tabāqāt-i Nāṣirī* (Persian), p. 49. Aybeg proclaimed himself as sultan in Lahore and spent his four and half year career as sultan, contesting Yildiz for Punjab and Ghazna.
52. ibid., pp. 47–8.
53. ibid., pp. 46–9.
54. ibid.
55. ibid.
56. Kumar, *The Emergence of the Delhi Sultanate*, p. 102.
57. ibid., p. 56. See also Syed Muḥammad Latif, *Early History of Multan* (Lahore, 1963), p. 18.
58. Daudpota, ed., *Cachnama*.
59. Fakhr-i Muddabir, *Tarikh-i-Fakhr-i-Muddabir*.

60. Written by Sadid al-Din Muḥammad Awfi.
61. Juzjānī, *Tabāqāt-i Nāṣirī* (Persian), p. 56.
62. ibid; Kumar, *Emergence of the Delhi Sultanate*, p. 102. His coinage was found in a hoard at Haryana. His bullion type coins bore the reflection of a horseman and Nandi bull. See also: Thomas, *The Pathan Kings*, p. 101.
63. Juzjānī, *Tabāqāt-i Nāṣirī* (Persian), p. 56.
64. ibid. It was the turbulent political situation of the Ghūrīd empire and *interregnum* that benefited Qabacha who rose to prominence in a short period of time and became a threat for both Ghazna and Delhi. Kumar, *The Emergence of the Delhi Sultanate*, p. 122.
65. Juzjānī, *Tabāqāt-i Nāṣirī* (Persian), pp. 56–7.
66. ibid., pp. 57–8; Iqtadar Hussain Siddiqui, *Perso-Arabic Sources of Information on the Life and Conditions in the Delhi Sultanate* (Delhi: Munshiram Manoharlal Press, 1992), pp. 2–4.
67. Juzjani, *Tabaqat-i Nasri I* (English), p. 532–4.
68. Peter Jackson, 'Jalal al-Din, the Mongols and the Khwarazmian conquest of the Punjab and Sind', *Iran*, Vol. 28 (1990): pp. 45–54. See also: Ghulam Rabbani Aziz, *A Short History of Khwarizm Shahis* (Karachi: n.p., 1956). For Mongol invasions in Khwārizm Shāhī territories see also: J. J. Saunders, *The History of the Mongol Conquests* (London: Routledge and Kegan Paul, 1971), pp. 61–2.
69. Juzjani, *Tabaqat-i Nasri I* (English), pp. 532–4.
70. ibid. For detail on the contest between Khwārzam Shāhīs and the Mongols see: Satish Chandara, *Medieval India: From Sultanate to the Mughals, Delhi Sultanate (1206–1526)* (New Delhi: Har-Anand Publications Pvt, Ltd, 1997), pp. 37–8.
71. Juzjani, *Tabaqat-i Nasri I* (English), p. 532–4.
72. Juzjānī, *Tabāqāt-i Nāṣirī* (Persian), p. 58.
73. ibid., Fakhr-i Muddabir, *Tarīkh-i Fakhr al-Dīn Mubārak Shāh*, p. 23; Hasan Nizami, *Taj al-Ma'asir: The History of India as Told by Its Own Historians* vol. 2 (Allahabad: Kitab Mahal, n.d.), translated by Elliot and Dowson, p. 227. He was raised to the senior positions after appropriate training. For details of about the Mu'izzī slave training see: Kumar, *The Emergence of the Delhi Sultanate*, pp. 80–2.
74. Juzjānī, *Tabāqāt-i Nāṣirī* (Persian), p. 58.
75. Mehrdad and Natalie H. Shkoohy, 'The Architecture of Baha' al-Din Tughrul in the Region of Bayana, Rajasthan', *Muqarnas*, Vol. 4 (1987): pp. 114–32.
76. Juzjānī, *Tabāqāt-i Nāṣirī* (Persian), p. 58.
77. ibid., p. 59.
78. ibid. The Persian evidence here seems very clear that he was not subservient to Aybeg, and there is no 'ambiguity' in the source as mentioned by Kumar, *The Emergence of the Delhi Sultanate*, p. 90.
79. Juzjānī, *Tabāqāt-i Nāṣirī* (Persian), p. 58.
80. Mehrdad and Natalie H. Shokoohy, *Rajasthan I* (London, 1986), pp. 51–3.

81. Since it was Iltutmish who purchased the elite slaves of Toghril (Nāṣir al-Dīn Ali Tamar al-Bahā'i and possibly Malik 'Izz al-Dīn Toghril Bahā'i) from his sons it is clear that Iltutmish outlived Toghril. Furthermore, the fact that they sold their father's slaves to Iltutmish indicates that the financial position of the progeny of Toghril was less than those of Iltutmish. See: Kumar, *The Emergence of the Delhi Sultanate*, p. 96.
82. ibid., p. 123.
83. Juzjānī, *Tabāqāt-i Nāṣirī* (Persian), pp. 59–60.
84. ibid.
85. ibid., pp. 60–1. For *iqṭā'* see: Kunwar Muḥammad Asharf, *Life and Conditions of the People of Hindustan (1200–1550)* (Karachi: Indus Publications, 1978), p. 74.
86. Juzjānī, *Tabāqāt-i Nāṣirī* (Persian), pp. 60–1.
87. ibid., p. 61. Quṭb al-Dīn Aybeg did not assume the title of sultan in the life time of Ikhtiyār al-Dīn Bakhtiyār Khaljī.
88. ibid.
89. ibid., pp. 61–2.
90. ibid., pp. 62–3.
91. ibid., p. 63.
92. ibid., pp. 62–9.
93. Juzjani, *Tabaqat-i Nāṣiri* (English), translated by Raverty, p. 559, fn. 3.
94. Peter Jackson, *The Delhi Sultanate*, p. 34.
95. ibid., p. 31.
96. Juzjani, *Tabaqat-i Nāṣiri* (English), translated by Raverty, pp. 558–9, fn. 9.
97. Juzjānī, *Tabāqāt-i Nāṣirī* (Persian), p. 65.
98. ibid., pp. 69–70; Juzjani, *Tabaqat-i-Nāṣiri* (English), translated by Raverty, p. 576, fn. 3.
99. Juzjānī, *Tabāqāt-i Nāṣirī* (Persian), pp. 70–2. According to inscriptions, Diwkot was a Muslim stronghold in West Bengal. Abdul Karim, ed., *Corpus of the Arabic and Persian Inscriptions of Bengal* (Dacca, 1992), pp. 48–53.
100. Juzjānī, *Tabāqāt-i Nāṣirī* (Persian), pp. 70–2.
101. ibid., p. 53; According to Juzjānī, Aybeg was able to win the favour of Sultan Shihāb al-Dīn when at one banquet the sultan bestowed presents consisting of gold, silver and ready money on his slaves. Quṭb al-Dīn distributed the share that he received to the Turks (these were probably the slaves of the sultan. The word 'Turk' usually meant slave: for details see Jackson, *The Delhi Sultanate*, Appendix Word Turk), janitors and other attendants. And nothing remained for himself. On hearing this, the sultan rewarded him with 'an honourable post among the important offices'.
102. Juzjani, *Tabaqat-i Nasri*, Vol. 1 (English), translated by Raverty, p. 512, fn. 4.
103. ibid.
104. Jackson, *The Delhi Sultanate*, p. 26.
105. Qadir, 'Chain of command', p. 6.
106. Juzjānī, *Tabāqāt-i Nāṣirī* (Persian), p. 53.

107. Jackson, *The Delhi Sultanate*, p. 12. Habib, 'Ruling Class', p. 5. The series of conquests attributed to Aybeg is as follows: In 588/1193 Delhi and in 589/1194 Kōl (modern Alīgarh) fell into Ghūrīd possession. In the same year, Shihāb al-Dīn came to invade the Gāhadavāla kingdom, the leadership of the vanguard was shared between the Ghūrī commander, 'Izz al-Dīn Husayn Khārmil and Quṭb al-Dīn Aybeg. In 594/1198 Badaun was taken by him. Around 592/1196, Aybeg advanced towards Gujarāt and Shihāb al-Dīn sent the reinforcements to aid him.
108. Siddiqui, *Perso-Arabic Sources*, pp. 168–9.
109. ibid.
110. ibid., p. 50.
111. Hasan Nizami, *Taj ul-Ma'thir* as quoted in Jackson, *The Delhi Sultanate*, p. 20.
112. Jackson, *The Delhi Sultanate*, p. 31.
113. ibid.
114. See Chapter 1 on the Umayyads.
115. Pushpa, *Sanskrit Inscription of the Delhi Sultanate*, pp. 4, 12, 218. Also see: Flood, *Objects of Translation*, pp. 113–15. For conceptualising otherness from the data extracted by study of inscriptions Cynthia Talbot, 'Inscribing the Other, Inscribing the Self: Hindu–Muslim Identities in Pre-Colonial India', *Comparative Studies in Society and History* 10/1995; 37 (04): 692–722.
116. Fakhr-i Muddabir, *Tarikh-i-Fakhr-i-Muddabir*, p. 26.
117. Juzjani, *Tabaqat-i Nāṣiri* (Persian), pp. 54–5.
118. Juzjani, *Tabaqat-i Nāṣiri* (Persian), pp. 53–5.
119. H.G. Raverty, *Ghaznan and its Environs: Geographical, Ethnographical and Historical*, ed. Ahmed Nabi Khān (Lahore: Sang-e-Meel Publications, 1995), pp. 40–1.
120. Jackson, *The Delhi Sultanate*, p. 26.
121. Siddiqui, *Perso-Arabic Sources*, p. 48.
122. Fakh al-Din Mubarik Shah, *Fakhr-i-Muddabir*, pp. 33–5, 73.
123. Sadiduddin Muḥammad Awafi, 'Jawami'ul Hikayat wa-Lavami'ur Rivayat', in Perso-Arabic Sources, p. 27.
124. Aziz Ahmad, *Political History and Institutions of the Early Turkish Empire of Delhi (1206–1290)* (Delhi: 1972), p. 146.
125. ibid.
126. Qadir, 'Chain of Command', p. 9.
127. Iqtidar Hussain Siddiqui, 'Social Mobility in the Delhi Sultanate', *Medieval India 1: Researches in History of India (1200–1750)*, ed. Irfan Habib (1992): p. 32.
128. Significantly, Balban used the same claim to acquire legitimacy to when he ascended the throne.
129. Jackson, *The Delhi Sultanate*, p. 31.
130. Hasan Nizami, *Taj al Maathir*, Eng. trans and ed. Elliot and Dowson, *The History of India as told by its own Historians*, Vol. 2, p. 57. This book covers the history *(manaqib)* of Ghūrīds from 1205 to 1228. For details see: Slama

Ahmad Farooqi, *A Comprehensive History of Medieval India: From Twelfth to Mid Eighteenth Century* (New Delhi: Dorling Kindersley, 2010), p. 7; Iqtadar H. Siddiqui, *Indo-Persian Historiography Up To The Thirteenth Century* (Delhi: Primus Books, 2010), pp. 40–52.

131. Jackson, *The Delhi Sultanate*, p. 19.
132. ibid.
133. Pushpa Prashad, *Sanskrit Inscriptions of Delhi Sultanate* (Delhi: Oxford University Press, 1990), pp. 4, 12, 218.
134. Kumar also identifies the problems of reliability of the Persian texts. He maintains that in the Persian textual sources of the Delhi sultanate 'the History of all the "Hindustan"... the Punjab, Ganga-Jamuna plain ... is observed through what is usually a very narrow prism. Interesting vignettes, together with broad generalisations, obscure the small human experience on which the authors of the *tawarikh* of the sultanate period usually base their narratives'. For details see: Kumar, *The Emergence of the Delhi Sultanate*, pp. 20–45. For general comments on the histories of Hasan Nizami and Fakhr-i Muddabir please see: Iqtadar H. Siddiqui, *Indo-Persian Historiography Up To The Thirteenth Century* (New Delhi: Primus Books, 2010); Fakhr-i Muddabir, pp. 17–28; Hasan Nizami, pp. 40–54.
135. Fakhr-i Muddabir, *Tarikh Fakhar ud Din Mubarik Shah* (London: n.p., 1927), p. 26.
136. See: Juzjani, *Tabaqat*, Vol. 1 (English), translated by Raverty, p. 529, fn. 4.
137. Jackson, *The Delhi Sultanate*, p. 42.
138. ibid; Habib, 'Formation of the Sultanate Ruling Class', p. 9. He quotes a paragraph from *Ṭabaqāt-i Nasri*: 'As the Quṭbi Turks and *amirs* gathered from all directions at Delhi, some of the Mu'izzī Turks and *amirs* gathered to oppose them, and pursued the path of enmity. They left Delhi and assembling in the environs, began a rebellion and insurrection'.
139. 'They were, however, defeated; and Iltutmish, the "mystic prince", ordered all of them beheaded'. Ibid., p. 9.
140. ibid.

Chapter 4 The 'Mystic Prince': Shams al-Dīn Iltutmish

1. Although the name Iltutmish is pronounced in multiple ways in the Delhi sultanate accounts, the correct pronunciation of the word is alike to Iltutmish and not Iletemish. Simon Digby, 'Iletemish or Iltutmish? A Reconsideration of the Name of the Delhi Sultan', *Iran*, Vol. 8 (1970): pp. 57–64.
2. Juzjānī, *Ṭabaqāt-i Nāṣirī* (Persian), p. 55; Juzjani, *Tabaqat*, Vol. 1 (English), p. 528; Juzjānī, *Ṭabaqāt-i Nāṣirī* (Urdu), pp 741–3. Later historical sources claim that he had no male issue. See: Juzjani, *Tabaqat-i Nasri I* (English), p. 529, fn. 4.
3. Juzjānī, *Tabaqat-i Nāṣirī* (Persian), pp. 81–2. There was a quarrel between various factions of *umarā'*. While the Mu'izzī *umarā'* were also present during

Quṭb al-Dīn's reign, there were Quṭbi *umarā'* as well. Letters were written to the governor of Badaun in order to replace him with the unwanted Ārām Shāh. Also see: Habib, 'Formation of the Sultanate Ruling Class of the Thirteenth Century', in *Medieval India 1: Researches in History of India (1200–1750)*, ed. Irfan Habib (New York: Oxford University Press, 1992), pp. 9–10.

4. Juzjānī, *Ṭabaqāt-i Nāṣirī* (Persian), pp. 81–2.
5. *Amīrs* of Quṭb al-Dīn Aybeg = Quṭbi *amīrs* and *amīrs* of Shihāb al-Dīn = Mu'izzī *amīrs*. Ibid., pp. 81–2.
6. ibid.
7. Juzjānī, *Ṭabaqāt-i Nāṣirī* (Persian), p. 55.
8. Habbibullah, *Foundation of the Turkish Rule*, p. 92. *Tabaqat-i-Akbari* mentions that he issued coinage and assumed the title of Sultan 'Alā al-Dīn, although no such coinage has been found.
9. Juzjānī, *Ṭabaqāt-i Nāṣirī* (Persian), p. 55.
10. Habbibullah, *Foundation of the Turkish Rule*, p. 92.
11. Juzjānī, *Ṭabaqāt-i Nāṣirī* (Persian), p. 82.
12. ibid.
13. ibid.
14. ibid., pp. 82–3.
15. Juzjānī completed his work under the patronage of Balban in the times of Nāṣir al-Dīn Mahmūd. He was born in 1193/589 in Fīrūz Koh. Due to Mongol invasions, many of the '*ulāmā*' and scholars came to the subcontinent and he was among them. In 1226, he joined the court of Qabacha. Later he came to Delhi and completed Juzjānī, *Ṭabaqāt-i Nāṣirī*. He wrote *Ṭabaqāt* at the times of Nāṣir al-Dīn Maḥmūd around mid-1240s/670s and completed it in the year 1260/658. Baranī, *Tārīkh-i Fīrūz Shāhī* (Persian), p. 64.
16. Juzjānī, *Ṭabaqāt-i Nāṣirī* (Persian), pp. 78–80.
17. ibid., pp. 79–81.
18. ibid., p. 80.
19. Juzjani, *Tabaqat-i Nasri I* (English), pp. 603–4, fn. 6.
20. ibid., p. 80.
21. Later, Ṭamghāj was killed in a battle between Aybeg and Yildiz. Ibid.
22. ibid., pp. 80–1.
23. ibid., p. 81.
24. ibid. For an alternative account of his manumission see: Qadir, *Ghori Chain of command*, pp. 6–7.
25. See Raverty for instance who provides a critique over the characteristics of various sultans. Juzjani, *Tabaqat-i Nasri I* (English), pp. 545–56.
26. ibid., pp. 77–8.
27. ibid.
28. ibid.
29. Nizami, *Religion and Politics*, p. 172.
30. Hasān 'Alā Sījzī, *Fawāid al-Fū'ād*, trans. Muhammad Sarwar (Lahore, 1973), p. 358; Ḥāmid ibn Fazalullāh Jamalī, *Sīrat-al-Ārifīn*, trans. Muhammad Ayūb

Qādrī (Lahore, 1989), p. 112; Baba Farid, *Fawaid al-Salikin* in *Hast Bahisht [A collection of eight Malfuzat of eminent Chishti Shaykhs]*, Urdu trans. Ansar Sabiri (Lahore: Progressive Books, 1996), p. 12.

31. For instance see: Sayyid Muhammad Mubārak 'Alvī Kirmānī Amīr Khward, *Siyar-al-Awaliyāh*, trans. Ejāz al-Haq Qūddūsī (Lahore: 1980); Naṣīr al-Dīn Mahmūd, *Khayr-al-Mājālis*, ed. Khalīq Ahmad Nizāmī (Aligarh: Muslim University Aligarh, n.d.); Muhammad Jamāl Qāwām, *Qāwām-al-Āqā'id: Hadrat Khāwājā Nizām ul-Din Awliyā kay Chasham dīd Hālāt*, trans. Nisār Ahmad Fārūqī (Delhi: n.p., 1994); Hāmid ibn Fazalullāh Jamalī, *Sīrat-al-Ārifīn*, trans. Muhammad Ayūb Qādrī (Lahore: n.p., 1989).
32. Irfan Habib, 'Formation of the Sultanate Ruling Class of the Thirteenth Century', in Irfan Habib (ed.), *Medieval India 1: Researches in History of India (1200–1750)* (Delhi: Oxford University Press, 1992), pp. 8–15.
33. ibid., p. 12.
34. Jackson, *The Delhi Sultanate*, p. 326. Peter Jackson's argument seems convincing that Juzjānī's use of the term 'Turk' was synonymous with elite military slaves.
35. Habib, 'Ruling Class', p. 10.
36. Baranī, *Tārīkh-i Fīrūz Shāhī* (Persian), pp. 32–8.
37. Jackson, *The Delhi Sultanate*, p. 61.
38. Although not all biographies specify the status of the slave, the usage of word Turk suggests a Turk slave. Ibid., p. 61.
39. Habib, 'Ruling Class', pp. 10–11.
40. Most of these slaves were not politically important during the reign of Iltutmish. For instance, Balban and Kushlü Khān occupied relatively insignificant offices of the royal household when the sultan died.
41. Habib, 'Ruling Class', pp. 10–11.
42. Kumar, 'When Slaves were Nobles', pp. 48–50.
43. Juzjānī, *Ṭabaqāt-i Nāṣirī* (Persian), pp. 150–1. Malik Hindu Khān served at the centre at the time of the death of Shams al-Dīn Iltutmish.
44. ibid., pp. 138–40. Malik Kabīr Khān held the *iqtā'* of Palwal at the time of the death of Shams al-Dīn Iltutmish.
45. Irfan, 'The Sultanate Ruling Class', p. 12.
46. Habib, 'Ruling Class', p. 11.
47. Otto Spies, *An Arab Account of India in India in the 14th Century: being a translation of the chapters on India from al-Qalqashandi's Subh ul-Asha* (n.p.: n.d), pp. 66–7.Wolsley Haig, *Cambridge History of India*, Vol. 3: *Turks and Afghans* (Delhi: n.p., 1958), p. 45.
48. Here again, the office of *muqṭa'* was irregular as far as work rules were concerned. The *muqṭa'* could hold as much territory as was assigned to him owing to his personal ability. See: Nizami, *Aspects of Religion and Politics*, pp. 124–5.
49. Habib, 'Ruling Class', p. 11.
50. ibid., fn. 62.
51. ibid., p. 12.

52. ibid., p. 11.
53. For instance see: William Irvine, *The Army of the Indian Moghuls: Its Organization and Administration* (New Delhi: Eurasia Publishing House, 1962), p. 28; Habib, 'Ruling Class', p. 11.
54. Kumar, 'When Slaves were Nobles', p. 47.
55. Habib, 'Ruling Class', p. 12.
56. Kumar, 'When Slaves were Nobles', p. 45.
57. Habib, 'Ruling Class', p. 12.
58. ibid.
59. Juzjānī, *Ṭabaqāt-i Nāṣirī* (Persian), pp. 134–216.
60. Habib, 'Ruling Class', p. 10.
61. The use of term 'Turk' was not ethnic but cultural, linguistic and political. Yehoshua Frenkel, *The Turkic People in Medieval Arabic Writings* (Oxford: Routledge, 2015), introduction: Osman Sayyid Ahmad Isma'il Al Bili, 'Prelude to the General: A Study of Some Aspects of the Reign of the Eighth 'Abbasid Caliph, Al-Mu'tasim Bi-Allah (218–227/833–842)' (Reading: Ithaca Press, 2001).
62. Jackson, *The Delhi Sultanate*, pp. 62–3. These included 'Izz al-Dīn Kabīr Khān Ayaz and Badr al-Dīn Sonqur who was later titled as Nuṣrat Khān.
63. The Khitais included Sayf al-Dīn Aybeg, Sayf al-Dīn Ikit Khān Aybeg-i-Khitai. The Qara-khitai's slaves were: 'Izz al-Dīn Toghan and Ikhtiyar al-Dīn Aytagin. Jackson, *The Delhi Sultanate*, p. 63; Kumar, 'When Slaves were Nobles', pp. 32–5 (Table).
64. These slaves included Qamar al-Dīn Qiran Temür, Tāj al-Dīn Sanjar Kirit Khān, Ikhtiyar al-Dīn Yuzbeg Toghril Khān, 'Izz al-Dīn Balban (Küshlü Khān) and Sayf al-Dīn Aybeg Shamsī-i Ajmī Jackson. *The Delhi Sultanate*, p. 63; Kumar, 'When Slaves were Nobles', pp. 32–4.
65. A sub-group of Qipchaq or possibly Qangli which included Bahā al-Dīn Balban or Balban-i Khward, Sayf al-Dīn Aybeg (Kishlī Khān) and Nūsrat al-Dīn Sanjar or Sonqur (Shīr Khān). Jackson, *The Delhi Sultanate*, p. 63; Kumar, 'When Slaves were Nobles', pp. 32–5.
66. Habib, 'Ruling Class', p. 10.
67. Jackson, *The Delhi Sultanate*, p. 62.
68. These included 'Izz al-Dīn Kabīr Khān Ayāz, bought from the family of Yildiz's *amīr-i-shikār*, Nāsir al-Dīn Aytemür al-Bahāi slave of Bahā al-Dīn Ṭoghril and Nūṣrat al-Dīn Tāīsī the slave of Mū'iz al-Dīn Ghurī. Jackson, *The Delhi Sultanate*, p. 63: Kumar, 'When Slaves were Nobles', pp. 32–4.
69. See the account of Hindū Khān in Juzjani, *Tabaqat-i Nasri II* (English), pp. 744–6 and fn. 6. According to Juzjānī, he belonged to Mihar. Raverty explains that there is no place such as this in Turkistan and he was probably a converted Hindu. However, according to Peter Jackson, this person was a local Indian and thus was given the title of Hindū Khān.
70. Jūzjānī mentions an incident of Sultan Shihab al-Dīn, when he endowed gold and silver as gifts to each of his slave present in his part at night. Juzjānī, *Ṭabaqāt-i Nāṣirī* (Persian), p. 53.

71. Kumar, 'When Slaves were Nobles', pp. 41–2.
72. ibid., pp. 45–6.
73. ibid., p. 47.
74. ibid., pp. 45–8.
75. Siddiqui, *Perso-Arabic Sources of Information on the Life and Conditions in the Delhi Sultanate* (Delhi: Munshiram Manoharlal Press, 1992), pp. 168–9.
76. Siddiqui, *Authority and Kingship*, p. 54. The designation of *kotwāl* was important since he was not only in charge of the fort as mentioned by U. N. Day, but also conveyed the public will to the sultans. U. N. Day, 'The Military Organization of the sultanate of Delhi (1206–1388)', *Journal of United Province Historical Society*, Vol. 14, No. 1 (1941): pp. 48–57.
77. Juzjānī, *Ṭabaqāt-i Nāṣirī* (Persian), p. 598.
78. ibid., pp. 77–8.
79. ibid., p. 78.
80. Wright, *The Coinage and Meteorology of the Sultans of Delhi*, p. 75. Mohd Abdul Wali Khan, *Gold and Silver Coins of the Sultans of Delhi: In Andhra Pradesh Museum Hyderabad* (Government of Hyderabad: n.p., 1974), pp. 21–3.
81. 'Jawama al Hukayat', in Iqtadar Hussain Siddiqui, *Perso-Arabic Sources*, pp. 22–4; idem, *Authority and Kingship*, p. 52.
82. Siddiqui, *Authority and Kingship*, p. 52. Saifal-Dīn Aybeg Yaghantut died during the life of the sultan; he had an intimate relationship with the sultan and was very influential. See: Juzjānī, *Ṭabaqāt-i Nāṣirī* (Persian), pp. 142–3.
83. Abu Baker bin Ali Usman al-Kasānī, *Farsi-Tarjuma-i Kitab-ul Saidna of al-Biruni*, ed. M. Sotudeh and Afshar (Iran 1352 Shamsi), pp. 11–13 in ibid.
84. Muḥammad Awfi, *Lubub al Albab*, ed. E. C. Browne and Mirza Muḥammad Qazvini, Part 2 (Leiden and London: 1903–6), pp. 114–15.
85. Jackson, *A Political and Military History*, pp. 36–8.
86. Juzjānī, *Ṭabaqāt-i Nāṣirī* (Persian), p. 87.
87. Habbibullah, *Foundation of the Early Turkish Rule*, pp. 87–112.
88. Habib, 'Formation of the Sultanate Ruling Class', p. 12.
89. ibid., p. 13. The Muslim rule in the Bihar region was rickety and uneven. While some regions were directly under the Muslim control, the others were under the administration of the locals. The control of the regions was frequently lost and then recaptured. For Bihar under the Delhi sultans see A. K. Thakur, *India and the Afghans: A Study of a Neglected Region (1370–1576)* (New Delhi: Janaki Prakashan, 1992), p. 42.
90. Habib, 'Formation of the Sultanate Ruling Class', p. 12.
91. Juzjānī, *Ṭabaqāt-i Nāṣirī* (Persian), p. 103.
92. ibid.
93. ibid., pp. 153–4.
94. ibid., p. 137.
95. ibid., pp. 138–40.
96. ibid., pp. 143–5.

97. Habib, *The Sultanate Ruling Class*, p. 12.
98. Juzjānī, *Ṭabaqāt-i Nāṣirī* (Persian), p. 166.
99. Habib, 'The Sultanate Ruling Class', p. 12.
100. ibid., p. 13.
101. Irfan Habib, 'Economic History of the Delhi Sultante – An Essay in Interpretation', *Indian Council of Historical Research*, Vol. 4, No. 2 (Jan. 1978), p. 293.
102. Wright, *The Coinage and Metrology of the Sultans of Delhi*, pp. 72–5. The sultan minted the bullion coins with the names 'sri shalifa' (Khalifa) over the bull and 'sri Hamir' (*amir*) over the horseman. The symbols of bull and horse were used in the earlier coins of Aybeg and Iltutmish. For more information on the coin issued after the caliph's investiture, see: M. M. Rahman, *Encyclopedia of Historiography* (New Delhi: Anmol Publishers, 2005), p. 198. 'Surviving specimen of early Delhi mint was dated 1230–1, the coin was executed in the standard Islamic format; Arabic legends, reference to the current caliph, name and title of the sultan. No influence of Indian culture was visible on the face of the coin'.
103. Juzjānī, *Ṭabaqāt-i Nāṣirī* (Persian), p. 85.
104. Siddiqui, *Authority and Kingship*, p. 260.
105. For more on authority in the sultanate era see: Peter Hardy, 'The Authority of Muslim Kings in Medieval South Asia', *Purusartha*, Paris, Vol. 9 (1986): pp. 37–55; J. F. Richards, *Kingship and Authority in South Asia* (Oxford: Oxford University Press, 1998).

Chapter 5 The Tale of the '40 Slaves': The Post-Iltutmish Interregnum

1. Translated extract from Baranī, *Tārīkh-i-Fīruz Shāhī* (Persian), p. 26.
2. Shamsī = Belonging to Iltutmish. Ibid.
3. Jackson, 'The Mamluk Institution in Early Muslim India', p. 341; Qadir, 'The Amiran-i-Chihalgan', pp. 57–146; Gavin Hambly, 'Who were the Chahilgani, The Forty Slaves of Sultan Shams Al-Din Iltutmish of Delhi?', *Iran Journal of the British Institute of Persian Studies*, Vol. 10 (1972), pp. 57–62.
4. Baranī, *Tārīkh-i-Fīruz Shāhī* (Persian), p. 27.
5. Opposition to Rukn al-Dīn Fīrūz Shāh brought together Shamsī slave Kabīr Khān with free Turkish *umarā'* (including 'Alā al-Dīn Janī), the Ghūri *amīr* Sālārī and presumably Tajiks amirs like Junaydī. Tājīks were included in the plan to remove Bahrām Shāh as well. Jackson, *The Delhi Sultanate*, p. 68.
6. ibid., p. 69.
7. Juzjānī, *Ṭabaqāt-i Nāṣirī* (Persian), pp. 90–1.
8. ibid., p. 95.
9. Jūzjānī's offers contradictory assignations of the position of chief queen. At one point he calls Shāh Turkan the chief wife and at another point, describes

Raḍiyyah's mother as chief queen. It can therefore be inferred that both the women were prominent and powerful. ibid., p. 91, 95 respectively.

10. After having him enthroned, the *umarā'* returned to their *iqtā'*. Juzjānī, *Tabaqat-i Nāṣirī* (Persian), pp. 92–3.
11. Juzjānī, *Ṭabaqāt -i Nāṣirī* (Persian), pp. 91–2.
12. ibid., p. 91.
13. Wright, *Coins and Meteorology*, p. 246.
14. ibid., p. 92.
15. ibid.
16. ibid.
17. Juzjānī, *Ṭabaqāt -i Nāṣirī* (Persian), p. 92.
18. For instance, while the *wazīr* Niẓām al-Mulk Junaydī was a free officer, Malik 'Izz al-Dīn Salāri was a Shamsī slave, and Malik 'Izz al-Dīn Khān Ayāz was a Mu'izzī slave. For more regarding the rebellion of the provincial governors and *wazīr* please see: Qadir, 'The Amiran-i Chihalgan', pp. 101–2.
19. Juzjānī, *Ṭabaqāt -i Nāṣirī* (Persian), pp. 92–3.
20. ibid. See also Jackson, *The Delhi Sultanate*, p. 46.
21. Juzjānī, *Ṭabaqāt -i Nāṣirī* (Persian), p. 93.
22. ibid.
23. Juzjani, *Tabaqat-i Nasri II* (English), p. 633, fn. 6.
24. Juzjānī, *Ṭabaqāt -i Nāṣirī* (Persian), p. 93.
25. ibid.
26. ibid., p. 634.
27. ibid.
28. The conflict started in Manṣūrpūr and Tarāī'n, with the Turk *amīrs* and royal household slaves later becoming party to it. They killed Tāj-ul Mulk Muḥammad, the *dabīr* (secretary), the son of Mushrif-i-Mamālik, and Bahā al-Dīn Hasan-i-Asharī, Karīm al-Dīn-i-Zahid, Ḍiyā' ul-Mulk, the son of Nizām ul-Mulk Muḥammad Junaydī, Nizām al-Dīn Shafurkanī, Khwājah Rāshid al-Dīn Maikanī, *amīr* Fakhr al-Dīn, the *dabīr*, and a number of other Tajik officials. Ibid., p. 93. For more on the conflict between Turks and Tajiks see: Jackson, *The Delhi Sultanate*, p. 66.
29. Juzjānī, *Ṭabaqāt -i Nāṣirī* (Persian), pp. 93–4.
30. ibid., p. 94.
31. For details on Radiyah see: Peter Jackson, 'Sultan Radiyya Bint Iltutmish', in *Women in the Medieval Islamic World: Power, Patronage and Piety*, ed. Gavin R. G. Hambly (Hampshire and London: Macmillan, 1998), pp. 181–97.
32. Juzjani, *Tabaqat-i Nasri II* (English), p. 634, fn. 9.
33. Juzjānī, *Ṭabaqāt -i Nāṣirī* (Persian), p. 96.
34. ibid.
35. ibid.
36. For details see: Sunil Kumar, *Emergence of Delhi Sultanate*, p. 43; Peter Jackson, *The Delhi Sultanate*, p. 64.

37. ibid.
38. Juzjānī calls her *'lashkar kash'*. Juzjānī, *Tabaqat-i Nāṣirī* (Persian), p. 95.
39. ibid.
40. ibid.
41. ibid. Kumar, *The Emergence of the Delhi Sultanate*, p. 187. Kumar correctly observes that the issue of succession was left in ambiguity, and it seems that by bringing his son Rukn al-Dīn along to capital he had resolved to the succession of his son and not his daughter.
42. Juzjānī, *Ṭabaqāt -i Nāṣirī* (Persian), p. 95.
43. Juzjānī, *Ṭabaqāt -i Nāṣirī* (Persian), p. 97. Jackson, *The Delhi Sultanate*, p. 47.
44. ibid., pp. 95–6.
45. However, when he crossed the Ganges River and the hostile *maliks* took him prisoner, affliction overcame him and what became of him is unknown; he was probably put to death Juzjani, *Tabaqat-i Nasri I* (English), p. 633, fn. 7.
46. He was a junior Shamsī slave, Kumar, *The Emergence of the Delhi Sultanate*, p. 160. After the death of Malik Saif al-Dīn Yaghantūt in 631/1233–4, governorship of the province of Lakhnawti fall in his hands. ibid., p. 173.
47. Juzjani, *Tabaqat-i Nasri II* (English), p. 641, fn. 8.
48. Juzjānī, *Ṭabaqāt -i Nāṣirī* (Persian), pp. 96–7.
49. Juzjānī, *Ṭabaqāt -i Nāṣirī* (Urdu), pp. 811–12.
50. Ḥaḍrat Khwājah Niẓām al-Din Awiliyah, *Fawa'id-al Fū'ād*, trans. Muḥammad Sarwar (Lahore: 'Ulāmā' Acadamy, 1991), p. 375.
51. Juzjānī, *Ṭabaqāt -i Nāṣirī* (Persian), p, 97.
52. Juzjani, *Tabaqat-i Nasri I* (English), p. 641, fn. 8.
53. Juzjānī, *Ṭabaqāt -i Nāṣirī* (Persian), p. 97: In 639/1241 he was a free *amīr* who became the *nāi'b-i mulk*. Sunil Kumar, *Emergence of the Delhi Sultanate*, p. 255.
54. Juzjānī, *Ṭabaqāt -i Nāṣirī* (Persian), p. 97.
55. ibid., p. 97.
56. Juzjānī, *Ṭabaqāt -i Nāṣirī* (Persian), pp. 97–8. See also Jackson, *The Delhi Sultanate*, p. 88.
57. In 1237 Sayf al-Dīn Aybeg Qutlugh Khān, the Turk deputy in command of Raḍiyya's army, died. However, this office was not given to a Turk but instead to Ghurī *amīr* Quṭb al-Dīn Ḥasan ibn 'Alī. See: Juzjānī, *Tabaqat-i Nāṣirī* (Persian), pp. 96–7; Jackson, *The Delhi Sultanate*, p. 67.
58. Habshī Jamāl al-Dīn Yaqūt was made *amīr-i-ākhūr* (intendant of royal stables). He was executed around 1240. Although we do not find any mention of any other African in Radiyya's court, it is still certain that Yaqūt was not the only one of his race in the royal court. Juzjānī, *Ṭabaqāt -i Nāṣirī* (Persian), pp. 96–7; Jackson, *The Delhi Sultanate*, p. 67.
59. Jackson, *The Delhi Sultanate*, p. 67. Ibid., p. 97. For work on gender construction in the sultanate historical sources with regards to Raḍiyyah see: Alyssa Gabbay, 'In Reality a Man: Sultan Iltutmish, His Daughter, Raziya, and

Gender Ambiguity in Thirteenth Century Northern India', *Journal of Persianate Studies*, Vol. 4, No. 1 (2011): pp. 45–63.

60. ibid., p. 97. For work on gender construction in the sultanate historical sources with regards to Raḍiyyah see: Alyssa Gabbay, 'In Reality a Man: Sultan Iltutmish, His Daughter, Raziya, and Gender Ambiguity in Thirteenth Century Northern India', *Journal of Persianate Studies*, Vol. 4, No. 1 (2011): pp. 45–63.
61. ibid., pp. 98–9; see also: Kumar, *The Emergence of the Delhi Sultanate*, p. 261.
62. Athar Ali, *Military Technology and Warfare in the Sultanate of Delhi* (1206–1398 AD) (New Delhi: Icon Publications PVT. LTD, 2006), p. 25.
63. Juzjānī, *Ṭabaqāt -i Nāṣirī* (Persian), p. 99.
64. ibid.
65. ibid., p. 100.
66. ibid.
67. ibid; See also: Kumar, *The Emergence of the Delhi Sultanate*, p. 261.
68. ibid., p. 101. It was certainly an attempt by the *umarā'* to formally become the stakeholders in the power structure. See: Jackson, *The Delhi Sultanate*, p. 67.
69. Juzjānī, *Ṭabaqāt -i Nāṣirī* (Persian), p. 101.
70. ibid.
71. ibid.
72. ibid., p. 102.
73. 'with one of his own brothers'; the use of word 'brother' by Juzjānī may be taken in metaphorical sense indicating the colleagues. See also Jackson, *The Delhi Sultanate*, p. 68.
74. Juzjānī, *Ṭabaqāt -i Nāṣirī* (Persian), p. 102.
75. ibid.
76. ibid., p. 103.
77. It seems that he came to the centre without the permission of the sultan and was consequently killed. Ibid; Jackson, *The Delhi Sultanate*, p. 68.
78. Juzjānī, *Ṭabaqāt-i Nāṣirī* (Persian), p. 104.
79. ibid., p. 103.
80. Juzjani, *Tabaqat-i NasriI I* (English), pp. 660–1.
81. ibid., pp. 660–1, fn. 1.
82. ibid.; Jackson, *The Delhi Sultanate*, p. 69.
83. Juzjani, *Tabaqat-i Nasri I* (English), pp. 660–1. Raverty seems justified here to consider the possibility that out of the two Balbans it is more likely that Balban-i Kushlü Khān was the son in law of Iltutmish and not Balban-i Khward, since *Ṭabaqāt-i Akbarī* and *Tarīkh-i Farishtah* indicate this fact.
84. Including Mallik Ikhtiyār al-Dīn Aytegin, Malik Tāj al-Dīn Sanjar. Ibid., p. 106.
85. Juzjānī, *Ṭabaqāt -i Nāṣirī* (Persian), p. 104.
86. ibid., pp. 106–7.
87. Juzjani, *Tabaqat-i Nasri I* (English), p. 661, fn. 2 (according to *Ṭabaqāt-i Akbarī* it was Nagor, Sind and Ajmair).
88. Juzjānī, *Ṭabaqāt -i Nāṣirī* (Persian), p. 106.

89. Laiq Ahmad, 'Kara, A medieval Indian City', *Islamic Culture*, Vol. 55 (1981): p. 85; See also: C. A. Bayly, *The Small Town and Islamic Gentry in North India: the Case of Kara in Collected Papers on South Asia: The City in South Asia: Pre-Modern and Modern*, ed. Kenneth Ballhatchet and John Harrison (London: Curzon Press, 1980), pp. 20–47.
90. Juzjānī, *Ṭabaqāt -i Nāṣirī* (Persian), p. 106.
91. ibid., p. 666, fn. 3.
92. Juzjānī, *Ṭabaqāt -i Nāṣirī* (Persian), p. 108.
93. ibid.
94. ibid. Qiran means the one who slaughters. As quoted by *Jackson, The Delhi Sultanate*, p. 63, n. 15.
95. Juzjānī, *Ṭabaqāt -i Nāṣirī* (Persian), p. 106.
96. ibid., pp. 107–8. Jackson rightly observes that that Juzjānī expresses gratitude in multiple places in his *Tabaqāt*. Balban's biography gets the largest space in *Tabaqāt* since it was Balban who was responsible for Juzjānī's important position in the sultanate. Jackson, *The Delhi Sultanate*, p. 48.
97. Juzjani, *Tabaqat-i NasriI I* (English), p. 663.
98. Juzjānī, *Ṭabaqāt -i Nāṣirī* (Persian), pp. 107–8, Juzjani, *Tabaqat-i Nasri II* (English), p. 665, fn. 15.
99. ibid., p. 108.
100. ibid., pp. 108–9.
101. Jackson, *The Delhi Sultanate*, p. 68.
102. Juzjānī, *Ṭabaqāt -i Nāṣirī* (Persian), p. 109.
103. ibid., p. 116.
104. Juzjani, *Tabaqat-i Nasri II* (English), p. 676, fn. 2.
105. It is interesting to note that the list of the *umarā'* in the chronicles of the Delhi sultanate was graphically explained, indicating the ethnicity, post and political influence, in addition to the title. In case of Nāsir al-Dīn Mahmūd it seems evident that the *umarā'* that are mentioned in the list were the veteran generals and *muqṭa*'s who had more administrative and military experience than the sultan. Juzjani, *Tabaqat-i Nasri I* (English), pp. 673–4.
106. ibid., p. 673, fn. 5.
107. Juzjānī, *Ṭabaqāt -i Nāṣirī* (Persian), p. 116.
108. ibid., p. 109.
109. ibid., p. 116, i.e. *Koshak-i Sabz*.
110. ibid.
111. ibid.
112. Also mentioned as Balban-i Khward (the younger Balban). Here onwards will be mentioned as Balban. Baranī, *Tārīkh-i-Fīruz Shāhī* (Persian), p. 26.
113. According to Nizamī, Juzjānī deliberated created a religious persona of Nāsir al-Dīn in order to justify Balban's dominance. Nizami, *On History and Historians*, pp. 82–3. According to Khurram Qadir, *Sultan Nasir ud-Din Mahmood* (unpublished). Nāṣir al-Dīn Maḥmūd's personality is wrongly reflected in later

historical sources due to Baranī's unreliable statements. According to Juzjānī he was not a powerless monarch. He was able to dismiss Balban at one point of his career, remaining busy in commanding military campaigns. It does not seem possible that he had left the affairs of state depending on Balban solely and copied Quran and stitched caps for living.

114. Juzjānī, *Ṭabaqāt -i Nāṣirī* (Persian), p. 117.
115. Juzjani, *Tabaqat-i Nasri II* (English), p. 677, fn. 6.
116. Juzjānī, *Ṭabaqāt -i Nāṣirī* (Persian), pp. 118–19.
117. Juzjani, *Tabaqat-i Nasri II* (English), pp. 679–80, fn. 5.
118. Juzjānī, *Ṭabaqāt -i Nāṣirī* (Persian), p. 160.
119. ibid.
120. ibid.
121. ibid.
122. Juzjānī, *Ṭabaqāt -i Nāṣirī* (Persian), p. 161.
123. Juzjani, *Tabaqat-i Nasri I* (English), pp. 688–9, fn. 4.
124. ibid.
125. ibid., Ḥasan Qurlugh was a Khwārzim Shāhī ally. Kumar, *The Delhi Sultanate*, pp. 139–40.
126. Juzjānī, *Ṭabaqāt -i Nāṣirī* (Persian), p. 122.
127. ibid.
128. Juzjani, *Tabaqat-i Nasri II* (English), p. 689, fn. 5.
129. Juzjānī, *Ṭabaqāt -i Nāṣirī* (Persian), p. 122.
130. ibid., See also: Kumar, *The Delhi Sultanate*, pp. 74–6.
131. Juzjānī, *Ṭabaqāt -i Nāṣirī* (Persian), p. 122.
132. ibid., p. 123.
133. ibid.
134. ibid.
135. ibid; Kumar, *The Emergence of the Delhi Sultanate*, pp. 281–2.
136. Juzjānī, *Ṭabaqāt -i Nāṣirī* (Persian), pp. 123–4.
137. ibid., p. 124.
138. ibid.
139. ibid.
140. ibid., pp. 124–5.
141. ibid., p. 698.
142. ibid.
143. ibid., p. 125.
144. ibid.
145. ibid.
146. ibid. For details about Rayhān and his associates, see: Kumar, *The Delhi Sultanate*, p. 269.
147. Juzjānī, *Ṭabaqāt -i Nāṣirī* (Persian), p. 125.
148. The sultan's response to this marriage suggests that the incident must have been recent.
149. ibid., p. 126.

150. ibid., pp. 126–7.
151. ibid.
152. ibid.
153. ibid.
154. ibid., p. 127.
155. ibid.
156. ibid., pp. 128–9. Kumar, *The Delhi Sultanate*, p. 269.
157. Juzjānī, *Ṭabaqāt -i Nāṣirī* (Persian), pp. 129–30.
158. ibid.
159. ibid.
160. ibid.; Kumar, *The Emergence of the Delhi Sultanate*, p. 269.
161. Juzjānī, *Ṭabaqāt -i Nāṣirī* (Persian), pp. 129–30.
162. ibid.; Jackson, *The Delhi Sultanate*, p. 112.
163. Juzjānī, *Ṭabaqāt -i Nāṣirī* (Persian), pp. 130–1.
164. ibid., pp. 131–3.
165. Juzjani, *Tabaqat-i Nasri II* (English), p. 714, fn. 7.
166. ibid.
167. ibid., pp. 716–17, fn. 5.
168. Jackson, *The Delhi Sultanate*, p. 70.
169. ibid.
170. Juzjānī, *Ṭabaqāt -i Nāṣirī* (Persian), pp. 177–216. For the section of Kushlü Khān his name will be Balban-i Khward.
171. Ibn Battūtah, *'Ajāib al-Asfār: Safarnāmāh-i Ibn-i Battūtah*, trans (Urdu) Mulvi Muḥammad Hussayn, vol. 2 (Islamabad: National Institute of Historical Research, 1983), p. 63.
172. Jackson, *The Delhi Sultanate*, p. 70.
173. ibid., p. 70.
174. ibid., p. 71.
175. Saeed Ahmad, *The Rise and Fall of Muslims: From the Pious Caliphs to Abbasid Spain and Moghal Dynasties* (Delhi: Adam Publishers and Distributors, 2004), p. 204–7.
176. Juzjānī, *Ṭabaqāt -i Nāṣirī* (Persian), pp. 166–70.
177. Jackson, *The Delhi Sultanate*, p. 70.
178. Juzjānī, *Ṭabaqāt -i Nāṣirī* (Persian), pp. 166–7.
179. Jackson, *The Delhi Sultanate*, p. 71.
180. ibid., p. 72.
181. See the account of Nāsir al-Dīn Mahmūd.
182. Juzjānī, *Ṭabaqāt -i Nāṣirī* (Persian), pp. 174–6.
183. Jackson, *The Delhi Sultanate*, p. 70.
184. Juzjānī, *Ṭabaqāt -i Nāṣirī* (Persian), pp. 166–7.
185. For patterns of promotions of the Samanid slaves see: Niẓām al-Mulk Tusī, *Siyasatnāmā*, pp. 121–3.
186. For patterns of promotions of the Ghaznawid slaves see: Bosworth, *The Ghaznavids*, pp. 98–106.

187. This is something that Ibn Battūtah must have heard in the streets a century later when he visited India. Thus, it is possible that the story of Balban's regicide was a truth popularly believed. Ibn Battūtah, *'Ajāib al-Asfār*, p. 62.
188. Baranī does mention that Nāsir al-Dīn was a puppet (*namoona*) in the hands of Balban. However, he does not mention anything about the murder of Nāṣir al-Dīn. Baranī, *Tārīkh-i-Fīruz Shāhī* (Persian), pp. 26–7.

Chapter 6 Blood and Iron, Poison and Dagger: Balban's Prescription for Successful Rule

1. The early title of Balban was Bahā al-Dīn Balban; he is also mentioned as Balban-i Khward and Balban's slaves were called the Ghiyāthī slaves due to his royal title Ghiyāth al-Dīn.
2. Baranī, *Tārīkh-i Fīrūz Shāhī* (Persian), p. 26. The statements of Baranī are undoubtedly biased and cannot be accepted without internal criticism of the evidence. For details see: Peter Hardy, 'The Orato Recta of Baranī's Tarikh-i-Firuz Shahi – A fact or fiction?', *Bulletin of the School of Oriental and African Studies*, Vol. 20 (1957), pp. 315–21; idem, 'Didactic Historical Writing in Indian Islam; Ziya al-Din Baranī's treatment of the reign of Muḥammad b. Tughluq (1324–1351)', in Friedmann, ed., *Islam in Asia*, I, pp. 38–59; Iqtadar Hussain Siddiqui, 'Fresh light on Diya al-Din Baranī; the Doyen of the Indo-Persian Historians of Medieval India', *Islamic Culture*, Vol. 63 (1989): pp. 69–84; K. A. Nizami, *On History and Historians in Medieval India* (New Delhi: Munshiram Manoharlal Press, 1983); Irfan Habib, 'Baranī's Theory of the History of the Delhi Sultanate', *Indian Historical Review*, Vol. 7 (1980–1), pp. 99–115.
3. Khaliq Ahmad Nizami, *Royalty in Medieval India* (Delhi: Munshiram Manoharlal Publishers Pvt. Ltd, 1997), pp. 90–1.
4. In these monologues, Baranī described the details of various confidential meetings, despite the absence of any witness to the captured scene. For details see: Gavin Hambly, 'Baranī's *orato racta* in Tarik-i-Fīrūz Shahi'.
5. Baranī, *Tārīkh-i Fīrūz Shāhī* (Persian), pp. 56–62.
6. ibid., pp. 81–92; Jackson, *The Delhi Sultanate*, p. 78.
7. Baranī, *Tārīkh-i Fīrūz Shāhī* (Persian), pp. 109–10.
8. ibid., pp. 57–9.
9. ibid., pp. 30–3. Tatār Khān died in 665/1266–1267 and the sultan was able to install his own officers in the province. Jackson, *The Delhi Sultanate*, p. 94.
10. See: Utbi, *Kitab-i-Yamini*, p. 21; *Tārīkh-i Fakhrudin Mubarik Shah*, p. 13; *Taj ul-Maasir*, p. 79; For an account of Juzjānī calling Iltutmish *Zil Ilah fil alimeen*, see: *Adab ul Harab*, fn. 113a, p. 165; In the same source, Nāṣir al-Dīn Maḥmūd is called *Saya-i Yazdan* and *Zil Ilah fil alimeen*, p. 205. Minhāj addresses Balban as such on p. 230. Amīr Khusraw calls him *Sayah-i-Yazdan Pak*, in *Qiran-us-Sadain*, p. 205; He is called *Zil-i Yazdani* in *Diwan*, p. 30; *Zil-i Ilahi* in *Qiran-*

us-Sadain, p. 25; As quoted in K. A. Nizami, *Some Aspects of Religion and Politics in India During the Thirteenth Century* (New Delhi: Caxton Press, 1961), p. 96.
11. ibid., pp. 95–6.
12. ibid.
13. Baranī, *Tārīkh-i Fīrūz Shāhī* (Persian), pp. 55–7. There was a deliberate effort to portray Mewāties as villains in the state records as they always remained a counter force against rulers of Delhi. Shail Mayaram, *Against History, Against State: Counter Perspectives from the Margins* (Columbia University Press, 2003).
14. Baranī, *Tārīkh-i Fīrūz Shāhī* (Persian), p. 57.
15. ibid.
16. ibid., pp. 57–9.
17. ibid., p. 57.
18. ibid; Also see: Jackson, *The Delhi Sultanate*, p. 135.
19. Baranī, *Tārīkh-i Fīrūz Shāhī* (Persian), p. 58.
20. ibid., p. 59.
21. ibid., pp. 65–6; Jackson, *The Delhi Sultanate*, p. 77.
22. Baranī, *Tārīkh-i Fīrūz Shāhī* (Persian), p. 61.
23. ibid., pp. 61–4. See also: Jackson, *The Delhi Sultanate*, p. 77.
24. Baranī, *Tārīkh-i Fīrūz Shāhī* (Persian), p. 66.
25. ibid., pp. 80–1; Jackson, *The Delhi Sultanate*, p. 94.
26. The sons of the sultan were allowed to keep their personalised staff, with which they cultivated the patrimonial relations. Prince Muḥammad was a great patron of scholars, poets and artists. Baranī, *Tārīkh-i Fīrūz Shāhī* (Persian), pp. 80–1.
27. ibid., p. 81.
28. ibid., p. 85; Jackson, *The Delhi Sultanate*, p. 78.
29. Baranī, *Tārīkh-i Fīrūz Shāhī* (Persian), pp. 84–9.
30. ibid., pp. 92–3.
31. ibid., p. 92.
32. ibid., pp. 107–8.
33. ibid., pp. 109–10. On Balban's Mongol policy see: Aziz Ahmed, *Studies in Islamic Culture in the Indian Environment* (Karachi: Oxford University Press, 1964), p. 14.
34. Jackson, *The Delhi Sultanate*, pp. 77–81.
35. ibid., pp. 76–9.
36. K. S. Lal, *Growth of Muslim Population in Medieval India* (Delhi: Research Publications in Social Science, 1973), p. 11.
37. In *c.*1279–1280, he was hanged as he had failed to suppress Toghril's revolt in Bengal. See: Jackson, *The Delhi Sultanate*, pp. 77–8.
38. ibid., p. 76.
39. Baranī, *Tārīkh-i Fīrūz Shāhī* (Persian), p. 61.
40. ibid., pp. 33–8.
41. ibid., p. 36.

42. Tanvir Anjum, 'Conceptualising State and State Control in Medieval India', *Pakistan Journal of Social Sciences*, Vols 24–6 (1998–2000), p. 97.
43. ibid., p. 36.
44. Baranī, *Tārīkh -i Fīrūz Shāhī* (Persian), p. 126.
45. Jackson, *The Delhi Sultanate*, p. 76.
46. ibid., p. 79.
47. Baranī, *Tārīkh-i Fīrūz Shāhī* (Persian), p. 29.
48. ibid., p. 29. Translated from Persian text.
49. Wink, *Al-Hind*, p. 83. quotes Marco Polo's words:

> the number of horses exported ... to India is something astonishing. One reason is that no horses are bred there, and another that they die as soon as they get there, through ignorant handling; for the people there do not know how to take care of them, and they feed their horses with cooked victuals and all sorts of trash ... and besides they have no farriers. In armies large number of horses are required. Due to above mentioned reasons the Indian armies consisted largely of non-professional peasantry, foot-soldiers and elephants.

50. Anjum, 'State and State Control', p. 91.
51. Baranī, *Tārīkh-i Fīrūz Shāhī* (Persian), p. 29.
52. ibid.
53. ibid.
54. Anjum, 'State and State Control', pp. 90–2.
55. Baranī, *Tārīkh-i Fīrūz Shāhī* (Persian), pp. 65–6.
56. Jackson, *Mamluk Institution*, p. 352; Jackson, *The Delhi Sultanate*, p. 77
57. Baranī, *Tārīkh-i Fīrūz Shāhī* (Persian), p. 65.
58. Prince Muḥammad and Bughrā Khān were serving at the north-western frontiers of the Delhi sultanate at the time of Toghril's revolt.
59. Jackson, *Mamluk Institution*, pp. 352–3.
60. ibid.
61. In the Calcutta edition it is Malik Butu. However, following the Aligarh edition, Malik Buqubuq is accepted here. Baranī, *Tārīkh-i Fīrūz Shāhī* (Urdu), translated by Sayed Moeen al-Haq, pp. 69, 94.
62. Baranī, *Tārīkh-i Fīrūz Shāhī* (Persian), p. 40.
63. Jackson, *Mamluk Institution*, p. 353.
64. Baranī, *Tārīkh-i Fīrūz Shāhī* (Persian), pp. 91–2.
65. ibid., p. 84.
66. ibid., p. 81.
67. Jackson, *Mamluk Institution*, p. 354.
68. Baranī, *Tārīkh-i Fīrūz Shāhī* (Persian), p. 118.
69. Jackson, *The Delhi Sultanate*, p. 76.
70. Baranī, *Tārīkh-i Fīrūz Shāhī* (Persian), p. 83.
71. This included his brother Kishlī Khān, the cousin Shīr Khān, the sons, Khān Shāhīd and Būghrā Khān. Interestingly, Balban's brother and cousin were Shamsī slaves whereas the status of his sons was that of *mawālzādāh.*

72. Jackson, 'Mamluk Institution', p. 354.
73. Idem, *The Delhi Sultanate*, p. 81.
74. Baranī, *Tārīkh-i Fīrūz Shāhī* (Persian), p. 122.
75. ibid., pp. 121–3.
76. ibid., p. 123.
77. For details about Fakhr al-Dīn see: B. S. Mathur, 'Malik-ul-Umara, Fakhr-u'd-din: The Kotwal of Delhi', *Islamic Culture*, No. 39 (1965): pp. 205–8.
78. Baranī, *Tārīkh-i Fīrūz Shāhī* (Persian), p. 131. Even Kaykquabad, despite his weakness, was able to patronise men of learning. Amir Khusraw started his career in the court of Delhi in the times of Kayquabad. For details see: Muḥammad Wahid Mirza, *Amir Khusraw* (Allahabad: Hindustani Academy UP, 1949), p. 104.
79. Jackson, *Mamluk Institution*, p. 354.
80. Baranī, *Tārīkh-i Fīrūz Shāhī* (Persian), pp. 131–2.
81. Jackson, *The Delhi Sultanate*, p. 81.
82. ibid.
83. Jackson, *Mamluk Institution*, p. 355.
84. Idem, *The Delhi Sultanate*, p. 81.
85. A. B. M. Habibullah, *The Foundation of Muslim Rule in India*, 2nd edn (Allahabad: Central Book Depot, 1961), pp. 194–6.
86. Baranī, *Tārīkh-i Fīrūz Shāhī* (Persian), p. 82.
87. ibid., p. 50–3.
88. ibid., pp. 51–2.
89. ibid., pp. 57; Jackson, *The Delhi Sultanate*, p. 135; Kumar, *Emergence of the Delhi Sultanate*, p. 336.
90. Baranī, *Tārīkh-i Fīrūz Shāhī* (Persian), p. 58.
91. ibid., pp. 83–6; Kumar, *The Emergence of the Delhi Sultanate*, p. 328.
92. Baranī, *Tārīkh-i Fīrūz Shāhī* (Persian), p. 93.
93. ibid., p. 61; Kumar, *Emergence of the Delhi Sultanate*, p. 308.
94. Baranī, *Tārīkh-i Fīrūz Shāhī* (Persian), p. 66.
95. ibid., p. 80.
96. ibid., pp. 66–9.
97. For details about the town of Baba Farid see Richard. M. Eaton, 'Court of Men, Court of God Local Perception of Shrine of Baba Farid Pakpatan, Punjab', in *Islam in India and Pakistan*, ed. Annemarie Schimmel (Leiden: E. J. Brill, 1982), pp. 44–61.
98. Baranī, *Tārīkh-i Fīrūz Shāhī* (Persian), p. 66.
99. ibid., pp. 65–6.
100. ibid., pp. 59–60.
101. For a detailed account of Balban's invasions in Doab see: ibid., pp. 57–60.
102. ibid., p. 64.
103. ibid., p. 108.
104. ibid., p. 56.

105. For details see Chapter 7.
106. Balban, warning his son Būghrā Khān in the wake of Toghril's revolt, explains the mindset of the sultan.
107. Baranī, *Tārīkh-i Fīrūz Shāhī* (Persian), pp. 40–1.

Chapter 7 When History Repeated Itself Repeatedly: Wealth, Betrayal and Success under the Khaljīs

1. Multiple opinions have been expressed on the ethnic background of the Khaljīs. For instance, see: Abdul Hai Habibi, 'Khaljis are Afghans', in Z. Ansari, ed., *Life, Times and Works of Amir Khusrau-i Dehlavi* (New Delhi: National Amir Khusrau Society, 1976), pp. 67–9.
2. See the previous chapter for details. Balban destroyed many strong Shamsī *umara*' and also many from his own patrimonial staff whom he distrusted.
3. 'Īṣāmī states that he was the Mīr Dād. See: Maulanā 'Īṣāmī, *Fūtūh-us Salātīn or Shāh Nāmah-i Hind of 'Īṣāmī*, (Persian), ed. A. S. Usha (University of Madras, 1948), p. 198.
4. Baranī, *Tārīkh-i-Fīruz Shāhī* (Persian), pp. 132–3.
5. 'Īṣāmī, *Fūtūh-us Salātīn* (Persian), pp. 196–8. For the ethnic heterogeneity of *umarā*' see: Sunil Kumar, 'Ignored Elites: Turks, Mongols and a Persian Secretarial Class in the Early Delhi Sultanate', *Modern South Asian Studies*, Vol. 43, no. 2 (2009): pp. 45–77.
6. For instance, two notable *umarā*' of Balban, Malik Shāhik the *muqta*' of Multan and Malik Tuzakī the *muqta*' of Baran who were killed on the inciting of Niẓām al-Dīn. Baranī, *Tārīkh-i-Fīruz Shāhī* (Persian), p. 172.
7. He had to drink the cup of poison that he had prepared for the sultan and thus he died the very same day. 'Īṣāmī, *Fūtūh-us Salātīn* (Persian), pp. 198–200; Baranī, *Tārīkh-i-Fīruz Shāhī* (Persian), p. 170.
8. See the resentment that arose regarding the rise of Khaljī in 'Īṣāmī, *Fūtūh-us Salātīn* (Persian), pp. 205–8; Baranī, *Tārīkh-i-Fīruz Shāhī* (Persian), p. 175.
9. Baranī says '*khward sāl*' meaning 'young' Baranī, *Tārīkh-i-Fīruz Shāhī* (Persian), p. 171; Yahya bin Ahmad ibn Abdullah Sirhindī, *Tarikh-i Mubarak Shahi*, p. 56; Abul Qasim Firishta, *Tarikh-i Farishta*, p. 76; He is called '*Tifl Sah sala*' or 'three-year-old child' in: 'Īṣāmī, *Fūtūh-us Salātīn* (Persian), pp. 205–6.
10. K. S. Lal, *The History of the Khaljis*, p. 6.
11. Baranī and Sirhhindi give his name as Kaikaus. 'Īṣāmī, gives the name as Kaimurth. See: Yahya bin Ahmad ibn Abdullah Sirhindī, *Tarikh-i Mubarak Shahi*, p. 56; Baranī, *Tārīkh-i Fīrūz Shāhī* (Persian), p. 171. 'Īṣāmī, *Fūtūh-us Salātīn* (Persian), p. 205.
12. Baranī, *Tārīkh-i Fīrūz Shāhī* (Persian), p. 172.

13. For a detailed discussion on ethnic origins of the Khaljīs see: Kishori Saran Lal, *History of the Khaljis A.D. 1290–1320* (Karachi: Union Book Stall, 1950), pp. 13–14.
14. Baranī, *Tārīkh-i Fīrūz Shāhī* (Persian), pp. 175–6.
15. ibid., p. 173.
16. ibid., pp. 10–11.
17. 'Īṣāmī, *Fūtūh-us Salātīn* (Persian), pp. 207–9.
18. Baranī, *Tārīkh-i Fīrūz Shāhī* (Persian), pp. 175–6. This city was certainly not built by Jalāl al-Dīn and was present since the earliest times of the Delhi sultanate. However, Kayquabād made the city his residence and later Fīrūz Khaljī also settled there.
19. K. S. Lal, *History of the Khaljis*, p. 16.
20. For an exhaustive account on Khaljī nobility, see: Siddiqui, 'Nobility under the Khalji Sultans', *Islamic Culture*, Vol. 37 (1963): pp. 52–66.
21. Baranī, *Tārīkh-i Fīrūz Shāhī* (Persian), p. 177.
22. Jackson, *The Delhi Sultanate*, p. 83., fn. 135.
23. K. S. Lal, *The Khaljis*, pp. 19–20.
24. Peter Jackson, *The Delhi Sultanate*, p. 84.
25. Baranī, *Tārīkh-i Fīrūz Shāhī* (Persian), p. 174.
26. In the time of Muḥammad b. Tughluq, Ibn Battūtah refers to a similar incident when many of the sons of a local raja died in fighting. The remaining sons surrendered and converted to Islam. They were given offices at the centre. 'Ibn Battūtah does not refer to them as slaves. For details see: Ibn Battūtah, *'Ajāib al-Asfār*, p. 163.
27. For Baranī's account of Malik chajju's revolt, see: Baranī, *Tārīkh-i-Fīruz Shāhī* (Persian), pp. 181–5.
28. Ḥasan Sijzī, *Fawā'id ul Fū'ād*, p. 164. I. H. Qureshi, *The Administration of the Sultanate of Delhi* (Karachi: Pakistan Historical Society, 1958).
29. Son of KishlīKhān.
30. *Muqṭa'* of Awadh Amir Ali *Sirjandar*, also known as Hatim Khān, was a *mawālzādā* (son of a freed slave) of Balban who supported Malik Chhajjū. For details see: Baranī, *Tārīkh-i-Fīruz Shāhī* (Persian), p. 181.
31. Jackson, *The Delhi Sultanate*, pp. 81–2.
32. Baranī, *Tārīkh-i Fīrūz Shāhī* (Persian), p. 181.
33. Jalāl al-Dīn Fīrūz Khaljī (1290–1296) is known for his mildness and compassion. Due to these characteristics many of his opponents blamed him as unfit to rule. For instance see: Shaikh Abdur Rashid, 'Jalal-ud-din Firuz Shah Khalji', *Muslim University Journal*, Vol. 1 (1931): p. 149.
34. Lal, *The Khaljis*, pp. 25–6.
35. Baranī, *Tārīkh-i Fīrūz Shāhī*, pp. 182–5; Jackson, *The Delhi Sultanate*, pp. 81–2.
36. Baranī, *Tārīkh-i Fīrūz Shāhī* (Persian), pp. 190–3.
37. ibid., p. 190.
38. For details of the incident see: Baranī, *Tārīkh-i Fīrūz Shāhī* (Persian), pp. 208–12; 'Īṣāmī, *Fūtūh-us Salātīn* (Persian), pp. 215–17; Sirhindī, *Tarikh-i Mubarak*

Shahi, pp. 65–7; Bakhshi, *Tabaqāt-i Akbari*, pp. 61–2; Al-Badauni, *Muntakhab-ut-Tawarīkh* (Ranking), Vol. 1, pp. 233–5; Farishtah, *Tārikh-i Farishtāh* (Urdu), Vol. 1, pp. 332–6; Abdur Rehman Chisti, *Mirat al-Asrār*, Vol. 2, pp. 282–3.

39. Riazul Islam, *Sufism in South Asia*, pp. 321–2, fn. 201. According to Simon Digby, it was one of the be-shar (that which did not follow Sharia) groups of Sufism. Simon Digby, 'Qalanders and Related groups: Elements of Social Deviance in the Religious Life of the Delhi Sultanate of the 13th and 14th Centuries', in *Islam in South Asia*, ed. Friedmann, Vol. 1: *South Asia*, p. 61.
40. According to the hagiographic accounts, even the sultan became convinced of the spiritual powers of the mystic after killing him. See: Abd al-Haqq, *Akhbār al-Akhyār*, p. 79.
41. Baranī, *Tārīkh-i Fīrūz Shāhī* (Persian), p. 210.
42. Baranī, *Tārīkh-i Fīrūz Shāhī* (Persian), p. 210. For details on Muwallah see: Riazul Islam, *Sufism in South Asia: Impact on Fourteenth Century Muslim Society* (Karachi: Oxford University Press, 2002), pp. 321–2, n. 201. According to a hagiographer, the sultan started believing in the spiritual powers of Sidi Muwallah after his death. See: Simon Digby, 'Qalanders and Related Groups: Elements of Social Deviance in the Religious Life of the Delhi Sultanate of the 13th and 14th Centuries', in *Islam in Asia*, ed. Friedmann, Vol. 1, p. 61.
43. Baranī, *Tārīkh-i Fīrūz Shāhī* (Persian), p. 189.
44. ibid., p. 213. 'Īṣāmī, *Fūtūh-us Salātīn* (Persian), pp. 238–9.
45. Baranī, *Tārīkh-i Fīrūz Shāhī* (Persian), pp. 218–19. The date of this expedition is not certain, since 'Īṣāmī mentions this event before the elimination of Sidi Muwallah. 'Īṣāmī, *Futuh-us Salatīn* (Persian), pp. 209–14.
46. According to Baranī, he was the grandson of Genghis Khān. Baranī, *Tārīkh-i Fīrūz Shāhī* (Persian), p. 219.
47. K. S. Lal, *History of the Khaljis*, p. 37.
48. K. S. Lal, *History of the Khaljis*, p. 38. fn. 80. All these areas are in the suburbs of Delhi on the west bank of river Kumna. Indrapat was in the north, Kelukherī was in the middle and Ghyathpūr was in the south. In Ghiyāthpūr lies the tomb of Nizām al-Dīn Awaliyāh and the region of Tuluka cannot be identified. The region of Mughalpura is still the name of a village near Delhi.
49. The massacre might have been an outcome of Ala-al Din's hostile stance against the Mongol invaders from the north-west that were a constant threat to the sultanate. The sultan must have been careful not to leave any potential supporters of them inside the capital. For details of the sultan's treatment of Mongols see: Sultan Hameed Warsi, *History of Alauddin Khalji* (Allahabad, 1930), p. 21. See also: Ahmad, *Islamic Culture*, pp. 15–16.
50. Baranī, *Tārīkh-i Fīrūz Shāhī* (Persian), p. 212.
51. Farishtah calls these people peasants. See: Farishtah, *Tārīkh-i Farishtah*, p. 238.
52. Baranī, *Tārīkh-i Fīrūz Shāhī* (Persian), p. 212.
53. Baranī, *Tārīkh-i Fīrūz Shāhī*, p. 87; Farishtah, *Tārikh-i Farishtah*, p. 235.

54. Jalāl al-Dīn seem to have made him an offer to be the *nā'ib*, which he declined, peacefully retiring to his *iqṭā'* in Kārā. It is unclear under which circumstances he defied authority. Jackson, *The Delhi Sultanate*, p. 82.
55. 'Alā al-Dīn is surrounded by many of the rebels and insurgents who supported Malik Chhajjū'. Lal, *The Khaljis*, p. 49. Baranī, *Tārīkh-i Fīrūz Shāhī* (Persian), p. 224.
56. Baranī, *Tārīkh-i Fīrūz Shāhī* (Persian), p. 223; 'Īṣāmī, *Fūtūh-us Salātīn* (Persian), pp. 233–4.
57. Baranī, *Tārīkh-i Fīrūz Shāhī* (Persian), p. 224.
58. ibid., p. 226.
59. ibid., p. 229.
60. ibid., pp. 228–38.
61. ibid., pp. 238–9.
62. ibid., p. 239. See also: Tanvir Anjum, *Chishti Sufis in the Sultanate of Delhi 1190–1400: From Restrained Indifference to Calculated Defiance* (Karachi: Oxford University Press, 2011), pp. 189–90.
63. Baranī, *Tārīkh-i Fīrūz Shāhī* (Persian), p. 244.
64. ibid., p. 239.
65. Amir Khusraw, *Khazain ul Futuh*, ed. Wahid Mirza (Calcutta, 1953), p. 38. For details about the life and times of Amir Khusraw see: S. Wahid Mirza, 'Hazrat Amir Khursraw' (PhD thesis, University of London, London, 1929).
66. Jackson, *The Delhi Sultanate*, p. 171; Siddiqui, 'Social Mobility', p. 25.
67. Including Ulugh Khān, Nuṣrat Khān, Zafar Khān, Baranī's uncle 'Alā-ul Mulk, Malik Sughrā Sār *dawāt dār*, and Malik Juna *dād beg* Baranī, *Tārīkh-i Fīrūz Shāhī* (Persian), p. 336.
68. Jackson, *The Delhi Sultanate*, p. 85.
69. For instance, Khwājah Khatīr was designated as *wazīr*, *qāḍi* Ṣadar Jahān Ṣadr al-Dīn 'Ārif was given the designation of *qāḍ at ul-mumālik*, Malik Juna was as *nāi'b wakīl-i dar*, and the designation of *diwan-i inshā'* remained with Baranī's uncle Umdā-tul Mumālik Malik, who later the next year was given the regions of Kara and Awadh as *iqṭā'*. The sons of 'Umdā-tul Mumālik Malik, Hamīd al-Dīn and Malik 'Izz al-Dīn's were promoted. Baranī's father was given the *iqṭā'* of Baran. Nuṣrat Khān who was earlier *nāi'b* Malik was made *kotwāl* of Delhi. Malik Fakhr al-Dīn Kūjī was made the *dād beg*, Zafar Khān was made *'ariḍ mumālīk*, Malik Abājī was made *ākhūr beg* and Malik Hirnmār was made *nāi'b barbeg*. Baranī, *Tārīkh-i Fīrūz Shāhī* (Persian), pp. 247–8.
70. Almas Beg is the Ulugh Khān in whose praise Amir Hasan Ala-Sijzi wrote poems and verses. See: Ḥasan Ala-Sijzī, *Dīwān-e-Ḥasan Alā Sijzī* (Hyderabad Deccan: Ibrahimia Machine Press, 1352 AH), pp. 22–3.
71. Amir Khusraw, *Mutla-i Anvar*, p. 35; Baranī, *Tārīkh-i Fīrūz Shāhī* (Persian), p. 283.
72. Baranī, *Tārīkh-i Fīrūz Shāhī* (Persian), p. 54.
73. Amir Khusraw, *Qiranus Sadain*, p. 35; Baranī, *Tārīkh-i Fīrūz Shāhī*, p. 78.

74. Baranī, *Tārīkh-i Fīrūz Shāhī* (Persian), p. 276. This brother was eliminated when the attempt of his elder brother to kill the sultan failed.
75. Baranī, *Tārīkh-i Fīrūz Shāhī*, p. 408.
76. For the rebellions of Umar and Mangu Khān see: ibid., pp. 77–8. For details about the murder attempt on the sultan by Sulaymān Ikht Khan see: ibid., pp. 272–8.
77. ibid., p. 337.
78. Jackson, *The Delhi Sultanate*, p. 174.
79. ibid., pp. 174–5.
80. For a detailed account on the transition of military technology and tactics see: Simon Digby, *War Horse and Elephant in the Delhi Sultanate: A Study of Military Supplies* (Oxford: Orient Monographs, 1971), pp. 74–82.
81. The word 'Temür' is a traditional Central Asian name, with the suffix '*sultānī*' generally denoting the status of the person as a royal slave, whereas the suffix 'Tagin', which means prince, is a common name found among Central Asian slaves (e.g. Alptagin and Sūbūktagin). Jackson, *The Delhi Sultanate*, p. 175. Also the sultan's army used stone balls and *manjniques* for warfare. Konstantin Nossov, *Indian Castles 1206–1526: The Rise and Fall of the Delhi Sultanate* (Oxford: Osprey Publishing House, 2006), p. 44.
82. Peter Jackson, 'Mamluks in Muslim India', *Journal of Royal Asiatic Society*, No. 2 (1990), p. 356.
83. ibid.
84. Agha Mahdi Husain, trans. and ed., *Futuhu's Salatin or Shah Namah-I Hind of Isami*, Vol. 1 (Aligarh: University Press of Aligarh, 1976), pp. 456–7. In Persian version see: 'Īṣāmī, *Fūtūh-us Salātīn* (Persian), pp. 281–3.
85. Amir Khusraw, *Khazinul Futuh*, trans. into English by Wahid Mirza (Lahore: United Printers, 1975), p. 35.
86. Baranī, *Tārīkh-i Fīrūz Shāhī* (Persian), pp. 272–7; Jackson, *The Delhi Sultanate*, p. 175; Kanhaiya Lall Srivastava, *The Position of Hindus under the Delhi Sultanate 1206–1526* (New Delhi: Munshi Ram Manoharlal Publishers, 1980), p. 32.
87. Taking the head of an important person as evidence of the death was probably the custom of that time.
88. Jackson, *The Delhi Sultanate*, p. 175.
89. ibid.
90. Lal, *The Khaljis*, p. 168.
91. Baranī, *Tārīkh-i Firuz Shahi* (Persian), p. 381.
92. 'Īṣāmī, *Fūtūh-us Salātīn* (Persian), pp. 301–8.
93. For Baranī's account of this revolt see: Baranī, *Tārīkh-i Fīrūz Shāhī* (Persian), pp. 278–82.
94. For 'Isāmī's account of this revolt see: Husain, *Futuhu's Salātīn*, p. 452.
95. According to Iqtadar H. Siddiqui, this event was a result of social tension emanating from urbanisation, education and awareness among the people. Siddiqui, 'Social Mobility', p. 35. However, the revolt seemed to

opportunistic, in the absence of the sultan who himself was a murderer of his predecessor. The slave had a following comprised of an unorganised and unruly mob, who wanted the current delegate of 'Alā al-Dīn deposed. There does not seem to have been any educated effort to reform or look for order.

96. Lal, *The Khaljis*, p. 90.
97. Malik Fakhr al-Dīn was a Tājīk *amīr* whose father Jamāl al-Dīn Nishāpurī had also served around 1257. According to Baranī the post of *kōtwāl* was held by the duo in succession for eighty years. Malik Fakhr al-Dīn was responsible for placing Kayqubād on the throne. This *amīr* remained in nobility after the Khaljī seizure of power. He died somewhere in the reign of Jalāl al-Dīn Khaljī. For fragments of information see: Jackson, *The Delhi Sultanate*, pp. 53, 58, 79, 84–5, 95, 172.
98. Lal, *The Khaljis*, p. 90.
99. Baranī, *Tārīkh-i Fīrūz Shāhī (Persian)*, pp. 278–9.
100. Lal, *The Khaljis*, p. 93.
101. Baranī, *Tārīkh-i Fīrūz Shāhī* (Persian), p. 382.
102. Siddiqui, *Authority and Kingship*, p. 85.
103. Siddiqui, 'Social Mobility', p. 35.
104. ibid.
105. Baranī, *Tārīkh-i Fīrūz Shāhī* (Persian), pp. 281–2.
106. ibid., pp. 366–9.
107. ibid., p. 337
108. ibid.
109. ibid.
110. Jackson, *The Delhi Sultanate*, p. 176.
111. Baranī, *Tārīkh-i Fīrūz Shāhī* (Persian), pp. 368–9.
112. ibid., p. 368.
113. Jackson, *The Delhi Sultanate*, p. 176.
114. Baranī, *Tārīkh-i Fīrūz Shāhī* (Persian), p. 372.
115. ibid., p. 374.
116. Lal, *Khaljis*, p. 270.
117. Baranī, *Tārīkh-i Fīrūz Shāhī* (Persian), p. 368.
118. Cambay was a port city of Gujarat in southern India. It underwent complete transformation after its annexation to the sultanate in 1300. It was inhabited by pockets of Muslim, Zoroastrian and Hindu traders, artisans and labourers. There seemed to have been a broad economic polarisation between the inhabitants of the city, resulting in extreme inequality. The rich even invested their money in Ghazna. See: Siddiqui, 'Social Mobility', pp. 29–30.
119. See: endnotes, Husain, *Futuhu's Salatin*, pp. 457–8. Later Peter Jackson also confirms this opinion. Jackson, *The Delhi Sultanate*, p. 177.
120. K. S. Lal provides this information by inference. Lal, *The Khaljis*, p. 71. He seems to be unfamiliar with this researched stance of Agha Mehdi Hussain, according to the version of *Futhu's Salateen* that he used. Whereas Peter

Jackson also considers Kāfūr a purchased slave of 'Alā al-Dīn. Jackson, *The Delhi Sultanate*, p. 175.

121. See: endnotes, Husain, *Futuhu's Salatīn*, pp. 457–8. Later Peter Jackson also confirms this opinion. See: Jackson, *The Delhi Sultanate*, p. 175.
122. ibid.
123. In a conversation between 'Alā-ul' Mulk and 'Alā al-Dīn, the former asked the latter to restore his control over the regions, extended on the eastern side from river Sarv to Sawālik and Janōr, Multan to Marilā (Damīrala) and whose western border stretched from Pālam to Lahore and Deopālpūr. Baranī, *Tārīkh-i Fīrūz Shāhī* (Persian), p. 269.
124. Such as Ranthambor, Chitor, Mandal Garh, Dahar, Ujjain, Mando, 'Alāīpūr, Chanderi, Erich, Sawanā and Jalor: ibid., pp. 323–4.
125. According to *Fūtūh us-Salātīn* the region was entrusted upon Malik Shāhīn. Jackson, *The Delhi Sultanate*, p. 198.
126. Baranī, *Tārīkh-i Fīrūz Shāhī* (Persian), pp. 323–4.
127. ibid.
128. For the history of Jhayin see: Satya Prakash Gupta, *Jhain of the Delhi Sultanate* in *Medieval India a Miscellany*, Vol. 3 (Aligarh: Aligarh Muslim University, 1975), pp. 209–15.
129. Baranī, *Tārīkh-i Fīrūz Shāhī* (Persian), p. 288.
130. For details see: I. H. Siddiqui, 'Espionage System of the sultans of Delhi', *Studies in Islam*, Vol. 1 (1964).
131. Namely, Sulaymān Ikhit Khān, Mangu Khān, 'Umar Khān and Ulugh Khān.
132. Baranī, *Tārīkh-i Fīrūz Shāhī* (Persian), p. 282.
133. ibid., pp. 283–4. See also: Riazul Islam, 'Theory and Practice of Jaziyah in the Delhi Sultanate (14th Century)', *Journal of the Pakistan Historical Society*, Vol. 50, No. 4 (2002): pp. 7, 18.
134. Baranī, *Tārīkh-i Fīrūz Shāhī* (Persian), p. 284.
135. ibid., pp. 284–6.
136. ibid., pp. 286–7.
137. ibid., pp. 287–9. The sultan also ordered construction of granaries to store surplus produce thus, enabling greater extent of economic control. Riazul Islam, 'Some Aspects of the Economy of Northern South Asia during the Fourteenth Century', *Journal of Central Asia*, Vol. 11, No. 2 (1988), p. 8.
138. Baranī, *Tārīkh-i Fīrūz Shāhī* (Persian), pp. 287–9.
139. ibid., pp. 288–9.
140. ibid., p. 302. For details on 'Alā al-Dīn's defence measures see: Dharam Pal, 'Ala-ud-Din Khalji's Mongol Policy', *Islamic Culture*, Vol. 21 (1947), pp. 255–63.
141. For details see: U. N. Day, 'The North West Frontier under the Khalji Sultans of Delhi', *Islamic Culture*, Vol. 39 (1963), pp. 98–108.
142. Baranī, *Tārīkh-i Fīrūz Shāhī* (Persian), p. 302. Siri is one of the six subcities of Delhi. Stephen Blake, *Shahjahanabad*, pp. 3–8.
143. Lal, *History of the Khaljis*, p. 257.

144. ibid. For a detailed account of Ala-al Din Khalji's economic policy see: C. Kenneth Kehrer, 'The Economic Policies of Ala-ud-Din Khalji', *Journal of the Punjab University Historical Society*, Vol. 16 (1963): pp. 55–66. For market reforms of Ala al-Din see: U. N. Day, *Some Aspects of Medieval Indian History* (Delhi: Low Price Publications, 2004), p. 84.
145. Sheikh Abdur Rasheed, 'Price Control Under Alauddin Khalji', in *Proceedings of the All Pakistan History Conference, First Session, Held at Karachi 1951* (Karachi, [n.d.]), pp. 203–10; P. Saran, 'The Economic Policy and Price Control of Alauddin Khalji', *Bharatiya Vidya*, Vol. 2 (1950): pp. 195–215.
146. Moreland, *The Agrarian System*, pp. 36–7.
147. For a detailed account of the economic reforms of Ala al-Din see: Baranī, Tārīkh-i-Fīruz Shāhī (Persian), pp. 304–20. Also see Irfan Habib, 'The price regulations of Ala al-Din Khalji – a defence of Zia Baranī', *Indian Economic and Social History Review*, Vol. 21 (1984), pp. 393–414.
148. ibid.
149. ibid., pp. 309–11.
150. ibid., pp. 313–16.
151. ibid., p. 303.
152. K. A. Nizami, ed., *Politics and Society during the Early Medieval Period: Collected Works of Professor Mohammad Habib*, Vol. 1 (New Delhi, 1974), p. 91. Although, according to Baranī, Ala al-Din was interested in founding a new religion, 'Ayn al-Mulk warned him against potential for mass resentment and he aborted the plan. Idem, *Supplement to Elliot and Dowson's History of India Vol. III* (Delhi: Idarah-i Adbiyat-i Delhi, 1981), p. 5.
153. Baranī's account of 'Alā al-Dīn focuses on the economic reforms of the sultan. Thus, he portrays the economic conditions under his rule as ideal.
154. Baranī, *Tārīkh-i Fīrūz Shāhī* (Persian), pp. 283–4, 288, 299.
155. K. S. Lal, *History of Khaljis*, p. 81.
156. ibid.
157. Baranī, *Tārīkh-i Fīrūz Shāhī* (Persian), pp. 303–4.
158. These regions came under the Muslim rule during the times of Shihab al-Din Khalji.
159. For details see: Chapter 1 and 2, section 1 entitled 'Arabs in India and Ghaznawids'.
160. For a general overview on the rise of Muslim power in Gujarat see: S. C. Misra, *The Rise of Muslim Power in Gujarat*, 2nd edn (New Delhi: People's Publishing House, 1982).
161. 'Alā al-Dīn Juvani, *Tarikh-i Jahan Kusha*, p. 87.
162. Misra, *The Rise of Muslim Power in Gujarat*, pp. 61–4; G. Buhler, 'A Jaina account of the end of the Vaghelas of Gujarat', *Indian Antiquary*, Vol. 26 (1897), pp. 194–5.
163. ibid.
164. Desai, 'A Persian-Sanskrit inscription of Karna Deva Vaghela of Gujarat', *Encyclopaedia Indica*, Arabic and Persian Supplement (1975), pp. 13–20.

165. Buhler, 'Jaina account', p. 195; Misra, *Muslim Power*, pp. 64–6. For 'Alā al-Dīn's Deccan policy see: Raj Kumar, ed., *The Deccan Policy of Alaud Din Khalji* in *Essays on Medieval India* (New Delhi: Discovery Publishing House, 2003), pp. 174–83.
166. Ibn Battūtah, *Tuhfat al-Nuzar fi Gharaibil-Amsar*, tr. H. A. R. Gibb, *The Travels of Ibn-i Battutah A.D. 1325–1354* HS, 2nd Series, Vol. 3 (Cambridge and London: Hakluyt Society, 1958–94), p. 672.
167. 'Manjhu Sikandar ibn Muḥammad, *Mirat-i Sikandari*, ed. S. C. Misra and Muḥammad Lutf al Rehman (Baroda, 1961), p. 42.
168. Ibn Battūtah, *Tuhfat al-Nuzar*, Vol. 4, ed. C. F. Beckingham, pp. 58, 59, 61.
169. H. C. Ray, *The Dynastic History of Northern India*, Vol. 1 (Calcutta: 1931–1935), p. 1046; D. B. Diskalkar, 'Inscriptions of Kathiawad', *New Indian Antiquary*, Vol. 1 (1938–1939), pp, 576–90. For details about Rānā Mamdalikka see: Buhler, 'Jaina account,' p. 194.
170. Baranī, *Tārīkh-i Fīrūz Shāhī* (Persian), pp. 276–7; 'Iṣāmī, *Fūtūh-us Salātīn* (Persian), pp. 271–4.
171. Baranī, *Tārīkh-i Fīrūz Shāhī* (Persian), pp. 254–8.
172. Jackson, *The Delhi Sultanate*, p. 197.
173. Amir Khusraw, *Khazain al-Futuh*, pp. 51, 54.
174. Amir Khusraw, *Diwal Rānī-yi Khiḍr Khan*, p. 66; *'Īsāmī, Futuh-us Salatīn*, p. 281–2.
175. Amir Khusraw, *Khazain al-Futuh*, p. 54; Also: Gupta, 'Jhain of the Delhi Sultanate'.
176. Buhler, 'Jaina account', p. 194.
177. Amir Khusraw, *Khazain al-Futuh*, pp. 60, 61–2, 63.
178. Padmavat is the first work in the Awadhi language. Muhammad Qasim 'Ali Barelvi, fl. 1850–1870, *Padmāvat Urdū* (Kanpur: Munshi Naval Kishor, 1873).
179. M. S. Ahluwalia, *Muslim Expansion in Rajasthan (The Relations of Delhi Sultanate with Rajasthan 1206–1526)* (Delhi: Yugantar Prakashan, 1978), pp. 97–9.
180. Khusraw, *Diwal Rani*, p. 67; Amir Khusraw, *Khazain al-Futuh*, pp. 63–4.
181. 'Īṣāmī, *Fūtūh-us Salātīn* (Persian), pp. 281–3.
182. This story is found in a Sanskrit epic and also is stated by Farishtah,
183. M. Habib and K. A. Nizami (eds), *The Delhi Sultanate (A.D.) 1206–1526)*, p. 371; Z. A. Desai, 'Inscriptions from the Victoria Hall Museum, Udaipur', *Epigraphia Indica Arabic and Persian Supplement* (1955–6), pp. 67–70.
184. Khusraw, *Diwal Rani*, p. 69.
185. Amir Khusraw, *Khazain al-Futuh*, pp. 68–72.
186. Yahyā ibn Ahmad Sirhindī, *Tarikh-i Mubarak Shahi*, ed. S. M. Hidayat Hussain (Calcatta: Asiatic Society of Bengal, 1931), p. 78.
187. Desai, 'Jalor Idgah inscription'.
188. Baranī, *Tārīkh-i Fīrūz Shāhī* (Persian), pp. 275–7.
189. Khusraw, *Diwal Rani*, pp. 67–8.
190. ibid., pp. 67–9. See also: Amir Khusraw, *The Campaigns of Alaud-Din Khalji being the Khaza'in ul Futuh (Treasures of Victory) of Hazrat Amir Khusraw of Delhi*,

Translated into English with notes and parallel passages from other Persian writers by Muḥammad Habib (Madras: Printed at the Diocesan Press, 1931), pp. 42–6.

191. Ibn Battūtah, *Tuhfaht us Sagar*, translated by Gibb and Buckingham, IV pp. 31, 786.
192. Amir Khusraw, *Khazain al-Futuh*, p. 75.
193. Ray, *Dynastic History*, pp. 905–6, 908; *Archaeological Survey of India*, *Annual Report on Indian Epigraphy* (1964–5), pp. 23–145 (nos. D 77–8).
194. For details see: K. H. Sherwani and P. M. Joshi, eds, *History of Medieval Deccan (1295–1724)*, Vol. 1 (Hyderabad: AP, 1973).
195. Baranī, *Tārīkh-i Fīrūz Shāhī* (Persian), p. 327.
196. Ibn Battūtah, *'Ajāib al-Asfār*, pp. 289–90.
197. ibid., pp. 289–301.
198. For a detailed account of 'Alā al-Dīn's Deccan campaigns see: P. M. Joshi and Agha Mehdi Hussain, 'Khaljis and Tughluqs in the Deccan', in Sherwani and Joshi, *History of Medieval Deccan*, Vol. 1, pp. 29–55.
199. Baranī, *Tārīkh-i Fīrūz Shāhī* (Persian), pp. 325–7; Khusraw, *Khazain al-Futuh*, pp. 64–8.
200. Baranī, *Tārīkh-i Fīrūz Shāhī* (Persian), p. 326.
201. Amir Khusraw, *Khazain al-Futuh*, pp. 122–4.
202. H. Nelson Wright, ed., *The Coinage and Metrology of the Sultans of Delhi* (London: Oxford University Press, 1936), pp. 89 (no. 305C), 91 (nos 321–2).
203. Amir Khusraw, *Nuh Sipihr*, ed. Wahid Mirza (London: Oxford University Press, 1950), pp. 62–73.
204. This wealth was even noticed by Marco Polo. For details see: Marco Polo, tr. Moule and Pelliot, *The Description of the World* (London: George Routledge & Sons, 1938), Vol. 1, pp. 381–6.
205. Baranī, *Tārīkh-i Fīrūz Shāhī* (Persian), pp. 333–5.
206. Shihāb al-Dīn Abd-Allah b. Izz al-Dīn Fadl-Allah Shīrāzi Wassaf, *Tajziyat al-Amsar wa Tazjiyat al-Asar*, lithograph edn (Bombay, 1269/1853), pp. 530–1; Khusraw, *Khazain al Futuh*, p. 127.
207. Amir Khusraw, *Khazain al-Futuh*, pp. 150–1.
208. Wassaf, *Tajziyat al-Amsar wa Tazjiyat al-Asar*, p. 351.
209. Vankataramanyya, *The Early Muslim Expansion*, pp. 93–4.
210. Baranī, *Tārīkh-i Fīrūz Shāhī* (Persian), p. 372.
211. ibid., pp. 371–3.
212. Jackson, *The Delhi Sultanate*, p. 177.
213. Baranī, *Tārīkh-i Fīrūz Shāhī* (Persian), pp. 372–3.
214. Namely Mūbashīr, Bashīr, Sālayh and Mūnīr Only 'Iṣāmī gives the names of these slaves. 'Iṣāmī, *Futuh us Salateen* (Persian), p. 349. Farishtāh also verifies the names of two of the slaves. See: Lal, *The Khaljis*, p. 321.
215. Ibn Battūtah, *'Ajāib al-Asfār*, p. 77.
216. Baranī, *Tārīkh-i Fīrūz Shāhī* (Persian), p. 277.

217. ibid., p. 376.
218. Jackson, *The Delhi Sultanate*, p. 177.
219. Baranī, *Tārīkh-i Fīrūz Shāhī* (Persian), p. 376.
220. ibid., pp. 288–9.
221. ibid., p. 377.
222. ibid., p. 389.
223. ibid.
224. For details about this conspiracy see: Lal, *The Khaljis*, p. 328.
225. I. H. Siddiqui, *Delhi Sultanate: Urbanisation and Social Change* (New Delhi: Viva Books, 2009), p. 21.
226. ibid., pp. 289, 292, 295.
227. Baranī, *Tārīkh-i Fīrūz Shāhī* (Persian), p. 387.
228. ibid., p. 377.
229. ibid., p. 381. For discussion on the origins and ethnicity of the tribe see: Lal, *The Khaljis*, p. 309.
230. Baranī, *Tārīkh-i Fīrūz Shāhī* (Persian), p. 377.
231. ibid.
232. ibid.
233. ibid., p. 390.
234. ibid., p. 281.
235. Baranī, *Tārīkh-i Fīrūz Shāhī* (Persian), pp. 396–7; Lal, *The Khaljis*, pp. 292–3.
236. Baranī, *Tārīkh-i Fīrūz Shāhī* (Persian), p. 391.
237. ibid., pp. 400–2.
238. Lal, *The Khaljis*, p. 303.
239. Footnotes, Ibn Battūtah, *'Ajāib al-Asfār*, p. 85.
240. Baranī, *Tārīkh-i Fīrūz Shāhī* (Persian), p. 405.
241. ibid., pp. 404–6.
242. ibid., p. 407.
243. Including 'Ayn al-Mulk Multānī, Malik Vahīd al-Dīn Qureshī, Malik Fakhr al-Dīn Juna, Malik Bahā al-Dīn Dabīr and sons of Qara Beg: Lal, *The Khaljis*, p. 312.
244. Baranī, *Tārīkh-i Fīrūz Shāhī* (Persian), p. 411.
245. Lal, *The Khaljis*, p. 313.
246. ibid.
247. Baranī, *Tārīkh-i Fīrūz Shāhī* (Persian), p. 410.
248. Lal, *The Khaljis*, p. 313.
249. Baranī, *Tārīkh-i Fīrūz Shāhī* (Urdu), pp. 411–12.
250. Lal, *The Khaljis*, p. 314.
251. ibid., p. 315.
252. Four months and four days.
253. Lal, *The Khaljis*, p. 315.
254. Baranī, *Tārīkh-i Fīrūz Shāhī* (Urdu), pp. 413–14.
255. Lal, *The Khaljis*, p. 317.
256. Amir Khusraw, *Tughluq Nama*, p. 29; Hussain, *Muḥammad Bin Tughluq*, p. 34.

257. Amir Khusraw, *Tughluq Nama*, p. 29; *Tarikh-i Mubarak Shahi*, p. 86; Hussain, *Muḥammad Bin Tughluq*, p. 36.
258. ibid.
259. Hussain, *Muḥammad ibn Tughluq*, pp. 35–6.
260. Lal, *The Khaljis*, p. 317.
261. Baranī, *Tārīkh-i Fīrūz Shāhī* (Urdu), pp. 317–18.
262. Lal, *The Khaljis*, p. 320.
263. Baranī, *Tārīkh-i Fīrūz Shāhī* (Urdu), pp. 419–21.
264. Lal, *The Khaljis*, p. 321.
265. Baranī, *Tārīkh-i Fīrūz Shāhī* (Urdu), pp. 420–1.
266. Lal, *The Khaljis*, p. 321.
267. ibid., p. 322.
268. ibid.

Chapter 8 From Megalomania to Chaos: The Tughluqs

1. Ibn Battūtah, *'Ajāib al-Asfār*, p. 144. For more on violence in his reign see: David Wains, 'Ibn Battutah on Shedding of Blood in the Delhi Sultanate', *Al Masaq Journal of Medieval Mediterranean*, Vol. 23, No 3 (2012): pp. 284–8.
2. Khurram Qadir, 'Public Opinion in Pre-Modern Times: Muḥammad bin Tughluq the Genesis of a Zalim Sultan', *Journal of the Pakistan Historical Society* part 1 and 2, July–September 2012.
3. For a detailed discussion of the origins of the word 'Tughluq' and its use by various sultans see: Mahdi Husain, *Tughluq Dynasty* (Calcutta: Thacker Spink and Co. 1963), pp. 52–60.
4. Mahomed Kasim Ferishta, *History of the Rise of the Mahomedan Power in India: till the Year A.D. 1612*, trans (English) John Brigges (Lahore: Sang-e Meel Publications, 2004), p. 185.
5. Jackson, 'Mamluks', p. 356.
6. According to Amīr Khusraw he was a nomad (*āwārā mardī*) and had arrived India during Jalāl al-Dīn Khaljī's reign. Amīr Khusraw, *Tughluq Nāmāh*, p. 25; Jackson, *The Delhi Sultanate*, p. 178.
7. According to Ibn Battūtah, Tughluq belonged to the Quranah Turk tribe that lives between Sind and Turkistan. He was a poor man who became a shepherd fora trader. In the times of 'Alā al-Dīn he became a *pā'īk* but ascending to high ranks he defeated the Mongols thirty-eight times. He was given the governorship of Deopalpur by Mubārak Khiljī. See for details, see: Ibn Battūṭah, *'Ajāib al-Asfār*, p. 86. See also: Iswari Prashad, *A History of the Qaraunah Turks in India* (Allahabad: The Indian Press Ltd, 1939).
8. According to 'Afīf, Abū Bakr, Rajab and Tughluq had come from Khorasan to Delhi in the reign of 'Alā al-Dīn and acquired high positions. Shams-i Sirāj 'Afīf, *Tārīkh Fīrūz Shāhī*, trans (Urdu) Muḥammad Fidā 'Alī Tālib (Karachi: Nafees Academy, 1962), p. 35.

9. According to Baranī, Ghiyāth al-Dīn considered the 'Alā'ī *umara'* 'as his *khwājatāshgān* (fellow slaves of the same master)' and gives no mentions of the Balban. He held these *umara'* 'in special esteem' and did not punish them for minor faults. The fact signifies that his primary loyalty was to the Khaljīs and not to the Ghāythids. Thus, it seems that Amīr Khusraw's assertion was true, that he was not a Balbanid slave. For details see: Baranī, *Tārīkh-i Fīrūz Shāhī* (Persian), p. 426.
10. ibid.
11. Jackson, 'Mamluk', p. 357.
12. Kulke, ed., *The State in India (1000–1700)*, p. 37.
13. Baranī, *Tārīkh-i Fīrūz Shāhī* (Persian), pp. 432–4.
14. The saint accepted Khusraw Khān's cash grant. Jamali, *Siyar al-'Ārifīn*, p. 87. Tripathi asserts that the saint's moral sympathies were aligned with Khusraw. However, it is important to remember that the saint preferred to stay detached from political events. R. P. Tripathi, *Some Aspects of Muslim Administration* (Allahabad: The Indian Press, 1936), p. 54; K. A. Nizami, *The Life and Times of Shiekh Nizam ud-din Awliya* (Delhi: Idarah-i Adbiyat-i Delli, 1991), p. 119, fn. 1. The conflict between Ghiyāth al-Dīn Tughluq and the saint occurred because the sultan demanded that the saint return the money endowed upon him by Khusraw. However, the saint had already spent the money in his charity and was unable to meet this demand. Khusraw Khān was trying to win the support of the urban elite of the Delhi sultanate. On the urban elite of the Delhi sultanate see: Rekha Pande, 'Pressure Groups and their Operation in the Delhi Sultanate', *Proceedings of the Indian History Congress*, 45th Session (1984): pp. 288–96. For an alternative view, that Khusraw Khān was unreliable for Hindus since he was a low cast and a converted Muslim, see: A. B. Pandey, *The First Afghan Empire in India, 1451–1526* (Calcutta, 1956), p. 19.
15. Hayati Gilani, ed., *Tughluq Nāmāh* (Persian) (Delhi: Indo-Persian Society, 1975), p. 29; 'Iṣāmī, *Fūtūh-us Salātīn*, fn. 378. Malik Mughallati the governor of Multan did not join him because the Malik considered him an *amīr* of a small principality of Deopalpur whereas he himself was the governor of Multan. Hussain, *Muḥammad b. Tughluq*, p. 35. For details on Ghīyāth al-Dīn Tughluq see: S. K. Bannerjee, 'Ghiasud-din Tughluq Shāh as seen in his Monuments and Coins', *Journal of Uttar Pradesh Historical Society*, Vol. 15, No. 2, p. 50.
16. Siddiqui, *Authority and Kingship*, p. 122.
17. For details about the defence of the frontiers of the Delhi sultanate under Tughluqs, see: Agha Hussain Hamdani, *Frontier Policy of the Delhi Sultanate*, pp. 139–53.
18. Jackson, *The Delhi Sultanate*, p. 180.
19. Baranī, *Tārīkh-i-Fīruz Shāhī* (Persian), p. 326. Baranī also praises the sultan for his immaculate moral character and his commitment to religion. For details see: Khalīq Ahmad Nizāmī, *Salatīn-i Dheli kay Madhabī Ru'jhānāt* (Delhi: Al Jami'at Press, 1958), p. 312.
20. Jackson, *The Delhi Sultanate*, p. 179.

21. ibid., pp. 179–80.
22. Baranī, *Tārīkh-i Fīrūz Shāhī* (Persian), p. 326. Baranī also praises the sultan for his immaculate moral character and his commitment to religion. For details see: Nizāmī, *Salatīn-i Dheli kay Madhabī Ru'jhānāt*, p. 312.
23. According to Baranī, he was known as Malik Fakhr al-Dīn Juna. See: Baranī, *Tārīkh-i-Fīruz Shāhī* (Persian), p. 14. According to Amīr Khusraw his name was Malik Fakhr ud-Daulah, Amīr Khusraw, *Tughluq Nāmāh*, p. 45.
24. Baranī, *Tārīkh-i-Fīruz Shāhī* (Persian), p. 428.
25. Peter Jackson, *The Delhi Sultanate*, p. 181.
26. Amīr Khusraw, *Tughluq Nāmāh*, p. 45.
27. Baranī, *Tārīkh-i-Fīruz Shāhī* (Persian), p. 428.
28. ibid., p. 424.
29. ibid., p. 423.
30. The Mongols were Rūmī, Rūsī and Tajiks from Khorasan. See: Peter Jackson, *The Delhi Sultanate*, p. 181.
31. Baranī, *Tārīkh-i Fīrūz Shāhī* (Persian), pp. 414–23; Sirhindī, *Tarikh-i Mubarak Shahi*, pp. 90–1; Khusraw, *Tughluq Nāmāh* (Persian), pp. 53–7.
32. 'Isāmī, *Fūtūh us Salātīn*, pp. 377–81.
33. Sirhindī, *Tarikh-i Mubarak Shahi*, pp. 89–90; Khusraw, *Tughluq Nāmāh*, pp. 47–51.
34. Sirhindī, *Tarikh-i Mubarak Shahi*, p. 90.
35. Baranī, *Tārīkh-i Fīrūz Shāhī* (Persian), p. 428.
36. Sirhindī, *Tarikh-i Mubarak Shahi*, pp. 89–90; Khusraw, *Tughluq Nāmāh*, p. 47–51.
37. 'Abdul Wali Maulvī, 'Life and letters of Malik 'Ayn u'l-Mulk Mahru, and side lights on Fīrūz Shāh's expeditions to Lakhnawtī and Jajnagar', *Journal of Asiatic Society of Bengal*, Vol. 19 (1923), pp. 253–90; Peter Jackson, *The Delhi Sultanate*, p. 180; 'Ayn al-Mulk Multānī is different from 'Ayn al-Mulk Ibn Mahru (whose correspondence is known as *Insha-yi Mahru*). See: Ayn al-Mulk Abd-Allah-i Muḥammad Sharaf Ibn Mahru, *Insha-yi Mahru*, ed. Sh. Abdur Rashid (Lahore, 1965). Ibn Mahru was the governor of Multan in the times of Muḥammad b. Tughluq and Fīrūz Shāh. 'Ayn al-Mulk Multānī belonged to a family of émigré Muslims while 'Ayn al-Mulk Ibn Mahru was an Indian whose father had converted to Islam. For details see: Peter Jackson, *The Delhi Sultanate*, p. 329; K. A. Nizami considers 'Ayn al-Mulk Multānī and 'Ayn al-Mulk Ibn Mahru the same person. K. A. Nizami, *On the History and Historians of Medieval India* (New Delhi, 1983), pp. 212–14.
38. Peter Jackson, *The Delhi Sultanate*, p. 179.
39. ibid.
40. Baranī, *Tārīkh-i Fīrūz Shāhī* (Persian), p. 426.
41. ibid., p. 450.
42. Peter Jackson, *The Delhi Sultanate*, p. 329.
43. Baranī, *Tarīkh-i Fīrūz Shāhī* (Persian), pp. 447–8.
44. 'Īṣāmī, *Fūtūh-us Salātīn*, pp. 393–9.

45. Baranī, *Tarīkh-i Fīrūz Shāhī* (Persian), pp. 334–8.
46. ibid., pp. 426–46.
47. Ibn Battūtah, *Ajā'ib al-Asfār*, pp. 92–3.
48. 'Īṣāmī, *Fūtūh-us Salātīn*, pp. 413, 420, 422, 425.
49. Baranī, *Tarīkh-i Fīrūz Shāhī* (Persian), pp. 456–60.
50. 'Īṣāmī, *Fūtūh-us Salātīn*, pp. 421–4.
51. Ibn Battūtah, *'Ajāib al-Asfār*, p. 204.
52. Peaceful transfer of power from Ghiyāth al-Dīn to Muḥammad b. Tughluq was a rare event in the Delhi sultanate. Usually the death of a king was followed by either a war of succession among the *umara'* or by the relatives of the deceased ruler.
53. Baranī, *Tārīkh-i Fīrūz Shāhī* (Persian), p. 446.
54. ibid., p. 454.
55. ibid., p. 527.
56. ibid., p. 139.
57. Ibn Battūtah, *'Ajāib al-Asfār*, pp. 42–8.
58. ibid.
59. Baranī, *Tārīkh-i Fīrūz Shāhī* (Persian), p. 454.
60. Ibn Battūtah, *'Ajāib al-Asfār*, pp. 92–3.
61. Jackson, *The Delhi Sultanate*, p. 182.
62. Ibn Battūtah, *'Ajāib al-Asfār*, pp. 92–3.
63. Baranī, *Tārīkh-i Fīrūz Shāhī* (Persian), pp. 649–50.
64. 'Īṣāmī, *Fūtūh-us Salātīn*, pp. 424–8, 431; Sirhindī, *Tarikh-i Mubarak Shahi*, p. 101. According to Ibn Battūtah he was the son of Ghiyāth al-Din's sister and he had refused to accept Muḥammad b.Tughluq as a ruler. Thus, the revolt occurred immediately after his enthronement. Ibn Battūtah, *'Ajāib al-Asfār*, p. 162.
65. 'Isāmī calls him Kishli Khān; however, the correct spelling is Kushlu Khān. 'Īṣāmī, *Fūtūh-us Salātīn*, pp. 426–42. According to Ibn Battūtah, Muḥammad b. Tughluqused to call him uncle and had great respect for him. Ibn Battūtah, *'Ajāib al-Asfār*, pp. 164–7.
66. Baranī, *Tārīkh-i Fīrūz Shāhī* (Persian), p. 478. According to Baranī the first revolt in Muḥammad b. Tughluq's reign was from Behrām Aybā. This *amir* had sided with Ghiyāth al-Dīn in his revolt against Khusraw Khān. Ghiyāth al-Dīn held him in great esteem and addressed him as brother.
67. Peter Jackson, *The Delhi Sultanate*, p. 162.
68. Patronisation towards the émigrés was one of the most striking feature of Muḥammad b. Tugluq for Ibn Battūtah. Since he mentions several émigrés working on important posts under the sultan. Ibn Battūtah, *'Ajāib al-Asfār*, pp. 4–5. For a general reference, see N. A. Baloch, 'An Account of Sind by Ibn Battūtah (Beginning from Muharram, 734 H/Sept.,1333 A.D.)', *Journal of the Pakistan Historical Society*, Vol. 54, No. 4 (2006): pp. 3–20.
69. Baranī, *Tārīkh-i Fīrūz Shāhī* (Persian), p. 499. Peter Jackson, 'The Mongols and the Delhi Sultanate in the Reign of Muḥammad Tughluq (1325–1351),' *Central Asiatic Journal* (1975): pp. 118–57.

70. Baranī, *Tārīkh-i Fīrūz Shāhī* (Persian), pp. 504–7. Baranī holds the sultan in great contempt for supporting the base born non-Muslims and the converts. See also, Riaz Ahmad, 'Political Philosophy of Zia-ud-Din Baranī', *Pakistan Journal of History and Culture*, Vol. 25, No. 1 (2004): pp. 35–71.
71. Arabic meaning 'dear' or 'relative'.
72. Arabic meaning 'poor' or 'destitute'.
73. Ibn Battūtah, *'Ajāib al-Asfār*, pp. 4–5.
74. ibid., pp. 213–14.
75. ibid., pp. 4–5.
76. ibid., pp. 218–19.
77. Baranī, *Tārīkh-i Fīrūz Shāhī* (Persian), p. 499.
78. Jackson, *The Delhi Sultanate*, p. 184.
79. ibid.
80. ibid.
81. Ibn Battūtah, *'Ajāib al-Asfār*, p. 217.
82. Baranī mentions the revolt of Kanya Naik in Warangal, due to which control of the area was lost. He also mentions another converted Muslim, who apostatised as soon as he reached Kampala and rebelled against the sultan. Thus, the control of that region was also lost. Baranī, *Tārīkh-i Fīrūz Shāhī* (Persian), pp. 484–5.
83. Ibn Battūtah, *'Ajāib al-Asfār*, pp. 10–11.
84. Baranī, *Tārīkh-i Fīrūz Shāhī* (Persian), pp. 503–7.
85. K. H. Kamdar, in *Proceedings of the all India Oriental Conference* (Baroda, 1933) pp. 629–33.
86. Baranī, *Tārīkh-i Fīrūz Shāhī* (Persian), pp. 503–7.
87. ibid.
88. 'Isāmī, *Fūtūh us-Salātīn* (Persian), p. 485. See also: M. Ifzar-ur-Rehman Khan, 'State Policy towards Non-Muslims in Medieval India', *Quarterly Journal of Pakistan Historical Society*, Vol. 54, No. 2 (2006): pp. 3–11.
89. Ibn Battūtah, *'Ajāib al-Asfār*, p. 238.
90. Shihāb al-Dīn Abu'l Abbas Aḥmad ibn-i Yaḥyā ibn Faḍl-Allah al-'Umrī, *Masālik al Absār fi Mamālikil-Amsār* (section on India) trans. Iqtadar Hussain Siddiqui and Qazi Muḥammad Ahmad, *A Fourteenth Century Account of India under Sultan Muhammad ibn Tughluq* (Aligarh: Siddiqui Publishing House, 1971), p. 37.
91. Ibn Battūtah, *'Ajāib al-Asfār*, p. 92.
92. ibid., p. 103.
93. *'Ajāib al-Asfār* and *Masālik ul-Absār* both make a mention of it. 'Mamluk' is the term specific for the elite military slaves. They were people of slave origins who were acquired in a systematic manner, followed by training and employment as soldiers. This term does not apply to all slaves who fought in wars, but only to the select few, whose lives revolved around elite military service. Interestingly, military slaves did not abandon their *mamluk* status even after they attained legal or actual freedom. The *mamluk* were dissimilar to the

menial slaves in many ways. The foremost difference was that of ownership. While even a destitute person could purchase an ordinary slave, only leading political figures, such as the ruler, his officials, and provincial leaders, could afford military slaves. Most military slaves, in fact, belonged to the ruler and the central or provincial government. Unlike ordinary slaves, who if employed in army were used as pawns, the *mamluk* formed an elite corps generally given the authority to command and conquer. For details about *mamluk* phenomenon see: Denial Pipes, *Slave Soldiers and Islam: The Genesis of a Military System* (London: Yale University Press, 1981); Andre Wink, *Al-Hind: The Making of the Indo-Islamic World: The Slave Kings and the Islamic Conquest 11th–13th Centuries*, Vol. 2 *(New Delhi: Oxford University Press, 1999), p. 92; David Aylon, 'The* Mamluk *of the Seljuks: Islam's Military Might at the Crossroads'*, *Journal of the Royal Asiatic Society.* Vol. 4 (London: Cambridge University Press, 1996), p. 305. For general reference see: idem, 'Aspects of the Mamluk Phenomenon, I. The Importance of the Mamluk Institution', *Der Islam*, Vol. 53 (1976), pp. 196–225; idem, *Studies on the Mamluks of Egypt (1250–1517)* (London: Variorum, 1977).

94. Jackson, *The Delhi Sultanate*, p. 183.
95. Ibn Battūtah, *'Ajāib al-Asfār*, pp. 9–11.
96. ibid., pp. 1–2.
97. Baranī, *Tārīkh-i Fīrūz Shāhī* (Persian), p. 481; Jackson, *The Delhi Sultanate*, p. 183.
98. ibid., p. 185.
99. 'Afīf, *Tārīkh-i Fīrūz Shāhī*, p. 267.
100. See notes in the margins, Ibn Battūtah, *'Ajāib al-Asfār*, p. 200.
101. Khuslü Khān was initially a friend of Muḥammad b. Tughluq and ruler of Sind. Later, he disobeyed the sultan who decided to kill him. Finding no escape from the wrath of the sultan the noble openly rebelled. He was ultimately killed. For details see: ibid., p. 165.
102. 'Afīf, *Tārīkh-i Fīrūz Shāhī*, p. 267; Jackson, *The Delhi Sultanate*, p. 185.
103. Jackson, *The Delhi Sultanate*, pp. 183–4.
104. Yar Muḥammad Khān, 'Relations of the sultans of Delhi with Foreign Rulers', *Journal of the Research Society of Pakistan University of Punjab*, Vol. 21, No. 3 (1984): p. 32.
105. Ibn Battūtah and 'Afīf also refer to some slave spies in their accounts.
106. Ibn Battūtah, *'Ajāib al-Asfār*, p. 179.
107. ibid., p. 176.
108. ibid., pp. 2–3.
109. The punishment given by Muḥammad b. Tughluq was generally capital punishment. Baranī, *Tārīkh-i Fīrūz Shāhī* (Persian), pp. 499–500.
110. Ibn Battūtah, *'Ajāib al-Asfār*, pp. 1–2.
111. ibid., pp. 241–3. Ibn Battūtah fell from the sultan's favour since he visited Sheikh Shihāb al-Dīn Sheikh Jām while the sultan was away on an expedition on Mabar.

112. Siddiqui, *Perso-Arabic Sources*, p. 131.
113. Ibn Battūtah, *'Ajāib al-Asfār*, p. 179.
114. ibid.
115. ibid.
116. *Nizāmī Bansūrī, Chahal Rozah.*
117. Ibn Battūtah, *'Ajāib al-Asfār*, pp. 92–3. For a similar view see also: Moinul Haq, 'Was Muḥammad B. Tughluq a Patricide?', *Muslim University Journal Aligarh* (1939).
118. 'Isāmī mentions the important role of Ahmed Ayaz in the reign of Muḥammad b. Tughluq. For instance see: 'Isāmī, *Fūtūh us-Salātīn*, pp. 413, 420, 422, 425.
119. 'Īṣāmī, *Fūtūh us-Salātīn*, p. 386.
120. Amir Khward, *Sayr al-Awlīyā'*, p. 218.
121. For instance see: 'Īṣāmī, *Fūtūh-us Salātīn*, pp. 413, 420, 422, 425.
122. Baranī, *Tārīkh-i Fīrūz Shāhī* (Persian), p. 522, For more on the rebellion against Fīrūz Shāh, see: ibid., p. 539.
123. The purpose of writing *Tārīkh-i Fīrūz Shāhī* was to reach out to Fīrūz Shāh. On several occasions Baranī laments over his career as a *nadīm* of Muḥammad b. Tughluq. Baranī, *Tārīkh-i Fīrūz Shāhī* (Persian), pp. 466–7, 509–13. He praises Sultan Fīrūz Shāh as a just, kind and efficient ruler. ibid., pp. 548–58. See also: K. A. Nizami, *On Sources and Source Material (Being Volume 1 of Historical Studies: Indian and Islamic)* (Delhi: Idarah-i Adbiyat-i Delhi, 1995), pp. 17–19. For a detailed note on Baranī see: idem, ed. *Politics and Society during the Early Medieval Period (Collected Works of Professor Mohammad Habib)*, Vol. 2 (Aligarh: Centre of Advanced Study, Department of History, Aligarh Muslim University, 1981), pp. 359–66.
124. Ibn Battūtah, *'Ajāib al-Asfār*, p. 241.
125. ibid., p. 343.
126. For the marriages among the nobility and slaves and distribution of female slaves (captives of war) see: ibid., p. 108. For the marriage of Khwājah Jahān's daughters with the sons of *qaḍi* Tirmiḍī, see ibid., p. 137.
127. For the *Eid darbār* where matters concerning to the social relations of the nobility were sorted out see, ibid., p. 107. For the surveillance of Ibn Battūtah see, ibid., p. 241.
128. For an account of the bloodshed ordered by the sultan, see: ibid., p. 144. For the elimination of Sheikh Shāhab al-Din, see: ibid., 145. For the murder of Sheikh 'Afīf al-Dīn, Sheikh Hood Qureshi and Sheikh Ali Hayder, see: ibid., pp. 150–5; Baranī, *Tārīkh-i Fīrūz Shāhī* (Persian), pp. 466–7. Alternatively, Ḥanīf believes that the sultan was not only just but also followed the examples of the Prophet Muḥammad in his dispensation of justice. See: N. Hanif, *Islamic Concept of Crime and Justice*, Vol. 1 (New Delhi: Sarup and Sons, 1990), pp. 77–8.
129. Agha Mehdi Hussain, The Rise and Fall of *Muḥammad bin Tughluq* (London: Luzac and Co., 1938), pp. 141–67.
130. Nizām al-Mulk Tusi, *Siyāsat Nāmāh*. trans. Shāh Hasan 'Atā (Karachi: Nafīs Academy, 1976), pp. 119–20.

131. Ibn Battūtah, *'Ajā'ib al-Asfār*, pp. 105, 112, 120.
132. Siddiqui, *Perso-Arabic Sources*, pp. 100–1, n. 34. Early Shi'is who came to the Delhi sultanate were of the Qaramathian sect. Since they were considered responsible for the murder of Shihāb al-Dīn Ghurī, they were suppressed by the early sultans of Delhi. 'Alā al-Dīn Khaljī had put their leaders to death.
133. 'Afīf Shams Sīrāj, *Tārīkh-i Fīrūz Shāhī* trans. (Urdu) Maulvī Muḥammad Fida 'Alī Tālib (Karachi: Nafees Academy, 1965), pp. 267–8.
134. ibid.
135. ibid., p. 268.
136. Jackson, *The Delhi Sultanate*, p. 185.
137. ibid.
138. ibid.
139. Afif, *Tārīkh-i Fīrūz Shāhī*, pp. 468–9.
140. Jackson, *The Delhi Sultanate*, pp. 186–9.
141. Ibn Battūtah, *'Ajāib al-Asfār*, pp. 10–11.
142. Afif, *Tārīkh-i Fīrūz Shāhī*, pp. 267–8.
143. Ibn Battūtah, *'Ajāib al-Asfār*, pp. 217–18.
144. The views of these historians cannot be accepted without criticism since 'Isāmī was writing in the south and his ancestors had been dislocated from Delhi to Dolatābād as a consequence of the capital's shift. See: Khaliq Ahmad Nizami, *On History and Historians of Medieval India* (Delhi: Munshiram Manoharlal Press, 1982), p. 114. Baranī on the other hand was dismissed from royal favour. See: ibid., pp. 129–30. Ibn Battūtah also witnessed the sultan's rage and displeasure owing to the fear of which he tendered his resignation from the position of *qaḍi* of Delhi. For more on this historian of the Delhi sultanate see: Peter Hardy, *Historians of Medieval India, Studies in Indo-Muslim Historical Writing* (London: Luzac,1960); Mohibul Hasan, ed., *Historians of Medieval India* (Meerut: Meenakshi Prakashan, 1968); B. N. Roy, 'The Transfer of Capital from Delhi to Dolatabad', *Journal of Indian History*, Vol. 20 (1941): pp. 159–80. This transfer of capital for a brief period of time resulted in the spread of Sufi (Chishti) Islam in the south. Eleanor Zelliot, 'A Medieval Encounter Between Hindu and Muslim: Eknath's Drama-Poem Hindu–Turk Samvad', in Richard M. Eaton, ed., *India's Islamic Traditions 711–1750* (New Delhi: Oxford University Press, 2003), pp. 67–8.
145. Ibn Battūtah, *'Ajāib al-Asfār*, p. 241.
146. ibid., pp. 144–5.
147. ibid.
148. ibid.
149. ibid., pp. 151–2. The relationship between the sultan and religious groups had grown embittered with time. Although the sultan had great reverence for Nizām al-Dīn Awlīyā', his relationship with the three great disciples of Sheikh Nizām al-Dīn Awlīyā' (Shaikh Nāṣir al-Dīn Chirāgh, Shaikh Qutb al-Dīn Munawār and Fakh ral-Dīn Zarradī) were far from cordial. See: K. A. Nizami, *Some Documents of Sultan Muḥammad bin Tughluq in Medieval India a Miscellany*,

Vol. 1 (Aligarh: Centre of Advanced Study, Department of History, 1969), p. 306. See also: Carl W. Ernst, 'From Hagiography to Martyrology: Conflicting Testimonies to a Sufi Martyr of the Delhi Sultanate', *History of Religions*, Vol. 24, No. 4 (May, 1985), pp. 323–4.

150. ibid., pp. 131–7.
151. Source: Iqtidar Hussain Siddiqui and *Qāzī* Mohammad Aḥmad, *A Fourteenth Century Arab Account of India Under Sultan Muḥammad Bin Tughluq (Being English Translation of the Chapters on India from Shihab al-Din al-Umari's Masalik al-absar fimamlik al-amsar)* (New Delhi: n.d.), pp. 38–9.
152. Siddiqui and Ahmad, *Masālik al-Absār*, p. 37.
153. Ibn Battūtah, *'Ajāib al-Asfār*, p. 144; Baranī, *Tārīkh-i Fīrūz Shāhī* (Persian), pp. 509–11; Sirhindī, *Tarikh-i Mubarak Shahi*, p. 119.
154. Baranī, *Tārīkh-i Fīrūz Shāhī* (Persian), pp. 475–6. For details on the token currency see: Simon Digby, 'The Currency System', in Raychaudhuri and Habib, eds, *Cambridge Economic History*, pp. 93–101; S. John Deyell, *Living Without Silver: The Monitory History of Early Medieval North India* (Oxford and Delhi: Oxford University Press, 1990).
155. Baranī, *Tārīkh-i Fīrūz Shāhī* (Persian), pp. 509–13. For a general note on the economy, see: Riazul Islam, 'Some Aspects of the Economy of Northern South Asia During the Fourteenth Century', *Journal of Central Asia*, Vol. 11, No. 2 (1988), pp. 5–39.
156. Baranī, *Tārīkh-i Fīrūz Shāhī* (Persian), p. 273.
157. Ibn Battūtah, *'Ajāib al-Asfār*, p. 242.
158. Hussain, *Muḥammad bin Tughluq*, pp. 141–67; Prashad, *Qaraunah Turks*, pp. 140–83.
159. Ibn Battūtah, *'Ajāib al-Asfār*, p. 273.
160. Baranī, *Tārīkh-i Fīrūz Shāhī* (Persian), pp. 489–91.
161. ibid., p. 491.
162. ibid., pp. 515–16, 523–4.
163. Jackson, *The Delhi Sultanate*, pp. 270–4.
164. Namely, Delhi, Deōgīr (Dolatābād), Multan, Kahrān (Kuhrām), Samanā, Swistān, Uchh, Hansi, Sarsutī, Mabar, Talingana, Gujarat, Badaun, Owadh, Kannauj, Lakhnāwatī, Bihar, Kara, Malwa, Lahore, Kalānor, Jājnagār and Dvārā Samudrā. Al-'Umarī, *Masālik al-Absār*, p. 87.
165. ibid.
166. Ibn Battūtah, *'Ajāib al-Asfār*, pp. 334–5.
167. Baranī, *Tārīkh-i Fīrūz Shāhī* (Persian), pp. 467–70.
168. This authority was one catalyst for the revolts against the sultan. The later part of Muḥammad's reign was marred by revolts of the provincial *amīr*s and *amīrān-i sadāh*. See: ibid., pp. 447–91.
169. The projects included: 1) increased taxation in Doab, 2) transfer of capital from Delhi to Dolatābād, 3) token currency, 4) annexation of Iraq and Khorasan, 5) retaining a large scale army and 6) expedition to Qarachil. The projects as described by Baranī are not in chronological order, and Baranī does not justify or

explain the rationale of the projects. ibid., pp. 469–781; Hussain, *Muḥammad bin Tughluq*, pp. 94–140; Prasad, *Qarauna Turks*, pp. 82–139; Jackson, *The Delhi Sultanate*, pp. 255–77. For general reference see: Sir Wolseley Haig, 'Five Questions in the History of the Tughluq Dynasty of Dihli', *JRAS* (1922), pp. 319–72; See also: Iqtadar Hussain Siddiqui, 'Sultan Muḥammad bin Tughluq's Foreign Policy: A Reappraisal', *Islamic Culture*, Vol. 62, No. 4 (1988): pp. 1–22.

170. Ibn Battūtah, *'Ajāib al-Asfār*, pp. 97–9; Baranī, *Tārīkh-i Fīrūz Shāhī* (Persian), pp. 457–63. Sirhindī, *Tarikh-i Mubarak Shahi*, pp. 118–19.

171. Drought in Delhi and its surroundings as well as the breakdown of the writ of the state in Sind region was an obvious outcome of the administrative misadventures of Muḥammad b. Tughluq. For a discussion of the impact of drought on the state see: Baranī, *Tārīkh-i Fīrūz Shāhī* (Persian), pp. 485, 473–4; Ibn Battūtah, *'Ajāib al-Asfār*, pp. 178–81, 202–3. For more about rebellions in Sind, see: Baranī, *Tārīkh-i Fīrūz Shāhī* (Persian), pp. 523–4.

172. ibid., p. 473. For a general discussion on sultanate economy and agriculture see: Irfan Habib, 'Agrarian Economy', in Raychaudhuri and Habib eds, *Cambridge Economic History*, pp. 48–76.

173. Sirhindī, *Tarikh-i Mubarak Shahi*, pp. 122–3.

174. For more on the loss of Warangal, see: Baranī, *Tārīkh-i Fīrūz Shāhī* (Persian), pp. 689–90. For more on the foundation of Bahamani Kingdom, see: ibid., pp. 513–15. For more on the rebellion in Bengal see: Fakhr al-Dīn (Fakhra), Perween Hasan, *Sultans and Mosques: The Early Muslim Architecture of Bangladesh* (London: I.B.Tauris, 2007), p. 11.

175. According to Ibn Battūtah, the sultan was disquieted by the people of Delhi writing insults on pieces of paper and throwing them into the royal residence. This offended the ruler, resulting in a change of capital. This justification does not seem reasonable to explain such a big move. However, this anecdote reflected what must have been the prevalent public impression. Ibn Battūtah, *'Ajāib al-Asfār*, pp. 158–9; 'Isāmī, *Fūtūh us-Salātīn*, pp. 446–7; B. N. Roy, 'The Transfer of Capital from Delhi to Dolatabad', *Journal of Indian History*, Vol. 20 (1941): pp. 159–80.

176. Baranī, *Tārīkh-i Fīrūz Shāhī* (Persian), p. 473.

177. ibid., pp. 479–80.

178. ibid.

179. Sirhindī, *Tarikh-i Mubarak Shahi*, p. 117.

180. Baranī, *Tārīkh-i Fīrūz Shāhī* (Persian), pp. 485–7.

181. ibid., pp. 484–5.

182. ibid.

183. ibid., p. 485.

184. ibid., p. 484.

185. Jackson, *The Delhi Sultanate*, pp. 262–6. For a general reference see: Irfan Habib, 'Non-agricultural production and Urban Economy', in Raychaudhuri and Habib, eds, *Cambridge Economic History*, pp. 76–93.

186. Its latitude lies between Somnath and Sarandib (Ceylon) up to Ghazna and its longitude from the port opposite to Aden to the wall of Alexander (the great Chinese wall) where the Indian Ocean meets the Pacific Ocean'. Al Umri, Masalik al-Absar, p. 10.
187. N. Venkata Ramanayya, 'The Date of the Rebellions of Tilang and Kampala against Sultan Muḥammad bin Tughluq', *Indian Culture*, Vol. 5 (1938–9): pp. 135–46.
188. Irfan Habib, 'Economic History of the Delhi Sultanate: An Essay in Interpretation', *Indian Council of Historical Research*, Vol. 4, No. 2 (Jan. 1978), p. 293.
189. Srivastava, *Hindus Under the Delhi Sultanate*, p. 153.
190. ibid.
191. Irfan Habib, *Essays in Indian History: Towards a Marxist Perception* (New Delhi: Pauls Press, 1995), p. 172.
192. Raychaudhuri and Habib, *Economic History*, p. 90.
193. Banerjee, *Fīrūz Shāh*, p. 135.
194. R.C. Majumdar, *An Advanced History of India* (London: Macmillan and Co, 1950), p. 400.
195. Ghulam Sarwar Khan Niazi, *The Life and Works of Sultan Alaud Din Khalji* (Lahore: Institute of Islamic Culture, 1990), p. 49.
196. Banerjee, *Fīrūz Shāh*, p. 135.
197. Raychaudhuri and Habib, *Economic History*, p. 90.
198. Srivastava, *Hindus Under the Delhi Sultanate*, p. 153.
199. Saiyid Muḥammad Mubarak Alvi Kirmani Amir Khward, *Sīrat al-Awlīyā'*, trans. Ejazul Huq Quddusi (Lahore: 1980), pp. 813–14.
200. Iqtidar Hussain Siddiqui and Qazi Mohammad Ahmad, *A Fourteenth Century Arab Account of India Under Sultan Muḥammad Bin Tughluq (Being an English Translation of the Chapters on India from Shihab al-Din al-Umari's Masalik al absar fi-mamlik al-amsar)* (New Delhi: n.d.), pp. 51–2.
201. Abdul Qadir Ibn-i Muluk Shāh Al Badaoni, *Muntakhabut-Tawārikh 1* (Calcutta: Baptist Mission Press, 1898), p. 89.
202. Muḥammad Aslam, *Malfuzātī Adab kī Tārīkhī Ahmīat* (Lahore:Idarah-yi Tahqiqat-i Pakistan,1995), p. 118.
203. Khalīq Aḥmad Niẓāmī, *Awraq-i Muswvīr: Ahd-i Wusta Kī Dillī* (Delhi: Delhi University, 1972), pp. 21–2.
204. 'Afīf, *Tārīkh-i Fīrūz Shāhī*, pp. 286–7.
205. Baranī, *Tārīkh-i Fīrūz Shāhī* (Persian), pp. 539–46; 'Afīf, *Tārīkh-i Fīrūz Shāhī*, pp. 48–9; Sirhindī, *Tarikh-i Mubarak Shahi*, pp. 123–6.
206. Baranī, *Tārīkh-i Fīrūz Shāhī* (Persian), p. 547.
207. Ibn Battūtah, *'Ajāib al-Asfār*, p. 137.
208. Baranī, *Tārīkh-i Fīrūz Shāhī* (Persian), pp. 547–8.
209. For the comparison of the two lists see: ibid., pp. 454, 527.
210. Tāj al-Dīn Turk as *nā'ib* Gujarat in the reign of Ghiyāth al-Dīn Tughluq. See: Baranī, *Tārīkh-i Fīrūz Shāhī* (Persian), p. 424.
211. Peter Jackson, *The Delhi Sultanate*, p. 188.

212. ibid.
213. ibid.
214. Baranī, *Tārīkh-i Fīrūz Shāhī* (Persian), pp. 583–4.
215. Peter Jackson, *The Delhi Sultanate*, p. 188.
216. ibid.
217. Khurram Qadir, *Sultan Muḥammad ibn Tughluq* (forthcoming). The sultan took measures to win the support of Sunni orthodox groups in order to punish the Shi'is and the *Mulhids* (apostates). For more see: *Fīrūz Shāh, Fūtūhāt-e-Fīrūz Shāhi*, ed. Sheikh Abdur Rasheed (Aligarh: Muslim University Aligarh, 1954), pp. 6–7. See also: K. K. Basu, 'An Account of Firoz Shāh Tughluq', *Journal of Bihar and Orissa Research Society*, Vol. 3, No. 22 (1936); Munazir Ahmad is of the view that Fīrūz Shāh ascended to the throne as a result of manipulation. Munazir Ahmad, *Sultan Firoz Shāh Tughluq* (Allahabad: 1978), p. 30. The sultan also was on cordial terms with the Sufis, Zafar al-Islam Islahi, *Salatin-i Delhi aur shari'at-i Islamiyah: ek mukhtasar jaizah* (Aligarh: Department of Islamic Studies Muslim University Aligarh, 2002), p. 94.
218. Baranī, *Tārīkh-i Fīrūz Shāhī* (Persian), pp. 579–80.
219. ibid., pp. 560–1.
220. ibid., pp. 576–8. A son of Fīrūz Shāh, Fateh Khān (1351–76) was given the government of Sind. See: 'Ain ud-Din 'Ain ul Mulk Abdullah bin Mahru, *Insha-i Mahru (Letters of 'Ain ud-Din 'Ain ul Mulk Abdullah bin Mahru)*, ed. Sh. Abdur Rasheed (Lahore: Research Society of Pakistan, 1965), pp. 2–8.
221. Peter Jackson, *The Delhi Sultanate*, p. 188.
222. ibid.
223. ibid.
224. 'Afif, *Tārīkh Fīrūz Shāhī*, p. 224.
225. Baranī, *Tārīkh-i Fīrūz Shāhī*, pp. 484–5.
226. ibid., p. 190.
227. 'Afif, *Tārīkh-i Fīrūz Shāhī*, p. 191.
228. Khurram Qadir, 'Firoz Shāh (Tughluq): A Personality Study', *Journal of Central Asia*, Vol. 9, No. 2 (December 1986): pp. 17–39. For a general reference see: Zafarul Islam, 'Fīrūz Shāh's Attitude towards non-Muslims – a Reappraisal', *Islamic Culture*, Vol. 64, No. 4 (1990): pp. 65–79; Zafarul Islam, 'The Fatawa Fīrūz Shāhi as a source for the socio-Economic History of the Sultanate period', *Islamic Culture*, Vol. 60, No. 2 (1986): pp. 97–117.
229. 'Afīf, *Tārīkh-i Fīrūz Shāhī*, p. 192.
230. Jamini Mohan Banerjee, *History of Firoz Shāh Tughluq* (Lahore: Progressive books, 1967), p. 136.
231. 'Afīf, *Tārīkh-i Fīrūz Shāhī*, pp. 191, 193.
232. ibid., p. 193.
233. ibid., p. 239.
234. Jackson, *The Delhi Sultanate*, p. 187.
235. ibid.

236. Banerji, *Fīrūz Shāh*, p. 135.
237. ibid.
238. ibid.
239. Jackson, *The Delhi Sultanate*, p. 187.
240. ibid.
241. Baranī, *Tārīkh-i Fīrūz Shāhī* (Persian), pp. 581–2.
242. ibid., p. 580.
243. ibid., p. 582.
244. 'Afif, *Tārīkh-i Fīrūz Shāhī*, p. 289.
245. ibid., p. 290.
246. ibid.
247. ibid., p. 291.
248. ibid., p. 293.
249. ibid., pp. 291–2.
250. ibid., p. 293.
251. ibid., p. 291; Jackson, *The Delhi Sultanate*, p. 306.
252. 'Afīf, *Tārīkh-i Fīrūz Shāhī*, p. 267.
253. ibid., p. 268.
254. ibid., p. 269.
255. ibid.
256. ibid.
257. ibid., pp. 269–71.
258. ibid., p. 270.
259. ibid., p. 284.
260. ibid.
261. Ayn al Mulk, *Insha-i Mahru*, pp. 1–12.
262. Muslim rule first arrived in these areas in the time of Muḥammad b. Qāsim. Therefore roughly six centuries had passed since the introduction of Muslim by this time.
263. Sehba Wahid, *Hindī-Islāmī Fan-i T'amīr 'Ahd-i Sultanate Main: Aik Tārīkhī aur Tehzībī Mut'ala* vol. II (Delhi: Urdu Academy, 1995), pp. 350–1.
264. Irfan Habib, 'Economic History of the Delhi Sultanate: An Essay in Interpretation', *Indian Council of Historical Research*, Vol. 4, No. 2 (Jan 1978), p. 292.
265. At one time the king became entirely dependent upon him for decision-making. See: Sirhindī, *Tarikh-i Mubarak Shahi*, trans. K. K. Basu (Karachi: Karimsons, 1977), p. 143.
266. ibid., p. 144.

Chapter 9 Vacillating between Order and Disorder: Amir Temür, Sayyids and Lodhis

1. Haji Dabir, 'Zafar ul-Walihbi Muzaffar Alih', in *An Arabic History of Gujarat*, Vol. 3, ed. Denison Ross (London: Murray 1910, 1921), p. 98. For more on the post-Timurid Fragmentation see: Simon Digby, 'After Timur Left', in

Francesca Orsini and Samira Sheikh (eds), *After Timur Left: Culture and Circulation in Fifteenth-Century North India* (Delhi: Oxford University Press, 2014).

2. The town of Kalpi was just such an example. I. H. Siddiqui, 'Kalpi in the 15th Century', *Islamic Culture*, Vol. 61, No. 3 (1987): pp. 90–120.
3. Sirhindī, *Tarikh-i Mubarak Shahi*, pp. 187–8.
4. Ibn Battūtah, *'Ajāib al-Asfār*, p. 217. The Arab *'ālims* were called *molanā*. ibid., p. 213. See also: Siddiqui, *Perso-Arabic Sources*, p. 136.
5. Sirhindī, *Tarikh-i Mubarak Shahi*, p. 189.
6. Sirhindī indicates that Temür appointed other officers in India; for instance, Lahore was given to Shaikha Khokhar who had joined Temür due to his enmity with another warlord Sarang Khān. Sirhindī, *Tarikh-i Mubarak Shahi*, p. 173.
7. Jackson, *The Delhi Sultanate*, p. 322.
8. Sirhindī mentions Khiḍr Khān as *Riyat-i 'Ala* while providing the account of Mubārak Shāh as 'Sultan-i A'zam-wa-Khudaigān-i Mu'azzm-Mū'iz-al-Duniya-wa-al-Dīn-Mubārak Shāh'. See: Sirhindī, *Tarikh-i Mubarak Shahi*, p. 199.
9. Muḥammad Bihamadkhani, *Tārīkh-i Muḥammadī*, partial tr (from 755/1354) Muḥammad Zaki (Aligarh, 1972), p. 95.
10. Bihamadkhani, *Tārīkh-i Muḥammadī*, p. 96; Abd al-Razzaq Samarqandi, *Matla' al-Sadayn*, ed. Shafi (Lahore, 1941–9, 2 vols), V, pp. 782–3.
11. ibid.
12. Tripathi, *Some Aspects of Muslim Administration*, p. 83.
13. ibid., p. 322.

BIBLIOGRAPHY

I – Primary Sources in Arabic, Persian, Urdu and English

'Abdullah. *Tarikh-i-Da'udi,* Edited by S. A. Rashid. Aligarh, 1954.

'Afīf, Shams-i Sirāj. *Tārīkh-i Fīrūz Shāhī* (Urdu). Translated by Muhammad Fidā 'Alī 'Tālib. Karachi: Nafīs Academy, 1962.

Al Badaunī, Abdul Qādir Ibn-i Mulūk Shāh. *Mūntakhab-ut-Tawārīkh.* Vol. 1. Calcutta: Baptist Mission Press, 1898.

Al Baihaki, Abul Fazl. *Tarikh-us-Subuktigin.* Translated and edited by H. M. Elliot and John Dowson. Lahore: Sang-e-Meel Publications, 2006.

Al Baihaqi, Abul Fazal Muhammad. *Tarikh-i-Masudi.* Tehran, 1324 AH.

Al Balazari, *Futuh al-Buldan.* Cairo, 1967.

Al Hamavi, Yaqut. *Mujam al-Buldan.* Cairo, 1324 AH.

Al Kasani, Abu Baker bin Ali Usman. *Farsi Tarjuma-i-Kitab ul Saidna of al Biruni.* Edited by M. Sotudeh and Afshar. Iran, 1352.

'Alā Sījzī, Hasān. *Kulliyāt-i Ḥasan 'Alā Sijzī.* Edited by Mas'ūd 'Alī Maḥwi. Hyderabad Deccan: Ibrahimia Machine Press, 1933.

________ *Fawā'id al-Fu'ād* (Urdu). Translated by Muhammad Sarwar. Lahore, 1973.

Al-Beruni. *Kitab al-Hind.* Leipzig, 1925.

Al-Idrisi. *Nuzhat al Mushtaq Fi Ikhtiraq al-Afaq.* Aligarh, 1954.

Al-Iṣtakhrī. *Al-Masalk wa 'l-Mumalik.* Leiden, 1927.

Al-Maqdisi, Bashshari. *Ahsan al-Taqasim fi Ma'rifat-al-Aqalim.* Leiden, 1877; 2nd edition.

Al-Masudi. *Muruj al-Dhahab wa Ma'adin al-Jawahir.* Baghdad, 1283 AH.

Al-Sayuti. *Tarikh al-Khulfa.* Lahore, 1892.

Al-Umri, Shihab al-Din abu Abbas. *A Fourteenth Century Arab Account of India Under Sultan Muhammad Bin Tughluq (Being English Translation of the Chapters on India from Shihab al Din al-Umari's Masalik al absar fi-mamlik al-amsar).* Translated by Iqtidar Hussain Siddiqui and Qazi Mohammad Ahmad. New Delhi, n.d.

Amir Khusraw. *The Campaigns of Ala ud-Din Khalji being the Khaza'in ul Futuh (Treasures of Victory) of Hazrat Amir Khusraw of Delhi Translated into English with Notes And Parallel Passages From Other Persian Writers* by Muhammad Habib. Madras: Diocesan Press, 1931.

________ *Nuh Sipihr*. Edited by Wahid Mirza. London: Oxford University Press, 1950.

________ *Tughluq Nama* (Persian). Edited by Hayati Galini. Delhi: Indo Persian Society, 1975.

________ *Khazain ul-Futuh*. Translated by Wahid Mirza. Lahore: United Printers, 1975.

Amīr Khward, Sayyid Muhammad Mubārak 'Alvī Kirmānī. *Siyar-al-Awaliyāh*. Translated by Ejāz al-Haq Qūddūsī. Lahore, 1980.

Amir Timur. *Tukaz-i-Timuri*. Ed. Abu Talib Husaini. Bombay: Fatehul Karim Press, 1307 AH.

________ *'Malfuzat-i Timuri*, or *Tuzak-i Timuri'. In The History of India as Told by its own Historians. The Posthumous Papers of the Late Sir H.M. Elliot*. Edited by John Dowson, 8–98. 1st edn 1867. Vol. 2, 2nd edn, Calcutta: Susil Gupta, 1956.

Arabshsh, Ahmad bin. *Kitab-i-Ajaib fi Akhbar-i-Timur*. Translated by J. H. Saunders. London: Luzac & Co., 1936.

Astarabadi, Farishtah. *Tarikh-i-Farishtah*. Vol. 2. Sindh University Library, n.d.

Awfi, Sadr al Din Muhammad. *Lubub al Albab*. Edited by E. C. Browne and Mirza Muhammad Qazvini, Part 2. Leiden and London, 1903–1906.

Baba Farid. *Fawaid al-Salikin* in *Hast Bahisht: A Collection of Eight Malfuzat of Eminent Chishti Shaykhs*. Translated by Ansar Sabiri. Lahore: Progressive Books, 1996.

Bakkari, Sayyid Muhammad Masum. *Tarikh-i Masumi*. Edited by Umar Bin Muhammad Daudpota. Poona: Bhundarkar Oriental Research Institute, 1938.

Baranī, Diyā' al-Dīn. *Tārīkh-i Fīrūz Shāhī*. Calcutta (Persian), 1862.

________ *Tarikh-i Firuz Shahi* (English). Translated by H. M. Eliot. *History of India*. Vol. 3. Delhi: Kitab Mehal, 1964.

________ *Tārīkh-i Fīrūz Shāhī* (Urdu). Translated by Sayyid Mu'īn al-Haq. Lahore: Shafiq Press, 1969.

________ *Fatawa Jahandari*. Translated by Atiq ur Rehman and Compiled by Riaz Ahmad. Islamabad: National Institute of Historical and Cultural Research, 2004.

Baranī, Zia ud Din, Shams-i-Siraj Afif. *Tarikh-i-Firoz Shahi*. Translated and edited by H. M. Elliot and John Dowson. Lahore: Sang-e-Meel Publications, 2006.

Barelvi, Muhammad Qasim 'Ali. *Padmāvat Urdū*. Kānpūr: Munshi Naval Kishor, 1873.

Chiragh, Sheikh Nasir ud din, *Khair-u'l- Majalis* {conversations of 9 ob. 1356}. Compiled by Hamid Qalandar and edited by Khaliq Ahmad Nizami. Aligarh: Muslim University Aligarh, n.d.

Clavijo, Gonzalez De. *Narrative of the Embassy of Ruy Gonzalez De Clavijo to the Court of Timur at Samarcand* A.D. *1403–6*. Translated by Clements R. Markham. London: Hakluyt Society, 1859. Reprint Lahore: Sang-e-Meel Publications, 2006.

Daudpota, U. M., ed. *Chachnama*. Hyderabad: Deccan, 1939.

Dowson, John. *The History of Sind (Being Vol 1 of Elliot's History of India) as Told by its own Historians: The Mohammadan Period Edited by John Dowson from the Posthumous Papers of the late H.M. Elliot*. Karachi: Karimsons, first edition Pakistan, 1976.

Fakhr-i Mudabbir. *Tarikh-i Fakhr al-Din Mubarak Shah*. Edited by E. D. Ross. London: Royal Asiatic Society, 1927.

Farrukhi. *Diwan Hakim Farrukhi Seistani*. Tehran, 1311 AH.

Fredunbeg, Mirza Lalichbeg. *The Chachnamah: An Ancient History of Sind.* Lahore: Vanguard Books, 1985.

Ghulam Hussain Salim, *Riyazu-s-Salatin: A History of Bengal.* Translated by Abdus Salam. Delhi: Idarah-i Adabiyat-i Delli, 1903. Reprint 1975.

Ibn al-Athir. *Kamil fi al-Tarikh.* Vol. 4. Cairo, 1801.

Ibn al-Wardī, Zayn al-Dīn ʿUmar ibn al-Muẓaffar. *Kharīdat al-ʿajāib wa-farīdat al-gharāib / Sirāj al-Dīn Abī Ḥafṣ ʿUmar ibn al-Wardī.* Cairo: Maṭbaʿat al-Himām (1302) 1884 (Arabic).

——— *Kharidat al Ajaib.* Cairo, n.d.

Ibn Battūtah. *Tuhfat al-Nuzar fi Gharaibil-Amsar.* Translated by H. A. R. Gibb: *The Travels of Ibn-i-Battutah* A.D. *1325–1354.* HS, 2nd Series, Vol. 3. Cambridge and London, 1958–94.

——— *'Ajā'ib al Asfār* (Urdu). Translated by Muhammad Hussain. Islamabad: NIHCR, 1983.

Ibn Hazam. *Jamharah Ansab al-ʿArab.* Cairo, 1245 AH.

Ibn Khaldun. *Kitab al-Ibar.* Vol. 2. Cairo, 1284 AH.

——— *Muqaddamah: An Introduction to History* (English). Translated by Frenz Rosenthal. Vol. 1. London: Routledge and Kegan Paul, 1958.

Ibn Shahriyar. Buzurk *Aja'ib al-Hind.* Cairo, 1336 AH.

Ibn Hauqal. *Kitab Surat al-Ard.* Leiden, 1938.

Īsāmī, Futuhu's Salatin or Shah Namah-i-Hind of Īsāmī (English). Translated and edited by Husain, Agha Mahdi. Vol. 1. Aligarh: University Press of Aligarh, 1976.

Isami, Maulana. *Futuhu's Salatin or Shah Namah-i Hind of Isami* (Persian). Edited by A. S. Usha. University of Madras, 1948.

Jamalī, Hāmid ibn Fazalullāh *Sīrat-al-Ārifīn.* Translated by Muhammad Ayūb Qādrī. Lahore, 1989.

Juvaini, Ata Malik. *Tarikh-i-Jahan Qusha.* Edited by Mirza Muhammad Qazwini. Part 2. Leiden, 1916.

Juzjani, Minhaj us-Siraj. *Tabaqat-e-Nasiri* (Urdu). Translated by M. Abdullah Chughtai. Lahore, 1952.

________ *Tabaqat-e-Nasiri.* Vols 1 and 2 (Urdu). Translated by Ghulam Rasool Mahar. Lahore: Urdu Science Board, 1975. Reprint 1985.

Kirmani, Muhammad ibn Mubarik (Mir-i-Khward). *Siyar al Awliyah fil Mahabbatil Haqq Jalla wa-Ala.* Delhi, 1302/1885.

Mahru, ʿAin ud-Din ʿAin ul Mulk Abdullah bin. *Insha-i-Mahru (Letters of ʿAin ud-Din ʿAin ul Mulk Abdullah bin Mahru).* Edited by Sh. Abdur Rasheed. Lahore: Research Society of Pakistan, 1965.

Manjhu, Sikandar ibn Muhammad. *Mirat-i-Sikandari.* Edited by S. C. Misra and Muhammad Lutf al Rehman. Baroda: University of Baroda, 1961.

Moinul Haq, S., ed. *Being a Critical Study of the Relevant Chapters of Tarikh-i-Firuz Shahi.* Baranī's History of the Tughluqs, by Ziya al-Din Baranī. Karachi: Pakistan's Historical Society, n.d.

Polo, Marco. *The Description of the World.* Translated by Moule and Pelliot. London, 1938.

Qāwām, Muhammad Jamāl. *Qāwām-al-Āqā'id: Hadrat Khāwājā Nizām ul-Din Awliyā kay Chasham dīd Hālāt.* Translated by Nisār Ahmad Fārūqī. Delhi, 1994.

Qazvini. *Athar al-Bilad wa –akhbar al-ʿibad.* Edited by Wusenfield. Gottingen, 1848/50.

Sachau, Edward C. *Alberuni's India: An Account of the Religion, Philosophy, Literature, Geography, Chronology, Customs, Laws and Astrology of India About* AD *1030*. Vol. 1. Lahore: Ferozesons, 1962.

Salim, Ghulam Hussain. *Riyazu-s-Salatin: A History of Bengal.* Translated by Abdus Salam. Delhi: Idarah-i Adabiyat-i Delli, 1975.

Saunders, J. H. *Tamerlane or Timur the Great, Life of Timur by Ahmad bin Arabshsh entitled Kitab-i-Ajaib fi Akhbar-i-Timur.* Translated from Arabic by Saunders. London: Luzac & Co., 1936.

Shah, Fakhr al-Din Mubarak. *Tarikh-i-Fakhr-ud-Din Mubarik Shah.* Edited by E. D. Rose. London: Royal Asiatic Society, 1927.

Shah, Firuz (Tughluq). *Futuhat-e-Firuz Shahi.* Edited by Sheikh Abdur Rasheed. Aligarh: Muslim University Aligarh, 1954.

Sirafi, Abu Zayd. *Silsilat al-Tawarikh* [*Ancient Account of India and China by Two Mohammedan Travelers 9th century* AD]. Translated from Arabic by Renaudot Eusebiu. Facsimile of 1733.

Sirhindī, Yahya Bin Ahmad Bin Abdullah. *Tarikh-i Mubarak Shahi.* Translated by K. K. Basu. Karachi: Karimsons, 1977.

Tusi, Nizām al-Mulk. *Siyāsat Nāmāh.* Translated by Shāh Hasan 'Atā. Karachi: Nafīs Academy, 1976.

Utbi. *Tarikh-i-Yamini.* Quoted by Henry Elliot, *The History of India as Told by its Historians (The Muhammadan Period).* Edited by John Dowson. 8 vols. Calcutta, 1952. 28.

Wassaf, Shihab al-Din Abd-Allah ibn Izz al Din Fadl-Allah Shirazi. *Tajziyat al Amsar wa Tazjiyat al-Asar.* Lithograph edn. Bombay, 1269/1853.

Ya'qubi. *Tarikh-i-Yaqubi.* Berinit, 1375 AH.

II – Secondary Sources

Ahmad, Aziz. *Studies in Islamic Culture in the Indian Environment.* Oxford: Oxford University Press, 1970.

________ *Political History and Institutions of the Early Turkish Empire of Delhi (1206–1290).* Delhi: Oriental Books Reprint Corps, 1972.

Ahmad, Manazir. *Sultan Firoz Shah Tughluq.* Allahabad: Chugh Publications, 1978.

Ahmad, Saeed. *The Rise and Fall of Muslims: From the Pious Caliphs to Abbasid Spain and Moghal Dynasties.* Delhi: Adam Publishers and Distributors, 2004.

Al Bili, Osman Sayyid Ahmad Isma'il. *Prelude to the General: A Study of Some Aspects of the Reign of the Eighth 'Abbasid Caliph, Al-Mu'tasim Bi-Allah (218–227/833–842).* Reading: Ithaca Press, 2001.

Alam Muzaffar, Francoise Nalini Delvoye and Marc Goboricau, eds. *The Making of Indo-Persian Culture.* Manohar: Indian and French Studies Centre de Sciences and Humanities, 2000.

Al-Hamdani, 'Abbas. *The Beginning of the Ismaili da'wa in Northern India.* Cairo, 1956.

Anjum, Tanvir. *Chishti Sufis in the Sultanate of Delhi 1190–1400: From Restrained Indifference to Calculated Defiance.* Karachi: Oxford University Press, 2011.

Ansari, Z., ed. *Life, Times and Works of Amir Khusrau-i-Dehlavi.* New Delhi: Seventh Century National Amir Khusrau Society, 1976.

Arnold, Thomas W. *The Caliphate.* New Delhi: Adam Publishers and Distributers, 2003.

Asharf, Kunwar Muhammad. *Life and Conditions of the People of Hindustan (1200–1550).* Karachi: Indus Publications, 1978.

Aslam, Muhammad. *Malfuzātī Adab kī Tārīkhī Ahmīyat.* Lahore, 1995.

________ *Muhammad bin Qasim aur us kay Janashin.* Lahore: Riaz Brothers, 1996.

Auer, Blain H. *Symbols of Authority in Medieval Islam: History, Religion, and Muslim Legitimacy in the Delhi Sultanate.* New York: I.B.Tauris, 2012.

Aylon, David. *Studies on the Mamluks of Egypt (1250–1517).* London: Variorum Reprints, 1977.

Aziz, Ghulam Rabbani. *A Short History of the Khwarizmshahs.* Karachi: Pakistan Historical Society, 1978.

Ballhatchet, Kenneth and John Harrison, eds. *The City in South Asia: Pre Modern and Modern* (Collected Papers on South Asia 3). London: Curzon Press, 1980.

Banerjee, Jamini Mohan. *History of Firoz Shah Tughluq.* Lahore: Progressive Books, 1967.

Barker, R. *Political Legitimacy and the State.* Oxford: Clarendon Press, 1990.

Bayly, C. A. *The Small Town and Islamic Gentry in North India: the Case of Kara in Collected Papers on South Asia: The City in South Asia: Pre-Modern and Modern.* Edited by Kenneth Ballhatchet and John Harrison. London: Curzon Press, 1980.

Bensman, Joseph. *Conflict and Control: Challenge to Legitimacy of Modern Governments.* London: Sage Publications, 1979.

Berker, R. *Political Legitimacy and the State.* Oxford: Clarendon Press, 1990.

Blake, Stephen. *Shahjahanabad: The Sovereign City in Mughal India, 1639–1739.* Cambridge: Cambridge University Press, 1993.

Bosworth, Clifford Edmund. *The Ghaznavids: Their Empire in Afghanistan and Eastern Iran 994–1040.* New Delhi: Munshiram Manoharlal Press, 1992.

________ *The Later Ghaznavids, Splendor and Decay: The Dynasty in Afghanistan and Northern India, 1040–1186.* Edinburgh, 1977. Reprint, New Delhi: Munshiram Manohalal, 1992.

Brice, William C, ed. *An Historical Atlas of Islam.* Leiden: E.J. Brill, 1981.

Chandara, Satish. *Medieval India: From Sultanate to the Mughals, Delhi Sultanate (1206–1526).* New Delhi: Har-Anand Publications Pvt Ltd, 1997.

Concermann, Stephen. *Die Beschreibung Indians in der 'Rihla' des Ibn Battuta: Aspekte einer herrschaftssoziologi. Einordunung des Delhi-Sultanatesunter Muhammad ibn Tughluq ... Untersuchungen)* (German Edition). K. Schwarz, 1993.

Crone, Patricia. Slaves *on Horses: The Evolution of the Islamic Polity.* Cambridge: Cambridge University Press, 1974.

Crone, Patricia and Martin Hinds. *God's Caliphs: Religious Authority in the First Century of Islam.* Cambridge: Cambridge University Press, 1986.

Daftary, Farhad. *The Ismailis: Their History and Doctrines.* Cambridge: Cambridge University Press, 1990.

Day, U. N. *Some Aspects of Medieval Indian History.* Delhi: Low Price Publications, 2004.

________ *The Government of the Sultanate.* 2nd edn. New Delhi: Munshiram Manoharlal Publishers Pvt Ltd, 1993.

De Bary, T. W., ed. *Sources of Indian Tradition.* New York: Columbia University Press, 1958.

Deyell, S. John. *Living Without Silver: The Monterey History of Early Medieval North India*. Oxford and Delhi: Oxford University Press, 1990.

Digby, Simon. *War Horse and Elephants in the Delhi Sultanate: A Study of Military Supplies*. Oxford: Oriental Monographs, 1971.

________ 'The Sufi Shaikh as a Source of Authority in Medieval India'. *Islam et Socie'te en Asie du Sud (Islam and Society in South Asia)*. Edited by Marc Gaborieau. Paris: L'École des Hautes 'Études en Sciences Socials, 1986.

________ 'The Currency System'. In Raychaudhuri and Habib, eds, *The Cambridge Economic History of India*. Vol. 1: *c.1200–c.1750*, 93–101. Cambridge: Cambridge University Press, 2004.

Eaton, M. Richard. *The Rise of Islam and the Bengal Frontier, 1204–1760*. Berkeley and Los Angeles: University of California Press, 1993.

________ 'Temple Desecration and Indo-Muslim States'. In Eaton, Richard M., *Essays on Islam and Indian History*. New Delhi: Oxford University Press, 2000.

________ ed. *Essays on Islam*. New Delhi: Oxford University Press, 2000.

Ernst, Carl W. *Eternal Garden. Mysticism, History and Politics at a South Asian Sufi Center*. New York: Albany, 1992.

Figgis, John Neville. *The Divine Right of Kings*. N.P.: Harper Torch Books, 1965. Reprint, New York: B.Y. Jove, 1990.

Frenkel, Yehoshua. *The Turkic People in Medieval Arabic Writings*. Oxon: Routledge, 2015.

Friedmann, Yohanan. 'A Contribution to the Early History of Islam in India'. In *Studies in Memory of Gaston Wiet*. Jerusalem, 1977.

________ ed. *Islam in Asia*. Vol. 1: I. *South Asia*. Jerusalem, 1984.

________ ed. *South Asia*. Vol. 1: *Qalanders and Related Groups: Elements of Social Deviance in the Religious Life of the Delhi Sultanate of the 13th and 14th Centuries*, by Simon Digby. Jerusalem: Magnes Press, Hebrew University, 1984.

Gaudefroy-Demombynes, Maurice. *Muslim Institutions*. Translated from French by John P. Macgregor. London: George Allen and Unwin Ltd, 1950.

Habib, Irfan. 'Formation of the Sultanate Ruling Class of the Thirteenth Century'. In *Medieval India 1: Researches in History of India (1200–1750)*, ed. Irfan Habib, (1992): 1–21.

________ *Essays in Indian History: Towards Marxist Perception*. New Delhi: Tulukia, 1995.

Habib, Mohammad and Khaliq Ahmad Nizami, eds. *The Delhi Sultanate (AD 1206–1526): A Comprehensive History of India*, Vol. 5. Delhi, 1970.

Habib, Mohammad. *Sultan Mahmud of Ghaznin: A Study*. Lahore: Universal Books, 1978 (first Pakistani Edition).

________ *Collected Works of Professor Mohammad Habib*. Edited by K. A. Nizami. Vol. 2: *Politics and Society during the Early Medieval Period*. Aligarh: Centre of Advanced Study, Department of History, Aligarh Muslim University, 1981.

Habibi, Abdul Hai, 'Khaljis are Afghans'. In Z. Ansari, ed., *Life, Times and Works of Amir Khusrau-i-Dehlavi*, Seventh Century National Amir Khusrau Society. New Delhi, 1976.

Habibullah, A. B. M. *The Foundation of Muslim Rule in India*. 2nd edn. Allahabad: Center Book Depot, 1961.

Haig, Wolseley. Turks and Afghans. Vol. 3: *The Cambridge History of India*. Cambridge: Cambridge University Press, 1928.

Hambley, R. G. Gavin. 'Twilight of Tughluqid Delhi', in R. E. Frykenberg, ed., *Delhi through the Ages: Essays in Urban History, Culture and Society*. Oxford and Delhi, Oxford University Press, 1986.

________ *Women in the Medieval Islamic World: Power, Patronage and Piety*. Hampshire and London: Macmillan, 1998.

Hamdani, Agha Hussain. *The Frontier Policy of the Delhi Sultans*. Islamabad: NIHCR, 1986.

Hamilton, Peter, ed. *Max Weber: Critical Assessments*, Vol. 2. 4 vols. New York: Routledge, 1991.

Hardy, P. *Historians of Medieval India: Studies in Indo-Muslim Historical Writings*. London: Luzak Publisher, 1960.

Hardy, Peter. 'Didactic Historical Writing in Indian Islam; Ziya al-Din Baranī's Treatment of the reign of Muhammad ibn Tughluq (1324–1351)', in Friedmann, ed., *Islam in Asia*, Vol. 1, 38–59.

________ *Historians of Medieval India: Studies in Indo-Muslim Historical Writing*. London: Luzac, 1960.

________ 'The Growth of Authority Over a Conquered Political Elite: Early Delhi Sultanate as A Possible Case Study'. In *Kingship and Authority in South* Asia, 2nd edn. University of Wisconsin-Madison: South Asian Studies, 1978. 216–41.

________ 'Is the Chach Nama intelligible to the historian as political theory?' In *Sind through the Ages: Proceedings of an International Seminar Held in Karachi in Spring 1975*. Edited by H. Khuhro. Karachi, 1981.

Hodivala, S. H. *Studies in Indo-Muslim History: A Critical Commentary on Elliot and Dowson*. 2 vols. Bombay, 1939–57.

Husayn, Sayyid Matlub. *Evolution of Social Institutions in Islam: During First Century of Hijrah*. Lahore: Islamic Book Foundation, 1986.

Hussain, Agha Mahdi. *The Rise and Fall of Muhammad ibn Tughluq*. London: Luzac and Co., 1938.

________ *Tughluq Dynasty*. Calcutta: Thacker Spink and Co., 1963.

Irvine, William. *The Army of the Indian Moghuls: Its Organization and Administration*. London: Luzac, 1903. Reprint New Delhi: Eurasia Publishing House, 1962.

Islahi, Zafar al-Islam. *Salatin-I Delhi aur Shari'at-I Islamiyah: Ek Mukhtasar Jaizah*. Aligarh: Department of Islamic Studies Muslim University Aligarh, 2002.

Islam, Riazul. *Sufism in South Asia: Impact on Fourteenth Century Muslim Society*. Karachi: Oxford University Press, 2002.

Jackson, Peter. *The Delhi Sultanate: A Political and Military History*. Cambridge: Cambridge University Press, 1999.

Jaffar, S. M. *Education in Muslim India being An Inquiry into the State of Education During the Muslim Period of Indian History (1000–1800 A.C.)*. Lahore: Ripon Printing Press, 1936.

Joshi, P. M. and Agha Mehdi Husain. 'Khaljis and Tughluqs in the Deccan'. In *History of Medieval Deccan*. Edited by Sherwani and Joshi. Vol. 1. 29–55. Hyderabad: The Government of Andhra Pradesh, 1973.

Karim, Abdul, ed. *Corpus of the Arabic and Persian Inscriptions of Bengal*. Dacca: Asiatic Society of Bangladesh, 1992.

Kern, Fritz. *Kingship and Law in The Middle Ages: I. The Divine Right of Kings and the Right of Resistance in the Early Middle Ages. II. Law and Constitution in the Middle Ages*. Translated by S. B. Chrimes. Oxford: Basil Blackwell, 1968.

Kulke, Hermann, ed. *The State in India (1000–1700).* Delhi: Oxford University Press, 1995.
Kumar, Raj. *Local Governments and Administration During Muslim Rule in India.* New Delhi: Anmol Publications Pvt Ltd, 2000.
________ *History and Culture Series: Essays on Medieval India.* New Delhi: Discovery Publishing House, 2003.
________ ed. 'The Deccan Policy of Ala ud Din Khalji' in *Essays on Medieval India.* New Delhi: Discovery Publishing House, 2003.
Kumar, Sunil. *Emergence of the Delhi Sultanate.* New Delhi: Permanent Black, 2007.
Lal, K. S. *History of the Khaljis* A.D. *1290–1320.* Karachi: Union Book Stall, 1950.
________ *History of the Khaljis* A.D. *1290–1320.* Karachi: Union Book Stall, 1950.
________ *Twilight of the Sultanate.* London: Asia Publishing House, 1965.
________ *Growth of Muslim Population in Medieval India.* Delhi: Research Publication in Social Sciences, 1973.
Lapidus, Ira M. *A History of Islamic Societies.* 2nd edn. Cambridge: Cambridge University Press, 2002.
Latif, Syed Muhammad. *Early History of Multan.* Lahore: Civil and Military Gazette Press, 1963.
Lewis, Bernard. *The Assassins: A Radical Sect in Islam.* Great Britain: Weidenfeld and Nicolson, 1967.
________ *Race and Color in Islam.* New York: Harper and Row, 1971.
Majumdar, R. C. *An Advanced History of India.* London: Macmillan and Co., 1950.
Mehta, J. L. *Advanced Study in the History of Medieval India.* Vol. I: *(1000–1526).* New Delhi: Sterling Publisher Pvt Ltd, 2007. Reprint.
Mirza, M. Wahid. *The Life and Works of Amir Khusrau.* Calcutta: Oriental Publishers, 1935.
________ *Amir Khusraw.* Allahabad: Hindustani Academy UP, 1949.
Misra, S. C. *The Rise of Muslim Power in Gujarat.* 2nd edn. New Delhi: People's Publishing House, 1982.
Mohib ul Hasan, ed. *Historians of Medieval India.* Meerut: Meenakshi Prakashan, 1968.
Moor, V. N. *Somnahth.* Calcutta, 1948.
Moreland, W. H. *The Agrarian System of Moslem India.* 2nd edn. Delhi: Oriental Books Reprint Ltd, 1968.
Mottahedeh, Roy P. *Loyalty and Leadership in an Early Islamic Society.* New Jersey: Princeton University Press, 1980.
Mubarikpuri, Qadi Athr. *Hindustan main Araboon Ki Hukoomatain.* Karachi: Education Press, 1967.
________ *Khilafat-i-Rashidah aur Hindustan.* Delhi: Nadwat al-Musannifin, 1972.
________ *Khilafat-i-Umvia aur Hindustan.* Delhi, 1975.
Mujamdar, K. *Chalukiyas of Gujarat.* Bombay: Bharatiya Vidya Bhavan, 1956.
Munshi, K. M., R. C. Majumdar, A. K. Majumdar and A. D. Pusalker. *The Delhi Sultanate.* History and Culture of the Indian People. Bombay: Bharatiya Vidya Bhavan, 1960.
Munshi, K. M. *Somnath: The Shrine Eternal.* Somnath: Somnath Board of Trustee, 1951.

Muumtaz Hussain Pathan, *ArabKingdom of al-Mansurah in Sind*. Sind: University of Sind, Institute of Sindhology, 1974.

Nadvi, Sayyid Suleyman. *Arab Hind ke Ta'lluqat*. Allahabad, 1930.

Nadvi, Zafar. *Tarikh-i- Sindh*. Azamgarh: Maarif Press, 1947.

Niazi, Ghulam Sarwar Khan. *The Life and Works of Sultan Alaud Din Khalji*. Lahore: Institute of Islamic Culture, 1990.

Nigam, S. B. P. *Nobility under the Sultans of Delhi A.D. 1206–1398*. Delhi: Munshiram Manoharlal, 1968.

Niyogi, Roma. *The History of the Gahadavala Dynasty*. Calcutta: Calcutta Oriental Book Agency, 1959.

Nizami, K. A. *Salatīn-i-Delhi kay Mazhabi Ru'jh'hānāt*. Delhi: Al Jami'at Press, 1958.

________ *Some Aspects of Religion and Politics in India During the Thirteenth Century*. New Delhi: Caxton Press, 1961.

________ ed. *Some Documents of Sultan Muhammad bin Tughluq*. Vol. 1: *Medieval India a Miscellany*. Aligarh: Centre of Advanced Study, Department of History, 1969.

________ *Awrāq-i-Muswvir: Ahd-i Wustā Kī Dillī*. Delhi: Delhi University, 1972.

________ *Supplement to Elliot and Dowson's History of India*. Vol. 3: *Historical Studies: Indian and Islamic*. Delhi: Idarah-i-Adbiyat-i-Delhi, 1981.

________ *On History and Historians in Medieval India*. New Delhi: Munshiram Manohar Lal, 1983.

________ *On Sources and Source Material*. Vol. 1: *Historical Studies: Indian and Islamic*. Delhi: Idarah-i-Adbiyat-i-Delhi, 1995.

________ *Royalty in Medieval India*. Delhi: Munshiram Manoharlal Publishers, 1997.

Nossov, Konstantin. *Indian Castles 1206–1526: The Rise and Fall of the Delhi Sultanate*. Oxford: Osprey Publishing House, 2006.

Nurul, Saiyed Hasan. *Religion, State, and Society in Medieval India: Collected Works of S. Nural Hasan*. Edited and translated by Satish Chandra. New Delhi: Oxford University Press, 2005.

Orsini, Francesca and Samira Sheikh, eds. *After Timur Left: Culture and Circulation in Fifteenth-Century North India*. Delhi: Oxford University Press, 2014.

Pandey, A. B. *The First Afghan Empire in India, 1451*–1526. Calcutta: Bookland, 1956.

Parashad, Ishwari. *A History of the Qaraunah Turks in India*. Allahabad: The Indian Press, 1963.

Pipes, Daniel. *Slave Soldiers and Islam: The Genesis of a Military System*. London: Yale University Press, 1981.

Prasad, Ishwari. *History of Mediaeval India: From* 647 *A.D. to The Mughal Conquest*. 2nd edn. Allahabad: The Indian Press Ltd, 1928.

________ *A History of the Qaraunah Turks in India*. Allahabad: The Indian Press, 1963.

Prashad, Pushpa. *Sanskrit Inscriptions of Delhi Sultanate*. Delhi: Oxford University Press, 1990.

al-Qazwini, Zakariya. *The History of India, As Told By Its Own Historian*. Translated into English by Henry Miers Elliot. London: Eli born Classic Series, 1952.

Qāwām, Muhammad Jamāl. *Qāwām-al-Āqā'id: Hadrat Khāwājā Nizām ul-Din Awliyā kay Chasham dīd Hālāt*. Translated by Nisār Ahmad Fārūqī. Delhi: n.p., 1994.

Qureshi, I. H. *The Administration of the Sultanate of Delhi.* Karachi: Pakistan Historical Society, 1958.

Ramanayya, N. Venkata. *The Early Muslim Expansion in South India.* Madras: University of Madras, 1942.

Raverty, H. G. *Ghaznin and its Environs: Geographical, Ethnographical and Historical.* Edited, revised and enlarged by Ahmed Nabi Khan. Lahore: Sang-e Meel Publications, 1995.

Ray, H. C. *The Dynastic History of Northern India.* 2 vols. Calcutta, 1931–1935.

Raychaudhuri, Tapan and Irfan Habib. Eds. *The Cambridge Economic History of India*. Vol. 1: *c.1200–c.1750*. Cambridge: Cambridge University Press, 2004.

Richards, J. F, ed. *Kingship and Authority in South Asia*. University of Wisconsin-Madison: South Asian Studies, 1978. 2nd edn, 1981.

Rose, Denison, ed. *An Arabic History of Gujarat*, Vol. 3 London: Murry 1910, 1921.

Saeed, Abdullah and Hassan Saeed. *Freedom of Religion, Apostasy and Islam.* Burlington, VT: Ashgate, 2004.

Saeed, Mian Muhammad. *The Sharqi Sultanate of Jaunpur: A Political and Cultural History.* Karachi: University of Karachi, 1972.

Sarkar, Jagadish Narayan. *The Art of War in Medieval India.* Delhi: Munshiram Manoharlal, 1984.

Segal, Judah Benzion. 'The Sabian Mysteries'. In *The Planet Cult of Ancient Harran, Vanished Civilizations*, ed. E. Bacon, 24–37. London: Thames and Hudson, 1963.

Sen, Asit Kumar. *People and Politics in Early Medieval India (1206–1398 AD).* Calcutta: Indian Book Distributing Co., 1963.

Seshan, Radhika, ed. *Medieval India: Problems and Possibilities.* New Delhi: Rawat Publications, 2006.

Shaban, M. A. *The Abbasid Revolution.* Cambridge: Cambridge University Press, 1970.

Sherwani, K. H. and P. M. Joshi, eds. *History of Medieval Deccan (1295–1724)*. 2 vols. Hyderabad: AP, 1973.

Siddiqui, Iqtadar Hussain. *Some Aspects of the Afghan Despotism in India.* Lahore: Funoon Press, 1969.

________ *Caliphate and Sultanate in Medieval Persia.* Karachi: Amiyat-ul Falah Publication, 1969.

________ ed. *Perso-Arabic Sources on the Life and Conditions in the Sultanate of Delhi.* Delhi: Munshi Ram Monoharlal, 1992.

________ 'Social Mobility in the Delhi Sultanate'. *Medieval India*, Vol. 1: *Researches in History of India (1200–1750)*, ed. Irfan Habib, 1992: 22–48.

________. *Authority and Kingship in the Delhi Sultanate.* New Delhi: Manohar Publishers, 2006.

Spellman, W. M. *Monarchies 1000–2000.* London: Reaktion Books Ltd, 2001.

Srivastava, A. L. *The Sultanate of Delhi (Including the Arab Invasions of Sindh), AD 711–1526.* Agra: Shiva Lal Agrawala & Co., 1950.

Srivastava, Kanhaiya Lall. *The Position of Hindus Under the Delhi Sultanate: 1206–1526.* New Delhi: Munshiram Manoharlal Publishers, 1980.

Stein, Burton. 'The Segmentary State in South Indian History'. In *Realm and Region in Traditional India*. Edited by R. J. Fox, 3–51. Durham: Duke University Press, 1977.

________ *The New Cambridge History of India Vijayanagra*. Cambridge: Cambridge University Press, 2003.

Syed, M. H. *History of Delhi Sultanate*. New Delhi: Mehra Offset Press, 2004.

Thapar, Romila. *A History of India*. Vol. 1. Baltimore: Penguin Books, 1966.

________ *Somnath* (Urdu). Translated by Riaz Siddiqui. Lahore: Fiction House, 2007.

Thomas, Edward. *The Chronicles of the Pathan Kings of Delhi*. London: Trubner and Co., 1871. Reprint Delhi: Munshiram Manoharlal Publishers, 1967.

Tripathi, R. P. *Some Aspects of Muslim Administration*. Allahabad: Central Book Depot, 1950.

Verma, H. C. *Dynamics of Urban Life in Pre-Mughal India*. Delhi: Munshiram Manoharlal Publishers, 1986.

Wahid, Sehba. *Hindi-Islami Fan-i-Tamir Ahd-i-Sultanate main: Aik Tarikhi aur Tehzibi Mutala*. Vol. 2. Delhi: Urdu Academy, 1995.

Warsi, Sultan Hameed. *History of Alauddin Khalji*. Allahabad: Rai Saheb Ram Dayal Agarwala, 1930.

Weber, Max. *Economy and Society: An Outline of Interpretative Sociology*. Edited by Guenther Roth and Claus Wittich. Berkeley: University of California Press, 1978.

Wink, Andre. *Al-Hind: The Making of the Indo-Islamic World: The Slave Kings and the Islamic Conquest 11th–13th Centuries*. Vols 2–3. New Delhi: Oxford University Press, 1999.

Wright, H. Nelson. *Catalogue of the Coins of the Indian Museum, Calcutta 2*. Oxford, 1907.

Zelliot, Eleanor. 'A Medieval Encounter between Hindu and Muslim: Eknath's Drama-Poem Hindu Turk Samvad'. In *India's Islamic Traditions 711–1750*, ed. Richard M. Eaton, 64–82. New Delhi: Oxford University Press, 2003.

III – Articles in Journals

'Abdul Wali, Maulvi. 'Life and letters of Malik 'Aynu'l-Mulk Mahru, and side lights on Firuz Shah's expeditions to Lakhnawti and Jajnagar'. *Journal of Asiatic Society of Bengal*, Vol. 19 (1923): 253–90.

Ahmad, Aziz. 'Mongol Pressure in An Alien Land'. *Central Asiatic Journal*, Vol. 6 (1961): 182–93.

________ 'The Sufi and the Sultan in Pre-Mughal Muslim India'. *Der Islam*, Vol. 38 (1962): 142–53.

________ 'Epic and Counter Epic in Medieval India'. *Journal of the American Oriental Studies*, Vol. 83 (1963): 470–6.

________ 'The Early Turkish Nucleus in India'. *Turcica*, Vol. 9 (1977): 99–109.

Ahmad, Laiq. 'Kara, A Medieval Indian City'. *Islamic Culture*, Vol. 55 (1981): 83–92.

Ahmad, Riaz. 'Political Philosophy of Zia-ud-Din Baranī'. *Pakistan Journal of History and Culture*, Vol. 25, No. 1 (2004): 35–71.

Ali, Athar. 'Military Technology of the Delhi Sultanate (13–14th C.)'. In *Proceedings of the Indian History Congress*, Vol. 50 (Gorakhpur, 1989) (Delhi, 1990): 166–82.

Anjum, Tanvir. 'Conceptualizing State and State Control in Medieval India'. *Pakistan Journal of Social Sciences*, Vols 24–6 (1998–2000): 85–101.

________ 'Temporal Divides: A Critical Review of the Major Schemes of Periodization in Indian History'. *Journal of Social Sciences, Government Collage University Faisalabad*, Vol. 1, No. 1 (2004).

________ 'Nature and Dynamics of Political Authority in the Sultanate of Delhi'. *Quarterly Journal of Pakistan Historical Society*, Vol. 54, No. 3 (2006): 30–59.

As-Sindi, B. M. B. K. 'The Probable Date of the First Arab Expeditions to India'. *Islamic Culture*, Vol. 20 (1946): 250–66.

Aylon, David. 'Aspects of the Mamluk Phenomenon, I. The Importance of the Mamluk Institution'. *Der Islam*, Vol. 53 (1976): 196–225; reprinted in his *The Mamluk Military Society*. London, 1979.

________ 'The *Mamluk* of the Seljuks: Islam's Military Might at the Crossroads'. *Journal of the Royal Asiatic Society*, Vol. 4. London: Cambridge University Press, 1996.

Baloch, N. A. 'An Account of Sind by Ibn Battutah (Beginning from Muharram, 734 H/ Sept., 1333 A.D.)'. *Journal of the Pakistan Historical Society*, Vol. 54, No. 4 (2006): 3–20.

Bannerjee, S. K. 'Ghias-u'd-din Tughluq Shah as Seen in his Monuments and Coins'. *Journal of Uttar Pradesh Historical Society*, Vol. 15, No. 2: 50.

Basu, K. K. 'An Account of Firoz Shah Tughluq'. *Journal of Bihar and Orissa Research Society*, Vol. 3, No. 22 (1936).

Blake, Stephen. 'The Patrimonial–Bureaucratic Empire of the Mughals'. *The Journal of Asian Studies*, Vol. 39, No. 1 (Nov. 1979): 77–94.

Blau, P. 'Critical Remarks on Weber's Theory of Authority'. *American Political Science Review*, Vol. 67 (1963): 305–23.

Bosworth, C.E. 'The Rise of the Karamiyyah in Khorasan'. *Muslim World*, Vol. 1 (Jan 1960): 5–14.

________ 'The Early Islamic History of Ghur'. *Central Asiatic Journal*, Vol. 6 (1961, Wiesbaden): 116–33.

________ 'The Imperial Policy of the Early Ghaznavids'. *Islamic Studies, Journal of Central Institute of Islamic Research Karachi*, Vol. 1, No. 3 (1962): 49–82.

Buhler, G. 'A Jaina account of the end of the Vaghelas of Gujarat'. *Indian Antiquary*, Vol. 26 (1897): 194–5.

Crane, Howard and Anthony Welch. 'The Tughluqs: Master Builders of the Delhi Sultanate.' *Muqarnas, a Journal of Islamic Art and Architecture,* Vol. 1. Yale: Yale University Press, 1984: pp. 123–66.

Day, U. N. 'The Military Organization of the Sultanate of Delhi (1206–1388)'. *Journal of United Province Historical Society*, Vol. 14, No. 1 (1941): 48–57.

________ 'The North West Frontier under the Khalji Sultans of Delhi'. *Islamic Culture*, Vol. 39 (1963): 98–108.

Digby, Simon. 'Iletemish or Iltutmish? A Reconsideration of the Name of the Delhi Sultan'. *Iran*, Vol. 8 (1970): 57–64.

________ 'The Sufi Sheikh and the Sultan: A Conflict of Claims to Authority in Medieval India'. *Iran*, Vol. 28 (1990).

Durrani, Ashiq Muhammad Khan. 'Sultan Mahmud and Multan'. *Journal of the Pakistan Historical Society*, Vol. 50, No. 4 (2002): 19–26.

Eisenberg, Andrew. 'Weberian Patrimonialism and Imperial Chinese History'. *Theory and Society*, Vol. 27, No. 1 (1998): 83–102.

Ernst, Carl W. 'From Hagiography to Martyrology: Conflicting Testimonies to a Sufi Martyr of the Delhi Sultanate'. *History of Religions*, Vol. 24, No. 4 (May 1985): 308–27.

Golden, B. P. 'The Olberli (Olperli): The Fortunes and Misfortunes of an Inner Asian Nomadic Clan'. *Archivum Eurasiae Medii Aevi*, Vol. 6 (1986 [1988]): 5–29.

Grafstein, R. 'The Failure of Weber's Conception of Legitimacy: Its Causes and Implications'. *Journal of Politics*, Vol. 43 (1981): 456–72.

Gupta, Satya Prakash. 'Jhain of the Delhi Sultanate'. *Medieval India: A Miscellany*. 3 vols (1975): 209–15.

Habib, Irfan. 'Economic History of the Delhi Sultanate: An Essay in Interpretation'. *Indian Council of Historical Research*, Vol. 4 (January 1978): 287–303.

________ 'Baranī's Theory of the History of the Delhi Sultanate'. *Indian Historical Review*, Vol. 7 (1980–1): 99–115.

________ 'The Price Regulations of Ala al-Din Khalji – a Defense of Zia Baranī'. *Indian Economic and Social History Review*, Vol. 21 (1984): 393–414.

Haig, Sir Wolseley. 'Five Questions in the History of the Tughluq Dynasty of Dihli'. *JRAS* (1922): 319–72.

Hambly, Gavin. 'Who were the Chihilgani: The Forty Slaves of the Sultan Shams al-Din Iltutmish of Delhi'. *Journal of the British Institute of Persian Studies*, Vol. 10 (1972): 57–62.

Hamilton, Gray G. 'Patriarchy, Patrimonialism and Filial Piety: A Comparison of China and Western Europe'. *The British Journal of Sociology*, Vol. 41, No. 1 (1990): 77–104.

Hardy, Peter. 'The Orato Recta of Baranī's Tarikh-i-Firuz Shahi – A fact or fiction?' *Bulletin of the School of Oriental and African Studies*, Vol. 20 (1957): 315–21.

________ 'The Authority of Muslim Kings in Medieval South Asia'. *Purusartha*, Paris, Vol. 9 (1986): 37–55.

Hussain, M. A. 'Six Inscriptions of Sultan Muhammad bin Tughluq Shah'. *Epigraphia Indica, Arabic and Persian Supplement* (1957–8): 29–42.

Ishaq, H. M. 'A Peep into the First Arab Expeditions to India Under The Companions of The Prophet'. *Islamic Culture*, Vol. 19 (1945): 109–14.

Islam, Riazul. 'The Rise of the Sammas in Sind'. *Islamic Culture*, Vol. 22 (1948): 359–82.

________ 'Some Aspects of the Economy of Northern South Asia during the Fourteenth Century'. *Journal of Central Asia*, Vol. 11, No. 2 (1988): 5–28.

________ 'Theory and Practice of Jaziyah in the Delhi Sultanate (14th Century)'. *Journal of the Pakistan Historical Society*, Vol. 50, No. 4 (2002): 7–18.

Islam, Zafarul. 'The Fatawa Firuz Shahi as a Source for the Socio-Economic History of the Sultanate Period'. *Islamic Culture*, Vol. 60, No. 2 (1986): 97–117.

________ 'Firuz Shah's Attitude towards non-Muslims – a Reappraisal'. *Islamic Culture*, Vol. 64, No. 4 (1990): 65–79.

Jackson, Peter. 'The Mongols and the Delhi Sultanate in the Reign of Muhammad Tughluq (1325–1351)'. *Central Asiatic Journal* (1975): 118–57.

________ 'Jalāl al-Dīn, the Mongols and the Khwarazmian Conquest of the Punjab and Sind'. *Iran*, Vol. 28 (1990): 45–54.

________ 'The Mamluk Institution in Early Muslim India'. *Journal of the Royal Asiatic Society* (1990): 340–58.

Kehrer, C. Kenneth. 'The Economic Policies of Ala-ud-Din Khalji'. *Journal of the Punjab University Historical Society*, Vol. 16 (1963): 55–66.

Khan, Ansar Zahid. 'Mahmud and Al-Biruni: A Reappraisal'. *Journal of the Pakistan Historical Society*, Vol. 54, No. 4 (2006): 21–54.

Khan, M. Ifzar-ur-Rehman. 'State Policy towards Non-Muslims in Medieval India'. *Quarterly Journal of Pakistan Historical Society*, Vol. 54, No. 2 (2006): 3–11.

Khan, M. S. 'A Thirteenth Century Persian Source For the Art of Warfare in Early Medieval India'. *Quarterly Journal of Pakistan Historical Society*, Vol. 38, No. 4 (1990): 293–307.

________ 'A Study of Fakhr Mudabbir's Thoughts on Avoidance of Warfare'. *Quarterly Journal of Pakistan Historical Society*, Vol. 43, No. 4 (1995).

Khān, Yar Muhammad Khān. 'Relations of the Sultans of Delhi with Foreign Rulers'. *Journal of the Research Society of Pakistan University of Punjab*, Vol. 21, No. 3 (1984).

Kumar, Sunil. 'When Slaves were Nobles: The Shamshi Bandagan in the Early Delhi Sultanate'. *Studies in History* (New Delhi), Vol. 10, No. 1 (1994): 23–52.

Levi, Scott C. 'Hindu Beyond Hindu Kush: Indians in the Central Asian Slave Trade'. *Journal of Royal Asiatic Society*, Vol. 12, No. 3 (November 2002): 277–88

Mathur, B. S. 'Malik-ul-Umara, Fakhr-u'd-Din: The Kotwal of Delhi'. *Islamic Culture*, No. 39 (1965): 205–8.

Moin, Mumtaz. 'Qadi Minhaj al-Din Siraj al-Juzjani'. *Journal of the Pakistan Historical Society Karachi*, Vol. 14, No. 3 (July 1967): 163–74.

Moinul Haq, Syed. 'Was Muhammad B. Tughluq a Patricide?' *Muslim University Journal Aligarh* (1939).

Moosvi, Shireen. 'Numismatic Evidence and the Economic History of the Delhi Sultanate'. *Proceedings of the Indian History Congress*, Vol. 50. Gorakhpur, 1989, 207–18. Delhi, 1990.

Nizami, K. A. 'Early Indo-Muslim Mystics and their Attitude towards the State'. *Islamic Culture*, Vol. 22 (1948): 387–98.

Oseni, Zakariyaul. 'A Study of the Relationship between al-Hajjaj ibn Yusuf al-Thaqafi and the Marwanid Royal Family in the Ummayed Era'. *Hamdard Islamicus Karachi*, Vol. 10, No. 3 (1987): 20–4.

Pal, Dharam. 'Ala-ud-Din Khalji's Mongol Policy'. *Islamic Culture*, Vol. 21 (1947): 255–63.

Pande, M. Rekha. 'Pressure Groups and their Operation in the Delhi Sultanate'. *Proceedings of the Indian History Congress*, 45th Session (1984): 288–96.

Qadir, Khurram. 'The Amiran-i-Chihalgan of Northern India'. *Journal of Central Asia*, Vol. 4 (1981): 59–146.

________ 'Firoz Shah (Tughluq): A Personality Study'. *Journal of Central Asia*, Vol. 9, No. 2 (December 1986): 17–39.

________ 'Implications of the Distinctive Features of the Ghori Chain of Command'. *Journal of History and Culture* 22 (January–June 2001): 1–14.

________ 'Indo-Muslim Historiography: The Delhi Sultanate'. *Pakistan Journal of History and Culture* XXIV, no. 12 (2003): 23–52.

Ramanayya, N. Venkata. 'The Date of the Rebellions of Tilang and Kampala against Sultan Muhammad bin Tughluq'. *Indian Culture*, Vol. 5 (1938–9): 135–46.

Richards, J.F. 'The Islamic Frontier in the East: Expansion into South Asia'. *South Asia*, Vol. 4 (1974) 94–8.

Rizvi, Rizwan Ali. 'The Sultanate was Real and Not a Legal Fiction'. *Journal of the Pakistan Historical Society*, Vol. 28, No. 1 (January 1980): pp. 37–9.

Roy, B. N. 'The Transfer of Capital from Delhi to Dolatabad'. *Journal of Indian History*, Vol. 20 (1941): 159–80.

Saran, P. 'The Economic Policy and Price Control of Alauddin Khalji'. *Bharatiya Vidya*, Vol. 2 (1950): 195–215; repr in *Studies in Medieval Indian History* (Delhi, 1952): 223–48.

Sen, Rangalal. 'Patrimonialism and Urban Development: A Reflection of Max Weber's Theory of the City'. *Bangladesh-e-Journal of Sociology*, Vol. 1, No. 1 (2004): 1–13.

Shaikh, Abdur Rasid. 'Jalal-ud-din Firuz Shah Khalji'. *Muslim University Journal*, Vol. 1 (1931).

________ 'Price Control Under Ala-u'd-din Khalji'. *Proceedings of the All Pakistan History Conference* (1951).

Sharma, S. R. 'Hindu Cooperation with Early Muslim Expansion in India'. *Proceedings of the Indian History Congress*, No. 8 (1945).

Shokoohy, Mehrdad and Natalie H. 'The Architecture of Baha' al-Din Tughrul in the Region of Bayana, Rajasthan'. *Muqarnas*, Vol. 4 (1987): 114–32.

Siddiqui, I. H. 'The Nobility under the Khalji Sultans'. *Islamic Culture*, Vol. 37 (1963).

________ 'Espionage System of the Sultans of Delhi'. *Studies in Islam*, Vol. 1 (1964).

________ 'Historical Information in the Thirteenth Century Collections of Persian Poems'. *Studies in Islam*, Vol. 19 (1982): 47–76.

________ 'The Afghans and their Emergence in India as ruling Elite during Delhi Sultanate Period'. *Central Asiatic Journal*, Vol. 26 (1982): 75–91.

________ 'Kalpi in the 15th Century'. *Islamic Culture*, Vol. 61, No. 3 (1987): 90–120.

________ 'Sultan Muhammad bin Tughluq's Foreign Policy: A Reappraisal'. *Islamic Culture*, Vol. 62, No. 4 (1988): 1–22.

________ 'Fresh Light on Diya al-Din Baranī: The Doyen of the Indo-Persian Historians of Medieval India'. *Islamic Culture*, Vol. 63 (1989): 69–84.

Stein, Burton. 'State Formation and Economy Reconsidered: Part One', Vol. 19, No. 3 (Special Issue: Papers Presented at the Conference on Indian Economic and Social History, Cambridge University, April 1984): 387–413.

________ 'Notes on "Peasant Insurgency" in Colonial Mysore: Event and Process'. *South Asia Research*, Vol. 5, No. 1 (1985): 11–27.

Stern, S. M. 'Ismaili Propaganda and Fatmid Rule in Sind'. *Islamic Culture*, Vol. 23 (1949): 298–307.

Theobald, Robin. 'Patrimonialism'. *World Politics*, Vol. 34, No. 4 (1982): 548–59.

Welch, Anthony, H. Keshani and A. Bain. 'Hydraulic Architecture in Medieval India: The Tughluqs.' *Environmental Design, Journal of the Islamic Environmental Design Research Centre*, Rome, Italy, Vol. 2 (1985): pp. 7–81.

________ 'Architectural Patronage and the Past: The Tughluq Sultans of Delhi'. *Muqarnas, An Annual on the Visual Culture of the Islamic World*, Vol. 10. Leiden: E. J. Brill, 1993: pp. 311–22.

________ 'A Medieval Muslim Center of Learning in India: the Hauz Khas Madrasa in Delhi'. in *Muqarnas, An Annual on the Visual Culture of the Islamic World*, Vol. 13. Leiden: E.J. Brill, n.d. pp. 165–190:

________ 'The Shrine of the Holy Footprint in Delhi'. *Muqarnas, An Annual on the Visual Culture of the Islamic World,* Vol. 14. Leiden: E.J. Brill, 1997: pp. 166–178.

________ 'Epigraphs, Scripture, and Architecture'. *Muqarnas, An Annual on the Visual Culture of the Islamic World*, Vol. 19. Leiden: E.J. Brill, 2002: 12–43.

IV – Inscriptions and Coins

Archaeological Survey of India. *Annual Report on Indian Epigraphy* (1964–5): pp. 23–145 (nos D 77–8).

Desai, Z. A. 'Inscriptions from the Victoria Hall Museum, Udaipur'. *Epigraphia Indica Arabic and Persian Supplement* (1955–6), pp. 67–70.

________ 'A Persian-Sanskrit inscription of Karna Deva Vaghela of Gujarat.' *Encyclopedia Indica, Arabic and Persian Supplement* (1975), pp. 13–20.

Diskalkar, D. B. 'Inscriptions of Kathiawad'. *New Indian Antiquary*, Vol. 1 (1938–9); pp. 576–90.

Kamdar, K. H. In *Proceedings of the all India Oriental Conference (Baroda, 1933).* Baroda, 1935.

INDEX

Abbasid(s), 9, 10, 12, 15, 18–22, 24, 26, 29, 38–40, 43, 57, 223, 231, 264, 270
Abd-al Malik b. Marwān, 15
Abu Bakr Baihaqi, 33
Abu Bakr Shah, 28
Abu Jafar, Caliph, 26
Abu Sufyān, 23
Abyssinian, 80
Afghanistan, 32, 43–4, 48, 50, 65, 178, 211, 213, 265
Afghanpurā, 127
Afghans, 4, 100–1, 108, 110, 122, 158, 185–6, 200, 222, 224, 236, 266, 275
'Afīf, 174–6, 248, 252–3, 257–9, 261
Afshīn, 43
ahl-i harb, 18
ahl-i-qalam, 5
ahl-i-saif, 5
Ahmad b. Ayāz, 162, 172, 174
Ahmad-i Chap, 116, 119
Ahmad-i Yenaltagin, 33
'Ainu'l Mulk Multani, 127
Ajmer, 45, 54
Akbar, 136, 206
Akhur Beg, Malik, 127
ākhūrbeg mainā, 116
'Alā al-Dīn Jānī, Malik, 70, 76, 78
'Alā al-Dīn Khalji, 8, 12, 68, 113–14, 116, 119–21, 124, 126–7, 130, 134–8, 140, 142, 148–9, 152–3, 156–7, 165, 175, 186, 189–90, 192–3, 200, 242–4, 247
'Alā al-Dīn Mas'ūd Shāh, 68, 83, 85–7
Ala al-Dīn Sikandar Shah I, 28
Alāfī(s), 17, 23
'Alā'ī, 121–7, 131–4, 137–9, 141–2, 145, 152, 154–5
'Alā'ī *umarā'*, 121, 152
Alam Shah, 28
'Alī, 39, 43, 52–3, 59–61, 82–3, 116, 125, 144, 154, 169–70, 179, 214, 227, 244, 248, 254, 261–2
'Alī Hussayn Nīshapurī, 43
'Alī Mardān, 52, 60
Aligarh, 123, 209, 214, 216, 222, 234, 240, 242, 251, 253, 255, 258, 260–4, 266–7, 269, 274
Allahabad, 36, 204, 215, 217, 235, 238, 247–8, 258, 264, 266, 268–9, 271
Alp Khān, 121, 125–6, 134
Altunapa (Altuniya), 80, 81
Amīr Hussayn, 178
Amīr Khusraw, 104–5, 120, 122, 136–7, 233, 247–9
Amīr Mu'āwiyāh, 15, 23
amīr-i ākhūr, 80, 93, 156
amīr-i dād, 59, 67, 104
amīr-i hājib/barbeg, 102
amīr-i shikār, 93, 174, 176
Amroha, 101, 105, 127–8, 159, 171
Arab, 6, 14, 16–20, 24, 29, 31, 36, 133, 138, 164–5, 184, 204–7, 222, 255, 257, 260–1, 263, 268, 270, 272–3
Arām Shāh, 26, 58–9, 221
Arhai Din Ke Jhomprā mosque, 54
'ārid, 51, 104, 106, 116, 155, 160
'ārid-i mumālīk, 114
Arsalān Khān, Sanjar-i Chist, 89
asabiyah, 186
Asam, 69

Asia, 5, 14, 22, 34, 43–4, 178, 184, 195, 203–4, 206, 215, 225, 229, 232, 238, 242, 255, 258, 265–70, 273–5
asylum of the universe, 67–8
Awadh, 76, 78, 90, 104–5, 116, 121–2, 127, 132, 155, 161, 166–9, 172, 174, 178–9, 237, 239
'Awafī, 68
Awar Khān, 64, 65, 70
Aybeg, 47, 49, 51–61, 64–5, 68, 70, 76, 80, 82, 86, 89, 90, 92, 94, 97, 104–5, 201, 216–19, 221, 223–5, 227
'Ayn al-Mulk, 137, 143, 155, 161–2, 166, 172, 178, 243, 246
Aytegin, 80–3, 105, 228
Aytemü r Kechhan, 106
Aytemü r Surkha, 106
Azīz the potter, 159

Badaun, 49, 55, 59, 69, 70, 75–6, 82, 84, 87–90, 101, 104, 115, 121, 123, 127–8, 132, 159, 176–7, 185, 219, 221, 255
Bada'yūnī, 92
Badr al-Dīn Sonqur, 82, 223
Badr al-Habashī, 160
Baghdad, 10, 24, 39, 46, 62, 94, 131, 208, 210, 261
bāgh-i jūd, 60
Baglana, 133
Bahā, 44, 47–8, 50–1, 62, 67, 70, 86–7, 92–3, 153, 157, 216, 218, 223, 226, 232, 246
Bahamanī, 179
Bahlul Lodhi, 185–6
Bahrām Shāh, 81–2, 93, 225
Bahrām-i Aybā, 154
Balāzarī, 18, 23, 207
Balban, 4, 8, 56, 63, 65, 67, 70, 77, 83–113, 115–17, 122, 124, 149, 151–3, 186, 189–90, 192–3, 201, 219, 221–3, 228–33, 235–7, 248
Balbanid, 151, 248
Balban-i Khward (junior Balban), 63, 229
Balban-i Kushlü Khān (senior Balban), 4, 70, 83
Baluchistan, 24, 29, 205–6
Banaras, 54, 179
Banbhina, 173
bandagān-i khās, 66
Bang, 52
Baniān, 87–8
Banū Hudayl, 23
Banū Sam'ā, 19, 22
Baq Temür the Ruknī, Malik, 90
Baran, 55, 61, 65, 69–70, 93, 120, 127, 168, 236, 239
Baranī, 2, 32, 61–2, 74, 87, 92, 94, 98, 99, 101–9, 115, 117–18, 120–5, 127, 129, 131–3, 136–8, 140, 143, 151–9, 161, 163–4, 166–8, 172–4, 189, 211, 221–2, 225, 229, 230, 232–59, 262–3, 269, 271, 273, 275
bārbeg, 105–6, 126
Barvārī, 142
Bayana, 47–8, 51, 64, 70, 89, 121, 128, 134, 217, 274
Begtars, 101–2, 105
Bengal, 2, 5, 51–2, 57, 65, 69–70, 80, 99, 101, 104, 107–8, 110, 113, 155, 168–9, 170, 177, 179, 186, 189, 191, 193, 218, 233, 244, 249, 256, 263–4, 266–7, 271
Bharaij, 85–6, 89–90
Bhatinda, 50
Bhattı, 109
Bhirān, 159
Bhojpur, 100, 108
Bihar, 52, 64, 69, 70, 155, 173, 185, 224, 255, 258, 272
Binbān, 69, 75
booty, 34, 37, 44–5, 52, 55, 57, 67, 88, 119, 133, 137, 140
Brahmanābād, 17, 23
Brahmans, 18
Buddhist(s), 15, 17, 22, 205, 208
Būghrā Khān, 92, 101, 106, 235
bulghakpūr, 107
Buqubuq, Malik, 111, 234
Burhān al-Dīn, 153
Byzantine, 65

caliphs, 9, 10, 12, 14–15, 19, 22, 26, 28–9, 231, 264–5
Central Asians, 158
Ceylon, 16, 257
Chachnāmah, 14, 18, 49, 206–7
Chanderi, 88, 122, 127, 137, 154, 242
chāshnigīr, 94
chatar (royal parasol), 71, 139, 185
Chenab, 33
Chhajjū, 105, 115–18, 237, 239
Chihilgānī, 73, 74
Chishti, 61–2, 222, 239, 254, 262, 264
Chitor, 122, 127, 135–7, 242
chōgān, 33
converts, 18, 120, 123, 173, 251
cursus honorum, 65

Dahar, 127, 242
Dailami, 33
Damascus, 22, 210
Dandahidesa, 134
Darya Khān, 178
Dāūdi Zāhirī, 21, 208

Dawarsumandara, kingdom of, 138
Daybul, 15, 17, 50, 205, 209
Deccan, 120, 127, 134, 138, 143, 160, 164, 167–8, 170–1, 205, 239, 244–5, 261–2, 267–8, 270
Delhi, 1–13, 25, 29, 31–2, 41–2, 47, 49, 51–60, 63, 65, 67–72, 75–9, 81–2, 84–94, 97–102, 105–11, 113–20, 122–4, 127–39, 141, 144, 146–8, 150–6, 158–64, 166–73, 177, 179, 181–91, 193–8, 201, 202–6, 210–75
Delhi sultanate, 1–7, 10–13, 31, 41, 55–7, 65, 68–71, 81, 90, 92–4, 98–100, 105, 107–8, 113, 119–20, 127–8, 131–7, 139, 146, 148, 150–1, 156, 158–60, 163–4, 167, 171, 177, 179, 182–4, 186–91, 193, 195–8, 204, 211, 213, 216–20, 222–3, 225–42, 244–52, 254–60
Delhi sultans, 1, 2, 11, 25, 29, 42, 107, 120, 127, 135–6, 191, 197, 224
Deōgīr, 119, 126, 133, 137–41, 154, 159, 166, 177, 255
Deopalpur, 104, 108, 127–8, 132, 144, 152–3, 156, 177–8, 185, 247–8
derwaish(es), 67, 83
Dhar, 137, 154
dhimmis, 21
Dinār, Malik, 123, 127, 142
dīwan khāna, 150
Diyā' al-Dīn Tūlakı, Malik, 45–6
Doab, 31, 37, 69, 87, 99, 101, 109, 127–8, 131, 166, 168, 178, 186, 189, 192, 235–6
Dolatābād, 8, 161, 166, 170, 172, 179, 254–6
dūrbāsh (trumpet), 55, 60, 71
dynasty, 4, 12–13, 19–22, 24, 29, 31, 35, 37–8, 40, 43–7, 49–50, 52, 72, 75, 94, 97, 101, 104, 106, 110, 112–14, 120, 132–4, 137–8, 146, 149–52, 156, 158–9, 179, 182, 184–5, 195–6, 200, 207, 214–15

Eastern Gangā, 179
Egypt, 10, 24, 29, 38, 62, 94, 105, 210, 252, 265
Erich, 122, 127, 137, 242

Fadal b. Māhān, 19–20, 22
Fakhr al-Dīn (also known as Fakhra), 58, 79, 106, 115–16, 125, 143–4, 152, 169–70, 179, 217, 226, 235, 239, 241, 246, 249, 256
Fakhr al-Dīn Juna, Malik, 143, 152, 246, 249
Fakhr al-Dīn Kōtwāl, 106
Fakhr-i Muddabir, 44, 58
Fakhruddin Mubārik, 49
Fakhr-ul Mulk Mirthī, 127
Farah, 46, 214
Faridkot, 108–9
Farishtāh, 61, 88, 92, 151, 238, 246
fatahnama, 17, 39, 72
Fatāwa-i Jahandāri, 32
Fatimid(s), 19, 22, 24, 29, 38
Firdusī, 43
Fīrūz Shāh, Tughlaq, 10, 28, 74–5, 83, 89, 114, 170, 172–5, 178–9, 181, 183, 190, 192, 194, 200, 225, 229, 232–46, 248–59
Fīrūzabad, 179
Fīrūzī Castle, 87
Fīrūzkūh, 45–6
Fūā'id ul-Fū'ād, 79
Fūtūh ul-Buldān, 18, 207

Gāgān, 23
Gahadāvālā, 57
Ganges, 37, 52, 79, 169, 227
Gardaiz, 48
Garjistān, 43
Garmsīr, 44, 214
Garshāsp, 153, 157
Genghis Khān, 50
Ghanza, 55
Gharjistān, 44–5, 214
ghāzī, 41
Ghāzī Malik, 143–6, 148, 151
Ghazna, 21, 24, 31, 34–5, 37–8, 43–5, 47–50, 55–6, 58, 60, 75–6, 88, 158, 211, 214, 216–17, 241, 257
Ghaznawid(s), 1, 11, 24, 29, 31–40, 43, 45, 56, 60, 232, 243
Ghazni, 108, 114, 212
Ghiyāth al-Dīn, Sultan, 4, 43–4, 46, 86, 103, 144
Ghiyāth al-Dīn Balban, 4, 8, 12, 27, 86, 103 (*see also* Balban; Balban-i Khward)
Ghiyāth al-Dīn Muhammad, 26, 44, 46
Ghiyāth al-Dīn Muhammad b. Sām, 44
Ghiyāth al-Dīn Tughluq, 151–2, 155, 156
Ghiyāth al-Dīn Tughluq II, 28
Ghiyāthī army, 154
Ghiyāthī *mawālzadgān* (sons of the freed slaves), 102
Ghiyāthid, 107, 113–16
Ghiyāthpūr, 118, 129, 238
ghulāms, 31, 36
Ghūr, 38, 43, 46, 49–50, 214

Ghūrī, 7, 31, 38, 41, 45–7, 49, 50, 52, 56–7, 62, 80, 83, 213, 219
Ghūrīd(s), 1, 11, 29, 40, 42–3, 45–7, 53, 55–7, 60, 64, 134, 215, 217, 219
Gnaur, 101
Gnosticism, 21
Gopalpur, 100
Gorakhpur, 179, 271, 274
Gramshīr, 51
Gujarat, 14, 29, 31, 44, 71, 79, 99, 101, 121–2, 125–8, 132–5, 142, 144, 152, 159–60, 171, 173, 176, 178, 185–6, 205, 241, 243–4, 255, 258, 260, 268, 270, 272, 276
Gwalior, 47, 51, 55, 61, 64, 67, 75, 78, 84, 88, 126, 173

Habīb, 64
Hāfiz 'Ibād Allah, al Munta-qīm min, 40
Hajjāj, 15, 16–17, 23, 207
Hājjī, 68, 121, 124–5, 128, 158
Hajjī Ilyas, 179
Hājjī Maulā, 68, 124–5, 128
Hamīd al-Dīn Amir-i Koh, Malik, 125
Hammiramahakavya, 71
Hanafite, 21, 43, 79, 208, 214
Hansi, 35, 69–70, 76, 89, 92–3, 102, 161, 170, 255
Hasām Adhung, 172
Hassam al-Dīn Olghbeg, Malik, 53
Hātim-i Tāi, 61
Hauz-i Ranī, 84
Haybat Khān, 104, 111, 122
Hazār Sūtūn Palace, 143
Helegu, 26
Herat, 44, 46, 174, 185, 214, 215
Hermeticism, 21
Hibariyāh Kingdom of al Mansūrāh, 20–1
Hind, 14, 19, 24, 29, 40, 204–9, 234, 236, 240, 252, 261, 263, 268, 271
Hindu(s), 15, 17, 20–2, 24, 30–1, 34–5, 37, 45, 49, 52, 54, 57, 63–5, 67, 80, 91, 102, 107, 109, 116, 126, 132, 142–4, 146, 148, 159, 164, 171, 186, 204–5, 212, 215, 219, 222–3, 240–1, 248, 254, 257, 270–1, 274–5
Hindustan(ī), 51, 53, 55, 60, 68, 91, 99, 162, 205, 206, 218, 220, 264, 268
Hizabr al-Dīn Yūsūf, 121
Hoysala king, Ballala III of Dvarasamudra, 139
Hoysalas, 138
Humayun, 136
Hurra-i Khuttālī, 37

Ibn al-Athīr, 52, 208
Ibn Battūtah, 94, 140, 151, 156–9, 161–5, 167, 170–1, 237, 245–7, 250–6, 258, 260
Ibn Hazm, 21
Ibn Hūqal, 21–2
Ibn Khuldūn, 21–2, 186
Ibrahīm, 119
Ikhit Khān, 121, 123, 242
Ikhtiyār al-Dīn, 51–3, 65, 70, 80–1, 88, 102, 105, 115–16, 122, 176, 228
Ikhtiyār al-Dīn Bakhtiyār Khaljı, 52
Ilkhān Mūsā, 159
Iltutmish, 5, 8–9, 12, 49, 50–1, 55–6, 58–78, 81–3, 85–6, 92–5, 97–9, 111, 113, 125, 134, 142, 149, 152–3, 186, 189–90, 192–3, 200–1, 218, 220, 222, 225–6, 228, 232, 272, 273
Iltutmish's progeny, 97
Ilyas Hajji, 170
'Imād al-Dīn Rayhān, 86, 90, 102
'Imād al-Mulk Shabīr, 176
'Imrān b. Mūsā Barmikī, 19
India, 1, 2, 12, 14–15, 16, 21–2, 24, 29–32, 35–45, 47–8, 50, 52–3, 55–7, 60, 63, 65, 69, 71, 92, 103, 107–8, 113, 127, 133, 136–7, 158, 166, 186–7, 203–6, 210–17, 219–22, 224–5, 228–9, 232–5, 240, 241–5, 247–9, 251, 254–5, 257, 260–2, 264, 265–76
Indrapat, 118, 129, 238
Indus, 36, 47–8, 50, 132, 218, 264
iqtā'(s), 7, 47–8, 52, 61–2, 63–7, 69–70, 75–8, 80, 82–4, 86, 88–94, 103–5, 107, 109, 111, 115, 120–1, 126, 128, 132, 137, 141–2, 144, 154–5, 163, 165, 169, 171–2, 175–6, 177–8, 183, 204, 218, 222, 226, 239
Iraq, 22–3, 52, 164, 168, 256
Irkalī Khān, 115, 117, 119
'Isāmī, 114, 121–2, 125, 136, 154, 156, 164, 171, 236–40, 244, 246, 248–51, 253–4, 256
Isfiza, 46
Ishāq Ibrāhīm b. Muhammad al-Farisī al-Istakarı, 22
Islamic law, 3, 61, 189
Ismā'lī, 23, 29, 36, 39
al-Istakhrī, 22, 24
'Izz al-Dīn, Malik, 76–9, 81, 84, 91, 116, 121, 218, 226

'Izz al-Dīn Kabīr, 77, 79–80, 223
'Izz al-Dīn Salārī, Malik, 76, 81
'Izz al-Dīn Tughan Khān Tughril, Malik, 66

Jahansūz, 46
Jaipāl, 31
Jalāl al-Dīn, 8, 27, 50, 55, 68, 82–7, 90, 113–21, 123, 146–8, 151, 169, 173, 189–90, 193, 217, 237, 239, 241, 247, 273
Jalāl al-Dīn Kashānı, 82
Jalāl al-Dīn Khaljī, 115
Jalāl al-Dīn Mingbarnī, 50, 55
Jalivān, 44
Jalor, 60, 242, 244
Jamna, 115, 118
Jāt(s), 17, 81, 109, 151
Jaunpur, 179, 185–6, 270
Jawami-'ul Hikayat, 49
jazyā, 18, 160
Jhayin, 121, 127–8, 135, 137, 242
Joseph, patriarch, 59
Juzjānī, 43, 46, 50, 52, 55, 58–65, 67–8, 70, 73–6, 78, 80, 82, 84–92, 94, 193, 213–18, 220–32

Kabīr Khān Ayāz, 63, 76, 223
Kabul, 15, 140, 184, 185
Kāfūr, Malik, 4, 12, 120, 122–3, 125–7, 137–44, 146, 148, 155, 194, 242
Kaithal, 81
Kalinjar, 36, 54
Kamāl al-Dīn 'Gurg' (wolf), 136, 140
Kamāl Mahyār, 103
Kampila, 164, 171
Kanbhaya, 126, 133
Kannauj, 22, 85, 87, 168, 177, 255
Kannū, 160, 164
Kanpal, 100, 108
Kara, 84, 89–90, 115, 127–8, 132, 134, 172, 177, 229, 239, 255, 265, 271
Kāramiyyah, 43
Karman, 24, 47
Karnadeva, King, 133
Karnataka, 171
Karosah, 179
al-Kasānī, 68
kashaf (reading minds), 62
Kashmandī, 52
Kashmir, 17, 22, 205
Katihar, 101, 128, 169
Kaykaūs, 61
Kaykhusraw, 102, 105, 113–14, 193
Kayqubād, 61, 92, 103, 105–6, 114–16, 119, 148, 193, 237, 241
Kayūmarth, 106
Kelukherī, 76, 91, 115, 118, 129, 238
Khalifa al-Wathiq Billah, 27
Khaljī(s), 8, 10, 12, 27, 41, 51–2, 53, 60, 68–9, 72, 102, 105–7, 112–17, 119–21, 124, 126–7, 130, 134–8, 140, 142, 146, 148–53, 156–7, 165, 168, 175, 186, 189, 190, 192–3, 200, 202, 218, 236–8, 241–5, 247–8, 254, 257, 261, 268, 271–5
khalq, 107, 109, 124
Khāmush, Malik, 116
Khān Jāhān, 172, 176–7, 181
Khān-i Khānān, 117
Khārjite(s), 24, 29
Kharosh, 179
Khawāja Hajjī, 155
Khawāja Jahān, 162, 164
Khidr Khān, 122, 125–6, 184–5, 213
Khidrabād, 136
khil'at (robe), 184–5
Khisli Khān, 86, 88
Khizr Khan, 28
Khokhar(s), 38, 81, 87, 109, 170, 260
Khorasan, 38–40, 43, 46–7, 49–50, 85, 92, 158, 168, 214, 248–9, 256, 272
Khorasanī, 51, 65, 67
Khusraw Khān, 4, 139, 142–6, 148, 150, 152, 192, 250
Khusraw Malik, 45, 75
Khusraw Shāh, 12, 38, 40, 143
khutba, 10, 19–20, 22, 26–7, 39, 41, 52–3, 56, 72, 117, 144, 188, 196, 207
Khwājah Jahān, 164, 170, 253
khwājatāshgān, 55, 104, 110, 151, 193, 248
Khwārzam Shāh, 46, 49
Khwārzam Shāhī, 45, 47, 50
Khwārzim, 40, 230
Khwajah Muhazzib, 82–4
al-Kirāj, 18
Kirk, 127
Kirmān, 24
Kishlī Khān, 90, 92, 94, 105, 157, 223, 235
Kīz, 23, 209
Koehlā, 127–8
Koh-i Jūd (salt range), 49, 87, 101, 109, 116
Koh-i Silmur, 91
Kol, 53–4, 76, 84, 101, 123, 127, 168
Kuhrām, 50, 54, 60, 104, 255
Kūjī, Malik, 76, 78–9, 239
kurtās, 22, 24
Kushlu, 4, 70, 77, 83–4, 86, 88–9, 91–3, 95, 154, 160, 164, 222, 231, 250

Lahore, 15, 31, 33, 38, 44–5, 48–50, 55–6, 60, 69–70, 75–6, 80, 82, 86–7, 89–91, 101, 104, 107–8, 127–8, 132,

167, 170, 177–8, 185, 207–9, 211–14, 216, 219, 222, 227, 240, 242, 247, 249, 255, 257–68, 270–1
lākh bakhsh, 61
Lakhnawatī, 52–3, 60, 65, 68, 70, 74, 76, 79, 84, 107–9, 111, 169, 179
Lamghān, 31
Lubāb al-Albāb, 49

Mabar, 139, 140, 150, 167, 169, 170, 179, 253, 255
M'ādān b. 'Isa, 23–4
M'adaniyā, Kingdom of Tīz-Makran, 19, 23–4
madrasahs, 43
Māhān, 20
Mahāniyā, Kingdom of Sanjān-Hind, 19, 22
Māhārāj, 24
Maharashtra, 19
Mahmūd, 14, 19, 21, 23–4, 29–40, 43–5, 51, 66–7, 74–5, 85–6, 88, 90, 93, 98, 108, 133, 141, 157, 184, 190, 192–3, 200, 210–13, 221–2, 229–32
Mahmūd of Ghazna, 14, 19, 21, 23, 29–30, 32, 43, 45, 67, 133, 184, 210–11
Mahmūd b. Muhammad, 28, 202
Mahmūd Nasir al-Dīn, 28
Māhrū, 125
Maimandi, 33
makātib, 43
Makran, 14, 15, 17, 19–24, 31, 40, 50
malīcha, 54
malikāh, 74
Malikā-i Jahān, 85, 86, 91, 119, 120
Malwa, 57, 69, 88, 99, 101, 132, 137, 142, 154–5, 159, 167, 178, 185–6, 205, 255
mamlūk, 62, 65–6, 94, 104–5, 151
al-Mamūn, 19
manaziras (religious debates), 62
Mandahīr, 109
Mandal-Khur, 137
Mandu, 137
Mandugārh, 137
manshūr, 188, 196
Mansur al-Mustansir Billah, 26
al-Mansūrāh, 18, 19, 20–2, 24, 209
Mansurpūr, 91
Manzar b. Zubair Hibari, 20
Maqbūl, 160, 164, 171–2, 176
Mas'ūd, 37–40, 97, 165, 212, 261
al-Mas'ūdī, 21, 24
Mawālzadāh Malik Qīrān-i 'Alā'ī, 122
mawālzadgān, 102–3, 105, 117
mawasāt, 69
M'āwiyah b. Hāris 'Alāfı, 23
Meeruth, 127
Meneyoan, 109
Mewāties, 100, 110
Mīds, 17
Mirath, 54
Mongol(s), 4–5, 49–50, 64, 68, 70, 75, 82, 85–8, 90, 92, 99, 101–2, 105, 107–8, 113–14, 118, 120, 123, 126, 128, 130, 132–4, 148, 152–5, 170, 174, 178, 185, 187, 196, 216–17, 221, 233, 236, 238, 242, 249, 251, 271, 273–4
Mubārak Shāh/Khān, 10, 28, 139, 140–3, 145–6, 148, 150, 152–3, 157, 217, 262
Mufarrih Sultanī, Malik, 178
Mughalpurā, 118
Mughaltaī, Malik, 154
Mūghīhth al-Dīn, Sultan, 104
Muhammad, 3, 8, 10, 16–23, 26, 28, 41, 44, 46, 53, 56, 76, 78, 82, 84, 101, 104–5, 109, 116, 122, 127, 135, 137–8, 144–5, 150–60, 162, 164–77, 179, 181–4, 186, 190, 192, 194–6, 200, 202, 204–12, 214–19, 222, 224, 226–7, 231–2, 235, 237, 244–5, 247–65, 267–75
Muhammad, Prince, 46, 101, 233, 234
Muhammad Alp Ghāzı, 46
Muhammad b. Qāsim, 16–17, 22–3, 205–7, 259
Muhammad b. Tughluq, 8, 10, 28, 137, 144, 151, 153–4, 156–9, 162, 165, 167–9, 172, 175–7, 183–4, 186, 190, 192, 194–5, 200, 202, 204, 232, 237, 248–50, 252–3
Muhammad Shāh, 28
Mu'izz al-Dīn (Almas Beg), 116; as the holy warrior sultan (*sultan-i ghāzi*), 55
Mu'izz al-Dīn Bahrām, 26, 81
Mu'izz al-Dīn Kaiqabad, 27
Mu'izzī(s), 47–8, 53–4, 58, 65–6, 78, 60, 69, 215, 220–1, 217
Muja'ā b. Sār Tamīmī, 23
Multan, 14–15, 17, 19, 21–4, 29, 31, 35–7, 39, 44, 47, 50, 64, 70, 76–7, 80–1, 87–9, 91–3, 101, 108, 114, 120–1, 127, 132, 144, 152, 154, 159–61, 164, 167, 170, 177–8, 209,

212–13, 216, 236, 242, 248–9, 255, 268, 272
Mumbai, 15, 19, 209
al-Muqaddasī, 21, 22
muqta'(s), 7, 64, 66, 76, 78, 80, 85, 87, 90, 93–4, 100–2, 104–7, 109, 116, 121–3, 127, 131–2, 134, 141, 144, 154–5, 159, 170, 173–6, 193, 222, 229, 236
murtīd, 39
Mushrif-i Mumalik, 78
Muslim, 1, 2, 5, 7, 10–11, 14–24, 29, 31–2, 34–7, 39, 42–3, 45, 47–52, 54–5, 58, 62, 67–70, 72, 94, 97, 100, 102, 107, 109, 114, 123, 126–7, 131–40, 143–4, 146, 164, 178, 186, 189, 205–10, 212–16, 218–19, 222, 224–5, 233, 235, 237–8, 240–5, 248, 251, 253–4, 256, 258–60, 262, 264–75
al-Mustakfi bi-Allah, 28
Mustansir Billah, 26
al-Mustasim Billah, 26
Musulman, 30
Mutāhir b. Rij'ā, 24
Mū'tasim, Caliph, 20
mutatāwī'a, 34
al-Mutawakkal Billah, 28
Mu'tazilites, 39
mystic prince, 61, 220

Nā'ib, Malik, 120, 122, 126, 139
nā'ib barbeg, 116, 153
nā'ib wazīr, 167
nāi'b-ghāi'bat, 78
Nānak, Malik, 123
Nāsir al-Dīn Aytemür, 64, 223
Nāsir al-Dīn Mahmūd Shāh, 26, 28, 47–8, 51, 60, 63–4, 67, 74–5, 83, 85–6, 88–90, 92, 98, 104, 118–19, 143, 184, 190, 192–3, 200, 213, 218, 221, 223, 229–32, 255
Nāsir Dīn Allah, 40
Nagaur(ī), 52, 69, 83, 88–9, 93
Nahrwala, 133–4
naib amir al-mumineen, 28
namāz (prayer), 79
Nasik region, 133
nasir amir al-mumineen, 26–7
Nathu Sudhal, 172
naubat, 82, 84
nīl (indigo), 36
Nirūn, 17, 209
Nizām al-Dīn, 39, 106, 114, 116, 148, 152, 154–5, 158, 162, 179, 226, 236, 238, 255
Nizām al-Dīn Awliyah, 79
Nizām al-Mulk, 78–9, 84, 94, 226, 232, 254, 264
Nizām al-Mulk Junaydī, 78–9, 226
nobility, 3–5, 7–9, 53, 73–6, 80, 83–4, 97, 101–3, 105, 110, 114–15, 118, 124, 140, 144, 147, 151–6, 158, 163–4, 172, 175, 186, 195, 197–9, 203–4, 212, 237, 241, 253
Nūr Tūrk, 79
Nusrat al-Dīn Tāī'sı, Malik, 64, 78
Nusrat Khān, 28, 86, 133–5, 153, 157, 172, 223, 239

Olberli(s), 2, 12, 42, 65, 68, 102, 115–16, 122, 124, 273

pā'ik, 103, 122–3, 140–1
Pandya/Mabar, kingdom of, 138
Pānipat, 183
parwanāh, 54
parwarish, 66–7
Patyāli, 100, 108
Persia, 5, 15, 43, 159, 173, 178, 208, 213, 270
Persian, 6, 15, 20–1, 24, 35–6, 38, 43, 45, 98, 158–60, 164, 196, 204, 210, 213–46, 248–53, 255–9, 261–4, 267, 273, 275–6
Peshawar, 31, 44, 56
Prithvi Rāj (Rai Pathurā), 45
Punjab, 19, 22, 31, 35–8, 40, 45, 48–50, 53, 60, 68, 80, 87–8, 108–9, 168, 170, 184, 205, 216–17, 220, 235, 243, 252, 273

Qabacha, 48, 49, 50, 56, 58, 60, 62, 69–70, 75, 217, 221
Qabtagha, 158, 174
Qabul Khilāfatī, 163
qadam (commuting supernaturally), 62
Qadar Khān, 116
Qadās, 44
qāḍi(s), 32, 33, 55–6, 67
Qadi ibn Abi Shwārib, 21
al-Qadir, 39
al-Qāi'm, Caliph, 40
Qadr Khān, 169
Qara-Khitai, 46, 77–8
Qara-Khitan, 78
Qarachomaq, Sipah Sālār, 102
Qaramathian(s), 29, 37, 39–40, 44, 79, 254
Qarāqash Khān, 63–5, 70, 80–1, 83
Qasr-i Bāgh, 86
Qasr-i Sufīd, 83
Qayqān, 23
Qirā Beg Ahmad-i Chhitam, 134
Qiran Safdar Malik, Malik, 160
Qiwāṃ al-Dīn Tirmidi, 174
Qur'an, 85, 87, 143, 214
Qur'anic, 100

Quraysh, 21–2
Qusdār, 40, 174
Qutb al-Dīn, Hussayn, Malik, 82
Qutb al-Dīn, 10, 47, 48, 51–3, 55–6, 59–61, 71, 76, 80, 83, 91, 139–41, 148, 150, 153, 192, 218–19, 221, 227, 255
Qutb al-Dīn, Sultan, 53, 140
Qutb al-Dīn Aybeg, 26, 47–8, 51–3, 55–6, 59–61, 71, 76, 219, 221
Qutb al-Dīn Mubarak Shah, 27, 146
Qutbī, 26, 60, 220–1
Qutbī slaves, 58
Qutlugh Khān, 68, 80, 89–91, 105, 170, 172, 227

Radiyyah, 26, 68, 74–5, 77–81, 92–5, 97, 189, 201, 226, 228
Rāi' Virabhanudeva III, 179
Raja Jaipāl, 31
Raja of Nārāyanpūr, 36
Raja Satal Deo, 136
Rajab, 153, 157, 248
Rajas, 15, 22
Rājpūt, 45, 60
Ram Chandara, 138
Ramadeva, King, 133, 139
Rāmādīva, the Yādavā King of Deōgīr, 126
Rānī Padmani, 135–6
Ranthambor, 60, 69, 87, 118, 121, 123–4, 134–6, 242
Rāshidūn, 14–15, 22, 43, 125, 210
Ratan, 159, 164
Raverty, 60, 75, 85–6, 88, 218–21, 223, 228, 270
Rawāfids, 29, 210
razīls, 63, 164
River Bayas, 91
Rukn al-Dīn, 68, 74–7, 83, 92, 97, 119, 173, 225, 227
Rukn al-Dīn Fīruz, 26, 68, 74–7, 225
Rukn al-Dīn Ibrahim, 27

Sabian, 21, 208, 270
Sachor, 133–4
Sadar ul-Mulk, Najam al-Dīn Abu Bakar, 90
Sadr ul-Mulk Najm, 84
Sadusān, 17
sagwān, 20
Sahu, 170 (rebel Afghan chief)
Saif al-Dīn Hasan Qurlugh, Malik, 88
Saifrud, 44
Saiyid Dynasty, 28
Sajistān, 24, 44, 49
saka (Rajput tradition to fight until death), 136
salaries (*mawājib*), 103
Sali Noyan, 92
Ṣāliḥ 'Abd al-Rahmān, the fiscal manager of Iraq, 18
Samana, 101, 104, 108–9, 114, 123, 127–8, 144, 154, 176–7, 255
Samanatasimh, 136
Samanids, 39
Samara, 159
Samarqand, 46
Sambhal, 160, 173
Sanān b. Salmā b. Mahbiq Huzailī, 23
Sanbhal, 87, 101
Sanjān, 19
Sanjar-i Chist, 90
Sankurān, 48
Sanskrit, 55, 58, 210, 219, 220, 244, 269, 276
Sargadwarī, 166, 172
sar-i jandār (royal guard), 61
Sayyids, 75, 184–6, 260
Shabankarā, 159
Shādī, Malik, 142, 145, 157
Shādī Dāwar, 153
Shādī Khān, 125
Shāh, 7, 45–7, 49, 68, 70, 74–8, 81, 85–6, 116–17, 121–2, 140–1, 144–5, 151–4, 163–4, 169–70, 172–8, 181, 184–5, 189–90, 200, 226, 236, 248, 254, 257–61, 264
Shāh Turkān, 74, 76–7
Shāhik Azhdar Khān, Malik, 106
Shāhīn, 122, 136, 141, 242
Shams, 8, 9, 12, 26–7, 50, 56, 58–61, 63, 69, 73, 75–6, 78, 83, 89, 91, 95, 97–8, 104, 106, 114–15, 124–5, 141, 170, 178–9, 189, 200–1, 220, 222, 225, 248, 254, 261–2, 273
Shams al-Dīn Iltutmish, 26
Shams al-Dīn Kaykaus, 27
Shamsī, 26, 56, 63–6, 70, 74, 77–9, 86, 92, 94–5, 98, 101–2, 104–5, 109, 111, 201, 223, 224–7, 235–6
Shamsī slaves, 63–6, 74, 92, 98, 102, 104, 235
Shansabānī, 38, 42–4, 46, 49, 215
Sharqi sultan, 184
Sher Khān, 4, 88–9, 101, 104, 107–10
Sherān Khalji, 53
Shihāb al-Dīn, 38, 40–8, 50–3, 55, 57, 60–1, 65, 67, 97, 116, 126, 141, 153, 163, 165, 184, 213–14, 218–19, 245, 251, 253–4
Shihāb al-Dīn, Sultan, 46
Shihāb al-Dīn Ghūrī, 38, 40, 41–8, 50–2, 57, 60, 65, 67, 97, 184, 213
Shi'i, 19, 22, 24, 38–9
Shi'ism, 38, 210
Shiva linga, 30
Sīdi Māwallih, 118

Sind, 14–24, 29, 36, 40, 44, 48–50, 54, 60, 68–70, 75, 87–9, 93, 101, 108–9, 113, 154, 159–61, 165, 167, 177–8, 205–10, 217, 229, 247, 251–2, 256, 258, 262–3, 267–8, 272–5
Sindhi, 16, 21
sipah sālār, 64
Sirhindī, 136, 249–50, 256–7, 260
Sistān, 44, 49, 174
slave, 2, 4, 19, 22, 44, 47–9, 53, 56–8, 60–7, 70, 74, 77, 83, 98, 100–2, 104–6, 108, 115, 122–6, 136, 140–2, 151, 153, 159–62, 165, 172, 175–6, 178, 182, 189, 192, 194, 200, 216–18, 222–5, 227, 237, 240–2, 248, 252
Somnath, 21, 30, 37, 210, 212, 257, 268, 271
Sonargaun, 169
Sonqur (Sonqar Rumı), 82, 86, 96, 104, 223
Subh ul-Asha, 64, 222
Sūbūktagin, 31, 240
Sudhal, 172
Sudharāh, 87
Sufi(s), 10, 11, 55, 61–2, 79, 117, 148, 163, 190, 192, 239, 254–5, 258, 264, 266, 271–2
Suhrawardiā, 61–2
Sulaymān, 121–2, 207, 240, 242
Sulaymān, Caliph, 18
sulh, 17
sultans, 1–13, 31, 36, 38, 41, 43, 48, 54, 65–7, 73–4, 79, 100, 105, 107, 114, 123, 128, 134, 138, 144, 146, 156, 158, 162, 173, 182–3, 186, 188–92, 195–7, 199, 211, 221, 224–5, 237, 242, 245, 247, 252, 254, 256
Sumana, 132
Sunam, 76, 101, 104, 108, 123, 127–8, 132
Sunni(s), 19, 24, 29, 38–9, 79, 210, 213–14, 258
Sūntī, Emperor, 160
Sursutī, 50
Swistān, 50, 127, 132, 144–5, 150, 154, 160, 168, 178, 255
Syrian troops, 17

Tabāqāt-i Nāsiri, 42, 56, 63, 213–14, 220–31, 238
Tabarhindāh, 50, 60–1, 69–70, 80–1, 89–90
Tagin, Malik, 127
Tāj al-Dīn Hoshang, 170
Tāj al-Dīn Kuchı, Malik, 116–17
Tāj al-Dīn Mūsawī, 83
Tāj al-Dīn Sanjar (Arsalān Khān), 51, 92
Tāj al-Dīn Sanjar Kezlik Khān, 66
Tāj al-Dīn Sanjar Qatulaq, Malik, 83, 84
Tāj al-Mulk Muhammad, 78
Tāj-ul Mulk, 153, 226
Tajik(s), 5, 41, 43, 62, 76, 192, 225–6, 249
Talinganā, 138
Tamar, Malik, 127
Tamghāj, 60–1, 221
Tarā'īn, 45, 49
Tārīkh-i-Ma'sumī, 16
Tatar Khān, 173
Tatik, 127
tawā'if ul mulukiat, 3, 4, 9, 183, 191, 196, 204
Tekish Khwārzam Shāh, Sultan, 46
Temür(id), 13, 84, 90, 122, 155, 158, 160, 175, 179, 182–4, 187, 195, 223, 240, 260
Thangīr, 47, 50
Tilang, 134, 138, 159–60, 164, 169, 170–1, 257, 274
Tīwar, 44
Tīz, 24, 209
Toghān Khān, 70, 78, 84
Toghril, 5, 44, 47–8, 50–1, 56, 64, 69–70, 77–8, 84, 99, 101, 104–5, 108, 111, 189, 193, 216, 218, 223, 233–4, 236
Tughluq(s), 2–3, 7, 10, 12–13, 27–8, 107, 122, 127–8, 136, 138, 144, 151, 153–7, 162, 168–9, 173–5, 177, 182–3, 186–7, 190, 192, 194, 196, 200, 202, 204, 245, 247–51, 253–9, 261–3, 264–5, 267, 269, 271–5
Tughluq Shāh, Malik, 127
Tulabugha Nagwrı, 155
turban wearers, 91
Turk(s), 39, 41, 44, 47, 62, 64, 70, 77, 79, 80–1, 84–5, 102–3, 114–15, 158, 160, 173, 192, 200, 208, 218, 220–3, 226–7, 236, 247, 254–6, 258, 266, 269, 271
Turkān Khātūn, 78
Turki, Malik, 106
Turkish, 5, 36, 41, 48–9, 62, 65, 73–4, 77–8, 80, 84–5, 96, 98, 102, 106, 114–17, 121–2, 151, 159, 165–6, 192, 215–16, 219, 221, 224–5, 264, 271
Turkistan, 16, 53, 70, 223, 247
Turushkas (Turks), 70
Tūsī's Shahnamah, 43

Ubayd-i Hakīm, 155
Uchh, 44, 47, 49, 64–5, 70, 76, 80–1, 85, 88–9, 91–3, 144, 154, 255
Ujjain, 127, 137, 154, 242
'ulāmā', 10–11, 32, 38, 43, 47, 55–6, 61–2, 75, 79, 87, 91, 100, 109–10, 172–3, 189–90, 192, 213, 221
Ulugh Khān, 91, 121, 127, 133–5, 153, 239, 242
'Umar b. Azīz al-Hibari, 20
umarā', 3–5, 7–9, 11–12, 31, 38, 53, 59, 61–2, 64, 67–9, 71, 73–4, 77–8, 80–1, 83–7, 90–1, 94, 99, 102–4, 106, 109–11, 113–21, 123–31, 140, 142–6, 148, 151–8, 160–8, 172–7, 183, 185, 189–90, 192–3, 195–6, 203–4, 212, 220–1, 225–6, 229, 236
al-Umarā', Malik, 105
al-Umarī, 165
Umayyad(s), 12, 14–19, 23, 29, 133, 204, 206, 219
'Utbi, 39
Uthman, Caliph, 22

Vadodara (Baroda), 134
Vaghela King Karnadeva, 133
Vira Pandya, 139

Waihind, 31
al-Walīd, 15, 16, 18
Warangal, 137–8, 155–6, 168, 251, 256
wazīr, 33, 75–6, 78–9, 82–4, 89, 92, 106, 116, 121, 133, 137, 142, 144, 154, 159, 162, 164, 167, 170, 172, 175–7, 226, 239

Yadavas, 138
Yaghantut, 64, 224
Yahyā, 21, 244, 251
Yakhlakhī, Malik,145
yamīn-ud-daulā-wa-amīn-ul-millāh, 39
Yaminu-d Daula Mahmud Bin Subuktigin, 30
Yāqūt, 21, 80–1
Yavanas (Westerners), 70
Yenaltagin, 33, 34
Yildiz, 47–50, 55–6, 58, 60, 66, 69–70, 216, 221, 223

Zafar Khān, 142, 173, 178, 239
Zafar Khān (II), 173
Zafarabād, 153
Zāhir Khalifat Allah amīr al Mumīnīn, 40
Zamindāwār, 44
Zinadiqā, 40
Ziyād, 23
Zuhrā Kalabī, 23